Dimensions of World Food Problems

# DIMENSIONS *of*

*University of Mid-America*

# WORLD FOOD PROBLEMS

E. R. DUNCAN, *Coordinating Editor*

*The Iowa State University Press,* AMES

THIS WORK was prepared in conjunction with a television series and other study materials by the University of Mid-America and the World Food Institute of Iowa State University, assisted by grants from the Lilly Endowment, Inc., and the National Institute of Education.



First edition, 1977
*Second printing, 1979*

---

**Library of Congress Cataloging in Publication Data**
Main entry under title:

Dimensions of world food problems.

Includes bibliographies and index.
1. Food supply—Addresses, essays, lectures.
I. Duncan, E. R.
HD9000.5.D55 338.1′9 77-1663
**ISBN 0-8138-1870-2**

---

# CONTENTS

# PREFACE

*Dimensions of World Food Problems* was written as part of a complete package of student materials designed especially for independent study at home. Through a joint project of the University of Mid-America and the World Food Institute of Iowa State University, and with the financial assistance of the Lilly Endowment, Inc., world food problems are addressed in this volume and in the companion materials in a way which avoids simplistic and overemotional responses to world food crises. This approach is evident throughout the study package, which includes also a self-instructional text and a series of television programs, in addition to this reference source written by seventeen of the nation's foremost experts in world food issues.

This volume was written and edited so that it could stand alone as a reference for the range of world food concerns in such diverse fields as population, food and nutrition, food production and distribution, and institutions affecting world food problems. The variety of opinion and knowledge represented in this book provides the reader with a comprehensive survey of many of the factors that must be considered in any study of this complex topic.

The complete multidisciplinary course on world food problems was designed and produced by a team of academic media specialists whose expertise was combined with that of the scholars commissioned to write the chapters of this volume. This team approach is exemplary of that employed by the University of Mid-America in its design and production of educational materials for independent study.

The University of Mid-America is governed by a consortium of midwestern state universities and funded principally by the National Institute of Education.

The contributions of several persons must be recognized in preparing this book for publication:

Dr. Walter Wedin, Director of the World Food Institute at Iowa State University for his encouragement, cooperation, and support.

Ms. Pamela Lassahn for her editing work and for providing a common form to each chapter.

The Senior Content Advisory Panel members for the World Food Problems project: Dr. Glenn Beck, Dr. Ercel Eppright, Dr. Roger Mitchell, Dr. John Murdock, and Dr. J. T. Scott for their generous time and insights in reviewing the early drafts of the manuscripts.

Each of the authors for his cooperation and understanding of the need for meeting deadlines.

Ms. Debbi Nelson for her typing of the several drafts and correcting all too obvious errors.

The advice and counsel of many others in conceptualizing the original dimensions of the problems to be incorporated into the book. The final selection of the subjects found in this book was the coordinating editor's alone.

# INTRODUCTION

## *A Focus on the Situation*

THE PROBLEM of feeding hungry people is not new or unique to our times; indeed, the history of humanity is essentially a story of peoples' attempts to feed themselves. Most major wars have been fought to gain and secure territory so that people could eat and live with some assurance of security. Until recently, food supplies generally increased with the increases in population, though vagaries of weather and diseases resulted in scattered and periodic shortages. But starting in the decade of the 1940s, a new factor was forced into the equation, that of a very rapidly expanding population caused largely by falling death rates and a rapid increase in the number of young people in the population. This situation is unique in human history.

When agriculture first started some 10,000 to 8,000 B.C., the population of the earth was probably about 8 million people, a number similar to the population of Buenos Aires or London but smaller than that of New York City or Paris. It may have required a million years to accumulate that many people. Today, however, there are more than 400 times that many people, and the population is increasing at the rate of 80 million per year. To put it another way, in less than three years there will be as many more people in the world as now live in the entire United States. There were an estimated one billion people in the world in 1830; by 1930 there were two billion. Thirty years later, in 1960, there were three billion, and 15 years later, in 1975, there were about four billion. Seven billion is estimated for the year 2000.

Authorities estimate the number of malnourished at between 400 and 800 million in the 1970s, and this is many more than any time in the past. Unfortunately, most of the malnourished are found in the developing nations where population growth is highest and food production per capita is lowest. Even if food were available in many countries, a large percentage of the people would not have the money to purchase it. Malnutrition affects young children most since they must have a known minimum of nutrition for normal mental and physical development.

Authorities do not agree on whether there was enough food in the world in 1976 to take care of all hunger and malnutrition, even if the food were properly distributed. If this assessment even approximates the situation now, what then will be the situation if the world's population doubles early in the next century?

The productive land area of the world is finite, as are the energy sources as we know them today. We are approaching the maximum sustainable level of aquatic harvest from the oceans. Vagaries of weather increasingly limit the genetic gains possible with crops and livestock in the short run. Higher fuel and food costs have reduced the foreign exchange available in most developing nations and have severely limited their internal development.

The considerable known technology available in the developed nations could be transferred to the developing nations. If applied, this technology would significantly increase and sustain new levels of food production. Unfortunately, any new technology has a cost. In this instance, the costs may range from changes in land tenure and ownership, changes in attitudes toward risk and uncertainty, infrastructure development, and changes in government policy toward agriculture to education for farmers.

World food demand (needs) has two principal components: population and per person consumption. Per person consumption, in turn, is related to income levels, prices, tastes, preferences, and dietary requirements.

World food supply consists of crops, animals and their products, seafoods, and manufactured products. Weather and economic factors at times influence food supply more than the more basic factors; energy may become a limitation in the years ahead.

Of the total foods produced in the world each year perhaps more than 30 percent is lost before, during, or after harvest. Plant diseases, birds, and rodents are part of the problem before harvest; lack of knowledge, skills, equipment, and rodents are sources of losses during harvest; while poor storage, rodents, insects, spoilage, spillage, and carelessness cause losses after harvest. Not only are physical losses involved in these processes; nutritional losses also occur.

Many constraints limit changes in existing methods and systems, especially in the developing nations. Some are social, some are economic, others are political, and all are made more difficult to eliminate by a low level of literacy that will take years to correct even with vigorous government action.

Among the self-appointed "authorities" addressing the population and food problems of the world today, opinions range from highly optimistic to discouragingly pessimistic. Some believe simple, effective solutions are available while others believe no solutions exist at all. Development of internal institutions, communications, and education are pressing problems. Cooperation within and between countries is essential but difficult to achieve. Nationalism and protectionism have always presented problems in cooperation between nations; with many new nations, the situation is even more difficult in the mid-1970s.

It is becoming increasingly apparent that no nation can exist for long above the subsistence level without products or other assistance from other nations. Throughout the written history of the world, famines, plagues, and political difficulties have periodically occurred. As the world population grows, we might expect the frequency of these events to increase. For the short run by historical reckoning, perhaps for the next 50 to 100 years, the outlook is not bright, but over the longer term we can be more optimistic.

The world has a large land area not now cultivated that can produce crops when we learn how, but costs will be higher. New sources of energy will be found; the sun, the wind, and the oceans are a vast potential; we must learn how to use them. Population will be stabilized at a manageable level, diseases will be reduced or eliminated, and incomes will rise so that the essentials of life will be available to most. We must, however, recognize that those things considered potentials today are far from realities. Technology can move rapidly; most of us can think back 25 years when 150 bushel maize and wheat yields, computers, moon walks, and progress in control of certain diseases would have been beyond the imagination. Similar progress can be made in the next 25 years. People and their institutions have not moved as rapidly, and there is no reason to expect that they will in the future.

It is entirely possible that the world of convenience and relative affluence that we know today may not hold even to the year 2000. The rising prices from 1974 to 1976, the high rate of inflation, reduced crop yields, shortage of fossil fuels, and high unemployment all serve to remind us that all changes are not favorable. News of droughts, hunger, malnutrition, starvation, and military takeovers also remind us that problems of other nations are more serious than those in the United States. Ours is a relatively fortunate situation as we move toward the year 2000.

The focus of this book is on the several principal dimensions of population and food problems and their interactions as they appear in 1976. The authors, all recognized authorities, present the problems in a factual, unbiased, and unemotional manner. They view the present situation as difficult and urgent, but certainly not as impossible. The emphasis of this book is on agriculture and providing food to hungry people to gain time for stabilizing the human population at a manageable level.

We believe this book can provide the reader with an informed background for understanding the world food problems and shows that there are no simplistic solutions to the complex problems.

E. R. Duncan

*October 18, 1976*

# Dimensions of World Food Problems

JIM HICKS

*A young Nigerian couple with their "farm equipment."*

# 1

# A Review of Population and Trends

E. R. DUNCAN

THE PROBLEMS of food and population cannot be separated; each affects the other. The most obvious relationship is that as population increases the total need for food also increases. The less obvious relationship is that when food is plentiful and people are well fed, death rates decline and life expectancy increases, which in turn also results in a greater total need for food.

Ever since 1798 when Malthus wrote his "Essay on the Principle of Population" there have been warnings that population would eventually outstrip food production. Indeed, this may eventually be true, but recent history shows that while the situation is precarious it is not disastrous except in a few instances. In the past two decades, world agricultural production in both the developed and the developing countries has actually increased by an average of 2.6 percent per year. In the developing countries, however, production has barely kept ahead of the increasing demand for food caused by the increasing population. In some countries and in some years it has lagged behind. Thus the developing countries are particularly vulnerable to any disruption in food supplies such as those caused by unfavorable weather and natural disasters. Their vulnerability is even more evident when we consider that almost all the developing countries depend on grain imports from a few countries, mainly the United States, Canada, and Australia.

Still another relationship between food and population is even less obvious. Some authorities believe that increasing local agricultural production, particularly in the developing countries, may be the best means of raising per capita incomes and thereby paving the way for the greater economic security and education that appear to result in a decline in population growth rates.

This chapter first examines the history of population, defining the terms needed to understand population statistics and pointing out what

E. R. DUNCAN, senior content specialist and coordinating editor for this book, is Professor Emeritus, Agronomy Department, Iowa State University. An educator and extension agronomist in crop production, he has been consultant in South American and African countries and Head, Plant Science Department, University of Ife, Nigeria.

factors determine population growth rates. Next, the dimensions of the problem are presented along with how the problem affects people's lives. The chapter then examines the differences in developed and developing countries and concludes with a discussion of the prospects of feeding more people.

POPULATION HISTORY. The world's history has been and continues to be a record of increasing population growth. Much of our information on prehistoric populations has been, at best, an educated guess. Even today population figures are estimates, which cannot be precise, especially for countries in which there is no census.

Census enumeration is not new. The first recorded census was taken more than 600 years ago in China for the purpose of relating numbers of people to needed food. Regular counts are comparatively recent. Sweden has had a regular census since 1750, the United States since 1790, England since 1800, and India since 1870. Russia has had irregular counts since 1897.

Today many countries still have no census information at all and among those who do inaccuracies persist. Coale suggests that population estimates in the eighteenth century erred by about 20 percent (3). The last census in the United States probably had errors in the range of 2 to 3 percent (10). Nigeria's careful census in 1974 showed that either their 1963 estimate was very poor or their actual count in 1974 was inaccurate. Political and social overtones will continue to limit census accuracy into the future.

Demographers (those who study population statistics) have compiled considerable data on population trends and estimates of population numbers for the past, present, and future, and these will be summarized briefly. Many of the statistics are presented in terms of *population growth rates,* which refers to births minus deaths plus migration. Demographers also use the term population increase, which refers simply to births minus deaths. If a growth rate is 4.4 per 1,000 per year, it may also be expressed as 0.44 percent per year.

PAST, PRESENT, AND FUTURE. Archaeologists recently unearthed evidence in the Rift Valley of southern Ethiopia and in Kenya that shows that a type of human being *(Homo erectus)* lived on the earth well over a million years ago. Prehistoric people and their offspring were forced to live by hunting and gathering edible berries, fruits, and plant parts. The sources of food and methods of obtaining it did not change until the beginning of agriculture (sometime between 10,000 and 8000 B.C.). As a result, population growth in the first 99 percent of human history was very slow with perhaps 8 million people on earth in 8000 B.C. With the advent of agriculture people could grow and store food thereby reducing the risk of starvation and hazards of hunting, and the population in-

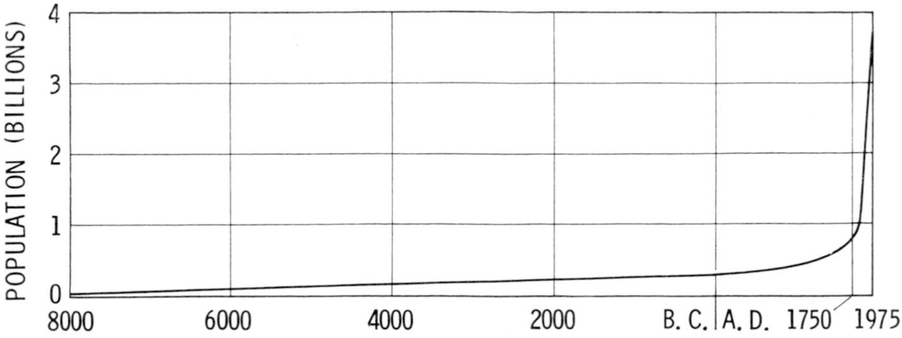


FIG. 1.1. Population growth from 8000 B.C. to 1975. Development of agriculture (about 8000 B.C.) resulted in a modest increase in population growth, but the Industrial Revolution starting about 1750 had a much greater effect.

creased somewhat more rapidly (Fig. 1.1). During the last 200 years of human history, however, population has increased very rapidly mainly because of improved medical knowledge and the ability to control disease epidemics. Durand estimated population growth rates of the four 50-year periods between 1750 and 1950 as approximately 4, 5, 5, and 8 per 1,000 per year (6). From 1950 to 1974 the growth rate was 18 per 1,000 per year—more than double that of the previous 50 years. The most recent growth rate estimate for the world is 22 per 1,000 per year.

Table 1.1 summarizes the current annual rate of increase for several countries based on United Nations' information (7). The Environmental Fund (10) has also reported estimates of current growth rates for the

TABLE 1.1. CURRENT (1973) POPULATIONS BASED ON UNITED NATIONS' ESTIMATES. (7)

| Area | People | Crude Birth Rate | Crude Death Rate | Annual Rate of Natural Increase |
|---|---|---|---|---|
| | *(millions)* | *(per 1,000 population per year)* | *(per 1,000 population per year)* | *(%)* |
| World | 3,860 | 33 | 13 | 2.0 |
| Developed countries | 1,120 | 17 | 9 | 0.8 |
| Underdeveloped countries | 2,740 | 39 | 14 | 2.5 |
| Africa | 375 | 46 | 19 | 2.7 |
| Asia (except Japan) | 2,100 | 38 | 14 | 2.4 |
| Latin America (tropical) | 265 | 38 | 8 | 3.0 |
| U.S. | 210 | 15 | 9 | 0.6 |
| Japan | 108 | 19 | 7 | 1.2 |
| Europe | 472 | 16 | 11 | 0.5 |
| U.S.S.R. | 250 | 18 | 8 | 1.0 |
| Others: Canada, Australia, New Zealand, Latin America (temperate) | 80 | 22 | 8 | 1.4 |

Source: Scientific American

world and for individual countries, and these estimates are presented in Table 1.2. Note that columns three and four (birth rate and death rate) are United Nations' figures, and those in columns one and two (population estimates and growth rates) are from the International Program Center, U.S. Bureau of the Census. Exceptions are noted. This table is included because it is the most comprehensive and current source of population information available. Population numbers for individual countries may be less precise than the comparisons between countries, but both are interesting and can be helpful. Some of the numbers shown in Tables 1.1 and 1.2 differ, in part because they represent different sources and different dates. This chapter uses the figures shown in Table 1.2 except when data are quoted from different sources.

Most reliable authorities believe that the number of people in the world will continue to increase for many years to come. Freedman and Berelson suggest three reasons for believing this (7). First, they point out that fertility itself is greatly resistant to change. Anyone who has been close to families and cultures in developing nations can understand why change will take place very slowly. Second, intervention in a family's fertility plan does not yet have a valid basis. Some may claim successes with family planning, but there is no evidence of mass adoption and at best the time needed for effective change is considerable. Third, population issues are changing. In some developing countries governments delay taking significant positive and effective policy action because the issue has become a political matter, especially when suggestions of need to limit population growth come from developed nations.

Few authorities are willing to admit that the increase in population will level out before 2050; the question is what level population will have reached by that time.

FACTORS AFFECTING POPULATIONS. The size of world population depends on two main factors: (1) birth rate and (2) death rate. The population increase is the amount by which the birth rate exceeds the death rate.

BIRTH AND FERTILITY RATES. When demographers study birth rates they usually examine, among other things, the general fertility rate, which is the number of live births in a designated year per 1,000 females of child-bearing age (usually defined as 15 to 44 years).

Differences in fertility among women are due to two factors: differences in exposure of women of childbearing age to the risk of childbirth through contact with a sexual partner and differences in rates at which live births occur among women having sexual contact. Among the many elements that influence fertility are age of marriage for both men and women, whether a woman marries, type of diet, and availability of fertility control measures.

Birth control measures of varying kinds were widely used in preliterate societies, and similar methods may still be used in remote tribes of

TABLE 1.2. 1976 WORLD POPULATION ESTIMATES (10).

| | Population Estimates (Millions) Mid 1976[1] | Growth Rate (%)[2] | Birth Rate (Per 1,000 Population)[3] | Death Rate (Per 1,000 Population)[3] | Number of Acres of Arable Land Per Person[4] | 1974 Production Cereal Grains (1,000 Metric Tons)[5] | 1948-1952 Net Exports Cereal Grains (1,000 Metric Tons)[6] | 1974 Net Exports Cereal Grains (1,000 Metric Tons)[7] |
|---|---|---|---|---|---|---|---|---|
| **WORLD[8]** | **4,240.7** | **2.2** | **35** | **14** | **0.8** | **1,333,864** | | |
| **AFRICA** | **431.9** | **2.8** | **46** | **21** | **1.2** | **67,921** | **–370** | **–6,936** |
| **NORTH AFRICA** | **99.4** | **3.0** | **44** | **17** | **0.7** | **17,940** | **35** | **–6,249** |
| Algeria | 16.2 | 3.3 | 39 | 17 | 1.0 | 1,346 | 183 | –1,774 |
| Egypt[9] | 37.9 | 2.3 | 44 | 16 | 0.2 | 7,908 | –561 | –2,860 |
| Libya | 2.5 | 4.1 | 46 | 16 | 2.3 | 173 | –20 | –401 |
| Morocco | 18.0 | 3.0 | 50 | 17 | 1.0 | 4,849 | 321 | –856 |
| Sudan | 18.9 | 3.2 | 49 | 18 | 0.9 | 2,527 | –15 | –61 |
| Tunisia[10] | 5.9 | 2.4 | 41 | 13 | § 1.9 § | 1,137 | 127 | –297 |
| **WEST AFRICA** | **137.5** | **2.5** | **49** | **24** | **1.4** | **14,701** | **–264** | **–2,079** |
| Benin (Dahomey) | 3.2 | 2.4 | 51 | 26 | § 1.2 § | 400 | (–5) | –15 |
| Cape Verde Islands | 0.3 | 2.3 | 29 | 9 | 0.3 | 13 | –11 | –35 |
| Gambia | 0.5 | 1.9 | 43 | 23 | § 1.0 § | 107 | –4 | –11 |
| Ghana | 10.3 | 3.0 | 47 | 18 | 0.2 | 877 | –27 | –153 |
| Guinea | 4.5 | 2.3 | 47 | 25 | § 0.8 § | 765 | –4 | –63 |
| Guinea-Bissau | 0.5 | 1.1 | 41 | 30 | 1.2 | 65 | 1 | –34 |
| Ivory Coast | 5.0 | 2.5 | 46 | 23 | 3.9 | 560 | –26 | –185 |
| Liberia | 1.6 | 3.1 | 50 | 21 | 0.2 | 208 | –3 | –47 |
| Mali | 5.8 | 2.3 | 50 | 27 | § 4.9 § | 891 | — | –232 |
| Mauritania | 1.3 | 2.2 | 44 | 23 | 0.5 | 34 | — | –126 |
| Niger | 4.7 | 2.9 | 52 | 23 | 7.9 | 847 | (–1) | –167 |
| Nigeria[11] | 83.8 | 2.5 | 50 | 25 | § 0.6 § | 7,806 | –12 | –354 |
| Senegal | 4.5 | 2.5 | 46 | 23 | § 3.1 § | 635 | (–167) | –464 |
| Sierra-Leone | 3.1 | 2.4 | 45 | 23 | 2.9 | 556 | –3 | –95 |
| Togo | 2.3 | 2.6 | 51 | 26 | 2.3 | 238 | –2 | –23 |
| Upper Volta | 6.1 | 2.0 | 49 | 29 | 2.2 | 699 | (0) | –75 |
| **EAST AFRICA** | **119.1** | **2.9** | **46** | **22** | **1.1** | **18,569** | **–155** | **–1,164** |
| Burundi | 4.1 | 2.4 | 48 | 25 | 0.6 | 552 | — | –7 |
| Comorros | 0.3 | 2.6 | 31 | 20 | § 0.7 § | 16 | 0 | –15 |
| Ethiopia[12] | 29.9 | 2.6 | 46 | 25 | 1.1 | 5,545 | 39 | –85 |
| Kenya | 14.1 | 3.7 | 48 | 18 | 0.3 | 2,118 | 43 | 65 |
| Madagascar | 7.7 | 2.2 | 46 | 25 | § 0.9 § | 2,093 | 2 | –161 |
| Malawi | 5.1 | 2.3 | 49 | 25 | 1.4 | 1,347 | –1 | 25 |
| Mauritius | 0.9 | 1.8 | 28 | 7 | § 0.3 § | 1 | –63 | –163 |
| Mozambique | 9.3 | 2.3 | 43 | 23 | 0.7 | 901 | –21 | –119 |
| Reunion | 0.5 | 2.0 | 28 | 7 | 0.3 | 12 | –34 | –88 |
| Rhodesia | 6.6 | 3.4 | 48 | 14 | § 0.7 § | 2,369 | –76 | –61 |
| Rwanda | 4.4 | 2.9 | 52 | 23 | 0.3 | 167 | — | –7 |
| Somalia | 3.2 | 2.4 | 46 | 24 | § 0.7 § | 325 | –6 | –24 |
| Tanzania | 16.0 | 3.0 | 47 | 22 | 2.3 | 1,031 | –9 | –430 |
| Uganda | 11.9 | 3.3 | 43 | 18 | 0.8 | 1,261 | 0 | –35 |
| Zambia | 5.1 | 3.2 | 50 | 21 | § 2.3 § | 831 | –29 | –59 |
| **MIDDLE AFRICA** | **47.1** | **2.6** | **45** | **25** | **1.5** | **2,833** | **107** | **–634** |
| Angola | 6.6 | 1.8 | 50 | 30 | § 0.3 § | 570 | 107 | –51 |
| Cameroon | 6.6 | 2.4 | 43 | 23 | 2.5 | 692 | –10 | –74 |
| Central African Republic | 1.8 | 2.6 | 46 | 25 | 8.0 | 119 | — | –14 |
| Chad | 4.3 | 2.4 | 48 | 25 | § 4.0 § | 577 | –8 | –46 |
| Congo | 1.4 | 2.7 | 44 | 23 | 1.1 | 14 | — | –62 |
| Equatorial Guinea | 0.3 | 1.9 | 35 | 22 | § 1.8 § | — | — | –2 |
| Gabon | 0.5 | 1.2 | 33 | 25 | § 0.6 § | 3 | — | –5 |
| Zaire[13] | 25.6 | 2.8 | 44 | 23 | § 0.7 § | 858 | 18 | –380 |
| **SOUTH AFRICA** | **28.8** | **3.0** | **41** | **17** | **1.2** | **13,878** | **–93** | **3,228** |
| Botswana | 0.6 | 1.9 | 44 | 23 | 2.1 | 55 | — | –44 |
| Lesotho | 1.1 | 2.1 | 39 | 21 | 0.8 | 211 | — | –64 |
| Namibia | 0.7 | 2.1 | 44 | 25 | 2.3 | 119 | –8 | 0 |
| South Africa | 25.9 | 3.1 | 40 | 17 | 1.2 | 13,390 | –85 | 3,347 |
| Swaziland | 0.5 | 3.2 | 52 | 24 | 0.8 | 103 | — | –11 |

TABLE 1.2. 1976 WORLD POPULATION ESTIMATES. *(Continued)*

| | Population Estimates (Millions) Mid 1976[1] | Growth Rate (%)[2] | Birth Rate (Per 1,000 Population)[3] | Death Rate (Per 1,000 Population)[3] | Number of Acres of Arable Land Per Person[4] | 1974 Production Cereal Grains (1,000 Metric Tons)[5] | 1948-1952 Net Exports Cereal Grains (1,000 Metric Tons)[6] | 1974 Net Exports Cereal Grains (1,000 Metric Tons)[7] |
|---|---|---|---|---|---|---|---|---|
| **ASIA** | **2,475.9** | **2.5** | **40** | **15** | **0.5** | **513,867** | **−5,845** | **−47,078** |
| **SOUTHWEST ASIA** | **90.4** | **2.9** | **43** | **16** | **1.1** | **24,179** | **135** | **−4,880** |
| Bahrain | 0.3 | 3.3 | 30 | [9] | 0.005 | — | — | −14 |
| Cyprus | 0.7 | 0.9 | 23 | 8 | 1.3 | 216 | −47 | −155 |
| Gaza | 0.4 | 3.6 | 44 | 8 | — | — | — | — |
| Iraq | 11.4 | 3.4 | 49 | 16 | 1.1 | 2,175 | 330 | −626 |
| Israel | 3.5 | 2.1 | 28 | 7 | 0.2 | 350 | −230 | −1,472 |
| Jordan | 2.7 | 3.6 | 48 | 16 | 1.0 | 261 | −29 | −169 |
| Kuwait | 1.1 | 6.1 | 43 | 7 | 0.002 | 0 | — | −203 |
| Lebanon[14] | 2.7 | 2.6 | 40 | 10 | 0.2 | 72 | −141 | −356 |
| Oman | 0.8 | 3.1 | [50] | [19] | 0.05 | — | — | — |
| Saudi Arabia[13] | 9.2 | 3.0 | 50 | 23 | 0.2 | 556 | (−101) | −693 |
| Syria | 7.6 | 3.4 | 48 | 15 | 1.8 | 2,335 | 191 | −336 |
| Turkey | 41.3 | 2.6 | 40 | 15 | 1.5 | 17,014 | 174 | −587 |
| U. A. Emirates | 0.2 | 3.6 | [50] | [18] | § 0.2 § | — | — | — |
| Yemen Arab Republic | 6.8 | 2.9 | 50 | 23 | § 0.4 § | 1,105 | — | −146 |
| Yemen Dem. Republic | 1.7 | 3.0 | 50 | 23 | § 0.4 § | 95 | −12 | −123 |
| **MIDDLE SOUTH ASIA** | **893.8** | **2.7** | **44** | **17** | **0.6** | **154,657** | **−4,164** | **−10,470** |
| Afghanistan | 19.7 | 2.5 | 51 | 27 | 1.0 | 4,702 | (0) | −16 |
| Bangladesh | 82.9 | 2.7 | [46] | [17] | 0.3 | 17,401 | — | −1,667 |
| Bhutan | 1.2 | 2.4 | [44] | [20] | § 0.01 § | 396 | — | 15 |
| India[15] | 652.7 | 2.6 | 43 | 17 | 0.6 | 108,199 | −3,576 | −5,374 |
| Iran | 36.0 | 3.1 | 45 | 17 | 1.1 | 6,348 | −50 | −1,948 |
| Nepal | 12.9 | 2.3 | 45 | 23 | § 0.4 § | 3,351 | (35) | 43 |
| Pakistan[16] | 74.2 | 3.6 | 51 | 18 | § 0.7 § | 12,315 | (39) | −559 |
| Sikkim[17] | 0.2 | 2.0 | 29 | 16 | § 0.1 § | 33 | — | −11 |
| Sri Lanka | 14.0 | 2.0 | 30 | 8 | 0.2 | 1,912 | −612 | −953 |
| **SOUTHEAST ASIA** | **338.4** | **2.7** | **44** | **16** | **0.5** | **73,455** | **1,413** | **−2,744** |
| Burma | 31.9 | 2.4 | 40 | 17 | 1.4 | 8,613 | 1,230 | 204 |
| Indonesia (Inc. W. Irian) | 143.4 | 2.3 | 48 | 19 | § 0.3 § | 25,560 | −464 | −1,714 |
| Khmer Republic | 8.7 | 3.2 | 45 | 16 | 0.5 | 705 | 0 | −223 |
| Laos | 3.5 | 2.7 | 42 | 17 | § 0.7 § | 930 | 0 | −88 |
| Malaysia | 12.7 | 2.7 | 38 | 11 | 0.2 | 2,062 | −642 | −1,000 |
| Philippines[18] | 45.9 | 3.3 | 45 | 12 | § 0.5 § | 7,883 | −278 | −794 |
| Portuguese Timor | 0.7 | 2.1 | 43 | 25 | 0.3 | 35 | 0 | −3 |
| Singapore[19] | 2.3 | 1.4 | 20 | 5 | 0.003 | — | — | −414 |
| Thailand | 42.7 | 3.1 | 43 | 10 | 0.7 | 15,855 | 1,291 | 3,547 |
| Vietnam, Dem. Rep. of[20] | 25.3 | 2.9 | 38 | 16 | § 0.2 § | 4,450 | (110) | −1,808 |
| Vietnam, Republic of | 21.3 | 2.6 | 43 | 8 | 0.4 | 7,362 | (166) | −451 |
| **EAST ASIA** | **1,153.3** | **2.3** | **35** | **12** | **0.3** | **261,572** | **−3,229** | **−28,882** |
| China[21] | 964.4 | 2.4 | 37 | 9 | § 0.3 § | 226,723 | (299) | −2,825 |
| Hong Kong | 4.4 | 2.1 | 19 | 5 | 0.006 | 7 | (−282) | −654 |
| Japan | 112.2 | 1.1 | 19 | 7 | 0.1 | 16,480 | −2,731 | −19,222 |
| Korea, Dem. Rep. of | 17.0 | 3.2 | 39 | 11 | § 0.3 § | 6,533 | (−55) | −531 |
| Korea, Republic of | 37.1 | 2.2 | 36 | 11 | 0.1 | 8,057 | (−543) | −2,676 |
| Macau | 0.3 | 2.2 | [25] | [7] | § 0.002 § | — | −25 | −25 |
| Mongolia | 1.5 | 3.1 | 42 | 11 | 1.3 | 358 | (−1) | −27 |
| Taiwan[22] | 16.4 | 2.0 | [23] | [5] | 0.2 | 3,414 | 109 | −2,922 |
| **NORTH AMERICA** | **245.3** | **1.3** | **14** | **8** | **2.3** | **235,958** | **22,481** | **76,374** |
| Canada | 23.1 | 1.3 | 16 | 7 | § 4.7 § | 31,478 | 8,492 | 11,658 |
| U.S.A.[23] | 222.2 | 1.3 | 14 | 9 | 2.1 | 204,480 | 13,989 | 64,716 |
| **LATIN AMERICA** | **333.5** | **2.6** | **39** | **10** | **0.8** | **76,840** | **1,160** | **−443** |
| **MIDDLE AMERICA** | **80.3** | **2.6** | **45** | **9** | **0.9** | **16,353** | **−448** | **−3,296** |
| Costa Rica | 2.0 | 2.3 | 29 | 5 | 0.3 | 178 | −23 | −93 |
| El Salvador | 4.3 | 3.1 | 40 | 8 | 0.3 | 520 | −21 | −50 |
| Guatemala | 6.2 | 2.8 | 42 | 13 | 0.5 | 723 | −23 | −139 |
| Honduras | 3.3 | 3.7 | 49 | 17 | § 0.6 § | 319 | −6 | −56 |

TABLE 1.2. 1976 WORLD POPULATION ESTIMATES. *(Continued)*

| | Population Estimates (Millions) Mid 1976[1] | Growth Rate (%)[2] | Birth Rate (Per 1,000 Population)[3] | Death Rate (Per 1,000 Population)[3] | Number of Acres of Arable Land Per Person[4] | 1974 Production Cereal Grains (1,000 Metric Tons)[5] | 1948-1952 Net Exports Cereal Grains (1,000 Metric Tons)[6] | 1974 Net Exports Cereal Grains (1,000 Metric tons)[7] |
|---|---|---|---|---|---|---|---|---|
| Mexico[24] | 60.5 | 2.2 | 46 | 8 | 1.1 | 14,047 | –369 | –2,850 |
| Nicaragua | 2.3 | 3.4 | 46 | 17 | 0.8 | 335 | 8 | –30 |
| Panama | 1.7 | 2.6 | 33 | 9 | 0.6 | 231 | –14 | –78 |
| **CARIBBEAN** | **27.4** | **2.2** | **33** | **10** | **0.5** | **1,519** | **–623** | **–2,537** |
| Bahamas | 0.2 | 3.8 | 22 | 5 | 0.025 | — | –6 | –19 |
| Barbados | 0.2 | 0.0 | 21 | 9 | 0.3 | 2 | –19 | –35 |
| Cuba | 9.4 | 1.8 | 25 | 6 | § 0.9 § | 540 | –397 | –1,474 |
| Dominican Republic | 5.1 | 3.1 | 49 | 15 | § 0.5 § | 270 | 4 | –247 |
| Guadeloupe | 0.4 | 1.7 | 28 | 7 | 0.3 | 1 | –19 | –49 |
| Haiti | 5.2 | 2.1 | 42 | 13 | § 0.2 § | 669 | –27 | –89 |
| Jamaica | 2.1 | 2.3 | 31 | 7 | § 0.3 § | 12 | –70 | –347 |
| Martinique | 0.4 | 1.4 | 22 | 7 | 0.1 | — | –18 | –44 |
| Netherlands Antilles | 0.2 | 1.7 | 20 | 5 | § 0.1 § | 6 | –11 | –35 |
| Puerto Rico | 3.2 | 3.0 | 23 | 7 | § 0.2 § | 3 | — | — |
| Trinidad/Tobago | 1.0 | 0.7 | 27 | 7 | 0.1 | 16 | –60 | –198 |
| **TROPICAL SOUTH AMERICA** | **183.0** | **3.0** | **40** | **10** | **0.6** | **32,556** | **–1,356** | **–4,616** |
| Bolivia | 5.6 | 2.6 | 44 | 19 | 1.3 | 508 | –70 | –211 |
| Brazil[25] | 113.0 | 2.9 | 38 | 10 | 0.6 | 26,404 | –886 | –1,266 |
| Colombia | 26.6 | 3.2 | 45 | 11 | 0.3 | 2,676 | –47 | –482 |
| Ecuador | 7.3 | 3.2 | 45 | 11 | 1.0 | 614 | 13 | –196 |
| Guyana | 0.8 | 2.3 | 36 | 8 | 2.5 | 229 | 5 | –23 |
| Peru | 16.0 | 3.0 | 42 | 11 | 0.4 | 1,139 | –225 | –1,101 |
| Surinam | 0.4 | 2.2 | 41 | 7 | 0.2 | 150 | 0 | –5 |
| Venezuela | 13.3 | 3.4 | 41 | 8 | 0.9 | 836 | –146 | –1,332 |
| **TEMPERATE SO. AMERICA** | **42.8** | **1.5** | **25** | **9** | **1.9** | **26,390** | **3,587** | **10,083** |
| Argentina | 26.3 | 1.4 | 23 | 9 | 2.2 | 23,160 | 3,558 | 11,292 |
| Chile | 10.8 | 1.7 | 26 | 9 | 1.3 | 1,706 | –34 | –1,291 |
| Paraguay | 2.6 | 2.6 | 45 | 11 | § 1.0 § | 332 | –37 | –77 |
| Uruguay | 3.1 | 1.1 | 21 | 10 | 1.4 | 1,192 | 100 | 159 |
| **EUROPE** | **475.8** | **0.6** | **15** | **10** | **0.7** | **235,076** | **–20,775** | **–28,470** |
| **NORTHERN EUROPE** | **81.4** | **0.3** | **14** | **11** | **0.5** | **35,328** | **–8,769** | **–7,961** |
| Denmark | 5.1 | 0.4 | 14 | 10 | 1.3 | 7,261 | –162 | 207 |
| Finland | 4.7 | 0.4 | 13 | 10 | § 1.4 § | 2,852 | –340 | –149 |
| Iceland | 0.2 | 0.9 | 20 | 7 | 0.013 | — | –9 | –34 |
| Ireland | 3.1 | 0.7 | 22 | 11 | 0.9 | 1,169 | –554 | –581 |
| Norway | 4.0 | 0.6 | 15 | 10 | 0.5 | 1,127 | –576 | –686 |
| Sweden | 8.2 | 0.4 | 14 | 11 | § 0.9 § | 6,651 | –246 | 610 |
| United Kingdom | 56.1 | 0.0 | 13 | 12 | § 0.3 § | 16,268 | –6,882 | –7,328 |
| **WESTERN EUROPE** | **153.4** | **0.5** | **12** | **11** | **0.5** | **72,017** | **–10,040** | **2,041** |
| Austria | 7.5 | 0.0 | 13 | 13 | 0.5 | 4,012 | –736 | –163 |
| Belgium | 9.8 | 0.4 | 13 | 12 | 0.2 | 2,012 | –1,292 | –3,609 |
| France | 53.3 | 0.8 | 15 | 10 | 0.8 | 41,070 | –1,033 | 16,876 |
| Fed. Rep. of Germany | 62.1 | 0.1 | 10 | 12 | 0.3 | 22,663 | –4,602 | –5,168 |
| Luxembourg | 0.4 | 0.6 | 11 | 12 | § 0.4 § | 134 | — | — |
| Netherlands | 13.8 | 0.9 | 14 | 8 | 0.1 | 1,314 | –1,588 | –4,445 |
| Switzerland | 6.5 | 0.5 | 13 | 9 | 0.1 | 812 | –789 | –1,450 |
| **EASTERN EUROPE** | **107.0** | **0.8** | **17** | **10** | **1.0** | **75,866** | **647** | **–6,710** |
| Bulgaria | 8.8 | 0.7 | 17 | 10 | 1.2 | 6,797 | (10) | –467 |
| Czechoslovakia | 14.9 | 0.8 | 20 | 12 | 0.9 | 10,599 | (7) | –1,066 |
| Dem. Rep. of Germany | 16.8 | —0.2 | 10 | 13 | 0.7 | 9,400 | (0) | –3,041 |
| Hungary | 10.6 | 0.6 | 18 | 12 | 1.2 | 12,855 | 349 | 1,461 |
| Poland | 34.4 | 1.1 | 18 | 8 | 1.1 | 22,983 | (195) | –3,922 |
| Romania | 21.5 | 1.0 | 20 | 9 | 1.1 | 13,232 | (86) | 325 |
| **SOUTHERN EUROPE** | **134.0** | **0.8** | **18** | **9** | **0.7** | **51,864** | **–2,613** | **–15,839** |
| Albania | 2.5 | 2.4 | 33 | 8 | 0.5 | 607 | (0) | –48 |
| Greece | 9.0 | 0.5 | 16 | 8 | 0.8 | 3,928 | –479 | –1,335 |

TABLE 1.2. 1976 WORLD POPULATION ESTIMATES. *(Continued)*

| | Population Estimates (Millions) Mid 1976[1] | Growth Rate (%)[2] | Birth Rate (Per 1,000 Population)[3] | Death Rate (Per 1,000 Population)[3] | Number of Acres of Arable Land Per Person[4] | 1974 Production Cereal Grains (1,000 Metric Tons)[5] | 1948-1952 Net Exports Cereal Grains (1,000 Metric Tons)[6] | 1974 Net Exports Cereal Grains (1,000 Metric Tons)[7] |
|---|---|---|---|---|---|---|---|---|
| Italy | 56.2 | 0.7 | 16 | 10 | 0.4 | 16,934 | −1,634 | −7,373 |
| Malta | 0.3 | 0.0 | 17 | 9 | 0.1 | 5 | −68 | −125 |
| Portugal | 8.5 | −0.4 | 19 | 11 | 1.0 | 1,601 | −318 | −1,788 |
| Spain | 36.0 | 1.1 | 19 | 8 | 1.1 | 13,158 | −260 | −4,523 |
| Yugoslavia | 21.5 | 0.9 | 18 | 8 | 0.8 | 15,631 | 146 | −647 |
| **U.S.S.R.** | **256.8** | **1.0** | **18** | **9** | **2.2** | **186,620** | **(2,050)** | **678** |
| **OCEANIA** | **21.5** | **1.8** | **23** | **10** | **5.3** | **17,583** | **3,158** | **6,947** |
| Australia | 13.7 | 1.4 | 18 | 9 | 8.1 | 16,822 | 3,389 | 7,264 |
| Fiji | 0.6 | 2.1 | 30 | 5 | 0.3 | 23 | (−11) | −52 |
| New Zealand | 3.2 | 2.2 | 21 | 9 | 0.6 | 730 | −173 | −82 |
| Papua/New Guinea | 2.8 | 2.6 | 42 | 18 | 0.1 | 5 | (−16) | −92 |
| Smaller Islands & Enclaves[26] | 1.2 | 3.3 | 31 | 7 | 0.5 | 3 | −31 | −91 |

POPULATION DOUBLING TIME

| Population Growth Rate % | Number of Years to double Population |
|---|---|
| 0.5 | 140 |
| 1.0 | 70 |
| 1.5 | 47 |
| 2.0 | 35 |
| 2.5 | 28 |
| 3.0 | 24 |
| 3.5 | 20 |
| 4.0 | 18 |

**Explanatory Remarks.** As in 1974, population estimates and growth rates are based on those prepared by the International Statistical Program Center, U.S. Bureau of the Census. The 1975 chart relied on U.N. data because the Census Bureau refused to release their estimates. Whether or not their findings will be released in 1976 is still in doubt (as of June 1, 1976). Our source is labeled "Preliminary Draft Not For Publication," December 12, 1975. In the few cases where we have departed from these figures, footnotes will indicate why we have done so.

The *1975 Estimates* included figures on urbanization, percentage of the population under 15 years of age, and energy consumption per capita. Rather than repeat these figures, we have substituted figures relative to the production, consumption, and export of cereal grains, which constitute 75%, or more, of the world's food supply.

Those who are interested in both the birth rates and growth rates of the early 1960s, for comparison purposes, should refer to the *1974 Estimates Sheet.*

**Footnotes.** (1) Unless otherwise indicated, all 1976 population estimates are from the International Statistical Program Center, U.S. Bureau of the Census. Figures derived from other sources are noted in footnotes.

(2) Unless otherwise indicated, growth rates are computed from the gain in population 1975–1976 as reported from the above source.

(3) Birth rates and death rates are from United Nations, *Population and Vital Statistics Report, Statistical Papers,* Series A, Volume XXVIII, Number 1, January 1976.

In cases where birth and/or death rates are not given by this source, the figures are taken from Census Bureau unpublished data *World Population: 1975,* March 10, 1976, and are in brackets.

(4) These figures are based upon arable land figures from the 1974 United Nations Food and Agriculture Organization (UNFAO), *Production Yearbook,* volume 28-1, Table 1.

In some cases, arable land was not separated from land under permanent crops, and the figure for the arable land is the sum of the two. These are marked with § §. Since permanent cropland is usually a small area relative to land under cultivation for any country, these combined figures are still useful.

(5) Data from 1974 UNFAO *Production Yearbook,* Volume 28-1, Table 12.

FAO's estimates are substantially greater than those made by USDA because FAO reports paddy rice, and USDA reports milled rice. Also, FAO figures sometimes include pulses and other crops with cereals (for instance the Chinese include potatoes).

(6) From 1960 UNFAO *Trade Yearbook,* Volume 14, Tables 14–21. Where data were not given, figures were taken from the 1955 and 1960 UNFAO *Trade Yearbook* for years in the early 1950s. These figures are printed in parentheses.

(7) 1974 UNFAO *Trade Yearbook,* Volume 28, Table 35.

(8) Includes the population of 27 smaller islands and enclaves not listed elsewhere.

(9) Birth rates and death rates from the 1970 United Nations *Demographic Yearbook,* because these correspond closely to rates derived by Egyptian demographers. See Footnote No. 2, 1974 Environmental Fund *World Population Estimates* for details.

Natural increase is probably above 2.8, but out-migration is substantial.

(10) Birth and death rates are from *Selected World Demographic Indicators by Countries, 1950–2000,* Population Division, United Nations Secretariat, Working Paper No. 55, May 28, 1975.

(11) According to the Nigerian census of 1973 (neither the Census Bureau nor the United Nations accepts this figure).

(12) The Census Bureau figure is 30.3 million, but there is now evidence that 500,000 people died of starvation in 1974. Census Bureau demographers tell us that their figure only reflects the 100,000 originally reported.

(13) Population and growth rate from 1974 United Nations *Demographic Yearbook,* Table 5.

(14) Birth and death rates from United Nations *Statistical Papers,* Series A, Volume XXVIII, No. 2, April 1976.

(15) Population and growth rate derived from *World Population: 1973,* U.S. Bureau of the Census.

(16) Birth and death rates from the 1972 United Nations *Demographic Yearbook.* Population and growth rate derived from the 1973 *Demographic Yearbook,* Table 4. See Footnote No. 8, 1974 Environmental Fund *World Population Estimates* for further details.

(17) Population and growth rates derived from 1974 United Nations *Demographic Yearbook,* Table 5. Sikkim became a state of India in April, 1975, and will not be reported separately hereafter.

(18) Population and growth rate from *Single-Year Population Estimates and Projections for Major Areas, Regions and Countries of the World, 1950–2000,* Population Division, United Nations Secretariat, Working Paper No. 56, October 6, 1975.

(19) Growth rate of 1.4 seems unlikely. United Nations sources give higher rates.

(20) Population and growth rates from 1974 North Vietnam census. See Footnote No. 17, 1975 Environmental Fund *World Population Estimates* for further details.

(21) Population estimates based upon Dr. John Aird's "intermediate model" for China prepared by the Foreign Demographic Analysis Division, Bureau of Economic Analysis, U.S. Department of Commerce, 1975. See Footnote No. 10, 1974 Environmental Fund *World Population Estimates.*

Birth and death rates are from United Nations *Statistical Papers,* Series A, Volume XXVII, No. 2, April 1975.

1974 Production and Net Exports of cereal grains are UNFAO figures for China minus figures for Taiwan obtained from other sources (see footnote 22). The U.N. stopped reporting Taiwan separately from mainland China in 1971.

(22) Arable land is obtained from the *World Data Handbook,* U.S. Department of State, 1973. 1974 production and net exports of cereal grains are obtained from the USDA Grains Division.

(23) Population includes official census figure of 215.7 million, plus verified undercount of 5.3 million, plus 1975–76 illegal immigration as reported by U.S. Immigration and Naturalization Service (1.2 million).

Growth rate was obtained from natural increase, 1.3 million (from HEW), plus net migration.

Birth and death rates published by HEW are slightly higher, because they are computed without including the verified undercount or the illegal aliens.

(24) Population figure of 61.3 million adjusted for out-migration to the U.S. of 800,000 (see footnote no. 23). The crude growth rate of 3.5 must be adjusted to 2.2 for the same reason.

(25) Population derived from CELADE figure for the 1970 Brazilian census including the undercount.

(26) Includes The British Solomons, New Caledonia, New Hebrides, Gilbert and Ellis Islands, Guam, The Pacific Islands, American Samoa, The Cook Islands, French Polynesia, Tonga, and Western Samoa.

Africa. As early as 1550 B.C. the Egyptians developed the basis for birth control that is used in clinics in England and the U.S. today (8). Prescriptions ranging from magical and ineffective procedures to practical techniques have been used for hundreds of years, with varying results. Among the most effective methods was *coitus interruptus,* which was used at least as early as biblical times and apparently compared favorably in effectiveness with the condom and diaphragm of today. In the 1600s birth control was not uncommon among the wealthy in France, parts of Italy, and northwestern Europe. On the other hand, effective birth control practices were probably not commonly used in the early western European rural regions, nor in the early United States, as they are not commonly used in developing nations today. Most family planning efforts in recent years have been based on education and have not been generally successful. There is some evidence that the lower number of births per woman in developed nations may be positively associated with gainful job opportunities, increased family income, changing lifestyles, and more effective birth control measures.

Death rates are just as important as birth rates in determining population growth. Indeed, the recent rapid population growth increase is more the result of falling death rates than increasing birth rates. The "population explosion" should be viewed in its proper context and properly related to its causes.

Death rates are influenced by nutrition, sanitation, health services, and education, among other factors. Each of these also has its influence on life expectancy.

Since before 1800 both fertility and death rates have generally declined. The average life expectancy in some countries now considered developed was no more than 35 years in the 1700s. In those same nations today it is approximately 70 years. A general but hardly dependable pattern of transition from high fertility:high death rates to low fertility:low death rates seems to emerge in developed countries. Lowered death rate came first, yielding an increased growth rate. This was followed very slowly by a decline in fertility rates resulting eventually in a slower population growth rate. This pattern appears to be underway in a few developing countries today, but verification will require several years. Certainly the pattern is not widely apparent in the developing nations.

The very rapid increase in population in the developing nations started about 1920, but has increased even more rapidly since 1940. World War II saw rapid strides in medical technology, development of applied health services, improved communications, more general awareness of human suffering, and a willingness and capability to respond to requests for assistance. These factors and others associated with them have been important in reducing human suffering and mortality and thereby have had a direct effect on increasing population. The problems associated with a delay in reducing fertility are less well known and will likely continue to be major concerns into the next century.

MIGRATION. Although it affects mainly the distribution of population, migration has also had an effect on total world population. New places to settle and frontiers to conquer reduced pressure to control fertility and kept death rates lower than if the total population had been crowded together.

Before World War I only a few affluent people had ever visited foreign continents, though many had come to this country from abroad. In most countries of the world it is still easy to find people who have not traveled beyond their state or regional boundaries.

Considering this lack of movement in recent years, it is interesting that prehistoric people found their way over much of the earth and that human beings *(Homo sapiens)* as known today, originating in Africa, reached North and South America more than 20,000 years ago and Australia 30,000 years ago (4). They achieved a wider distribution than any other animal, probably because of their ability to adapt to a wide range of conditions and food. History is replete with the movement of invading armies long before Christ. Many of the soldiers settled and intermarried in the lands they conquered. Nomads, with their livestock, moved virtually the length of the African continent.

The more familiar exploits of the Vikings, Spanish, Portuguese, English, and Italians found their way into the U.S. history books. It has been estimated that up to 10 million, mostly African, slaves were imported into slave-using countries between 1450 and 1870. Between 1840 and 1930, more than 50 million people emigrated voluntarily from Europe. Most came to North America but some went to South America, southern Africa, and Australia, and lesser numbers to many other countries (4). Since the seventeenth century, these people came from and went to the temperate climate regions. They emigrated to escape the grinding poverty, oppression, and even near starvation of their homelands. Some, of course, were adventurers.

It is of interest that with the millions of people who have emigrated from Europe and the British Isles only Ireland showed a population decline. Figure 1.2 compares what might have happened without emigration with what actually happened (4).

Essentially, the entire white population of North America, South America, Australia, and New Zealand came from European countries. This massive movement of people made possible the rapid development of many of the now developed nations. While many of the immigrants to the United States and other temperate zone countries were classified as unskilled, they were usually venturesome, courageous, and therefore well suited to the rigors of pioneering. Petty criminals and debtors also were imported to work on the early plantations, but their numbers were relatively small.

Davis has reported that nearly 17 million Indians left India in the nineteenth century and at least a fourth did not return (4). Several million Chinese left China; nearly a million people left Java. Consid-

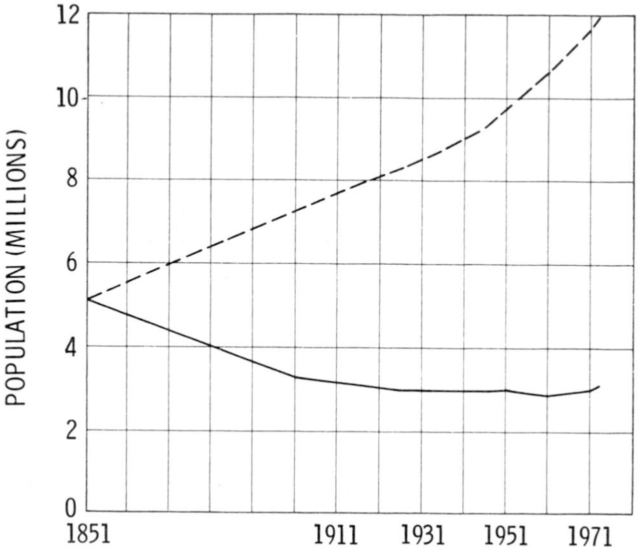


FIG. 1.2. The impact of emigration on the population of Ireland. The solid line shows the actual population, while the broken line shows the projected population if emigration had not occurred, assuming unchanged birth and death rates. From "The Migration of Human Populations" by Kingsley Davis. Copyright © 1974 by Scientific American, Inc. All rights reserved.

ering the movement out of other tropical countries, the total numbers from Asia may have exceeded those of the slave migration from Africa. It is interesting that only a small percentage of the immigrants from temperate zone countries moved to tropical regions. Except for the slaves, few of those from tropical countries found their way to the temperate zones.

Over the years migrations have had effects on intermixing within the human species. In the process of the vast movements of people, some groups probably became extinct, many were hybridized, and some made gains. From 1750 to 1930, the numbers of Caucasians increased more than five times, Asians more than twice, and blacks less than twice. See Davis' article (4) for a more complete discussion of human migration.

DIMENSIONS OF THE POPULATION PROBLEM. Sometimes it is hard to bring statistics into focus. For example, the world population as of 1976 was more than 4 billion and this number is projected to double in less than 35 years. But just what do these figures mean in terms of human beings? Consider doubling the population of the town you live in or a nearby large town in the next 30 years. Think about the problems that would be associated with doubling that population: housing, transportation, schools, water and sanitary facilities, etc. And remember most of the increase would be in young people not yet earning their own living or paying taxes to support the required services.

To bring the doubling concept more sharply into focus, take a chess or checker board, write the number 1 in the lower left-hand square, double the number to 2 in the second square, and continue to double the number in each succeeding square across the board and back again until as many squares as you want to consider are covered. Even if you use only the dark colored squares the final figure is quite amazing. Doubling the world population in 35 years is frightening, especially considering that the world's population has doubled only about four times since 1 A.D.

Population growth, whether of a family, village, tribe, nation, or the world, impinges on virtually all activities of individuals and in turn on all of society. The dimensions of the population problem need to be seriously considered in any knowledgeable discussion of population and food supplies. Brown and his co-authors have presented a stinging indictment of the situation and make some proposals (1):

> With the exception of the population-food relationship, population studies have been pursued mainly by demographers who have succeeded in clarifying those human aspects of the population equation that are quantifiable. They have measured population sizes, rates of growth, composition, and fertility levels, and devised techniques for building models and projecting population trends. This single-minded focus on demographic analysis has been at the expense of attention to the many consequences of population growth that might properly concern economists, ecologists, meteorologists, political scientists, urban planners, and many other specialists. Because the implications of population growth embrace so many disciplines, they have been the primary focus of almost none.
>
> The food dimension of the population threat remains paramount, yet in their Malthusian mindset, population analysts often neglect the threat's numerous other, often newer, manifestations.

In the paper, Brown et al. propose 22 dimensions of the population problem, including hunger, that deserve attention. They selected the topics on evidence that population growth contributes to some degree to each of them and that rising affluence, economic mismanagement, and inappropriate technologies may also contribute. The 22 dimensions considered are: literacy, ocean fisheries, natural resources areas, pollution, inflation, environmental illness, hunger, housing, climate change, overgrazing, crowding, income, urbanization, deforestation, political conflict, minerals, health services, water, unemployment, endangered species, energy, and individual freedom.

Undoubtedly others could be added and some are much more important than others. But all 22 deserve attention and sober consideration.

In the countries where the population growth rate is most rapid, the numbers of people reaching adulthood as illiterates is increasing rather than decreasing. This happens because these countries have less to spend on education and there are neither facilities nor teachers to handle the vast numbers needing attention. What efforts are made do gradually increase the absolute numbers of people able to read and write but the percentage continues to decline.

The problems are most acute in the Arabian and African states, where estimates indicate that 80 percent of the women and 60 percent of the men are illiterate. Even in countries with universal primary education the difference in illiteracy between men and women continues to widen because families give boys preference for educational opportunities. This pattern is likely to continue as long as education is directed toward opportunities for upward economic mobility. Many believe that upward mobility cannot continue to be the primary or only goal for an education; education is essential for human, social, economic, and political development.

Housing is becoming a critical aspect of the increasing population problem. Housing is bad enough in the villages, but migration to the cities creates problems that are impossible to solve in the short run. Large U.S. cities have their slums, but at least some sanitation facilities exist, fuel is available, and the water supply is clean. In the slums of most cities in the developing countries none of these "essentials" is available. The warm temperatures of the tropics allow people to exist under conditions that would not sustain life in the temperate climates but also create greater disease, insect, and rodent problems. Well over 50 percent of the population living in large cities of developing countries probably cannot afford the lowest cost housing being built. One study has shown that in India 85 percent of the households cannot finance ownership of a housing unit, and the situation is much the same in other parts of Asia, Africa, Latin America, and southern Europe (1).

As large numbers of people are crowded into the same space, many old problems intensify and new problems are created. Laboratory experiments with animals have shown the behavioral changes that take place as crowding increases. Similar stresses are created among the human population, even when food and satisfactory shelter are available. Crowding's side effects include excessive competition, aggression, high blood pressure, skin disorders, alcoholism, child abuse, and homicide (1).

Besides the human physical changes that occur with crowding, pressures on water and fuel supplies increase, the environment is more rapidly degraded, parks are overcrowded and deteriorate, forests and wildlife are reduced, and the distance to jobs increases. The physical problem of moving food from where it is produced and processed to where it is needed is monumental. Periodically, typhoons, volcanic eruptions, floods, and droughts cause large losses of life. But the question could be raised whether fewer lives would be lost in these "natural" disasters if people were not crowded into locations where such events are expected to happen.

The problem of unemployment is a significant dimension of the population and food problem because no job means no income to buy food, shelter, or medical services even when they are available. The United States is concerned about an unemployment rate of 6 to 7 percent. But in the developing countries, unemployment is far worse. Between 1950 and 1965 in Latin America, the visible unemployment rate moved from less than 6 percent to more than 11 percent and is increasing rapidly. At least 15 percent of the labor force is jobless in southeast Asia. In the developing nations as a whole, the International Labor Office estimated that 27.7 percent of the labor force was either unemployed or underemployed in 1970 and expects the figure to rise to about 30 percent by 1980 (1). Table 1.3 shows the projected job situation in both developed and developing nations of the world.

Some of the controlled-economy countries have shown that the job situation can be handled. Controlling the economy is an alternative, but the one thing the developed nations prize most highly, their independence, is the first thing lost under communist type systems. Even the controlled-economy countries cannot handle unlimited populations since as numbers of people increase, problems of caring for them also increase. Of these countries, only the German Democratic Republic has a zero population growth but a few other countries (Austria and Portugal, for example) have reached or fallen below the zero level (Table 1.2).

DIFFERENCES BETWEEN DEVELOPED AND DEVELOPING COUNTRIES. Of the approximately 4 billion people in the world, 3 billion live in the developing countries. Of this number, 28 percent live in China, 33 percent in southern and western Asia, 14 percent in southeast Asia, 14 percent in Africa, and 11 percent in Latin America.

Birth rates in developing countries are two to three times greater than those in developed nations, while the death rates are only one and a half to two times higher. This difference plus the high population base causes the growth rate and population differences between devel-

TABLE 1.3. Projected growth in world labor force from 1970 to 2000

| | 1970 | 2000 | Additional Jobs Required | Percent of Change 1970 to 2000 |
|---|---|---|---|---|
| | | *(millions)* | | |
| Developed nations | 488 | 644 | 156 | +32 |
| Developing nations | 1,011 | 1,933 | 922 | +91 |

Source: International Labor Office

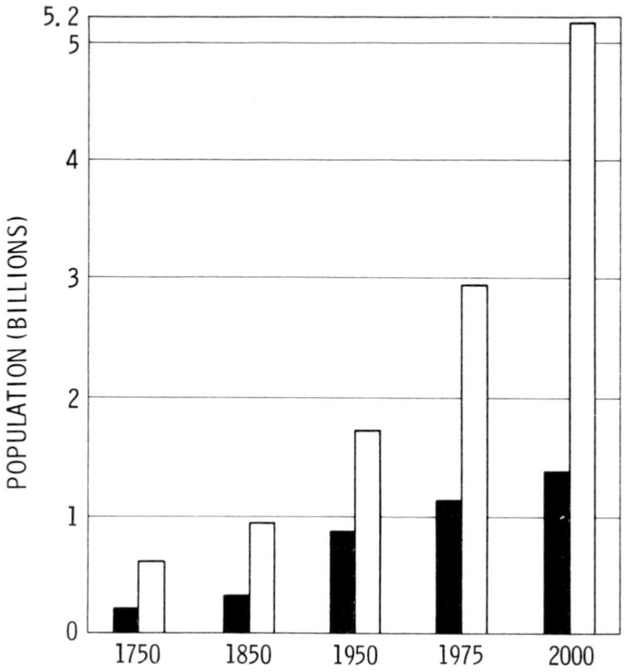


FIG. 1.3. World population increases since 1750 and projections to 2000 for developed (black) and developing (white) countries. From "The Populations of Underdeveloped Countries" by Paul Demeny. Copyright © 1974 by Scientific American, Inc. All rights reserved.

oped and developing countries shown in Table 1.1. The reduction of death rates since 1920 has been much more rapid in the developing countries than in the developed countries.

On a global scale, Figure 1.3 shows the emerging differences in numbers of people in the developing and developed countries (5). The projection to the year 2000 is based on United Nations' figures and is considered conservative.

Experts believe that growth rates are relatively uniform among the developing regions but vary between countries. As more information about China has become available, it now appears that its growth rate may be lower than that shown in Table 1.2. The present growth rates of the developing countries may be as high as or higher than any time in the past. The state of knowledge regarding growth rates in many countries is uncertain.

In contrast, the most significant demographic feature of the developed countries is the low population growth rate (from a little over 1 percent to less than .25 percent), and for most countries the rate is still declining. Figure 1.4 shows the historical downtrend in birth and death rates in the developed regions of the world (14). This downtrend may

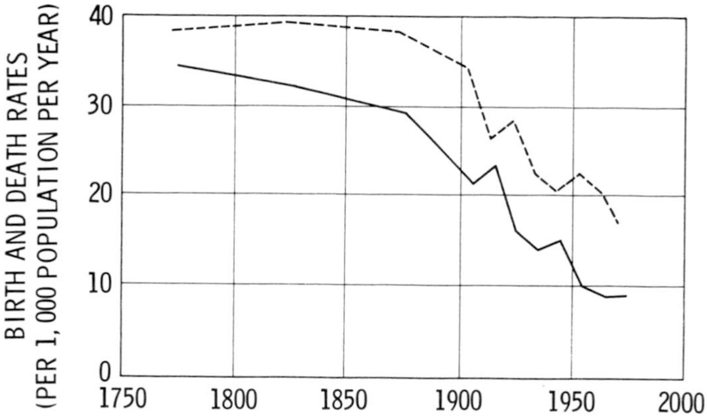


FIG. 1.4. Historical downtrend of birth rates (dotted line) and death rates (solid line) per 1,000 population per year are compared for the currently developed regions of the world. Short-lived baby booms following both world wars produced the two peaks in birth rates. From "The Populations of the Developed Countries" by Charles F. Westoff. Copyright © 1974 by Scientific American, Inc. All rights reserved.

not continue since the birth rate has increased sharply in the past, particularly after World Wars I and II. But concerns of people in developed nations today make it less likely to happen. The attitudes of women in the developed countries toward family size have changed recently. As of the early 1970s, women in the United States expected to have about one-third the number of children a similar age group had 15 years earlier, and contraceptives have been a factor in making this change possible (12).

The age group composition of the population in developed countries is also changing. In 1900 the United States had the characteristics of a fast growing population: birth and death rates were high; about one third of the population was under 15 years of age; and life expectancy was under 60 years (Fig. 1.5) (14). This situation results in a steadily increasing rise in the population as the increasing number of young people reach reproductive age. By 1970 the U.S. population had changed significantly, with fewer young people especially in the 1- to 9-year-old age groups and a higher percentage of people in the age group over 40 years (Fig. 1.6). This transition from a population characterized by high birth and death rates to one with lower birth and death rates is being felt especially in the primary schools. By 1980 fewer students are expected in high schools and universities.

The people living in countries described today as developed have longer life, better health, and more education than those in developing countries. But a large percentage of the people in these countries did not have all these advantages as recently as half a century ago and some do not have them today.

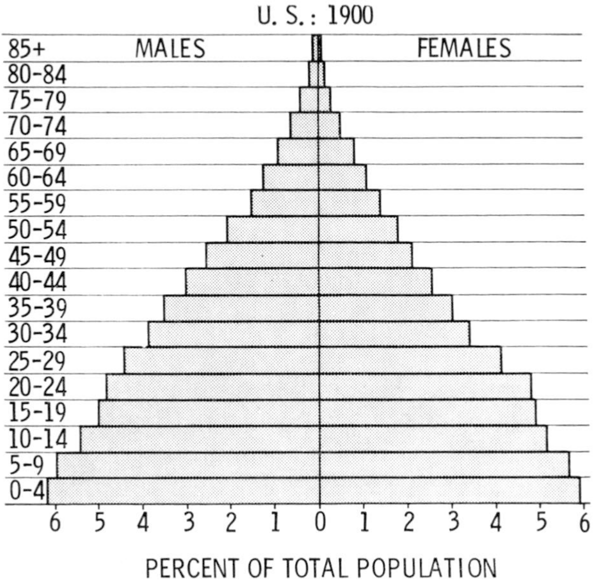


FIG. 1.5. Age composition of the U.S. population in 1900. The shape of this pyramid is characteristic of a fast-growing population with high birth and death rates where the average life expectancy is under 60. A third of Americans were under 15 years of age. From "The Populations of the Developed Countries" by Charles F. Westoff. 

Per capita income in developed countries is measured in thousands of dollars while the people in developing nations have incomes of hundreds of dollars or even less. Life expectancy at birth is above 70 years in some developed countries and little more than half that in many developing countries.

For those who have traveled widely and observed conditions in places such as Quito, Caracas, Algiers, Addis Ababa, Lagos, Kinshasa, Bombay, and Calcutta, problems facing the developing nations are quite apparent. Malnutrition, unemployment, low pay, poor housing, and lack of sanitary and health services are a few of the obvious problems. And the rural areas of the countries in which these cities are found are frequently more depressed.

There is no question that countries such as the United States can feed, house, and clothe many more people. An expanding population still brings concerns about jobs, adverse environmental effects, education, and social problems. Ryder expects that fewer U.S. families will have more than two children in the years ahead and that a small proportion may even choose to have none at all (12). At this time many people in developed nations appear to recognize the problems associated with large families and a large population, though governments apparently do

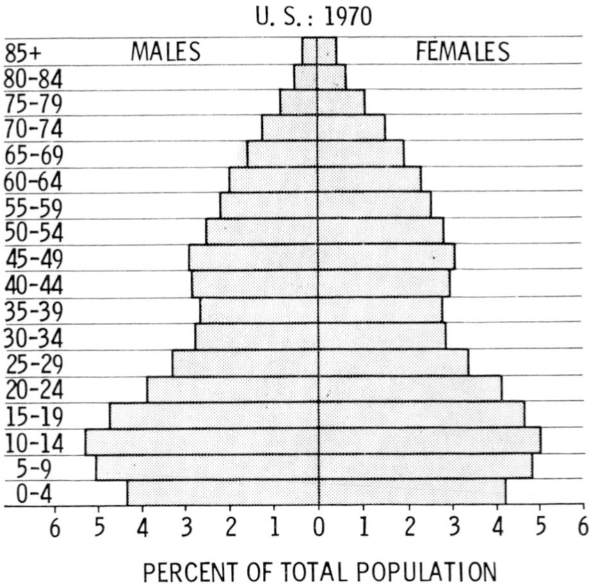


FIG. 1.6. Age composition of U.S. population in 1970. The sides of this pyramid are pinched in because of the low birth rates that prevailed during the years of the Great Depression. The bulge centered on the 10- to 14-year-old age group is a consequence of the postwar baby boom. From "The Populations of the Developed Countries" by Charles F. Westoff. Copyright © 1974 by Scientific American, Inc. All rights reserved.

not. The problem, as such, was not even discussed by the presidential candidates in the 1976 campaign. The developed nations in general and the United States in particular do not have to have a zero population growth rate at this time, but the time when they will have to consider it may not be far away.

Among the developing countries, only Brazil and some countries in Africa have significant amounts of additional land for more people. The countries with largest populations tend to have the least land for their increasing numbers. This suggests critical population-food problems for at least the next quarter century.

Ryder suggests that eventually society will not tolerate either a negative population growth nor an excessively high positive growth (12). Governments may act in three different ways to influence population growth though there are undesirable consequences to each. One action might be to legislate against more than two children. Another could be to take advantages away from large families and give them to small families. As a third alternative, the government could create an institutional alternative to the family as a source of individual emotional support.

Ryder does not believe that any of these three alternatives is suitable in a free society. Some action may be necessary and indeed some actions by governments have already been taken. The age of marriage can be changed; Germany has done this. Abortion can be made easy and legal; a number of nations including the United States have taken this step. Couples with more than two children can be denied public housing as in Sri Lanka. Early marriage and having more than two children are punishable offenses in China. India has moved toward compulsory sterilization. Reverse situations also exist such as baby bonuses in Canada and income tax deductions in the United States. The above represent only a few of the types of actions taken and being considered by governments.

In most countries, developed and undeveloped, the major emphasis on population control has been on education. Considerable effort and money have gone into education and action on fertility control by some governments and other interested groups. But a change in attitudes is essential if a significant reduction in fertility is to occur. Population growth rates are the result of the reasoning, decisions, and actions of the people causing them.

Demeny has pointed out that the force of the demographic transition can be summarized in a single sentence: "In demographic matters, as in others, people tend to act in accordance with their interests as they best see them" (5). Bohlen has discussed these attitudes in greater detail in Chapter 16.

PROSPECTS FOR FEEDING MORE PEOPLE. It is very difficult for most people in the developed countries to understand the fact and reason that more than half of the world population is preoccupied with getting food to satisfy day-to-day needs. This is not a new situation in the world, but the islands of affluence in a hungry world have enlarged from a few individuals to a few families to segments of populations in countries to entire nations. In developed countries only a small percentage of people have experienced hunger for prolonged periods of time while in developing countries only a small percentage of people know any other way of life. This situation exists for several reasons: there are too many people for the existing food supply, too few people have resources to purchase adequate food, food production methods are primitive, yields are low, and governments have not provided the facilities and the incentives that favor increased food supplies.

Since 1972 when poor crops occurred simultaneously in the U.S.S.R., China, Australia, southeast Asia, and the Sahelian region of Africa, the seriousness of the population:food problem has been brought into focus. The 1972 condition was primarily the result of unfavorable weather, but following 1972 increased economic activity in the developed countries, worldwide inflation, sharply higher energy costs, and reduced supplies of fertilizer all occurred at a time when potential and actual demands for food were expanding.

As a result of a drastically lowered store of surplus food grains in the exporting nations, several important conferences were convened to study the situation with an eye to needed action.

The United Nations World Population Conference held in August 1974 in Bucharest, Romania, was attended by representatives of 137 countries and numerous groups and organizations. While the conference devoted its major efforts to demographic and population problems it recognized agricultural problems and recommended actions that would increase food production and improve the lot of rural people in developing counrties. In the conference report *(Action Taken at Bucharest),* 21 resolutions were adopted (2). Of these, 11 offered specific recommendations and three of those 11 were concerned with rural development, food production, and food and fertilizer shortages.

In November 1974 the United Nations convened a World Food Conference in Rome, Italy. It was attended by leaders from most countries of the world. The urgency of considering world food needs arose as a result of the low level of production in 1972 and the reduced storage stocks that followed. In its assessment of the world food situation the conference report made the following comments: "History records more acute shortages in individual countries, but it is doubtful whether such a critical food situation has ever been so worldwide" and (in spite of good yields in 1973 and reasonable yields in 1974) "Thus, the world's food situation has suddenly become exposed to an uncertainty of unacceptable proportions" (13). The situation was considered to be a *crisis.*

It is indeed fortunate that cereal grains and root crops are the principal and acceptable sources of food in most of the developing countries (see Chapter 2). Worldwide the period from about 1950 to 1971 saw a doubling of cereal grain production, while population increased by only half that amount. United States corn yields more than doubled during this period and the dwarf high-yield varieties of rice and wheat were introduced in many countries. While the cereal production per person increased by at least 50 percent during this period, most of the grain remained in the developed nations. Less than half of the increase was unevenly available to the poorest 2.6 billion people of Latin America, Asia, and Africa. In the period 1965 to 1975, the increase in production per unit area of land was very slow while population increased dramatically. The result was a clouded outlook. The Rome conference projected the world food demand to 1985 to increase at 2.4 percent per year, with 2 percent representing population increase and 0.4 percent increased purchasing power. Averages tell only part of the story, for the developed nations are expected to show an increased demand of 1.5 percent per year and developing nations more than 3.5 percent. But it is possible that a country with a rapid population increase and a rapid growth in income—some of the smaller oil exporting nations, for example—could double its food demand by 1985. At the other extreme it is expected that more than 30 countries, because of continuing poverty, could have an effective demand for food that would fall short of food energy requirements. The conferees believed the projections of increased demand by the developing countries of 3.3 percent for cereals, 4.7 percent for fish, and 4.4 percent for meat per person per year were conservative. It is more difficult to project supplies, but an estimate of 2.6 percent increase per year has been made for developing countries. This would require increasing levels of imports by the developing nations if food needs are to be met.

The many constraints to increasing food production, especially in the developing countries, are hard to overcome, but more difficult in the near term may be the removal of constraints that work against getting food to the hungry people. These constraints were considered at both the Rome World Food Conference and The World Food Conference of 1976 held at Iowa State University (11). They are also discussed in some detail in Chapters 4, 5, 10, 11, 12, 13, 14, 15, 16, and 17 in this book.

Faced with the knowledge that as much as one-fourth of the world's population does not have enough food to meet physiological requirements and at least half a billion seldom have the minimum requirements, it is natural that knowledgeable people would have a wide range of opinions regarding possible solutions. Some forecast starvation or malnutrition related deaths occasionally in the millions range. Others believe that there is now, and will continue to be, enough food produced and that distribution and ability to purchase that food are the main problems. A few would abandon the countries whose prospects for improvement are at best questionable and concentrate assistance on those whose prospects are considered better (triage). By and large, most agricultural scientists believe that scientific information and resulting technology will be able to meet the challenge of needed food production. The potentials for meeting food production requirements are considerable.

Millions of hectares of land suitable for farming and grazing remain unused or underused. This land is largely in South America and Africa. The problems and costs of bringing it to a useful state are discussed in Chapter 7 and by Chandler, Khan, Luykx, and Obeng (11). There are still limited opportunities for bringing more land into production in North America and other developed countries. The difficulties of bringing new lands into production in the tropics revolve around costs and lack of appropriate research and technology. Irrigation for existing cultivated lands and for new lands holds considerable potential, but irrigated agriculture is labor and management intensive, development costs are high, and usually energy needs are great. The potential, however, is there.

There are vast potentials for increasing livestock and livestock products for food. Much of this potential can be realized, especially with ruminants, through improving herd health, upgrading quality through genetic improvement, and improving the feed base. These things can be accomplished on lands that cannot produce significant amounts of food crops. Livestock opportunities are discussed in Chapter 8 and by Conrad, El-Shazly, Pagot, and Wittwer (11).

Much has been written of the potential for "harvesting the sea" and inland waters. Reduction of the fish catch in the early 1970s suggests that significant research and coordinated management are needed if this potential is to be realized. Chapters 3 and 8 consider this matter.

The potential of cereal crops and seed legumes is the main hope for feeding the expanding population. Agricultural scientists are optimistic and progress in the past quarter century is justification for optimism. Crop and seed quality improvement methods are known. Production procedures need adaptive research especially outside the temperate zones. Serious questions arise concerning availability of fertilizers, pesticides, and herbicides. These chemicals are energy costly and environmentally suspect. It is the lack of these essential ancillary needs that may delay realizing the potential production of food crops. Potentials for increasing food crop production are discussed in Chapters 3, 9, and 10 of this book. Burton, Okigbo, Olembo, Sprague, and Winkelmann also consider this important subject (11). The potential for increasing total food supplies in the world exists, but the prospects for getting enough food to all people in the next two decades are hardy optimistic. And even if more total food is produced, the rapidly increasing population may mean fewer kilograms or pounds of food per individual after the year 2000.

There is no question that there will be more people on this earth in the years ahead. The question is whether they can be adequately fed and have a better quality of life than their forebears. The alternatives to optimism are not pleasant to contemplate, but to build hopes only on *potentials* for improvement does not appear realistic; the potentials must be realized. Increased production of food is not a final solution but can be used to buy time for population growth to stabilize at a manageable level.

It seems appropriate to consider again the deliberations of Thomas Malthus, the English clergyman who had given human population and food considerable thought before 1800. His treatise, "An Essay on the Principle of Population" (9), was very unpopular at the time, but through the years he has been the most widely quoted writer on the subject. He presented three propositions in his essay and believed he proved them:

1. Population is necessarily limited by means of subsistence.
2. Population invariably increases where the means of subsistence in-

crease unless prevented by some very powerful and obvious checks and that these checks are all resolvable into moral restraints, vice and misery.

3. The preventive and positive checks are inversely related. (Interpreted in today's language, fertility and mortality can either be both high or both low.)

Most commonly quoted is an interpretation of an example he used in discussing population and food: that population tends to increase geometrically and food supplies increase arithmetically. If this thesis is valid, it is obvious that a collision course is established and it is only a matter of when, not if, a starvation condition will occur. The stated principle may be valid, but Malthus could not foresee the innovations in agriculture that would allow food production to proceed at more than arithmetic rates or the voluntary controls on birth rate that cause population to increase at less than a geometric rate.

In many of the developing nations in the 1970s, per capita food supplies are decreasing while population is increasing geometrically. Only a few countries including Canada and the United States produce an exportable surplus (see Chapters 3 and 9), but competition for that surplus causes it to move not to the very hungry people but to those who can afford to pay for it (see Chapter 17).

SUMMARY. This chapter has attempted to present a brief history of the world's population and the factors involved in creating the numbers of people we have today. It has compared the developed and developing nations and has shown projections for numbers of people for the next 25 years based on available evidence. It has shown the relationships between people and food and discussed the problems of feeding a rapidly expanding world population.

Obviously, none of the demographic considerations could be discussed in detail. The writer hopes that readers will be challenged to pursue their specific areas of interest in greater detail. The references cited are only a sample of the available literature, the authors are among the world's most respected authorities, and their articles are as current as can be found.

There can be no question that the lives of all persons will be affected directly or indirectly by the increasing numbers of people and attempts to feed them over the next quarter century. Some people will only pay a bit more for their food; others will be hungry; still others malnourished; and some may die. The Rome conference considered the situation of crisis proportions. The least that can be said is that population and food is worthy of greater study and understanding.

## REFERENCES

1. Brown, Lester R.; McGrath, Patricia L.; and Stokes, Bruce. Twenty-two Dimensions of the Population Problem. In Worldwatch Paper 5, Worldwatch Institute, March 1976.
2. Centre for Economic and Social Information. Action Taken at Bucharest. United Nations World Population Conference. CES 1/WP4-22, November 1974.
3. Coale, Ansley J. The History of the Human Population. Scientific American 231 (3): 40–51, September 1974.
4. Davis, Kingsley. The Migration of Human Populations. Scientific American 231 (3): 92–105, September 1974.
5. Demeny, Paul. The Populations of Underdeveloped Countries. Scientific American 231 (3): 148–159, September 1974.
6. Durand, John D. A Long Range View of World Population Growth. Annals of the American Academy of Political and Social Science, January 1967.
7. Freedman, Ronald, and Bernard Berelson. The Human Population. Scientific American 231 (3): 30–39. September 1974.
8. Himes, Norman. Medical History of Contraception. New York: Shocken Books, 1970.
9. Malthus, Thomas R. An Essay on the Principle of Population. 5th ed. Homewood, Ill.: Richard D. Irwin, Inc., 1963.
10. 1976 World Population Estimates. Washington, D.C.: The Environmental Fund, 1976.
11. Proceedings of The World Food Conference of 1976. Ames: Iowa State Univ. Press, 1977.
12. Ryder, Norman B. The Family in Developed Countries. Scientific American 231 (3): 123–132, September 1974.
13. United Nations World Food Conference. Assessment of the World Food Situation: Present and Future. Rome, November 1974.
14. Westoff, Charles F. The Populations of the Developed Countries. Scientific American 231 (3): 108–120, September 1974.

E. R. DUNCAN

*One step in changing cassava to gari, a high carbohydrate food.*

# 2

# Human Nutritional Needs and Food Sources

JOHN N. HATHCOCK *and* JOSEFA S. EUSEBIO

An interim report of the National Research Council made in 1975 estimated that 94 percent of the people who receive insufficient calories and protein live in developing countries. A conservative view suggests that 61 developing countries were deficient in food energy supplies in 1970. They also estimate that 25 to 30 percent of the population in the Far East and Africa suffer from significant malnutrition. Malnutrition affects at least half a billion people and quite possibly more.

The incidence of malnutrition is higher in southern Asia and central Africa, but poor people suffer wherever they are. The very large numbers who have minimal diets and health are just not able to cope with the stresses from infection and temporary food shortages. In many developing countries nearly a quarter of the population with the lowest income may have only half of the per capita energy intake of the top 10 percent. If these figures are valid, the degree of malnutrition of the poor is much worse than national averages indicate.

It is important, if not essential, that as many people as possible understand human nutritional needs and the food sources that supply these needs.

Human nutritional needs can be considered from two main points of view: (1) that food and the nutrients it contains are needed for life, growth, and development, and for maintenance throughout life; and (2) that food and nutrients are required to prevent certain specific diseases and build resistance to others. Research on nutritional deficiency diseases has contributed much knowledge about the role of nutrition in normal growth and development and maintenance of life. Besides satisfying the biological needs of people, food also serves psychological and social needs.

John N. Hathcock, researcher in nutritional status methods, nutrient utilization, and toxicological influences on nutrition, is Associate Professor, Food and Nutrition Department, Iowa State University. He has also been researcher and teacher at University of the Philippines.

Josefa S. Eusebio is Assistant Professor, Institute of Human Ecology, University of the Philippines and currently a graduate student in nutrition at Iowa State University.

Many food supplement and nutrition improvement programs have been designed to prevent visible symptoms of malnutrition. Only recently have the impacts of nutrition on the individual's work capacity, on the economic productivity of the labor force, and on other health services been considered in planning for national development.

Countries with little visible malnutrition can afford to include the benefits of good nutrition in their nutrition planning. But in many countries with high incidences of one or more of the diseases of malnutrition, the immediate goal must be to prevent these diseases.

BENEFITS OF GOOD NUTRITION. The nutrients and energy provided by an adequate, balanced diet are necessary for life, reproduction, growth, physical and mental development, and body maintenance. But good nutrition alone is not enough. Many other factors such as infectious diseases, also influence health and development.

Nutritionally deprived children may develop recognized symptoms of malnutrition, but many are only smaller, less developed physically, and perhaps retarded in mental and social development. The exact cause of the retarded mental development that can occur in severely undernourished children is not an entity but a complex deeply intermingled with poor nutrition. Experiments with animals indicate that inadequate intake of protein or calories can cause slowed physical development and maturation of the brain. This could cause mental retardation. But severely undernourished young children are also frequently listless, lethargic, and relatively unresponsive to environmental stimuli. This lack of attention to events and circumstances around them slows the process of learning. So whether a malnourished child cannot learn normally because the brain has not developed normally, or because malnutrition has interfered with the necessary energy and interest to learn is an unanswered question. Either way, the immediate consequences are the same: retarded mental development leads to delayed or impaired emotional and social development. Poor mental, social, and emotional development of many individuals undoubtedly also can impair the cultural and economic development of a nation, although data to prove this relationship are incomplete at present.

Good nutrition is essential for healthy, thriving individuals, families, and nations but by itself cannot assure these benefits. Nutrition planning, therefore, should be an important part of any government's health, agricultural, and economic policies.

MALNUTRITION AND ITS IDENTIFICATION. Strictly speaking, malnutrition means "bad nutrition," which includes both excess and deficiency.

The most common types of malnutrition resulting from excessive intake are obesity resulting from overeating foods (fats, carbohydrates, and proteins), atherosclerosis from excessive intake of cholesterol and animal fats, high blood pressure from excessive salt intake, and toxicity diseases from eating food inappropriately processed, stored, and preserved.

Obesity and atherosclerosis are diseases of the middle class and of the affluent, not of the very poor. In developed countries, such as the United States and those of Western Europe, even a person receiving government assistance may be quite affluent compared with a slum-dweller in Calcutta or Caracas.

Malnutrition in most areas of the world, however, results from an inadequate supply of nutritious food. Many dietary deficiency diseases have been identified: for example, beriberi, cheilosis, pelagra, scurvy, endemic goiter, and xerosis, which result from single deficiencies of thiamin, riboflavin, niacin, vitamin D, vitamin C, iodine, and vitamin A, respectively. Other diseases may be caused by either a single deficiency or combined deficiencies of specific nutrients. Anemia can result from deficiencies of iron, folic acid, vitamin $B_{12}$, or other nutrients. Rickets is related to deficiencies in calcium, phosphorus, and vitamin D. Such specific nutrients are needed in small amounts, and deficiencies may be the result of improper food storage, processing, and lack of variety, or simply inadequate amounts of food. The major functions and important sources of critical nutrients are listed in Table 2.1.

The most common kinds of malnutrition in the world are protein-calorie malnutrition, xerophthalmiz, nutritional anemias, and endemic goiter. Protein-calorie malnutrition (PCM) is caused by a protein deficiency, a calorie deficiency, or both, and presents the most difficult problems to solve. Clinical manifestations of PCM in children have been classified as kwashiorkor, marasmus, or marasmic-kwashiorkor, and the less acute forms as growth retardation or nutritional dwarfism.

Historically, the word kwashiorkor (k wäsh ē 'or ker) was introduced into the nutritional and medical vocabulary by Dr. Cicely D. Williams in 1933 when she was working in the Gold Coast (now Ghana) of West Africa. To the Ga people with whom Dr. Williams worked, kwashiorkor was a specific name given to a specific disease of the displaced baby when the next one is born. The symptoms of the disease are delayed growth, swelling of feet and legs, irritability, changes in hair color, severe and rather characteristic skin disorders, enlarged fatty livers, and in many cases diarrhea and eventually death. After investigating the backgrounds of such patients, she concluded that the disease was probably caused by protein deficiency, since patients had diets with substantial amounts of energy (calories) but little protein.

Marasmus is the term used to describe a severe growth retardation and wasting of the muscle mass. Marasmic children appear literally to be "skin and bones," except for a bloated abdomen. In severe cases, the visible muscle of the arms and legs may nearly disappear. Often, the

TABLE 2.1. SOURCES AND FUNCTIONS OF SOME NUTRIENTS.[a]

| Nutrient | Important Sources | Major Functions |
|---|---|---|
| Energy | carbohydrate, fat, protein | body warmth, physical work, life processes |
| Carbohydrate | wheat, corn, rice, potatoes, cassava, sugars, etc. | energy, blood glucose |
| Fat | cooking oils, butter, margarine, lard, fat meats | energy, essential fatty acids |
| Protein | meats, poultry, fish, milk, cheese, beans, peas, and many cereal staple foods | body structure, life processes |
| Vitamins: | | |
| A | liver, butter, fortified milk, dark green leafy vegetables, yellow and orange vegetables and fruits | maintenance of skin and mucous membranes, night vision, bone and tooth development |
| D | fortified milk, fish oils, exposure of skin to sunlight | absorption of calcium and phosphorus, bone mineralization |
| E | vegetable oils, wheat and rice germ, green leafy vegetables | protects membranes, needed for normal reproduction |
| K | liver, leafy vegetables, synthesis in intestine | blood clotting, perhaps needed in energy utilization |
| C | fresh fruits and vegetables | cartilage formation, blood vessel formation, amino acid metabolism, iron absorption |
| $B_1$ (thiamin) | whole-grain and enriched cereal products, green vegetables, liver | carbohydrate metabolism |
| $B_2$ (riboflavin) | meats, whole-grain and enriched cereal products, milk, eggs | carbohydrate, fat and protein metabolism, life processes |
| Niacin | meats, whole-grain and enriched cereal products | carbohydrate, fat and protein metabolism, life processes |
| $B_6$ (pyridoxine) | meats, potatoes, vegetables | protein metabolism, life processes |
| Folacin | meats, eggs, whole-grain cereals, dark green leafy vegetables | protein metabolism, life processes, maturation of red blood cells |
| $B_{12}$ (cobalamin) | meats, milk, eggs | protein metabolism, red blood cell maturation |
| Minerals: | | |
| Calcium | milk, dairy products, dark green leafy vegetables, meats containing bone | bone and tooth structure, blood clotting |
| Phosphorus | milk, meat, cereal products | bone and tooth structure, energy metabolism |
| Iron | meats, eggs, whole-grain cereal products, leafy vegetables | hemoglobin formation, life processes |
| Iodine | iodized salt, seafood, foods from iodine-rich soils | thyroid hormone formation |

[a]This table does not list all known nutrients.

marasmic child is too weak to be irritable or cry. Most commonly these children receive severely inadequate amounts of food.

During the last several years, dietary surveys in India have failed to clearly distinguish between the diet composition patterns that lead to kwashiorkor and those that lead to marasmus. Instead, the recent trend, which is supported by nutritional studies from many areas of the world, is to recognize kwashiorkor as a very acute (severe) form of PCM and marasmus as a more chronic (long-lasting) form. Kwashiorkor is often precipitated in children one to five years old by some infectious disease (such as measles) or by intestinal parasites. Marasmus, often accompanied by diarrhea and dehydration, often occurs earlier than kwashiorkor and is often associated with early weaning, inadequate amounts of breast milk from the mother, or improper bottle feeding with very dilute formula.

In many developing countries, prepared bottle formulas for infants are advertised to appeal to status, progress, and general Western civilization life-styles. When people switch to such formulas without adequate income to buy enough and without knowledge of how to use them, the too common result is a baby who becomes marasmic before weaning. Under these conditions, breast feeding is the best insurance against malnutrition.

Ignorance and misinformation often contribute to the development of PCM in children even in families with adequate food. Many cultures teach that meat, eggs, and other protein rich foods are bad for young children, especially when they are sick. This belief generates a vicious cycle: children are sick because they are not properly fed and then they are not properly fed because they are sick. The results are often tragic.

Malnutrition is often difficult to identify, because it commonly occurs with, and may be aggravated by, other diseases. The reverse is also true: other diseases may be made more severe by malnutrition.

Four major ways to assess nutritional status or condition and to identify malnutrition are (1) dietary surveys, (2) clinical examination, (3) anthropometric assessment (body measurements), and (4) biochemical tests. The most accurate assessment comes from use of as many of these as technically and economically possible.

Dietary surveys that ask people to recall what was eaten and food composition tables can be used to calculate estimated intakes of food energy and nutrients. Intakes can be compared with requirements and recommended allowances to estimate probable dietary adequacy or quality. The primary difficulties with this method are (1) the lack of precise knowledge of the composition for many foods and prepared dishes, (2) the reluctance of many parents to admit that they had not provided well for their child, and (3) the lack of precise knowledge of nutrient requirements and efficiency of use in a child or adult who is also burdened with infectious disease or parasites.

Clinical examination may reveal swelling; enlarged liver; skin disorders; tongue, hair, gum, and eye changes, and many other signs of malnutrition. Examination is extremely useful, partly because it often reveals the unexpected. Clinical aspects of a nutritional survey should be performed by a physician who has special training in the symptoms of malnutrition.

Body measurements, such as height, weight, arm and head circumferences, and skin-fold thicknesses at various sites of the body, are very useful in assessing protein-calorie status, but less so for assessing vitamin and mineral status. These data are often used in conjunction with biochemical tests.

Biochemical methods for urine and blood analysis are the most specific and objective way to assess nutritional status for many nutrients. These tests can also detect preclinical malnutrition, i.e., malnutrition that is not severe or prolonged enough to cause clinically visible symptoms.

EFFECTS OF INADEQUATE NUTRITION ON POPULATIONS AND NATIONS. Malnutrition of large numbers of individuals must ultimately be reflected in adverse effects on whole populations and nations. But in many countries, accurate figures on how many people suffer and die from malnutrition are almost impossible to obtain. Much infant mortality and early adult death in developing countries is not attributed directly to diagnosed malnutrition. Instead, health statistics list measles, whooping cough, sleeping sickness, malaria, influenza, pneumonia, or unknown as the cause of death. Furthermore, in many countries the census accuracy is so poor that the population size and number of births and deaths in any given year can only be a guess.

Studies have shown, however, that malnutrition is correlated with high total death rates and high death rates from infectious diseases. And since healing processes and resistance to infection depend on adequate nutrition, malnutrition undoubtedly contributes substantially to the death rate attributed to infectious disease.

Besides direct effects on vital and health statistics, malnutrition has many other adverse effects on nations. There is a strong association between early malnutrition and below-normal performance at school. Malnutrition interferes with motivation, concentration, and ability to learn. Malnourished children also miss more days of school than normal children. Regardless of whether there is a permanent effect on the brain, the malnourished child is permanently handicapped because of an irreversible loss of opportunity.

In jobs that require physical prowess, malnutrition is a severe handicap. In many other jobs, malnutrition may decrease performance because of decreased attention, precision, and stamina. Malnutrition is also correlated with decreased working life span.

From a developmental policy viewpoint, therefore, a nation invests food, resources, labor, and time in rearing children into adults. If malnutrition decreases the return in terms of the quantity or quality of productive adulthood, then the nation's resources are being poorly invested.

REQUIREMENTS AND ALLOWANCES FOR CRITICAL NUTRIENTS. Nutritional requirements are the minimum amounts of energy and nutrients required to support optimum health and performance. Exact requirements vary from individual to individual and can be specified only for any specific person at a specific time. The factors that affect the requirements will be given in the following section. In this section, how requirements and recommended allowances are arrived at will be examined.

Because of individual differences, the recommended daily allowances for specific nutrients include an extra allowance to provide a margin of safety. The only exception to this rule is energy. The recommended energy intake is the lowest value that provides for the activity and maintenance of good health for the average individual in a particular sex and age group, and for the needs of such processes as growth and reproduction. No margin of safety is provided because consistent and cumulative excessive intakes usually lead to obesity. Likewise, any deficiency in energy intake leads to weight loss. Therefore, allowances must be individually adjusted over the long term to provide the precise energy requirements and stable body weight. Adults should especially avoid gradual accumulations of weight that come with age or changes in life-style.

Protein requirements are more difficult to state than other nutrient requirements. Not only is a margin of safety required, but the exact protein requirement must be adjusted for variations in protein quality.

Protein is made up of 22 amino acids and the body can synthesize all except 8, which are commonly called "essential" amino acids. These essential amino acids, therefore, must be obtained from food. To be well nourished, a person must consume all 8 at the same time and in sufficient quantities. The proportions of essential amino acids found in most animal products more nearly match human body requirements (are higher quality) than the proportion commonly found in plants. Protein quality not only varies with content of amino acids but also with the digestibility of the protein.

For a high quality protein, then, the minimum required daily intakes will be relatively low, and for poor quality proteins, the minimum required intakes will be considerably higher. Recommended dietary allowances for protein are based on the assumption that the diet provides a variety of foods containing protein of varying quality, but with an intermediate average quality.

The minimum requirements for several specific vitamins and minerals are known with considerable accuracy. And since for most of these there is relatively little risk of toxicity from excess intake from food sources, the recommended dietary allowances are set reasonably high to provide a substantial margin of safety. There are several vitamins and minerals that are not given in tables of recommended dietary allowances because even though we know they are required, we do not know what their exact minimum requirements in humans are. Fortunately, these nutrients are usually abundantly supplied in most diets, relative to the probable required amounts. Hence there is small risk of accidental deficiencies of these nutrients in human beings.

Standard recommended dietary allowances are set and periodically revised by the following two groups, as well as several others: the Food and Nutrition Board of the National Research Council in the U.S., and the joint Expert Group of the Food and Agriculture Organization and the World Health Organization (both of the United Nations) in the developing countries of the world. Often there are discrepancies between the dietary recommendations made by these two sources. Many of these differences are legitimate differences in scientific method and opinion. Sometimes, however, the United States, in the comfort of its abundance of food, is accused of setting the recommended dietary allowances wastefully high. Conversely, local committees in some developing countries and the United Nations group have been accused of obscuring food shortages by setting recommended dietary allowances too low to provide for optimal health. In summary, there is no complete general agreement on how much total food and its components the world requires.

WORLD POPULATION AND FOOD SUPPLY. The ratio of world food production to population has remained remarkably stable over the last 20 years. Despite major improvements in agricultural methods and materials and consequent increases in food production, the per capita food supply in developing countries has not increased appreciably because of the rapid population growth rates.

While the United States, Japan, the countries of Western Europe, and a few other countries have substantially decreased their population growth rates in recent years, the developing countries have made little progress in this respect and the world population is still increasing by more than 2 percent per year. Even with food imports from the more prosperous nations and improved agricultural practices, the developing countries remain unable to feed themselves adequately.

In the developed nations generally characterized by affluence, there has been a shift toward diets higher in animal protein. Feed grain and oilseed demands have increased and world trade among these nations has accelerated. On the other hand, in the less developed countries, people largely depend on cereals and other plant foods for their major nutrients. In several Asian countries, where diets are primarily based on rice and some grain legumes, protein supplementation may be useful and even necessary.

The population in the developing nations was almost three times as great as that in the developed countries in 1975 and will be nearly four times as great by the year 2000. Asia's population increase is critical since the population base in these countries is already so large. Estimates indicate that in the developing countries a 135 percent increase in food production will be needed by year 2000 if the expanding population is to be adequately fed. For the developed countries, a 60 percent increase will be needed.

The Food and Agriculture Organization of the United Nations recognizes the long-term need to increase caloric levels to meet minimum energy needs and to upgrade protein value of diets by increasing the amount of animal protein and higher quality vegetable proteins consumed in the developing countries. Fortifying foods with vitamins and minerals continues to be an important need. In the last two decades the development of protein-rich foods or mixtures has made a significant contribution in preventing and treating malnutrition among the very young. Unconventional food sources, such as algae, single cell proteins, and leaf proteins, are also being developed to supplement food supplies and as possible alternative protein sources.

But regardless of any and all improvements in agriculture and food production, malnutrition will remain unless population growth rates are decreased and eventually stopped. Many claim that population can be controlled only through national development, while others claim that development is too slow a method for population control. Humane resolution of this problem is probably the greatest challenge ever faced by mankind.

FACTORS INFLUENCING NUTRITIONAL NEEDS. Tables of recommended dietary allowances include differences based on influences of age, sex, body size, pregnancy, and lactation. Some differences in nutritional needs between males and females relate to body size, some to metabolic patterns and body composition, and others to physiological functions, such as growth, pregnancy, lactation, and menstruation during which substantial amounts of iron are lost in bleeding.

During periods of rapid growth, children have very high nutritional requirements because of the needs for increasing body size as well as accomplishment of the basic life processes. Good nutrition during pregnancy is especially important to prevent adverse effects on the developing child. During pregnancy, folic acid needs nearly double for some unknown reason. The need for increased nutrient intake during lactation is obvious because nutrients, especially calcium and protein, are needed in large quantities to produce milk, and a considerable amount of energy is used in the process.

Some substances in food affect the digestion, absorption, and use of nutrients. For example, raw soybeans contain a substance that inhibits protein digestion, while cooked soybeans do not; whole grain cereal products contain a substance that decreases zinc, iron, and calcium absorption; and moldy peanuts and cereal grains may contain poisonous substances (aflatoxins). Some of these substances merely increase the amounts of certain nutrients needed in the diet to provide adequate nutrition, whereas other substances, such as aflatoxins, make the food unfit for consumption by humans or animals and may cause death. Also, as we saw earlier, protein quality affects the amount of dietary protein needed.

Many infectious diseases increase the need for protein and other nutrients. Likewise, deficiencies of certain nutrients increase a person's susceptibility to infectious disease. Intestinal or urinary tract infections may cause substantial iron and protein loss. Intestinal tract infection and diarrhea can dramatically lower the efficiencies of digestion and nutrient absorption. Hookworm and roundworm infestations can cause very high rates of iron and protein loss through bleeding.

Prior nutritional status also affects immediate nutritional needs. For example, higher nutrient intakes are required to recover from malnutrition than to merely maintain adequate nutritional status in a well-nourished person. A malnourished body requires corrective measures before it can be maintained in good health.

Climate and activity markedly affect the minimum nutritional requirements, especially for energy. Large numbers of calories are used to regulate body temperature in very cold climates and to support prolonged, intense physical activity.

TREATMENT OF MALNUTRITION. How much the effects of malnutrition can be reversed depends on their severity, the duration and the time or age at deprivation, and more importantly, on the kind of malnutrition. Mild vitamin A deficiency may cause only temporary night blindness, whereas severe and prolonged vitamin A deficiency can destroy the normal structure of the eye and result in permanent, total blindness. Even severe but temporary protein deficiency in an adult may cause only weight loss, whereas the same deficiency in a young child could cause clinical PCM and perhaps brain damage. In general, milder forms of malnutrition, especially those of shorter duration, are mostly reversible by proper nutrition. Severe or protracted forms of malnutrition are likely to cause irreversible damage or to prevent physical or mental development, depending on the type of deficiency and age of the person involved. For example, malnutrition during prenatal stages can affect later life. Brain growth, which is most rapid during the last three months of prenatal life and first six months of postnatal life, can be retarded if the pregnant mother or the newborn baby is poorly nourished.

Body size cannot usually be changed substantially if malnutrition persists through puberty. But once the diet becomes consistently adequate, earlier malnutrition does not necessarily mean that the expected life span will be shortened. Such dramatic changes in dietary pattern, however, are unusual. Symptoms of persistently inadequate food intake may become less obvious as a child grows into adulthood because adults have lower nutrient requirements per unit of body size and because adults tend to show fewer symptoms than children, even when the condition is quite severe.

FOOD SOURCES OF NUTRIENTS. Foods eaten by people around the world are strikingly varied (Table 2.2). Food habits among population groups have developed over generations based mainly on which foods are available. But custom, religion, and physical differences also affect food habits. Following are some examples. Vegetarian diets are more common among people in South Asia and in the Near and Middle East. For religious reasons, Hindus avoid meat and Jews and Muslims do not eat pork. Superstitions, such as fish causing worms, eggplant causing leprosy, eggs causing sterility, and a certain combination of foods causing illness, have originated as specific beliefs. Frogs, snails, and horse meat are delicacies in France, whereas buffalo-beef and beetles sometimes contribute significant amounts of protein in Asian countries. Certain populations in tropical zones are unable to tolerate milk because they lack the enzyme necessary to digest milk sugar. Most places in the world raise food capable of providing all the nutrients needed for good health. A few areas (e.g., parts of India and Africa) do not, and if the people are too poor to buy imported foods, malnutrition and starvation result. Imports, however, are not always necessary and can, in fact, adversely affect food habits. For example, importing canned and processed foods into some South Pacific islands has resulted in local people no longer growing many traditional foods that were once the source of adequate nutrients. Again, malnutrition has resulted.

ENERGY. Carbohydrate and fats in foods supply approximately 80 to 90 percent of the total energy requirements of an individual or population group, with protein supplying the rest. Carbohydrate-rich foods are the main component of man's diet and are often referred to as staples. They are the cheapest source of energy and come almost entirely from plants. They provide needed bulk in the diet as well as calories.

Around the world, cereal grains and cereal products are the most widely consumed source of carbohydrates, but root crops are also eaten in substantial amounts. Wheat flour and potatoes are the staples in

TABLE 2.2. SOURCES OF FOOD NUTRIENTS IN TYPICAL DIETARIES AROUND THE WORLD.[a]

| | Africa (Masai Diet) | Polynesia | India (vegetarian) |
|---|---|---|---|
| Carbohydrates | milk | taro, breadfruit, bananas | chick pea, chapati, mangoes, potatoes, peas, oranges |
| Fats | meat, milk | fish, coconuts | ghee, lamb |
| Proteins | milk, meat, blood | fish, coconuts | lamb, dahl, chapati, curds |
| Vitamins | milk, meat, wild fruits | fish, taro leaves, breadfruit, taro | lamb, chapati, dahl, cabbages, curds, carrots, oranges, potatoes, maize, ghee |
| Minerals | milk, blood, meat | taro leaves, fish, bones | dahl, curds, chapati |

| | Guatemala | Japan | France | USA |
|---|---|---|---|---|
| Carbohydrates | tortillas, black beans, papaya, squash, pineapple | rice, oranges | bread, potatoes, artichokes, turnips, wine | bread, corn, potatoes, apples, cucumbers |
| Fats | cheese, chicken | raw & cooked fish, soybean soup | cheese, chicken | beef, butter, milk |
| Proteins | chicken, black beans, cheese, tortillas | raw & cooked fish, shrimp, soybean soup | chicken, cheese, snails, bread | beef, bread, milk, corn |
| Vitamins | black beans, tortillas, chicken, chard, papaya, carrots, cheese, pineapple | seaweed, raw & cooked fish, rice, shrimp, oranges, strawberries | spinach, bread, tomatoes, cheese, potatoes, artichokes | bread, string beans, potatoes, corn, beef, milk, butter, tomatoes |
| Minerals | black beans, chard, cheese, tortillas | shrimp, raw & cooked fish, seaweed, green onions, soybean soup | snails, bread, spinach, cheese, artichokes | bread, milk, beef, corn |

[a] Adapted from W. H. Sebrell, Jr., and J. J. Heggarty, Food and Nutrition (New York: Time Inc., 1975).

Europe and the United States. In certain parts of the Near and Middle East parboiled or plain milled wheat is very popular. During parboiling, the nutrients normally concentrated in the outer husk are driven into the wheat kernel, where they remain when the husk is removed. The cereal becomes enriched by its own nutrients. Rice typifies the diets of the Chinese, Japanese, Korean, Indonesian, Malaysian, and Filipino peoples. Cassava (from which tapioca comes) and plantain (a relative of the banana) provide the mainstay of diets in many countries of Africa. The root crop taro, which is cooked into "poi," is the staple in the South

Pacific Islands. Corn and corn products remain the important staple in Central and South America.

Fats contain the highest energy of any dietary component: 9 calories per gram, compared with 4 calories per gram of carbohydrates and proteins. Although they are the most concentrated form of energy, fats are generally less available and more expensive than carbohydrates.

Fats are sometimes divided into visible and invisible categories. Visible fats, such as oils, butter, margarine, lard, hydrogenated fats, salad oils, and fat parts of meat cuts, contribute significantly to the energy levels of the diet. The invisible fats come from high intakes of lean meat, fish, poultry, dairy products, and eggs, and can represent as much as 65 percent of the total fat intake in western diets. Milk contains approximately 3 percent fat, cheese 30 percent, and meat and meat products 20 to 25 percent. In general, fish has a lower fat content than meats and eggs, but can contribute significant amounts if enough is eaten. Eskimos eat such large quantities of fish and meat that a very large proportion of their energy comes from the fats and proteins in them.

Among the plant sources, soybeans have exceptionally high fat content (17 to 20 percent), while other leguminous seeds contain much less fat. Coconut oil and coconut milk contribute substantial fat in Asian diets. Cereal grains may contain significant amounts of fats, ranging from 2 to 9 percent; but almost half of the fat content is lost when the germ is removed during milling and processing.

Oils from such plants as corn, cotton, and soybeans, are particularly important to man since they are rich sources of essential fatty acids. Fish, poultry, and meat, on the other hand, furnish only small amounts of these essential nutrients. Animal foods do, however, furnish much cholesterol, which when consumed in large amounts may cause atherosclerosis and related diseases.

Ideally, carbohydrates should furnish about 50 percent of man's caloric needs. In developing countries, however, people often derive as much as 70 to 80 percent of their energy from carbohydrates, particularly cereals, which are low in fat content. When most of the energy in a person's diet is derived from carbohydrate sources, the sheer physical bulk eaten limits the intake of other important foods, including fats. Even when diets include large amounts of fish and grain legumes, fat levels may be low. The problem of high fat intake is peculiar to western developed countries, and exists because of a high intake of animal products.

PROTEIN. Protein and energy consumption is a major indicator of the nutritional sufficiency of either a developing or underdeveloped country. Whenever energy and protein intakes are adequate, other nutrients are usually also adequate, since many energy and protein rich foods are also good sources of other nutrients. However, many people in the developed countries and the more affluent in the developing countries may consume an excessive amount of energy and protein foods unless they also consume fruits and vegetables.

The richest sources of protein, ranging from 12 to 30 percent protein, are meats, fish, poultry, eggs, dried milk, and milk products. Dried fish and meats are important sources of concentrated protein in many Asian and African countries. Generally, cereals, cereal products, and legumes are satisfactory sources of protein when sufficient amounts are consumed. Soybeans are an excellent source of high-quality protein. Human milk is a very important source of high-quality protein for infants. Vegetables and fruits furnish the least amount of protein.

In the developed countries, much of the protein is supplied by meats and poultry. This is also true of the upper socioeconomic classes in the developing countries. Most of the diets in developing countries depend primarily on plant proteins. In a typical Asian diet, for example, cereal grains and cereal products can supply as much as one-third to one-half of the total protein intake. This is not because rice or corn is so rich in protein, but simply because large amounts of these cereals are eaten everyday. Even so, rice is a better source of protein than root crops and plantains, which gives the Asians an advantage over the Africans and South Pacific Islanders who depend on the plantains and root crops. Grain legumes, lentils, pulses, groundnuts (peanuts), soybeans, blade beans, chick-peas, mung beans, etc., are an important protein source in many developing countries. For example, the widely eaten Indian "dahls" are made from green and red gram (e.g., chick-peas) and peas. Soybean milk and fermented soybean products (e.g., soy sauce) are widely used in diets in China, Japan, Taiwan, and Indonesia.

When animals are available in the developing world, they are used completely. In Asia, all parts of the pig from the brain to blood and intestines are cooked in various ways and eaten. In China, there are at least 70 different ways of using various parts of a Peking duck for a meal. In Africa, especially among the Masai people, blood meal is as common a protein source as milk is in Europe.

As explained earlier, animal products contain higher quality protein than plants. Thus, it is generally considered easier to obtain adequate protein if some animal products are eaten. To get the correct supply of amino acids from plant sources only, an individual should eat a variety of plants with complementary amino acids. For example, the amino acids in grains and grain legumes complement each other. The essential amino acids must be eaten at the same time and in the proper amounts to form a complete protein.

A breakthrough in improving the protein quality of cereals through plant breeding was the discovery in 1963 of the mutant gene that produces "opaque-2" corn, which contains increased quantities of the essential amino acids lysine and tryptophan. During the last decade, breeding research has produced encouraging improvement in the protein content of wheat, rice, and corn. The average of 6 to 8 percent protein has been raised to levels as high as 12 to 14 percent. Other ways of improving the protein intake in developing countries are being tried. For example, high protein bean flours are being used on an experimental basis to replace rice and mung bean flour and improve the protein content and quality of noodles.

VITAMINS. Vitamins, while required in fairly small amounts in contrast to protein, carbohydrates, and fats, are essential to each individual's health.

The form of vitamin A that is directly usable by the body is called retinol and exists only in foods of animal origin. The body can, however, synthesize usable vitamin A from carotenes, a group of yellow and orange pigments widely distributed in fruits and vegetables. Yellow sweet potatoes, yams, squash, papayas, carrots, and many dark green leafy vegetables are very good sources of vitamin A. As a rule, the deeper yellow the fruit and the greener the vegetable, the richer it is in carotene. Cereals like yellow corn, however, contain small quantities of carotene. In other fruits, such as tomatoes and prunes, the yellow color is obscured by other pigments.

Meat liver and fish liver are especially rich in the retinol form of vitamin A. Eggs also contain significant amounts, but meat and carcass fat contain only traces. Milk and cheese usually contain relatively small amounts, but may contain considerable amounts depending on the feed given to the cow. In many countries, margarine, butter, and milk are fortified with retinol or carotene.

In arid regions, such as Afghanistan and parts of Africa and India, vitamin deficiency can be a serious problem because few fruits and vegetables are available. In developing countries, the problem of obtaining adequate amounts of vitamin A is aggravated by low fat intakes. Fats are necessary for the body to adequately absorb vitamin A.

Foods of plant origin do not contain vitamin D. In fact, most natural foods are poor sources of vitamin D. Fish liver oil is a good source and only small amounts are present in egg yolk, liver, and fish. In the more advanced countries, all evaporated and fresh milk are fortified with vitamin D. This vitamin has also been added to a number of other foods, such as cereals and margarine. In tropical countries, where sunlight is plentiful, the body uses the sun's ultraviolet light to synthesize its needed vitamin D. In communities where sunlight is limited, especially during long winters, or where custom, habit, or environmental conditions, discourage exposing children to sunlight, rickets can be a nutritional problem. Fortification of foods with vitamin D, therefore, becomes necessary.

Vitamin E is derived mainly from plant sources, especially vegetable oils, wheat, and rice germ. Appreciable amounts are also present in dark green leafy vegetables, nuts, and legumes. Foods of animal origin are low in vitamin E; human milk does provide adequate vitamin E for the infant, whereas cow's milk is low.

Green leafy vegetables and pork liver are the most important dietary sources of vitamin K. Cereals, fruits, and other vegetables are poor sources. This vitamin can, however, be synthesized to some extent by the bacteria in the human intestines.

Fruits, especially citrus fruits, are rich sources of vitamin C (ascorbic acid). Guavas, papayas, and passion fruits are also excellent sources in tropical countries where these abound. Melons, tomatoes, and fresh green vegetables such as broccoli and leafy greens, are good sources. However, much of the vitamin C in green vegetables may be destroyed during preparation and cooking. Root vegetables, such as potatoes and taro, are fairly good sources of vitamin C because they are eaten in such large quantities. Meats, fish, eggs, milk, and fresh legumes contain little vitamin C. Human fresh milk and cow's milk provide vitamin C at levels sufficient for the newborn infant, but it can be easily destroyed if the cow's milk is heated. Dried grain legumes are practically devoid of ascorbic acid, but when sprouted, as in mung bean and soybean sprouts, the vitamin C content becomes significant.

Unprocessed natural foods usually contain significant amounts of thiamin (vitamin $B_1$). Pork, among animal sources, and whole grain cereals, among plant sources, contain the highest amounts of thiamin. Grain legumes, and nuts are good sources. Significant amounts of thiamin are found in yeast, and therefore in homemade beers. The thiamin is destroyed, however, in commercially produced beers and wines. Polishing rice and refining wheat remove most of the thiamin. In many countries where bread is made from highly milled wheat, law requires the enrichment of flour with added thiamin. But the enrichment of polished rice has not been successful in Asian countries because of technical and political problems. In other countries in the East and Far East, low thiamin levels of the traditional rice diet have been supplemented by considerable intakes of soybeans, mung beans, and other grain legumes. The process of parboiling wheat, common in India and Pakistan, causes more thiamin and other B-vitamins and minerals to be retained in the grain and less removed in the processing of milling.

Niacin and riboflavin are both widely distributed in most foods. Meats, especially liver, are rich sources of niacin, as are whole grain cereals and legumes. Niacin is present in corn, but as niacytin—a form the body cannot use. If during cooking, corn is treated with alkali, the niacin becomes usable to the body. In Mexico, for example, tortillas are prepared by treating maize flour with lime water before cooking, thus releasing niacin and making it more available to the body tissues. Milk, although a poor source of niacin, is a pellagra preventative because of its high tryptophan content. This amino acid can be slowly converted in the body to niacin.

Yeast is an exceptionally good source of riboflavin, and eggs, fish, and milk are useful sources. The riboflavin content of milk, however, depends on the source of feed for the animals producing the milk. Most grain-legume seeds and nuts are rich in riboflavin, but green leafy vegetables vary greatly in content. Riboflavin is destroyed during the drying of milk, and is low in milled or refined cereal flours. Considerable amounts may be present in beer.

The other vitamins of the B-complex group are required in lesser quantities in the diet than thiamin, riboflavin, and niacin, and are generally found in cereal grains, legumes, nuts, and dark green leafy vegetables. Inclusion of a wide variety of these foods in the diet can generally provide adequate amounts of these nutrients, but care must be taken to assure adequate folic acid and vitamin $B_{12}$ intake during pregnancy when their requirements are about doubled.

MINERALS. Like vitamins, minerals are essential for health. Some care must be taken to obtain adequate amounts of foods containing calcium and phosphorus, iron, and iodine. Other so-called trace minerals are widely distributed in foods and, therefore, are not usually lacking in human diets.

Calcium is widely distributed in varying amounts in natural foods. Milk and milk products and fish eaten with bones are very rich in calcium. In countries where little milk is available to the children, much calcium may be provided by fish, clams, oysters, and shrimp. Certain dark green leafy vegetables are also important sources when they are eaten frequently, but some vegetables have substances that prevent the body from absorbing the calcium present. Excess fat and phosphates also chemically combine with calcium and prevent the body from absorbing calcium as efficiently.

In Asia, small fish and shrimp are fermented in salt to preserve them and are added to vegetables or eaten with rice; these are good sources of calcium. The practice among rural women of chewing betel nuts and leaves together with lime adds to the daily calcium intakes.

Even though calcium is required for growth, the failure to grow and the small bone structure of certain populations with low intakes of milk cannot be attributed entirely to the lack of dietary calcium. When a diet is low in protein, less of the bone matrix on which minerals are deposited is formed.

Phosphorus is also widely distributed in foods, with milk, meat, and fish being the most important contributors. A diet that furnishes adequate protein and calcium will nearly always provide sufficient phosphorus. Fruits and vegetables contain only small amounts of phosphorus.

Iron is widely distributed in all foodstuffs and may seem to be adequately consumed by most of the world's population, but iron-deficiency anemia is quite common, especially among certain populations. This is because not all iron in food is in a form available to the body. Some foods, such as whole grain cereals, have a substance that prevents the body from absorbing iron. Daily iron intakes come mostly from lean meat, dark green leafy vegetables, and whole grain or enriched cereals and bread. Milk and milk products are poor sources of iron whereas eggs, liver, organ meats, dried fruits, legumes, shellfish, and molasses are iron-rich foods. In Asia and Africa, blood meal contributes considerable iron.

Some iron and other minerals are lost when large amounts of water are used in cooking and then discarded. Refined foods also generally contain less iron. Recent studies in South and Central America indicate that fortification of foods, such as sugar and salt, with available forms of iron may be useful in countries where iron-deficiency anemia is very prevalent.

Among the natural unfortified foods, the best sources of iodides are seafoods and vegetables grown in iodide-rich soils. Most cereal grains, legumes, and root crops have low iodine contents. The use of iodized salt in iodine-poor regions has been successful and is widely adopted.

Fluorides are found in seafoods and tea, and ingestion of cooking and drinking water containing one part per million of fluorine can protect a population from widespread tooth decay.

TRANSLATING NUTRITIONAL NEEDS INTO FOODS. For the recommended dietary allowances to be useful to the world's population, they must be interpreted in terms of foods locally available from farm, garden, or market. Since the average consumer or homemaker can become easily confused by the many units, such as kilocalories, milligrams, grams, and international units, in which recommendations are expressed, they should be expressed in terms that are easy to understand and use. They should also be available to people with different levels of purchasing power and different customs and traditions.

To help overcome these problems, nutritionists have identified what are known as the Basic Food Groups, which serve as guide categories in planning and evaluating diets.

The number of groups into which the foods are divided varies from country to country, depending on the availability of food and the food habits of the people. For instance, in Asia milk and milk products do not constitute a basic food group in the same way they do in the United States, Colombia, or India.

Table 2.3 shows examples of two different basic food groupings, the Basic Four from the United States and the Basic Three from the Philippines. When the number of servings indicated for all groups is eaten each day, the foundation of a satisfactory diet will be assured for most healthy adults. Additional servings of any foods will be needed for energy. The daily number of servings is more in the United States group-

TABLE 2.3. EXAMPLES OF BASIC FOOD GROUPINGS

| Basic 4—United States | Basic 3—Philippines |
|---|---|
| 1. *Milk Group*<br>2–4 cups. Milk products can supply part of the milk.<br>2. *Meat Group*<br>2 or more servings. Meats, poultry, eggs, grain legumes, or nuts. (1 serving=2–3 oz.)<br>3. *Vegetable–Fruit Group*<br>4 or more servings. Dark green or yellow vegetables, citrus fruits or tomatoes, other fruits and vegetables, including potatoes. 1 serving = ½ cup cooked vegetables or 1 medium size fruit)<br>4. *Bread and Cereal Group*<br>4 or more servings. Enriched or whole grain. (1 serving = 1 slice bread, ½–¾ cup cooked grains or 1 oz, dry cereal) | 1. *Protein Rich Food Group*<br>3 or more servings. Children need 2–3 cups of milk. Fish, meat, grain legumes, eggs or poultry, and milk. (1 serving = 1 egg or 1 oz. cooked meat/fish or ½ cup cooked dry beans)<br>2. *Energy Rich Food Group*<br>3 or more servings. Rice, corn or root crops, bread with fats or oils. (1 serving = ½ cup cooked cereal plus 1 tablespoon fat)<br>3. *Vegetable–Fruit Group*<br>4 or more servings. Dark green or yellow vegetables, citrus fruits, guavas, mangoes, and other fruits and vegetables. (1 serving = 1 cup raw or ½ cup cooked vegetables or 1 medium size fruit) |

ing because they are larger people on the average and, therefore, require larger amounts of nutrients.

Food within each group has similar nutrients, making it easier to tell if needed nutrients have been included in the day's diet. Recommendations then take the form of number of servings needed from each group each day. Thus, the grouping facilitates an understanding of how to meet the total daily nutrient needs; but, to be used effectively, knowledge of the exchangeability of food in the various groups must be acquired.

## BIBLIOGRAPHY

Aykroyd, W. R. The conquest of famine. New York: The Reader's Digest Press, 1975.

Berg, A. The nutrition factor: Its role in national development. Washington, D.C.: The Brookings Institution, 1973.

Berg, A.; Scrimshaw, N. S.; and Call, D. L., eds. Nutrition, national development and planning. Cambridge, Mass.: The M.I.T. Press, 1973.

Food and Agriculture Organization of the United Nations. Handbook on human nutritional requirements. FAO Nutritional Studies No. 78. Rome: United Nations Food and Agriculture Organization, 1974.

Grossman, R. A.; Harinasuta, C.; and Underwood, B. A. Nutrition and some related diseases of public health importance in the lower Mekong Basin: A review. Cambridge, Mass.: The M.I.T. Press, 1973.

National Research Council. Recommended dietary allowances. 8th ed. Washington, D.C.: National Academy of Sciences, 1974.

National Research Council. Food science in developing countries. Washington, D.C.: National Academy of Sciences. 1974.
Pyke, M. Man and food. New York: McGraw-Hill, 1970.
Robson, J. R. K.; Larkin, F. A.; Sandretto, A. M.; and Tadayyon, B. Malnutrition: Its causation and control. New York: Gordon and Breach, 1972.
Sebrell, W. H., Jr., and Haggarty, J. J. Food and nutrition. Life Science Library. New York: Time Inc. 1975.
Science. (Special issue on food, May 9, 1975) 188(4188).
Williams, C. D., and Jelliffe, D. B. Mother and child health. London: Oxford University Press, 1972.

3

# The Food-Producing Regions of the World

LOUIS M. THOMPSON

ALTHOUGH the oceans occupy two and one-half times the space occupied by the land, they provide only about 2 percent of human food energy. Over 97 percent of people's energy is derived directly or indirectly from plants grown on the land (1). This relationship will not change in the future despite ideas that we will "farm the oceans." The maximum possible sustained fish catch is estimated to be only twice the present catch (4), and thus the earth's soils, along with increasing inputs of capital and technology, will continue to supply most of people's food demands. This chapter, therefore, will emphasize the land-based food producing regions and the potentials and limitations of each.

PRINCIPAL SOURCES OF FOOD ENERGY. Human beings began agriculture by cultivating crops that produced seeds. Seed crops are important because protein and minerals concentrate in the seeds, which can be dried and stored without refrigeration and eaten until the next crop can be produced. Seeds still are the foundation of the human diet as indicated by Figure 3.1. The cereal crops consumed directly as food provide slightly more than half of man's calorie intake and grain legumes provide another 13 percent. Thus, plant seeds, cereals and legumes provide almost two-thirds of the human food energy supply, in contrast to the 22 percent provided by animal products, that is, meat, eggs, milk, and butter. All other foods, including potatoes, sugar, fruits, vegetables, and nuts, provide about 14 percent of the human energy supply.

This high percentage from cereals and grain legumes is expected to become even larger in the future.

## PRINCIPAL PRODUCTION REGIONS

THE GRAIN PRODUCING REGIONS. About 72 percent of the nearly two billion acres of cropland in the world is used to produce grain (cereal)

LOUIS M. THOMPSON is Professor and Associate Dean of Agriculture, Iowa State University. He specializes in teaching soil fertility and researching technology and weather factors in crop production.

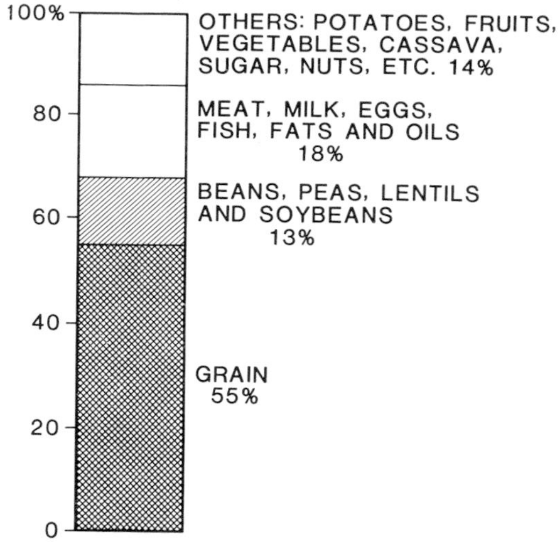


FIG. 3.1. Sources of food energy (9)

crops as shown in Figure 3.2. Wheat is the leading crop, followed by rice, and then corn (maize).

The cereal crops are commonly divided into two groups—food grains and feed grains. Food grains are wheat, rye, and rice; and feed grains are oats, barley, corn, and grain sorghums. The groupings are based on what each grain is primarily used for. Some feed grains are used as food for human consumption; likewise, surplus food grains are fed to livestock.

About 40 percent of the world production of cereal crops is fed to

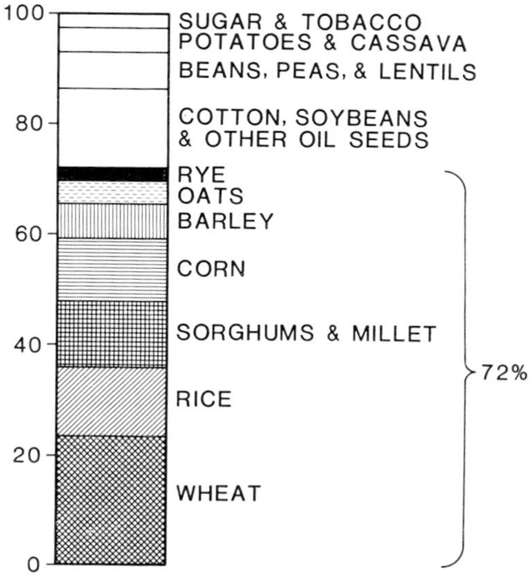


FIG. 3.2. World area of principal crops (9)

livestock, although this varies from year to year with supply. As human food needs are met, the remaining grain is fed to livestock. When cereal grains become plentiful and cheap, as from 1969 to 1972, livestock production is expanded, and when grain supplies decrease and prices rise, livestock production is cut back. For example, U.S. cattle numbers decreased 3 percent in 1975 (the first reduction since 1967) because of high grain prices in 1974 and 1975.

So, as we look at the world's food supply in perspective, the livestock supply is the principal reserve food supply. When grain is in short supply, less grain is fed to livestock and more livestock is slaughtered for food.

The cereal crops are best adapted to those regions of the world where soils developed under tall grasses, the so-called prairie regions. The regions are characterized by temperate to cool temperate, and subhumid to humid climate where the precipitation to evaporation ratio is less than one. Nearly all these areas lie between the 30th and 55th parallels in both and northern and southern hemispheres and are known as the middle latitudes.

Most wheat is grown in the middle latitudes (see Fig. 3.3) even though it is grown so widely that it is harvested somewhere in the world every month of the year. The United States produces only 15 percent of the world's wheat but exports more than half of the wheat that moves from country to country in world trade. Less than 15 percent of the world's wheat crop moves in world trade since most wheat is used where it is produced.

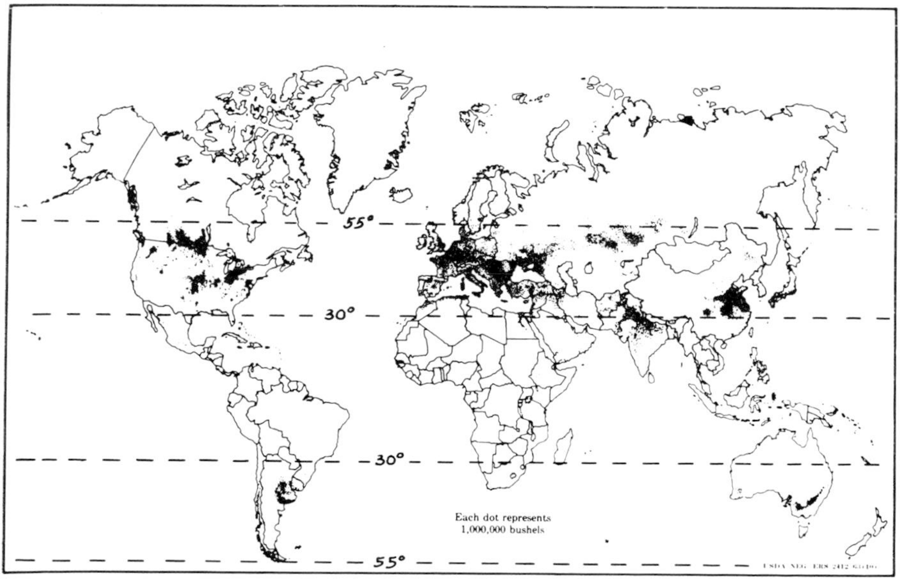


FIG. 3.3. World wheat production (3)

Although wheat is best adapted to the middle latitudes, some has always been grown in the areas between 20 and 30 degrees latitude in both hemispheres. Both Mexico and India have been increasing their wheat production, particularly since 1966 when the short stemmed high yield varieties were developed in Mexico and were quickly accepted in India.

Winter wheat is grown in the latitudes from 20 to about 45 degrees where it is planted in the fall and harvested in the late spring or summer. Above 45 degrees, the winters are too severe for winter wheat so spring wheat, which is planted in the spring and harvested in late summer and fall, is grown.

Rice is the most important cereal crop in the warm band around the earth between the equator and the 30th parallel (Fig. 3.4). However, some rice is grown at higher latitudes. For example, some rice is grown around Sacramento, California, which is near 38 degrees north latitude, but this area's climate is greatly affected by the nearness to the Pacific Ocean and low elevation. Likewise, rice is grown in the 30 to 40 degree latitude in China, Korea, and Japan where climate is moderated by low elevation and nearness to the Pacific.

About 96 percent of the world's rice crop is consumed as human food in the countries where it is produced. Therefore, only about 4 percent of the world's rice crop moves in world trade with most being exported by the United States even though it produces only 2 percent of the world's rice crop.

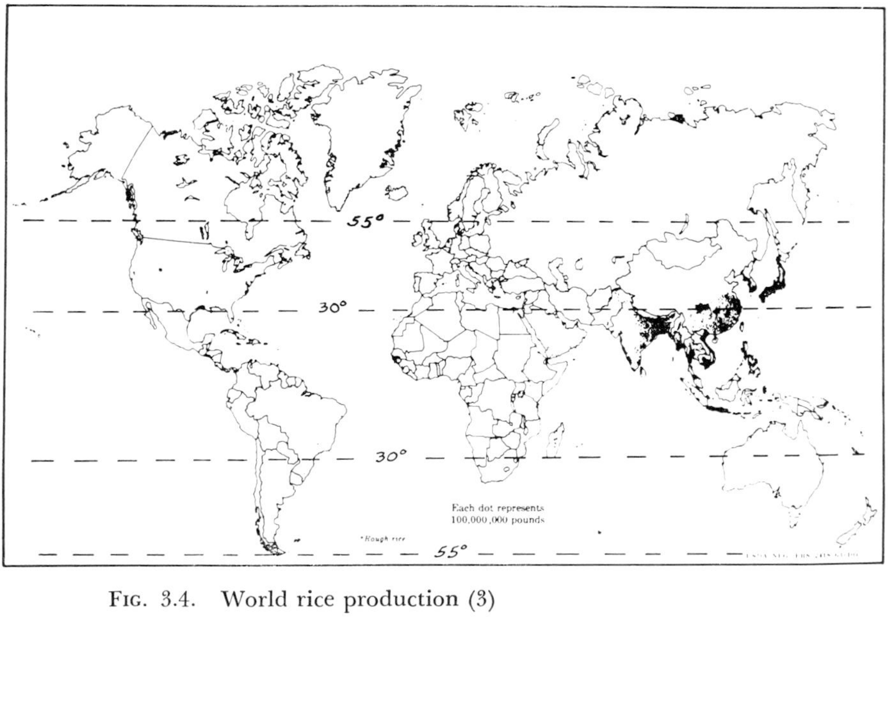


FIG. 3.4. World rice production (3)

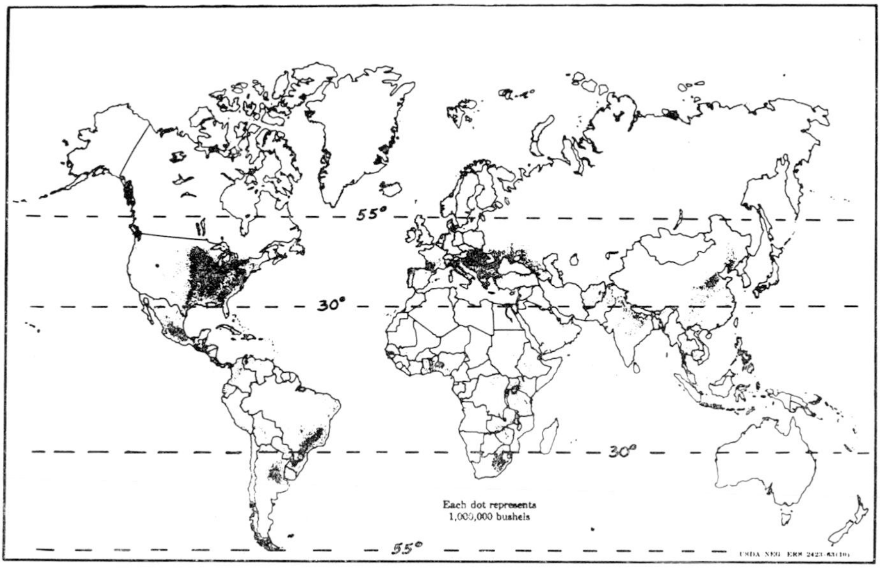


FIG. 3.5. World corn production (3)

Most of the world's corn (maize) is grown between the 30th and 45th parallels (see Fig. 3.5). At higher latitudes, growth is limited by the length of the growing season and at lower latitudes by high summer nighttime temperatures. The optimum average temperature for summer months is about 72 degrees (10) with an optimum range from 50 degrees at night to 86 degrees in the daytime. Corn is best adapted to dark-colored soils rich in organic matter and deep enough to allow the storage of about 10 inches of plant-available soil moisture (about 2 inches per foot of depth). Such soils are found in a large area in the central part of the United States, known as the Corn Belt. Because of its soils and climate the United States produces nearly half the world's corn. Europe, China, Argentina, Brazil, and South Africa produce most of the other half (see Fig. 3.5), but some corn is also grown in lower latitudes where the summer temperatures are favorable because of higher elevations or moderated by winds off the oceans.

Barley and oats are grown in the same climates as wheat and corn and are mainly used as feed grains although they are also used for food products for human consumption. Barley production is second to wheat production in Canada.

Grain sorghum is an important feed grain grown in latitudes below about 40 degrees in subhumid regions where there is a long growing season. This crop is more drought tolerant than corn and, therefore, can tolerate higher summer temperatures. In the United States grain sorghums are grown only about as far north as Lincoln, Nebraska; farther north frost usually occurs before the crop matures. With the development of hybrid grain sorghums this crop yields almost as many pounds of grain per acre as corn in the western part of the Corn Belt. Grain sorghums are also important in Africa and India. The United States is the principal producer and exporter of the world's grain sorghum.

THE LEGUME SEED PRODUCING REGIONS. The most important legume seeds of the world are soybeans, ground nuts (peanuts), peas, and beans. Soybeans, long an important food crop in China, Korea, and Japan, became popular in the United States about 50 years ago as a source of vegetable oil and meal for livestock feed. Soybeans prefer about the same length of growing season and summer temperatures as corn (11) and are grown throughout the Corn Belt. The United States grows about 60 percent of the world's soybeans and supplies about 75 percent of the soybeans exported. China and Brazil each produce about 20 percent of the world's soybeans. This crop became important in Brazil only during the last decade, and the short world supply of soybeans in 1973 caused Brazil to expand its production rapidly.

Ground nuts (peanuts) are important food crops in India, Africa, and China and are best adapted to warm climates and to sandy soils that permit harvesting without damaging shells. Peanuts are grown in latitudes as high as 40 degrees, but are concentrated in latitudes from 10 to 30 degrees. India produces about 33 percent of the world's peanuts, and Nigeria and Senegal are the leading peanut producers in Africa. The United States produces peanuts along the Gulf Coastal region from Texas to North Carolina but produces only about 5 percent of the world's peanuts.

Peas and beans are most popular as home garden crops throughout the world, but there are significant acreages of these crops for commercial production scattered throughout the world.

POTATOES. Potatoes are popular in the American and European diets. Ninety percent of the world's 250 million tons of this crop is grown in Europe (including Russia). Russia alone produces about 40 percent of the world's potato crop.

SUGAR. Either sugar cane or sugar beets are grown in nearly all countries of the world below 50 degrees latitude. About 30 percent of this production is traded on the world market with Cuba, Philippines, Brazil, France, and the Dominican Republic the major exporters. World sugar production is now over 70 million metric tons a year (a metric ton equals 2200 pounds).

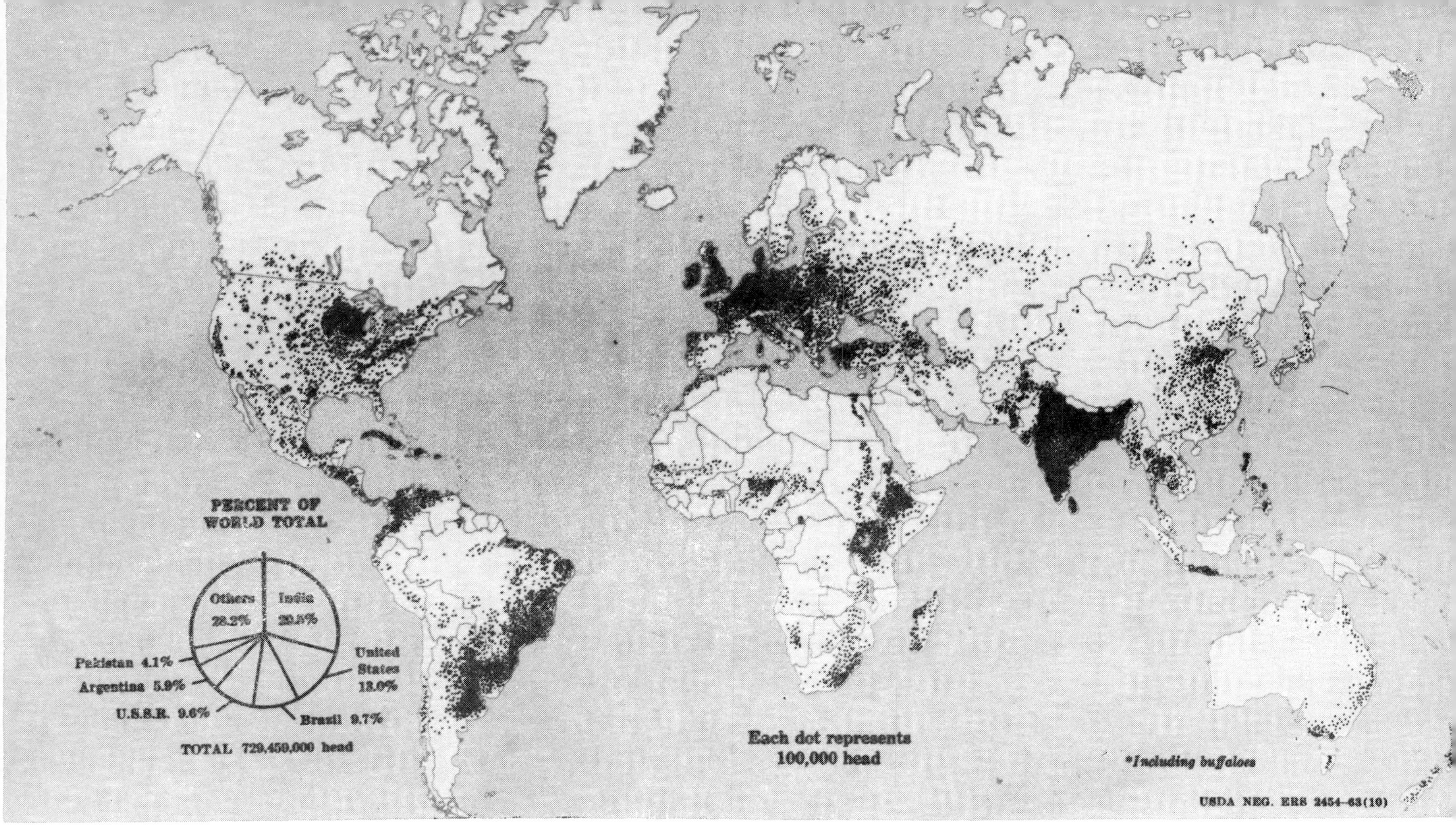


FIG. 3.6. World cattle production (3)

LIVESTOCK PRODUCING REGIONS. Livestock is raised on two different kinds of land in the world: (1) land unsuitable for cultivation, and (2) land where feed grains could be grown.

Cattle can be produced wherever grass and legume forages will grow, which is all the way from the equator to the 55th parallel (see Fig. 3.6). The breeds of cattle best known in the United States (Hereford, Angus, and Holstein, for example) are best adapted in the middle latitudes, but breeds, such as the Brahman and Water Buffalo, are adapted to the tropical and subtropical climates.

Ruminant animals, such as cattle and sheep, can digest plant cellulose and use it for energy. The human digestive system cannot, however, use this kind of plant material. Thus the ruminant animal is an important food source when used to forage lands unsuitable for cultivation. For example, hundreds of millions of acres of grassland in the Great Plains of the United States are used to produce sheep and cattle. The cattle raised on this land, however, are usually moved to the north central and other areas of the country to be fattened. Therefore, they also depend on grain grown on some of the best producing cropland in the United States.

Sheep are better foragers than cattle since they can digest shrubby plants as well as grass and thus can survive on lowest producing rangelands that are rocky, mountainous, or semiarid. Sheep are also better adapted to the climates of the middle latitudes, and a high percentage of the world's sheep numbers are above the 30th parallel.

Hogs, with a digestive system more nearly like that of human beings, must eat foods similar to those required by people and tend to be concentrated in the middle latitudes where corn is grown. The leading producers of hogs are the United States, Europe, Russia, China, and Brazil. In the United States, hogs are concentrated in the Midwest. Iowa produces almost 20 percent of the corn and 25 percent of the hogs grown in the United States.

The world's livestock population, as well as the amount of red meat consumed per person, has been increasing over the last decade. But it is unlikely that this trend will continue because as the world's human population continues to grow, more grain will be consumed directly by people and less will be available to feed livestock. More and more of the world's animals, particularly cattle, will be raised on rangeland. And the carrying capacity of rangelands (that is, the number of animals the land can support without damaging grazing) cannot be economically increased significantly because carrying capacity is related more to weather and climate than to fertilizer use or grass types. What little grain is available for livestock will be fed to animals that are more efficient in converting that food to protein. (See also Chapter 8.)

Population pressures will also affect the amount of grain available to each person in the future. Figure 3.7 shows that grain production has

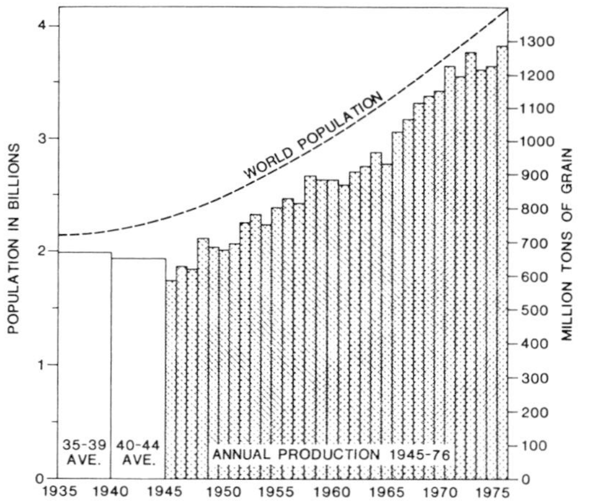


FIG. 3.7. World production of cereal grain plotted against population growth (9)

doubled from 1945 to 1975 while population increased only 80 percent resulting in a small gain in available food. But it is very unlikely that grain production can continue to increase as fast as population from 1975 until the year 2000.

## FISH PRODUCTION

THE OCEANS AS A SOURCE OF FOOD. Oceans cover two and one-half times the area occupied by land and contain huge amounts of plant life. Yet only about one million tons of this plant material is harvested to help feed man and animals or for industrial uses. This is small indeed when compared with the 1200 million tons of grain produced each year. The main energy source from oceans is fish, which supply 2 percent of people's energy.

Fish are found all the way from the equator to the cold waters of the polar regions and are part of a complex ecological chain. The ultimate source of energy for fish is produced by photosynthesis in plants living in the oceans, particularly in a floating microscopic form called phytoplankton or plankton. Small fish consume plankton and, in turn, are eaten by larger fish forming a chain of relationships among species that tend to remain in balance from year to year unless disturbed by man or changed by climatic variability. The ocean waters circulate because of the earth's motion and the differentials in temperature caused by warming near the equator and cooling toward the polar regions. Thus, the variability of the climates in the oceans influences the production of certain species of fish from one decade to another. For example, the drop in production of anchoveta off the coast of Peru in 1973 was the result of a change in ocean climate of the region. (Anchoveta is most important as a protein source for livestock feed, but there are some varieties highly prized as food and known as anchovy.)

The most important species of fish caught for food are tuna, salmon, sardine, shrimp, lobster, and crab. About 64 million tons of fish were caught from the oceans each year in the early 1970s (1). This was three times as much fish as was caught before 1945. Fish production has grown faster than grain production during the past 30 years. Much of this growth can be attributed to the development of the anchoveta industry off the coast of Peru, but there is little prospect that the anchoveta catch will increase above the present level of about 10 million tons annually (1).

Estimates are that some species of fish production could be doubled by 2000, but this would be near the productive capacity of the oceans. Further depletion would upset the ecological balance and might cause extermination of some species. Furthermore, the increased catch of fish will mean a lower percentage of the more valued species, such as tuna and salmon, and a greater percentage of the less valued species, such as krill and anchoveta. Krill is a small shrimp-like animal that is important in the food chain for whales. The reduction of whales by overfishing during this century may be one reason for the increase in krill. Exploitation has reduced the present annual harvest of whales to only 15 percent of what it could have been with prudent management (1).

AQUACULTURE. Aquaculture (fish farming) is almost as old as agriculture and has been practiced in Asia for thousands of years but developed slowly until the 20th century. About 5 million tons of fish are produced annually by aquaculture, compared with 65 million tons caught from oceans. Approximately 80 percent of world fish production by aquaculture is in Asia where the most popular fish grown is carp (8).

Only recently has aquaculture become popular in the United States. The Agriculture Experiment Station in Alabama pioneered in the development of "catfish farming" in the 1930s. By 1971 there were about 43,000 acres of ponds in this country producing about 38 million pounds of catfish annually (13). This is only 0.4 percent of the fish produced by aquaculture in the world but it represents great potential. Hundreds of thousands of acres of ponds could be made productive. Furthermore, hundreds of thousands of acres of land not suitable for cultivation could be developed into ponds.

While the world's catch of fish from oceans will probably not double by the year 2000, production of fish by aquaculture could be increased ten times, from 5 million tons to 50 million tons within the same time frame.

But even with the growth in fish production just described, world population will grow enough so that fish will still provide only about 2 percent of the human food supply by the year 2000.

HISTORICAL ROLE OF CLIMATE AND WEATHER. Two very important aspects of recent climate have had a significant effect on food supply. First, the earth's climate has been relatively more favorable since 1800 than in the previous 400 years. Second, from 1956 to 1973 this country had a period of unusually favorable weather when the yields of wheat, corn, and soybeans climbed dramatically and reached peak levels (7). In the future we should expect the more variable weather experienced from 1890 to 1955 and not the highly favorable, rather benign weather enjoyed from 1956 to 1973.

Evidence of human beings on earth goes back beyond a million years, but their history and the development of agriculture go back only about 10,000 years. These developments are associated with the present interglacial period, which goes back about 15,000 years. There is now good evidence from studies of deep sea cores that during the last million years there were glacial periods about every 100 thousand years. Indeed, there was glacial ice in northern Iowa as late as 13,000 years ago. The earth warmed rapidly after the last glacial period until it reached a temperature somewhat higher than our present temperature about 5,000 years ago.

We are believed to be at, or near, the peak of that interglacial period, but this period has had a series of warming and cooling periods. Figure 3.8 shows this variation in climate for the last 1000 years. From about 1400 A.D. until about 1800, there was a period known as the "little

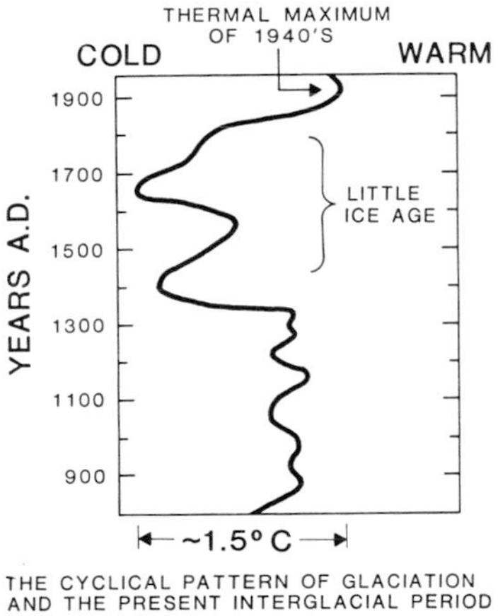


FIG. 3.8. The cyclical pattern of glaciation and the present interglacial period (2)

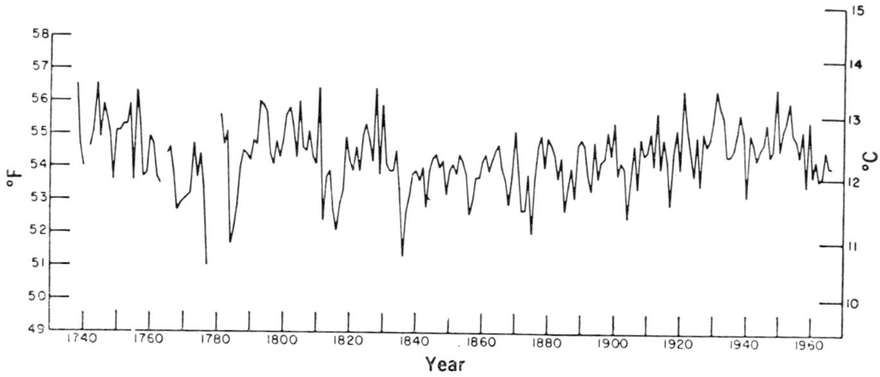


FIG. 3.9. The temperature trend in the Atlantic seaboard area centered on Philadelphia (6)

ice age," and natural productivity in the middle latitudes about 40 degrees was considerably below that of recent years because of the shorter growing season and greater variability of weather. A warming trend followed this cold period and continued until 1940. Since then there has been a cooling trend that has prompted many to suggest that we are approaching another little ice age. But as Figure 3.9 indicates, there were several cooling trends 10 to 20 years long during the overall 100-year warming trend from 1800 to 1940. Thus, climate is constantly changing, and while human beings will notice the year-to-year variations, they are less aware of the overall climate change during their lives.

CYCLICAL WEATHER PATTERNS IN THE MIDDLE LATITUDES. Weather in the middle latitudes has an irregular cyclical pattern with severe droughts occurring about every 20 years (12). The Great Plains of the United States has had nine drought periods since 1800, and droughts occurred at nearly the same time in Russia, China, Australia, and Argentina.

Droughts may be related to the sunspot cycle, which has averaged about 11 years since 1700. The cycle is characterized by the appearance of large spots of very strong magnetic fields on the face of the sun. The spots increase in size and number for several years and then decrease for several years until there are virtually none for several months. The period of few or no sunspots is referred to as a "quiet year of the sun," and these are the years that occur approximately 11 years apart but vary from 9 to 14 years apart.

J. W. King has reported that 29 of 68 famines (caused by drought) since 1700 have occurred in a quiet year or the year preceding the quiet year. The probability that this occurred by chance would be one in ten thousand (5).

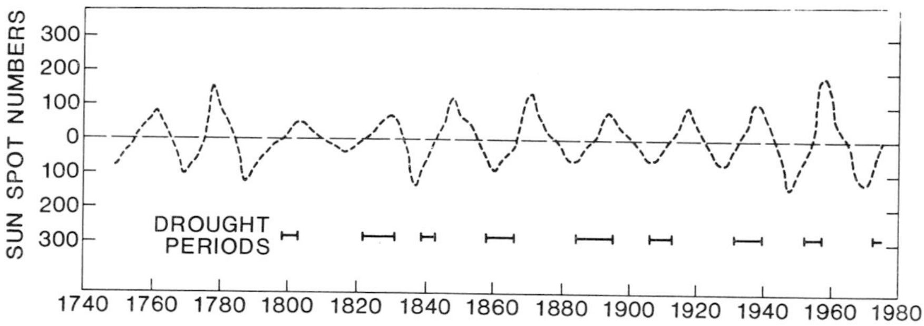


FIG. 3.10. Drought in Nebraska related to the double sunspot cycle (12)

Sunspots have a magnetic field associated with them. In one 11-year cycle the direction of the magnetic fields is positive and in the following 11-year cycle it is negative. Thus, a full cycle is really 22 years. That is, it takes 22 years for the sunspots to go through both positive and negative cycles and return to their original direction.

Figure 3.10 shows this cycle since 1800 plotted with the drought periods in Nebraska (12). The droughts have occurred in the same phase of the double cycle for nine consecutive times since 1800. The droughts tend to center on every other quiet year.

IMPLICATIONS OF CYCLICAL WEATHER. "Food scares" occur about every 10 years as in 1965 and again in the mid-seventies. Since most of the world's food supply is produced in the middle latitudes where cyclical weather patterns are more prominent, "food scares" tend to coincide with drought years. Nearly all the grain produced each year is consumed by people or fed to livestock and when grain supplies are reduced, farmers begin to reduce livestock numbers, and there is fear of continued shortage.

The probability is that drought will be followed by a decade of surplus production, but it is important to recognize that drought and possible famine might occur every 10 to 20 years and that surplus production should be stored to meet people's needs in years of scarcity. For more information on weather and climates see Chapter 6.

## PRODUCTION TRENDS IN THE FUTURE

THE MIDDLE LATITUDES. Nearly three-fourths of the world's grain supply is produced in the middle latitudes (between 30 and 50 degrees). And since 1956 grain production in this area has nearly doubled because of the development of inexpensive nitrogen fertilizer and sustained favorable weather. It is unlikely that this trend will be maintained, however. But since the middle latitudes are also where most of the developed countries are and where population growth is least, food production will continue to meet this area's needs and even produce some surplus.

THE HIGHER LATITUDES. It is above 50 degrees north latitude where there is greatest concern for future growth in production. This area includes most of Canada, most of Russia, the Scandinavian countries, England, most of Germany, and most of Poland. The short growing season in these countries plus the greater weather variability limits the choices of cereal crops and while the nearness to the oceans moderates Western European climates, interiors of large land masses, such as Canada and Russia, have widely varying rainfall, snowfall and temperature, making crop production in these areas undependable. Spring wheat, barley, and rye are the important cultivated crops. Hay and pasture crops are also important in these regions with short growing seasons.

THE TROPICAL AND SUBTROPICAL LATITUDES. The tropical and subtropical regions lie between the equator and about the 30th parallel. Most of the world's population also lives in this area, which includes nearly all of Africa, most of India, most of South America, and most of Australia. This warm band around the earth encompasses most of the developing and undeveloped countries where population is growing at rates above the average of 2 percent.

This warm band, however, has a long growing season and where water is sufficient for irrigation, two or more crops a year can be grown. Many crops are also adapted to the warm climate. Soils in this region, however, have a low productivity. Also, this region has serious insect and disease problems, and most of the area lacks the economic development needed to supply capital to improve soil fertility and agricultural production.

THE SOIL FACTOR. The soils of higher latitudes—above 40 degrees—have been influenced by the cyclical pattern of glaciation that exposes less-weathered soil material with each glacial cycle. In lower latitudes, however, glaciation has not rejuvenated the soils. Furthermore, the warmer the climate, the more rapid is the range of chemical weathering of the mineral matter making up the soil. Also the warmer the climate, the faster organic matter decomposes and the less organic matter accumulates in the soils.

As soils undergo long periods of weathering (decomposition) under warm climate, the minerals that supply plant nutrients decompose and nutrients leach out of the soil leaving only the minerals most resistant to weathering. The clay that develops in such a situation is high in aluminum and iron oxides and is bright yellow and red. These red and yellow soils require heavy applications of lime and fertilizer to improve their fertility. Organic matter is needed to help improve their physical condition for cultivation and their water absorption and holding properties for plant use. The soils also require more nitrogen fertilizer over the years to replace the declining nitrogen previously obtained from decomposing organic matter. All these factors mean that the warm band around the world will increase in productivity only if sufficient capital is made available.

Presently the population in these areas is growing faster than capital is being generated to produce more food from agriculture. Even so, productivity will increase more in the warm band than in the middle latitudes during the next 25 years as more land, now under natural vegetation, is cultivated and more soil fertility practices, particularly use of fertilizer, are instituted.

INCREASING CROPLAND. Estimates are that the world's cropland could be doubled to about 4 billion acres over the next 25 years. Most, about 1400 million acres, of the increase lies between the equator and the 30th parallel. This is also where the need is the greatest because of growing population demands. The middle latitudes (from 30 to 50 degrees) are already well developed leaving less land for further increase. But with land reclamation, irrigation, and drainage another 500 million acres could be brought under cultivation. The least potential for further increase is in the regions above 50 degrees latitude because of weather variability, shorter growing season, and the limited number of crops adapted to this area. Only about 100 million more acres could be brought under cultivation.

ANOTHER PERSPECTIVE OF WORLD PRODUCTION AND FOOD CONSUMPTION. This chapter has demonstrated that for food production and consumption latitude is the major influence, but in import-export relations the longitudinal influence has dominated since 1930. The world can be divided in two groups: (1) the New World with North and South America and Oceania (Australia and New Zealand), and (2) the Old World with Europe, Asia, and Africa.

In both of these "worlds" the population growth rate is about 2 percent a year, but the amount of cropland available per person is very different. In the New World there is about one acre of cropland per person, but in the Old World that figure is less than 0.5 acre. Thus, as population continues to grow there is a growing deficit of food in the Old World that amounts to about 3 to 4 million tons of grain a year with the current population growth. The increasing dependence of the Old World on the New is clearly illustrated in the import-export balance (Fig. 3.11). From 1934 to 1938 Europe was the only region importing grain. All other regions were exporting grain. But by 1970 Europe, Asia, and Africa had all become dependent on the New World surpluses to

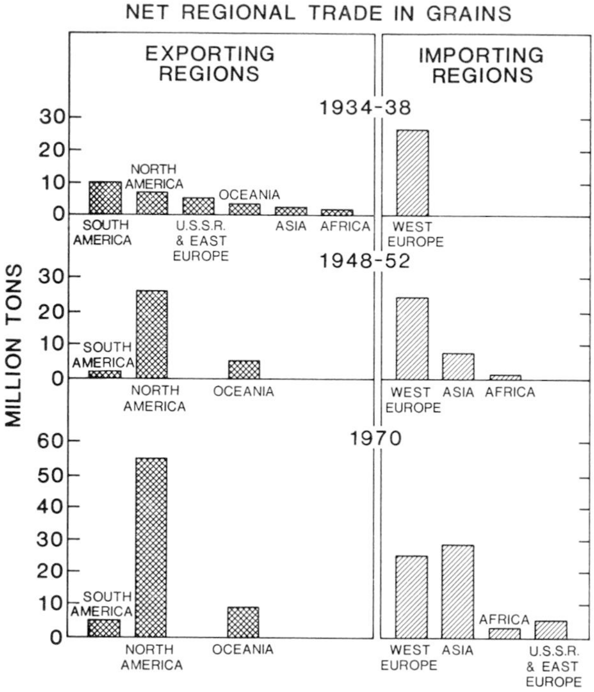


FIG. 3.11. The trend in world import-export balance (9)

help feed their population. Wheat surpluses exist in the United States, Canada, Australia, and Argentina; corn surpluses are in the United States, Argentina, and South Africa; and soybean surpluses exist in the United States and Brazil.

In summary, the United States is the world's leading supplier of food because of (1) a vast area of naturally productive land and relatively favorable climate, (2) a supply of capital to develop agriculture, and (3) a smaller and a more slowly growing population demanding its production.

## REFERENCES

1. Allen, K. Radway. Little Likelihood of Seas Solving World Food Problems. Australian Fisheries, April 1975.
2. Federal Council for Science and Technology. Report of the Ad Hoc Committee on the Present Interglacial. Washington, D.C.: National Science Foundation, August 1974.
3. Guidry, Nelson P. A Graphic Summary of World Agriculture. Miscellaneous Publication 705. Washington, D.C.: USDA, 1964.
4. Johnson, James. Paper read at conference on World Food Supply in Changing Climate, Sterling Forest, N.Y., December 2–5, 1974.

5. King, J. W. Sun Weather Relationships. Aeronautics and Astronautics 13 (4): 10–19, 1975.
6. Landsberg, H. E. Man Made Climatic Change. Science 170:1265–1274, December 18, 1970.
7. McQuigg, James, and Thompson, Louis M. The Influence of Weather and Climate on United States Grain Yields—Bumper Crops or Drought. Committee Report to the National Oceanic and Atmospheric Administration, U.S. Department of Commerce, December 1973.
8. Nelson, Philip R. Four Thousand Years of Farming. Farm Pond Harvest 7 (3): 8–9, 1973.
9. Thompson, Louis M. The World Food Situation. Journal of Soil and Water Conservation 27 (1): 4–7, 1972.
10. ———. Weather and Technology in the Production of Corn in the U.S. Corn Belt. Agronomy Journal 61:453–456, 1969.
11. ———. Weather and Technology in the Production of Soybeans in the Central United States. Agronomy Journal 62:232–236, 1970.
12. ———. Cyclical Weather Patterns in the Middle Latitudes. Journal of Soil and Water Conservation 28 (2): 87–89, 1973.
13. U.S. Department of Agriculture. That We May Eat. 1975 Yearbook of Agriculture. Washington, D.C.: USDA, 1975.

JIM HICKS

*A small farm in Nigeria. Getting a tractor is seldom the next step.*

# 4

# Energy Use in Food Production

DAVID PIMENTEL *and* ELINORE CRUZE TERHUNE

ENERGY is defined as the capacity to do work. It exists as light, heat, sound, electricity, chemical energy, mechanical energy, nuclear energy, radio energy, and magnetism, and is governed by the laws of thermodynamics (the theory of the relationships between heat and mechanical energy). The First Law of Thermodynamics states that energy can be converted from one form to another but can never be created or destroyed. For example, you can, using a furnace, change the chemical energy in fossil fuel into heat energy, which is used to drive a turbine, which supplies the mechanical energy to operate a generator, which supplies us with electricity. None of these conversions is 100 percent effective; some energy is always lost as heat (the Second Law of Thermodynamics). These laws are sometimes summarized as (1) you can't win, and (2) you can't even break even.

Energy is measured in several different units. Throughout this chapter, the common unit of energy measurement will be the kilocalorie (kcal), which is often used as a unit of heat energy and is equal to the Calorie of nutrition. Other commonly used units of energy are the horsepower-hour (hph) and the kilowatt-hour (kwh). The horsepower-hour is based on the amount of work a horse can do in each hour of a 10-hour day; one hph is equal to 641.56 kcal. A human can do only about one-tenth as much work as a horse, so that a person can do work equivalent to about one-tenth hph or about 64 kcal in one hour. A kilowatt-hour is a commonly used unit of electrical energy; it is equal to 860 kcal or about 1.34 hph.

Fossil fuels constitute a tremendous concentration of the ability to do work. A few calculations may give some feeling for the magnitude of energy units in terms of a person's ability to do work. For example, one

DAVID PIMENTEL is Professor, Entomology Department, Cornell University and an active member of committees and councils of National Academy of Sciences, Environmental Protection Agency, and Department of Health, Education, and Welfare.

ELINOR CRUZE TERHUNE is a Postdoctoral Fellow at Cornell University. She earned the Ph.D. at Stanford University in 1975 with emphasis on population biology, and ecology.

gallon of gasoline is generally assumed to have 36,000 kcal. Assume that the gasoline is used to run a mechanical engine and that the conversion from chemical energy to mechanical energy is only 20 percent efficient. The gasoline will thus produce about 7,200 kcal of work (36,000 $\times$ .20). Since 1 hph equals 641.56 kcal, this is equivalent to 11.2 hph of work (7,200/641.56). Hence, from one gallon of gasoline we can get approximately the work we would get from a horse working 11 hours or about 10 people each working an 11-hour day. In other words, one gallon of gasoline produces as much work as one person working an 8-hour day, 5 days a week for 3 weeks!

All energy resources valuable to humans contain highly concentrated, available energy. The energy in these natural resources is finite and cannot be recycled. When work is performed, the resources are transformed from a state of high energy *availability* into work waste products and unavailable energy. Pollutants and waste products are therefore the direct and inevitable result of degrading available, high energy resources to perform work (20). The waste products cannot be reassembled into their former high energy state, nor can the energy in a barrel of petroleum be used again. Although the energy efficiency of combustion and other processes can no doubt be improved, no technical innovations can alter the Second Law of Thermodynamics: the amount of energy that actually performs work must be less than the energy available in the original resource.

INTERDEPENDENCE OF POPULATION, FOOD, LAND, WATER, AND ENERGY. The amount of energy required to produce the world's food depends on complex interrelationships among population, land, and climate (including water availability). Each of the five factors of energy, population, food, land, and water affects and is affected by every other factor. The interrelationships are actually even more complicated because labor, which is a subdivision of both energy and population, additionally affects all five factors. Indeed, all the factors can be subdivided further, and these interrelationships become exceedingly complex as they are examined in detail.

World agricultural yields actually increased by an average of 2.6 percent per year between 1954 and 1973 (63), but further gains are limited by the amount of available energy, land, water, and genetic manipulation of plants. Recently total food demand has kept up with or exceeded gains in food production, particularly in developing countries (6, 22). Population is currently increasing by 2.5 percent per year in developing countries (38) while overall food production in these countries, outside China, increased only by 1.9 percent between 1954 and 1973 (60). Per capita food production in Africa has actually *declined* over the past 20 years (15). All the developing nations are now net food importers.

Currently most of the world's people live on about 2,100 kcal (47) per day compared with the United State's average of 3,300 kcal (59). An estimated half-billion of the world's 4 billion people are protein-calorie malnourished (19), and the situation is not expected to improve as world population grows to a projected 6 to 7 billion around the year 2000 (37), with 200,000 new mouths (38) to feed each day (see Chapter 1).

The amount of available land is also a limit to food production. Even though there are an estimated 13.4 billion hectares (1 ha = 2.47 acres) of land area in the world (19), only 11 percent is suitable for cultivation (18), the rest being too dry, too cold, and/or too steep to raise food crops. About 182 million ha of this arable land is in the United States. More land might be cultivated throughout the world (see Chapter 3), but the cost in terms of energy would be immense.

Available land depends not only on climate, but also on population and land use policies (46). For example, at least 240,000 ha of U.S. cropland is lost annually to urban development, transportation networks, reservoirs, and flood control projects (15). Each new person born in the United States is responsible for an estimated loss of about 1 ha that is used for these projects (22). Elsewhere in the world, population pressures cause deforestation, overgrazing, and erosion, resulting in land loss. Hillside forests are cut for fuel, allowing disastrous erosion of the slopes and flooding of the low-lying croplands.

Estimates of just how much land it takes to feed a person an adequate diet depend on the type of diet and on the amount of energy used. Worldwide, an estimated 0.57 ha (1.4 acres) is needed to provide 2,350 kcal per day; the land required would triple if the calories were produced from animals (27) (see also Chapter 8). On the other hand, using the high energy technology of the United States, only about 0.5 ha (1.25 acres) is required to produce a diet of 3,300 kcal per capita per day that includes animal products (60). (Note that in this chapter data on industrialized agriculture are primarily for the United States but the conclusions apply where this technology is used—Canada, western Europe, U.S.S.R., South Africa, New Zealand, Australia, etc.). Whatever the actual land *requirements* are for per capita food production, only 0.36 ha (0.88 acres) of arable land per person is actually *available* worldwide (18).

At the same time that an increased number of people is demanding more energy to produce food, the people added each year demand that finite energy supplies be available for other uses involved in raising the standard of living. Clearly all the demands on land and energy cannot be met.

FOSSIL ENERGY USE. Global energy use has been increasing faster than population (Figure 4.1). The world population has doubled in the last 30 years, but *world energy consumption has doubled within the last 10 years.* Energy use in the United States has doubled in the past 20

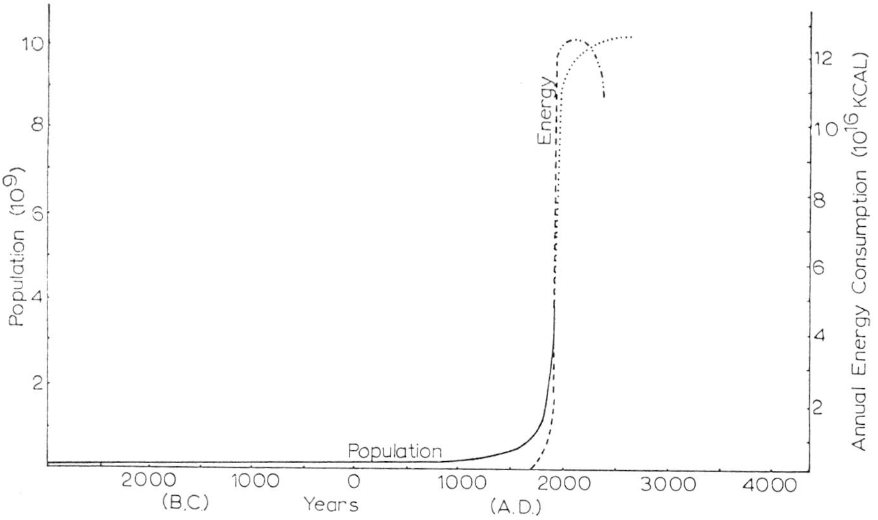


FIG. 4.1. Estimated world population numbers (————) from 1600 to 1975 and projected numbers (........) to 2250. Estimated fossil fuel consumption (------) from 1650 to 1975 and projected consumption (–··–··–) to 2250 (43)

years, while it has taken about 60 years for our population to double. Energy use in the United States is now the highest in the world on a per capita basis (13). Today the United States annually consumes 34 percent of the world's energy (23).

Since the mid-1800s, fossil fuels have replaced wood as the United State's major energy source. In 1850 wood provided 91 percent of the energy needs of the U.S. (62). By 1972 fossil fuels supplied about 96 percent of the energy, with petroleum, mostly for transportation, supplying 43 percent; natural gas, 33 percent; and coal, 20 percent; water power supplies 3 percent of the energy (23). Today wood supplies only a tiny fraction of U.S. energy requirements, even though the United States burns about 25 percent as much wood now as in the late 1800s (52).

The energy in fossil fuels has been used to control the human environment by reducing disease and increasing food production. Lower death rates have resulted, but there has been no corresponding decrease in birth rates. We have, in effect, used fossil energy to raise the human population above the natural carrying capacity of the earth. In many parts of the world DDT (a chemical that requires over 48,000 kcal per kg to produce and formulate) (30, 44) was used to control malaria-carrying mosquitoes. Death rates fell from 20 to 14 per thousand in Ceylon (Sri Lanka) and from 27 to 15 per thousand in Mauritius within one year of spraying (40), but birth rates did not decline, resulting in explosive population increases.

Energy in the form of labor, machinery, gasoline, fertilizers (nitrogen, phosphorus, and potassium), irrigation, pesticides, herbicides, etc., has increased crop yields, particularly in the developed countries. Energy use has been increasing faster in agriculture than in many other sectors of the world economy. For example, energy inputs into U.S. corn production more than tripled between 1945 and 1970 (44). It now takes about 890 liters (235 gallons) of oil equivalent per year to feed each person in the United States or the United Kingdom (29). The United States devotes about 3 to 5 percent of its energy to this task. The energy needed for processing, distribution, and preparation raises the oil equivalent per person per year to 1,250 liters (330 gallons) (45) or about 15 percent of the total U.S. energy (25, 27).

In the 1960s high-yielding strains of dwarf wheats and rices were introduced to food-deficit countries. These strains were the basis of the so-called Green Revolution. They were capable of doubling yields (6) provided they were heavily fertilized; they also required increased use of pesticides because some are more susceptible than native varieties to attack by pests (39). If high energy inputs are not maintained for some Green Revolution varieties, yields may be lower than those from native varieties.

Although the developing countries use less of the world's energy resources per capita than the United States does, about 60 percent of the energy used in the developing countries goes into food production (49). Overall, the world's food systems use nearly 25 percent of all energy consumed (41). Despite this heavy energy input, world food demand still exceeds world food production; the demand for food and energy is not likely to decrease.

ENERGY RESOURCES. Fossil fuel supplies, however, are rapidly dwindling. More than half the known world reserves of petroleum and natural gas are expected to be depleted by the year 2000; coal reserves are expected to be half depleted by about 2100 (26).

To illustrate the relation between decreasing energy supplies and the demands of food production, assume that the world's petroleum supplies were used only for food production. Assume also that U.S. food production technology were used to feed a U.S. diet to the 4 billion people in the world. The known petroleum reserves, estimated about 87 trillion liters (23 trillion gallons) (28), would last about 13 years:

$$\frac{76\% \text{ of 87 trillion liters is convertible to fuel}}{\text{4 billion people} \times \text{1,250 liters/person/year for U.S. diet}} = \text{13 years}$$

Of course, this scenario is unlikely because the U.S. agricultural technology and food distribution network cannot be duplicated instan-

TABLE 4.1. Energy analysis of subsistence and shifting agriculture. Data given are long-term annual averages that include fallow periods (29). None of the energy budgets that follow include solar energy as an input. Only because of this omission is it possible to get an output that is higher than "input," which the reader should recognize is clearly contrary to the Second Law of Thermodynamics.

| Area | Crop | Input/ha/Year | | Output/ha/Year | | | Kcal Output/ Kcal Input |
|---|---|---|---|---|---|---|---|
| | | Labor (hours) | Kcal[a] | Crop Yield (kg) | Kg Protein | Kcal | |
| Dayak | rice[b] | 217 | 41,462 | 190 | 15.2 | 685,454 | 16.5 |
| Dayak | rice[b] | 166 | 31,717 | 160 | 12.8 | 577,979 | 18.2 |
| Iban | rice[b] | 75 | 14,330 | 56 | 4.5 | 203,009 | 14.2 |
| Tanzania | rice[c] | 204 | 38,978 | 252 | 20 | 909,959 | 23.3 |
| Africa | maize[d] | 450 | 85,980 | 896 | 85 | 3,248,149 | 37.8 |
| Africa | millet[d] | 250 | 47,767 | 478 | 53 | 1,733,938 | 36.3 |
| Africa | sweet potato[d] | 580 | 110,819 | 3057 | 46 | 3,475,042 | 31.4 |
| Africa | cassava[d] | 935 | 178,648 | 7115 | 50 | 10,890,852 | 61.0 |
| Africa | yams[d] | 1160 | 221,638 | 4895 | 98 | 5,087,174 | 23.0 |
| Africa | groundnut[d] | 758 | 144,829 | 558 | 84 | 1,853,356 | 12.8 |
| New Guinea[e] | total all crops[f] | | 227,329 | | | 3,733,366[h] | 16.4 |

[a]Calculated from Leach (29, p. 133) using Leach's assumption of 0.8 megajoules (191.07 kcal) expended per hour of labor.
[b]Cropped one year in 10 years.
[c]Cropped 1½ years out of 10.
[d]Assumed to be cropped 5 years out of every 10. Original source gave range of 3 to 7 years out of 10. Leach did not specify whether the land was cropped consecutive years or not.
[e](48).
[f]Long fallow (20 to 25 years).
[g]Based on actual expenditure of energy during clearing, cultivation, and harvesting.
[h]Includes portion of the crop fed to pigs.

taneously throughout the world. It is included only to show the energy limitations that will prevent use of U.S. technology to solve the world food problems.

ENERGY USE AND FOOD PRODUCTION. Major resources used in crop production are energy (machinery, fuel, chemicals, irrigation, etc.), labor, and land. Within limits these inputs can be substituted for each other. For example, fossil energy can be used to reduce human labor and vice versa. Likewise, energy or labor inputs reduce the land required to produce a given amount of food. This is *intensive* land use.

Conversely, where land is abundant compared with population, *extensive* land use prevails. Shifting cultivation, or fallow agriculture, uses burning to release minerals bound up in the vegetation, making nutrients available to the crop planted in the ashes. A minimum of human energy is required since stumps are not removed, the seeds or tubers are simply scratched into the soil with a digging stick, and the plots are not weeded much. The plot is cultivated for 1 to 4 years, until soil fertility declines and yields diminish, and encroaching forest plants make cultivation increasingly difficult. The plot is then abandoned and not cultivated again for about 20 years. Such methods are used primarily in rain forests and savannahs and allow people maximum amount of leisure time, with minimum expense and work (5).

When plots remain in use longer and fallow periods become shorter weeds must be removed to prevent their competition with crop plants. Cultivation with hoes or plowing with draft animals or both become necessary. Fertilizers, animal manures, or decayed vegetation must also be added to the land to offset declining soil fertility.

Subsistence agriculture and shifting cultivation systems have a high ratio of edible energy output to energy input (Table 4.1) (29). This Energy Ratio (Er) is large primarily because farmers use only their own labor and none of the high-energy inputs, such as fertilizer, machinery, draft animals, and fuel. The average Er for rice production systems with fallow periods of about 9 years is about 18.8, and for single crops grown in Africa, using shorter fallow periods, the Er averages about 33.3 overall. These Ers are vastly greater than the ones for semi-industrial and industrial systems. The calculated Er of a semi-industrial system in Mexico using oxen is only 3.38 (Table 4.2) and for some highly industrialized farming in the U.S., the Er drops to 2.69 (Table 4.3). Much of the energy used in U.S. farming is consumed as fuel, machinery, and the highly energy dependent fertilizer nitrogen.

If the three food production systems are examined on the basis of output per *worker hour,* however, the picture is reversed (Table 4.4). The output per worker hour in industrialized farming systems is many times higher than that of shifting cultivation systems, which is just what one would predict from the earlier discussion of the interrelationships

TABLE 4.2. ENERGY INPUTS IN CORN PRODUCTION IN MEXICO USING OXEN (42).

| Input | Quantity/Hectare | Kcal/Hectare |
|---|---|---|
| Labor[a] | 383 hrs[b,c] | 208,448 |
| Oxen[d] | 198 hrs[b] | 693,000 |
| Machinery[e] | 41,400 kcal | 41,400 |
| Seeds[f] | 10.4 kg | 36,680 |
| TOTAL | . . . | 979,528 |
| Corn yield[g] | 941 kg[b] | 3,312,320 |
| Energy ratio (Er)—kcal return/kcal input: 3.38 | | |

[a]Assuming a farm worker consumes 21,770 kcal per week (3,110 kcal per day) and works a 40-hour week. $\frac{333 \text{ hrs}}{40 \text{ hrs}} \times 21{,}770 \text{ kcal} = 208{,}448 \text{ kcal}$

[b](31).

[c]Excluding labor used to tend oxen.

[d]Oxen weighing about 315 kg consume 20,000 kcal/day (140,000 kcal/week) when working (36). Oxen were assumed to work about 8 hours per day and to work a 5 day week. $\frac{198 \text{ hrs}}{40 \text{ hrs}} \times 140{,}000 = 693{,}00$

[e]Machinery assumed to weigh about 10 kg/ha, to last 5 years, and to require 20,700 kcal/kg for construction (42). $\frac{20{,}700}{5} \times 10 = 41{,}400 \text{ kcal}$

[f]1 kg corn seed = 3,520 kcal (58). 10.4 kg × 3,520 kcal = 36,608 kcal/ha

[g]1 kg corn was assumed to contain 3,520 kcal (58).
941 kg × 3,520 kcal = 3,312,320 kcal/ha

TABLE 4.3. ENERGY INPUTS IN CORN PRODUCTION, INDUSTRIALIZED AGRICULTURE (U.S.), 1970 (43).

| Input | | Kcal/Hectare |
|---|---|---|
| labor[a] | | (12,103) |
| machinery[b] | | 1,078,000 |
| fuel | 206 liters/ha × 10,000 kcal/liter | 2,060,000 |
| nitrogen | 125 kg/ha × 15,180 kcal/kg | 1,897,500 |
| phosphorus | 25 kg/ha × 3200 kcal/kg | 112,000 |
| potassium | 67 kg/ha × 2200 kcal/kg | 147,400 |
| seeds | 21 kg/ha × 3520 kcal/kg | 147,840[c] |
| irrigation[d] | | 187,000 |
| insecticides[e] | | 82,790 |
| herbicides[e] | | 82,790 |
| drying[f] | | 296,400 |
| electricity | | 380,000 |
| transportation | | 172,900 |
| total, not including labor | | 6,644,220 |
| including labor | | 6,656,323 |
| corn yield: 17,881,600 kcal/ha | | |
| energy ratio (Er) except labor: 2.69; including labor: 2.69 | | |

[a](44).

[b]About 244,555,000 kcal are required to produce the average 11,700 kg of machinery used to farm 25 ha. Repairs were assumed to be 10 percent of production requirements, and the machinery (tractors, trucks, and miscellaneous) were assumed to last 10 years.

[c]Includes higher energy use for production of hybrid seed.

[d]Only 3.8 percent of the 1964–70 corn acreage was irrigated, and about 4,921,166 kcal are required to irrigate 1 ha of corn for one season.

[e]1 kg/ha @ 24,200 kcal/kg + 49,720 kcal for application.

[f]30 percent of the corn in 1970 was dried, using about 198.5 kcal/kg.

TABLE 4.4. OUTPUT PER WORKER HOUR IN SOME AGRICULTURAL SYSTEMS (29).

| Agricultural System | Output (kcal/hour) |
|---|---|
| Preindustrial Systems | |
| Kung bushmen, hunter-gatherers | 1100 |
| Subsistence rice (tropics)[a] | 2600 to 4500 |
| Subsistence corn, millet, sweet potatoes (tropics)[a] | 6000 to 7200 |
| Peasant farming (China) | 9600 |
| Semi-industrial Systems | |
| Rice (tropics) | 9600 |
| Corn (tropics) | 5500 to 11,500 |
| Industrialized Systems | |
| Rice (U.S.) | 668,700 |
| Cereals (U.S.) | 726,000 |
| Corn (U.S.) | 907,600 |

[a]See also Table 4.1.

among land, energy, and labor. Fossil energy inputs in industrialized agriculture vastly improve yields per hectare and per labor hour, but at the expense of energy efficiency.

The high output per worker in Chinese peasant farming (1935–37, Table 4.4) was attained through high inputs of energy in irrigation and manure and because of considerable intercropping and multiple cropping.

The semiindustrial systems present a problem in energy analyses. Many of the data available do not include the human labor required to maintain draft animals; that is, to round them up, to build enclosures, and to care for them, their harnesses, and field implements. Thus, the calculations on energy efficiency are ambiguous, and further research is needed on energy use in systems that use only animal power and in those that are making a transition to mechanization.

Because increasingly intensive systems require very hard work, there is some evidence that farmers prefer to continue shifting cultivation systems. Boserup pointed out that "there are many examples of government offers to supply ploughs and draught animals being turned down because the cultivators found it easier to continue with the system of forest fallow" (5). Perhaps farmers only undertake more demanding technology when all other efforts have failed to increase yields on soils of ever declining fertility. In addition, some governments in developing countries maintain policies that keep food prices low as a subsidy to urban dwellers; farmers thus have no economic incentive to undertake the harder work required by more intensive food production methods.

ENERGY USE FOR PRESERVATION AND PREPARATION OF FOODS. Considerable energy goes into the preservation, processing, and preparation of foods. Some foods (e.g., grains and pulses—beans, peas, lentils, etc.) must be dried before they can be stored safely (see Chapter 11). Where the climate is suitable, energy from the sun has long been used to dry meat, fish, coconut meat (copra), fruits (raisins, prunes, apricots), and most forage crops (hay). Large amounts of energy are often used, particularly in developed countries, to machine dry some grains. For example, about 5,040 kcal is required to reduce the moisture content of 1 bu of corn from 26.5 to 13 percent (12).

In the United States substantial energy goes into packaging materials, including paper, plastic (made from petroleum and natural gas), metals, and glass. A 12-ounce aluminum can takes almost twice as much energy (1,875 kcal) to produce, transport, and fill as does a steel can (1,058 kcal) (4), due to the large amount of energy used to refine aluminum. When three types of disposable half-gallon milk containers were compared, the energy requirements were 2,159 kcal for a plastic bottle, 1,058 for a plastic pouch, and 1,669 for a paper carton.

The energy required for paper packaging materials ranges from 10.1 million kcal per ton for unbleached kraft paper to 11.5 million kcal per ton for set-up boxes (4). For glass containers the range is 1,204 to 1,333 kcal per container depending on size, although the relation between size and energy requirements is not a simple one.

Processing food for packaging or canning uses additional energy; for example, about 85 kcal are required to husk, prepare, fill, and heat the contents of a single can of corn during canning and about 900 kcal for the can itself, compared with 187 kcal required to grow the corn (Table 4.5) (8). In 1963 food processing accounted for 7.2 percent of the total U.S. energy use (25).

Food preparation in the home (cooking, refrigeration, and freezing) and shopping by automobile accounted for 30.5 percent of the food-related energy use in 1963, compared with 17.9 percent for agriculture. In the same year, household energy use, including the energy to produce and deliver the necessary fuels and appliances, cost $6.1 billion and used 471.2 trillion kcal (25).

In areas of the world where combustible materials are in short supply and/or expensive, animal dung is widely used as cooking fuel. Almost half of India's 770 million metric tons of recoverable cattle manure is burned as cooking fuel each year, providing the thermal equivalent of 38.5 million metric tons of coal (24) or about 270 million kcal. Cow dung is also preferred over other fuels because it "burns with a clean,

TABLE 4.5. Energy used to produce a can of corn (8).

| Production Stage | Kcal |
|---|---|
| Growing corn | 187 |
| Processing (husk corn; prepare, fill and heat can) | 85 |
| Produce can | 900 |
| Transportation from store to consumer's home | 11,437 |

TABLE 4.6. ENERGY EFFICIENCY OF FREIGHT TRANSPORT SYSTEMS (32).

| Freight Transport Type | Cargo Ton Miles per Gallon of Fuel |
|---|---|
| Air | |
| Boeing 707[a] | 8.3 |
| Boeing 747[b] | 11.4 |
| Surface | |
| Sixty 250-hp, 40-ton trucks | 50.0 |
| Fast 3000-ton, 40-car freight train | 97.0 |
| Three 5000-ton, 100-car freight trains | 250.0 |
| Large pipeline, 100 miles, 2 pumps | 500.0 |
| Water | |
| 60,000 gross tons inland barge | 220.0 |
| 100,000-ton supertanker, 15 knots | 930.0 |

[a]160 tons, 30,000 hp aircraft, one-half of which is attributable to carrying freight.
[b]360 tons, 60,000 hp aircraft, one-fourth of which is attributable to carrying freight.

slow long-lasting flame" (24). There is, however, a conflict in developing countries because the manure is sorely needed for fertilizer.

ENERGY USE FOR DISTRIBUTION AND MOVEMENT OF FOODS. The energy efficiency for various methods of transportation has been measured (Table 4.6). Except under emergency conditions, such as circumventing blockades or for famine relief, air freight is not normally used to transport food, and pipeline transport is shown only for comparison. Of the two remaining land transport systems, trains are about five times more energy efficient than trucks. Some trucks must be used, however, to haul produce between farms and rail depots or processors; trucks are also used to move processed foods for retail distribution.

Because energy has been abundant and cheap, some very inefficient transport patterns have occurred, particularly in the United States. For example, it is economically feasible to transport a head of lettuce from California to the East, consuming 1,140 kcal, even though the lettuce, which is 95 percent water, contains only 47 kcal.

The least efficient link in the chain of food transport from the farm to the consumer is the passenger automobile (see Table 4.5). The average distance traveled from home to grocery store is about 4 km (2.5 miles), requiring at least 1.39 liters of gasoline (11,437 kcal) for a round trip (8).

PROJECTED ENERGY DEMAND FOR DIFFERENT FOOD SYSTEMS. Americans each consume 312 grams of meat daily or 114 kg (250 lbs) per person annually (61). Each American consumes, on the average, 53 kg of beef, 30 kg of pork, 6 kg of fish, 23 kg of chicken and turkey, 2 kg of veal and lamb, 129 kg of dairy products, and 285 eggs (36 kg) per year. Out of a total of 96 grams of *protein* consumed per

TABLE 4.7. ENERGY ANALYSIS OF VEGETABLE PROTEIN PRODUCTION. DATA ARE GIVEN PER HECTARE, AND ARE FOR THE U.S. EXCEPT WHERE INDICATED (45).

| | Outputs | | | | Inputs | | | | | |
|---|---|---|---|---|---|---|---|---|---|---|
| | | | | | Labor | | | | | |
| Crop | Yield (kg) | Yield in Food Energy ($10^6$ kcal) | Protein Yield (kg) | Protein Yield ($10^6$ kcal) | Worker Hours | Energy Equivalents ($10^6$ kcal) | Fossil Energy ($10^6$ kcal) | Total Input ($10^6$ kcal) | Kcal Protein Yield/ Kcal Fossil Energy Input | Kcal Protein Yield/Energy Input Including Labor |
| Alfalfa | 6,451 (dry) | 11.4 | 710 | 2.8 | 9 | .005 | 2.694 | 2.699 | 1.04 | 1.04 |
| Soybeans | 1,882 | 7.6 | 640 | 2.6 | 15 | .008 | 5.285 | 5.293 | .49 | .49 |
| Brussels Sprouts | 12,320 | 5.5 | 604 | 2.4 | 60 | .033 | 8.492 | 8.525 | .28 | .28 |
| Potatoes | 26,208 | 20.2 | 524 | 2.1 | 60 | .033 | 8.907 | 8.940 | .24 | .23 |
| Corn | 5,080 | 17.9 | 457 | 1.8 | 22 | .012 | 6.644 | 6.656 | .27 | .27 |
| Corn silage | 30,200 | 24.1 | 393 | 1.6 | 25 | .014 | 5.493 | 5.507 | .29 | .29 |
| Rice | 5,796 | 21.0 | 388 | 1.6 | 30 | .016 | 15.536 | 15.552 | .10 | .10 |
| Dry beans | 1,457 | 5.0 | 325 | 1.3 | 15 | .008 | 4.478 | 4.486 | .29 | .29 |
| Oats | 1,900 | 7.4 | 276 | 1.1 | 6 | .003 | 2.978 | 2.981 | .37 | .37 |
| Wheat | 2,284 | 7.5 | 274 | 1.1 | 7 | .004 | 3.770 | 3.774 | .29 | .29 |
| Hay | 5,000 (dry) | 8.6 | 200 | .80 | 16 | .009 | 3.115 | 3.124 | .26 | .26 |
| Corn (Mexico) | 1,944 | 6.8 | 175 | .70 | 1144 | .219 | 0.053 | 0.272 | 13.2 | 2.57 |
| Rice (Philippines) | 1,654 | 6.0 | 111 | .44 | 576 | .110 | 0.582 | 0.692 | .76 | .64 |
| Wheat (India) | 821 | 2.7 | 99 | .40 | 615 | .118 | 0.256 | 0.374 | 1.6 | 1.07 |
| Sorghum (Sudan) | 900 | 3.0 | 99 | .40 | 240 | .046 | 0.079 | 0.125 | 5.1 | 3.2 |
| Cassava (Tonga) | 5,824 (dry) | 19.2 | 58 | .23 | 1284 | .245 | 0.016 | 0.261 | 14.4 | .88 |

TABLE 4.8. Energy analysis of animal protein production per hectare in the U.S. and Africa (45).

| Product | Protein Yield ($10^6$ kcal) | Feed Energy Input ($10^6$ kcal) | Fossil Fuel Inputs in Feed and in Animal Management ($10^6$ kcal) | Labor | | Total Energy Input ($10^6$ kcal) | Kcal Protein Output/ Kcal Input |
|---|---|---|---|---|---|---|---|
| | | | | Hours | $10^6$ kcal[a] | | |
| milk | .236 | 6.963 | 8.561 | 23 | .0125 | 15.536 | .015 |
| eggs | .728 | 14.406 | 9.560 | 174 | .0947 | 24.061 | .030 |
| broilers | .464 | 8.886 | 10.233 | 38 | .0207 | 19.140 | .024 |
| catfish | .204 | 5.007 | 7.068 | 55 | .0299 | 12.105 | .017 |
| pork | 260 | 17.021 | 9.212 | 28 | .0152 | 26.248 | .010 |
| beef (feedlot) | .204 | 24.952 | 15.845 | 31 | .0169 | 40.814 | .005 |
| beef (rangeland) | .00880 | 1.420 | .089 | 1 | .0005 | 1.510 | .006 |
| lamb (rangeland) | .00680 | .128 | .011 | 0.2 | .0001 | .139 | .005 |
| Zebu cows, African rangeland—milk, blood, and meat | .00304 | .040 | 0.0 | 34 | .0065 | .046 | .066 |

[a]See Table 4.6.

capita per day, 66 grams is animal protein. Americans consume a total of 5.3 million metric tons of animal protein per year (45).

In an animal carcass, the actual amount of usable protein (dry weight) is only about 15 percent of the usable meat, and the meat itself is only a fraction of the carcass. About half the energy in the food eaten by an animal is used for metabolism, and energy also goes into nonedible parts such as hides, bones, and offal.

Only the last quarter of an adequately fed animal's food intake is used for weight gain, fat storage, and milk production; half-starved animals have no energy reserves with which to produce meat and milk. In areas of the developing nations where livestock herds have expanded beyond the carrying capacity of the ranges, milk and meat production could actually be increased substantially by reducing herd sizes by about half (15).

To compare the energetic cost of producing plant and animal protein, energy-rich carbohydrates were omitted from the calculations for Tables 4.7 and 4.8. (The ratios in these tables, thus, correspond only in a general way to Ers in Tables 4.1 to 4.3 and should not be compared directly with them.) It takes at least 30 kcal of energy input to produce 1 kcal of animal protein—10 times the 3 kcal required for 1 kcal of plant protein.

Furthermore, by comparing the protein yield (in kcal) columns in Tables 4.7 and 4.8 we see that typical vegetable protein yields per hectare are about five times that produced by animals. That is, about five times more land is required to produce a given amount of protein from animals.

Of the protein produced from all sources in the United States in 1975, fully 76.5 percent was fed to livestock. For the world, 29.5 percent of the protein produced was fed to livestock. The distribution of high protein foods is also important; the developing nations annually export to the generally well-fed industrial nations some 3.5 million tons of animal protein (fish meal, shrimp, oilcakes, and soybeans) (16) for use as livestock or pet fodder or as luxury foods.

About 5 percent of all protein fed to livestock in the United States is consumed by about 100 million dogs and cats (63). If this food could be processed and distributed effectively in developing nations, an adequate diet could be provided for perhaps 100 million people.

Indeed, if distribution problems were resolved, we could feed an increased number of human beings by reducing the consumption of animal products in developed nations. A better alternative would be to use the grains and other foods that would be released to feed a smaller number of humans at a higher nutritional level. Table 4.9 shows that if the world's peoples ate only vegetarian diets, about one fourth less protein would have to be produced than if we continued to feed animals as we do today.

We are by no means suggesting that the United States should stop

TABLE 4.9. ESTIMATED AND PROJECTED PROTEIN PRODUCED, FED TO LIVESTOCK, AND AVAILABLE AS HUMAN FOOD (45).

| | U.S. | World | | |
|---|---|---|---|---|
| | 1975 | 1975 | 2000 | Vegetarian Diet 2000 |
| | | *(million metric tons)* | | |
| Total cereal, legume, & other vegetable protein produced | 27.1 | 131 | 228 | 179 |
| fed to livestock | 24.6 | 45 | 59 | 0 |
| available to people | 2.5 | 86 | 169 | 179 |
| Total livestock protein produced | 6.0 | 33 | 43 | 25 |
| fed to livestock | 0.7 | 3 | 4 | 0 |
| available to people | 5.3 | 30 | 39 | 25 |
| Total fish protein[a] produced | 1.0 | 9 | 12 | 12 |
| fed to livestock | 0.8 | 3 | 4 | 0 |
| available to people | 0.2 | 6 | 8 | 12 |
| Total protein produced | 34.1 | 173 | 283 | 216 |
| fed to livestock | 26.1 | 51 | 67 | 0 |
| available to people | 8.0 | 122 | 216 | 216 |

[a]Includes all seafoods and allows for a reduction in the protein that is actually available due to cleaning fish for human consumption.

producing animal protein. Protein from animals is of higher nutritional quality than that from plant sources and is especially needed by children (see Chapter 2). Also, much of the world's surface is not suited to cropping and can be used only for grazing. Animals provide the only practical way of converting the grasses and other plants on these lands to human foods. The energy costs of range-fed beef, however, can be high when herding is done with pickup trucks, as in the western United States. (See Chapter 8 for further discussion of animal contributions, efficiency, and competition with people for food.)

ENERGY REQUIREMENTS FOR IRRIGATION. Only about 12 percent of the world's cultivated land is irrigated (17). Irrigation can be used to increase food production, especially in warm climates, but requires enormous inputs of energy. For example, in the subtropics it takes about 12.2 million liters of water to produce 5,000 kg of corn per ha. Pumping this much water from a depth of about 90 feet uses about 20.6 million kcal (45). In California irrigation accounts for some 68 percent of all the electricity used in agriculture (2). Energy is required for excavation and other construction, surface networks, delivering systems, pipe and construction materials, pumping, and human labor. Depending on the system, electricity or animal labor or both are also used.

When irrigation makes multiple cropping possible, production can be substantially increased. The Taiching District in Taiwan has fertile soil, skilled farmers, and relatively warm winters. Using irrigation, plots of land can be effectively tripled in size by growing spring rice and summer rice, plus a winter crop such as wheat, cabbages, sweet potatoes, or rapeseed (in addition to raising poultry and other livestock) (50).

Irrigation causes the loss of 200,000 to 300,000 ha of land annually throughout the world (15). When land is irrigated, small amounts of minerals present in the water accumulate as salt deposits on the soil unless leached to lower levels or flushed into streams. If proper drainage is not provided, water tables rise and waterlogging compounds the problem of salinization.

Irrigation systems can be effective only when the water supply is reliable. In many parts of the world, impoverished people seeking firewood and land to cultivate disrupt vital river flow. Rivers that formerly flowed year round (as in Peru) tend to be sediment-laden torrents during the rainy season, and to dry up entirely during the dry season (15). Heavy silt loads also render expensive reservoirs useless. For example, the Anchicaya Dam in Colombia was completely filled with sediment 7 years after completion, and its multimillion dollar hydroelectric power generating system now operates solely on stream flow, at one-third its planned capacity (15). India and Pakistan in particular had relatively few sites suitable for dam construction, and once these reservoirs are filled with sediments, no additional sites can be created.

ALTERNATIVES FOR ENERGY CONSERVATION IN DEVELOPED AND DEVELOPING COUNTRIES. Between 1950 and 1970, a barrel of oil cost only about $1.50; this was equivalent to having two human "energy slaves" working for about a year for a dollar (29). Because labor was expensive in comparison, Western agriculture used mechanization and chemical pest control to reduce labor inputs drastically. From 1945 to 1970, for example, the number of hours worked per ha in U.S. corn production declined from 52 to 22 (44).

MACHINES, ANIMALS, AND HUMAN LABOR. Human labor can almost always accomplish a given task using less energy than machinery. For example, using a tractor and sprayer to apply herbicides requires 65 times as much energy as a person using a hand sprayer (44).

Even so, developed countries are not likely to replace machine labor with human labor as long as labor remains so expensive relative to fossil energy. As fossil energy becomes more expensive, it must be used more efficiently. The horsepower of tractors, for instance, could be matched more closely to the task to be performed, and fuel can be saved by keeping tractors tuned up. Another scheme to reduce energy use by machines is minimum tillage, but this method results in pest problems requiring increased chemical use (9).

In the developing countries, agriculture can be made more intensive by using more labor, although surplus labor is not always available where and when it is needed.

Draft animals (oxen, bullocks, water buffalo, and horses) also offer energy advantages over mechanization. A water buffalo uses about 800 kcal of energy per hour of work, whereas a tractor requires about 90,000 kcal (43); draft animals, however, take about 8 to 12 times longer to perform a given task (55). Farmers also have to care for the animals when they are not working, although they can be fed rice straw and other crop remains, and can graze along paths, along streams, on steep slopes, and on other land not used for crops (57). Draft animals do serve as an additional source of protein in the form of milk and meat—an important consideration to people who would otherwise subsist on a largely vegetarian diet. These animals also provide manure for fertilizer and fuel.

FERTILIZER. In industrialized agriculture, nitrogen fertilizer is a major energy input. In U.S. corn production, for example, nitrogen was the second largest input in 1970 (Table 4.3). Not only is more nitrogen used than phosphorus and potassium, but nitrogen also requires substantially more energy to produce (about five times as much as phosphorus and seven times as much as potassium). Alternate technologies that decrease the use of nitrogen fertilizer, therefore, could save energy in industrialized agriculture.

Manure is one substitute for nitrogen fertilizer. It also adds valuable organic material to the soil, thereby increasing beneficial soil organisms, making plowing easier, improving the soil's water-holding and percolation capacity, reducing soil erosion, and improving the ratio of carbon to nitrogen in the soil (1, 11, 56). The 125 kg of nitrogen usually applied to a hectare of corn can be replaced by the manure produced in a year by 3 cows or buffaloes, 22 hogs, or 207 chickens (3, 14, 34, 35, 54). Using a tractor and spreader to haul and spread 900 kg of manure within 0.8 to 0.6 km of the source would require 40,000 kcal (33). To fertilize a hectare of corn entirely with bovine manure would require 22,400 kg of manure (produced in a year by 3 animals), yielding 125 kg of nitrogen. Spreading this amount would require about 1,000,000 kcal (100 liters of gasoline), but the energy cost of hauling and spreading could be reduced by using animal or human labor.

Legume crops that are plowed under also add nitrogen to the soil. For example, legumes could be planted between corn rows in late August and plowed under in the spring. Winter vetch used this way yields about 150 kg of total nitrogen per hectare of corn (51) and would require about 8 percent of the energy needed to make and apply an equivalent amount of commercial nitrogen (43). *Sesbania aculeata* (another legume) can be planted with rice and uprooted and worked into the soil as the rice matures, adding about 96 kg of nitrogen per hectare (21). Legumes can also add nitrogen when used as part of rotation schemes. (See Chapter 9 for research on legumes and nitrogen-fixation.)

PEST CONTROL. Energy inputs for chemical pest control can be reduced by emphasizing alternative methods of controlling insects and mites, diseases, and weeds. Breeding resistant strains of crop plants, using biological controls, and improving cultivation techniques and timing have all been used to good advantage. High prices for chemical pesticides are also influencing growers' use; apple growers in New York, for example, are becoming increasingly sophisticated about applying sprays only when needed, rather than according to fixed schedules recommended by chemical companies.

Weeds can be controlled by mechanical cultivation, chemicals, humans operating hand tools, or a combination of all three. Manufacturing and applying chemical herbicides (pre-and postemergence) uses more energy (258,800 kcal per hectare) than cultivating three times with a rotary hoe (180,000 kcal). Use of hoes or other hand implements requires only about 3 percent of the energy required by herbicides (43).

The greatest opportunities for conserving fossil energy in agricultural production exist in the developed countries, where use is presently highest. Meats, fluid milk, bakery products, and beverages are very expensive in terms of energy; alcoholic beverages alone account for 10 percent of the total use of energy by the food industry in the United States (25). Also, as noted earlier, home use of energy for food purchase, storage, and preparation is much greater than the energy used on farms to produce the food. Clearly, advances can be made by designing stoves, refrigerators, and freezers to function more efficiently and by reducing the number of trips to the supermarket.

Developing nations are faced with shortages of fossil and other fuels, and high prices. Of the possible inputs (land, energy, labor) needed to raise food production, then, only labor is really available. Ironically, fuel and fertilizer inputs have a greater impact on yields in developing nations. An additional pound of fertilizer applied in industrialized nations only produces about an additional 5 pounds of grain, whereas the same pound of fertilizer in India, Brazil, or Indonesia produces at least 10 pounds of additional grain (7).

ALTERNATIVE ENERGY SOURCES. All methods of harnessing energy to convert it into work require materials and equipment and energy to construct the equipment. As long as some forms of energy are *priced* cheaply, it will be economically feasible to use energy to extract energy.

With few exceptions, most of the alternative energy sources being developed in the United States would produce electricity and heat, which are not used to propel tractors or as the raw material for nitrogen fertilizer. These alternatives include nuclear fission and fusion; geothermal energy; direct use of solar energy; indirect use of solar energy as wind, tidal, and wave power; coal gasification; increased use of wood; and more efficient use of wastes. Although U.S. agriculture uses electricity for such things as lighting, electric motors, milking machines, and irrigation and other pumps, the major energy inputs in crop production are for fertilizers, machinery, and fuel (see Table 4.3). Of the alternative energy sources being developed, only coal gasification, methane generation from manure and municipal wastes, and increased use of manures or other wastes for fertilizers can make a *direct* contribution to energy supplies available for agriculture.

National priorities may have to be established for apportioning the remaining supplies of petroleum, reserving petroleum and natural gas for those uses for which it is uniquely suitable, such as feedstock for nitrogen fertilizer, essential plastic products, and petroleum-based drugs, as well as fuel for essential self-propelled vehicles. Electricity from alternative energy sources can relieve the pressure on dwindling petroleum reserves by supplying residential and commercial energy needs (particularly space heating and cooling), which consume about 20 percent of all energy used in the United States (32). Better energy efficiency in transportation is also crucial to preserve petroleum for those uses for which no alternative supplies have been developed.

Development of a cheap solar device for cooking foods would be a major technical breakthrough, helping to stop forest and arid land destruction. Current devices cost from $35 to $50 (15), making them beyond the reach of the people who need them most. The problem of storing energy cheaply for use during cloudy weather also needs to be solved.

SUMMARY. Fossil energy inputs in the food system (production, preservation, and distribution) and in human disease control have allowed the human population to expand to 4 billion. The critical question facing the planet in the last quarter of the twentieth century is how adequately a growing population can be supported as the fossil energy supplies are exhausted.

At the present annual rate of increase the world population will double in about 37 years. To double food production to meet this demand on presently cultivated land will require about a threefold increase in energy use within the next 25 years because of declining soil fertility, increased need for irrigation, and the diminishing returns from additional fertilizers. Tripling the energy used in agriculture would consume 35 to 40 percent of the total energy used worldwide each year by the year 2000, compared with 25 percent used now. Furthermore, as the quality of land declines because of population pressure and soil erosion, the proportion of the total energy needed for agriculture will increase even more.

Considerable additional energy and materials would be required to produce the capital equipment—farm machinery, fertilizer and agricultural chemical factories, oil tankers, refineries, railroads, trucks, highways, etc.—necessary for energy intensive agriculture. Whether this equipment *can* be assembled soon enough in the 37-year population doubling-time to be effective is, of course, another question and one that will have to be faced in the near future.

Food production in developing countries can be raised through increased energy inputs, especially fertilizers and irrigation. The potential for using irrigation to increase food production, however, is seriously threatened by deforestation due to population pressures. Reducing herd sizes to a more productive level in overgrazed areas would also make a major contribution to the food supply.

The reasonable course would be to reduce wasteful energy-use practices, particularly in transportation, in the industrialized nations to free world energy resources for use in areas where hunger is most widespread. It remains to be seen whether the political and social will exists to do this in time to avert widespread food shortages in the world, and whether population growth itself will be halted by more humane methods than by an increase in the death rate.

## REFERENCES

1. Andrews, N. B. The response of crops and soils to fertilizers and manures. 2nd ed. State College, Miss., 1954.
2. Batty, J. C.; Hamad, S. N.; and Keller, J. Energy inputs to irrigation. Utah State University, Department of Agricultural and Irrigation Engineering. 211(d)–8, 1974.
3. Benne, E. J.; Hoglund, C. R.; Longnecker, E. D.; and Cook, R. L. Animal manures: What are they worth today? Mich. Agr. Exp. Sta. Cir. Bull. 231, 1961.
4. Berry, R. S., and Makino, H. Energy thrift in packaging and marketing. Technology Review 76 (4): 32–43, 1974.
5. Boserup, E. The conditions of agricultural growth. Chicago: Aldine-Atherton, 1965.
6. Brown, L. R. The world food prospect. Science 190:1053–1059, 1975.
7. Brown, L. R., and Eckholm, E. P. By bread alone.
8. Brown, S. J., and Batty, J. C. Another perspective of energy and America's food system. Trans. Amer. Soc. Agr. Eng., in press.
9. CAST. Potential for energy conservation in agricultural production. Prepared by a task force of the Council for Agricultural Science and Technology, January 24, 1975.
10. Cervinka, V.; Chancellor, W. J.; Coffelt, R. J.; Curley, R. G.; and Dobie, J. B. Energy requirements for agriculture in California. Calif. Dept. of Food & Agr., Univ. of Calif., Davis. 1974.
11. Cook, R. L. Soil management for conservation and production. New York: John Wiley and Sons, Inc., 1962.
12. Corn Grower's Guide. Aurora, Ill.: W. R. Grace and Co., 1968.
13. Darmstadter, J.; Teitelbaum, P. D.; and Polach, J. G. Energy in the world economy. Baltimore: Johns Hopkins Press, 1971.
14. Dyal, R. S. Agricultural value of poultry manure. In Natl. Symp. on Poultry Ind. Waste Mgt. Nebr. Ctr. for Continuing Ed., Lincoln, Nebr., 1963, (unpaged).
15. Eckholm, E. P. Losing ground: Environmental stress and world food prospects. New York: W. W. Norton & Company, Inc., 1976.
16. Ehrlich, P. R., and Ehrlich, A. H. Population, Resources, Environment: Is-

sues in human ecology. 2nd ed. San Francisco: W. H. Freeman and Company, 1972.
17. Food and Agriculture Organization, United Nations. Production yearbook 1969. Vol. 23, 1970.
18. Food and Agriculture Organization, United Nations. Production yearbook 1972. Vol. 26, 1973.
19. Food and Agriculture Organization, United Nations. Assessment of the world food situation. World Food Conference, Rome, November 1974.
20. Georgescu–Roegen, N. Energy and economic myths. The Southern Economic Journal 41 (3): 347–381, 1975.
21. Ghose, R. L. M.; Ghatge, M. B.; Subrahmanyan, V. Rice in India. New Delhi: Indian Council of Agr. Res., 1956.
22. Hall, C. A. S. The biosphere, the industriosphere and their interactions. Bull. of the Atomic Scientists 31 (3): 11–21, 1975.
23. Hammond, A. L. Energy options: Challenge for the future. Science 177: 875–876, 1972.
24. Harris, M. Cows, pigs, wars and witches: The riddle of culture. New York: Vintage Books, Div. of Random House, 1975.
25. Hirst, E. Food-related energy requirements. Science 184:134–138, 1974.
26. Hubbert, M. K. Man's conquest of energy: Its ecological and human consequences. In The Environmental and Ecological Forum 1970–1971, pp. 1–50. Oak Ridge, Tenn.: U.S. Atomic Energy Commission, Office of Information Services, 1972.
27. Ingraham, E. W. A query into the quarter century on the interrelationships of food, people, environment, land and climate. Wright-Ingraham Institute, Colorado Springs, Colorado. Workshop, Cabo San Lucas, Mexico, Jan. 15–17, 1975.
28. Jiler, H. Commodity Yearbook. New York: Commodity Res. Bur., Inc., 1972.
29. Leach, G. Energy and Food Production. London: International Institute for Environment and Development, 1975.
30. Leach, G., and Slesser, M. Energy equivalents of net work inputs to food producing processes. Glasgow: Strathclyde University, 1973.
31. Lewis, O. Life in a Mexican village: Tepoztlán revisited. Urbana: Univ. of Ill. Press, 1951.
32. Lincoln, G. A. Energy conservation: Some challenges are proposed for science and technology. Science 180:155–162, 1973.
33. Linton, R. E. The economics of poultry manure disposal. Cornell Extension Bull. 1195. Ithaca, N.Y.: Cornell Univ., 1968.
34. Loehr, R. C., and Asce, M. Animal waste—a national problem. J. San. Eng. Div., Proc. Amer. Soc. Civil Eng. 2:189–221, 1969.
35. McEachron, L. W.; Zwerman, P. J.; Kearl, C. D.; and Musgrave, R. B. Economic return from various land disposal systems for dairy cattle manure, Cornell Univ. Conf. on Agric. Waste Mgt., 1969, pp. 393–400.
36. Morrison, F. B. Feeds and feeding. Ithaca, N.Y.: Morrison, 1946, pp. 50, 429.
37. National Academy of Sciences. Rapid Population Growth. Vols. 1 and 2. Baltimore: Johns Hopkins Press, 1971.
38. National Academy of Sciences. Population and food: Crucial issues.
39. Oka, I. Personal communication, 1973.
40. Political and Economic Planning. World population and resources. London, 1955.
41. Pimentel, D. Energy use in world food production. Environ. Biol. Cornell University, Ithaca, N.Y. Report 74–1, 1974.
42. ———. Food, nitrogen, and energy. Proc. Intern. Symposium on Nitrogen fixation, mimeographed. Pullman, Wash., June 6, 1974.

43. Pimentel, D. The energy crisis: Its impact on agriculture. Milan, Italy: Scienza & Tecnica, Mondadori Press, in press.
44. Pimentel, D., et al. Food production and the energy crisis. Science 182: 443–449, 1973.
45. Pimentel, D.; et al. Energy and land constraints in food protein production. Science 190:754–761, 1975.
46. Pimentel, D.; et al. The effects of land degradation on food and energy resources. 1976. (Science, in press).
47. President's Science Advisory Committee. Report of the Panel on the World Food Supply. Vols. 1 and 3. Washington, D.C.: The White House, 1967.
48. Rappaport, R. A. The flow of energy in an agricultural society. Sci. Amer. 225 (3): 117–132, 1971.
49. Royal Swedish Academy of Sciences. Energy uses. Manuscript. Energy conference, Aspenasgarden, Oct. 27–31, 1975.
50. Ruthenberg, H. Farming systems in the tropics. Oxford: Clarendon Press, 1971.
51. Sprague, H. B. The value of winter green manure crops. New Jersey Agr. Sta. Bull. 609, 1936.
52. Steinhart, C. E., and Steinhart, J. S. Energy: Sources, use, and role in human affairs.
53. Steinhart, J. S., and Steinhart, C. E. Energy use in the U.S. food system. Science 184:307–316, 1974.
54: Surbrook, T. C.; et al. Drying poultry waste. In Proc. Int. Symp. Livestock Wastes. St. Joseph, Mich.: Amer. Soc. Agr. Eng., 1971.
55. Terhune, E. C. Prospects for increasing food production in less developed countries through efficient energy utilization. Proc. 1st Energy and Agriculture Conference, Center for the Biology of Natural Systems, St. Louis, Mo., June 16–19, 1976. New York: Academic Press, 1976.
56. Tisdale, S. L., and Nelson, W. L. Soil fertility and fertilizers. 2nd ed. New York: MacMillan, 1966.
57. United Nations Panel of Experts on the Protein Problem Confronting Developing Countries, Strategy statement on action to avert the protein crisis in the developing countries. New York: U.N. Publication, 1971.
58. U.S. Department of Agriculture, Consumer and Food Economics Res. Div., ARS. USDA Agr. Handbook No. 8, 1963.
59. U.S. Department of Agriculture. Agricultural statistics 1973. Washington, D.C.: U.S. Govt. Printing Office, 1973.
60. U.S. Department of Agriculture. Our land and water resources. Current and prospective supplies and uses. Econ. Res. Serv. Misc. Publ. No. 1290, May, 1974.
61. U.S. Department of Agriculture. National Food Situation. Economic Research Service, NSF–151, 1975.
62. U.S. Department of Commerce. Historical statistics of the U.S. colonial times to 1957. Washington, D.C.: U.S. Govt. Printing Office, 1960, pp. 354–5.
63. Wittwer, S. H. Food production: Technology and the resource base. Science 188:579–584, 1975.

## BIBLIOGRAPHY

Brown, L. R. The world food prospect. Science 190:1053–1059, 1975.
Brown, L. R., and Eckholm, E. P. By bread alone. New York and Washington: Praeger, 1974.

Eckholm, E. P. Losing ground: Environmental stress and world food prospects. New York: W. W. Norton & Company, Inc., 1976.

Georgescu-Roegen, N. Energy and economic myths. The Southern Economic Journal 41 (3):347–381, 1975.

Hirst, E. Food-related energy requirements. Science 184:134–138, 1974.

National Academy of Sciences, Committee on World Food, Health and Population. Population and food: Crucial issues. Washington, D.C.: National Academy of Sciences, 1975.

Odum, H. T. Environment, power, and society. New York: Wiley-Interscience, Division of John Wiley & Sons, Inc., 1971

Owen, D. F. Man in tropical Africa: The environmental predicament. London: Oxford University Press, 1973.

Pimentel, D.; Dritschilo, W.; Krummel, J.; and Kutzman, J. Energy and land constraints in food protein production. Science 190:754–761, 1975.

Pimentel, D.; Terhune, E. C.; Dyson-Hudson, R.; Rochereau, S.; Samis, .R; Smith, E.; Denman, D.; Reifschneider, D.; and Shepard, M. The effects of land degradation on food and energy resources. Science, in press.

Steinhart, C. E., and Steinhart, J. S. Energy: Sources, use, and role in human affairs. Belmont, Calif.: Duxbury Press, 1974.

# 5

# Land Ownership and Tenure

PETER DORNER

THE SETTING. Those of us who grew up in the United States, especially in the country's midsection, have a particular conception of a farm that has little relevance in most of the world. We consider a farm a fenced rectangular area of land, divided into fenced rectangular fields. At least one side of this farm is bordered by a road, and the farmstead—the house, the barns, the silos, and the sheds—is located near this road. In terms of world agriculture, especially in the developing countries, this is a unique pattern, originating only because of the way the United States was settled.

In the spring of 1785, the U.S. Congress spent several months vigorously debating the disposition of the public lands and how they might best be settled. These debates resulted in the great Land Ordinance of May 20, 1785, which determined how land would be surveyed and divided all the way to the Pacific (2). This system led to our familiar 80-, 120-, 160-, 240-acre farm sizes. Between 1800 and 1900, over 5 million farms were marked out on the public lands.

With some exceptions in the East, parts of the South, and the far West, most of the country was settled this way, resulting in family-owned and -operated farms. Farms were registered in the owner's name, and owners received a clear title to a tract of land easily identified and located both physically and on maps. A clear title gave farmers great freedom. Land could easily be purchased and sold with titles transferred and again registered in the new owner's name. The record discouraged disputes, and could be used for land taxation and other purposes.

This system is uncommon in the developing countries. Variations among countries and regions are very great, but several generalizations are possible. First, the system we take for granted in the United States is absent, and land is not marked off in square mile units or rectangular

PETER DORNER is Professor of Agricultural Economics and Director of Land Tenure Center, University of Wisconsin at Madison. He has also been a teacher and researcher in foreign countries and consultant to presidential committees, United Nations Development Program, Food and Agriculture Organization, and Committee on Agrarian Reform.

shaped farms. Indeed, units of measurement vary widely, especially for land area. Officially, however, the metric system, with a kilometer equivalent to 0.6 of a mile and a hectacre equivalent to 2.47 acres, is most common. Individual farmsteads are not usually scattered throughout the countryside. Instead, people commonly live in villages (or at least a clustering of houses) and must walk or travel by ox cart to their tract of land. The most common beast of burden is not the horse or mule (although donkeys are very common) but the ox or cow, the water buffalo, or the camel.

There is also very little fencing—at least wire fencing. Why? First, fencing is expensive relative to the incomes of most farmers. Second, livestock is frequently raised away from crop farming and is not as common as in the United States. Third, labor is plentiful and cheap, and children can help watch livestock and keep them out of the crops. Finally, farms are frequently very small (or composed of several scattered plots), and since there are no roads, people must travel across, or at least along, the edges of others' lands to get to their own land.

Records of land ownership and registered titles to land are frequently nonexistent. Even where they do exist, the boundaries between farms are not always clear, leading to many disputes over ownership and over boundaries. The more powerful in the community are more likely to have their claims validated.

In the wheat-growing regions of northern India, there are vast fields of wheat, but these fields are cultivated not by a single family but by perhaps 100 or more families. Some families may own a parcel or several parcels (2–3 hectares) of land, while others, under some form of rental or sharecropping arrangement, operate land owned by others. Similarly, in some of the major rice-producing regions, large contiguous areas are planted to rice, but this represents many individual family plots or farms. Visible in such fields are land ridges, or bunds, that frequently form the boundaries of individual family plots and hold irrigation water within the plot. By contrast, in many Latin American countries land is commonly owned and operated in very large units—hundreds, even thousands of hectares. Such farms may be operated largely by a hired work force or by people renting small plots from the owner of the large farms. Such renters also frequently work for wages in the fields of the large farm owner.

In tropical areas of Africa, Asia, and Latin America, a method of agriculture known as "slash and burn" has been practiced for many centuries. Here, on farms or plots of highly irregular shapes and sizes, crops are grown amid the nutrient-rich debris that remains after cutting down and burning the trees and brush. The land will be farmed 2 or 3 years until the nutrients are exhausted and then will be abandoned for long periods.

These, then, are some of the contrasts we must remember: The U.S. farm image does not represent most of the world's agriculture. U.S. agriculture developed when there was plentiful land and a scarcity of labor; thus the major emphasis for agricultural improvement was placed on developing mechanical devices and improved tools and equipment that would save labor. The reverse situation, an overabundance of labor and a scarcity of land, characterizes most of the developing countries. While less than 5 percent of the U.S. population is engaged in farm production, in most developing countries 50 to 80 percent of the population is so engaged.

LAND TENURE AND OWNERSHIP FORMS. Land tenure system refers to (1) the arrangement by which people gain access to productive opportunities on the land and (2) the rules and procedures governing how the basic resources of land and water are used and controlled. Land tenure arrangements may be legal and contractual or they may be merely customary. Either way the system helps determine how income is distributed in the farming areas and who will be employed in farming and under what terms and conditions.

Africa, Asia, and Latin America provide many examples of the wide variety of agricultural conditions and institutional arrangements found in the developing countries. The colonial experiences of these regions were quite different and have left their mark on the national development policies. Also since the three areas emerged from colonial rule at different times, they are in different stages of coping with the transition.

In Africa (Africa here refers to the tropical, sub-Sahara regions), European-drawn political demarcations sometimes cut across well-recognized ethnic boundaries, sometimes becoming a major source of hostility and conflict between neighbors and certain ethnic groupings (3). European concepts of land tenure and ownership were introduced in areas where plantation crops were grown and also in some areas of general farming where private land concessions were granted. On the other hand, in the hinterland areas, the traditional customary practices of dealing with land were undisturbed and still remain. Thus, many of the new governments, who have only recently won their independence and are trying to implement development plans, find their claims to sovereign authority challenged by local, traditional tribal authorities.

In traditional, customary land tenure systems throughout much of Africa, the sovereign ownership of land is vested in the local group or tribe. Individuals have only usufructuary (use) rights, and persons have these rights simply because of their membership in the group. A share of the family land is a birthright and is not lost by living away from the home village. Although strangers (nonmembers) may receive land allotments, they do not have the same privileges, especially regarding inheritance of land by their children (6).

Many Asian countries, like African countries, have just emerged from colonial rule. Here colonialism had a profound impact on agrarian structure and village organization. The Europeans frequently introduced a high degree of administrative centralization (often for political purposes). In some instances, the traditional local authorities of the village communities had little role to play and consequently their authority languished. Sometimes colonial administrators installed special tax collectors who later became recognized as the proprietors of the land. At other times large estates were assigned to members of the local aristocracy as rewards for their cooperation. Thus in Asia there are few areas of tribal lands and customary tenures. And except where major land reforms have occurred, landlords now own much of the land, which is farmed by sharecroppers and tenants in small, independently operated units.

Most Latin American nations have been independent for well over a century, but present land tenure structures originated with the Spanish colonial system, and these basic forms were reinforced after independence. Large land grants to the early colonizers set the pattern for a system dominated by the *latifundia* (very large farms, including plantations, traditional large estates or haciendas, and large cattle ranches or *estancias)* and by *minifundia* (extremely small, subsistence holdings) whose holders provide much of the labor for the large estates. Most of the large estates used hired labor, and the permanent farm workers often have their homes on the estate and receive certain land-use privileges in return for their work on the estate.

In all Latin American countries family-sized farms exist or even predominate. Some traditional forms of land tenure, similar to those described for Africa, occur in the Indian communities of the Andean countries. In other areas land reform has taken place. The Mexican ejido, a communal type of tenure created by that country's land reform, was intended to reconstruct and build upon a traditional form. In the ejidos, land is communally held and cannot be bought or sold, but most land is worked by individual families in small units. Still, despite these exceptions, most agricultural land continues to be held in large estates, with the small, subfamily units holding relatively little land but serving as a refuge for most of the rural population.

The situation within every tenure group is affected by the availability of and access to alternatives. So long as economic development continues to expand opportunities and improve incomes by providing alternative employment, the power of one party over the other in a landlord-tenant relation is limited. Incomes earned by either party are influenced more by the relatively impersonal conditions in factor markets (land, labor, and capital) than by the personal ability of one party to dominate the other. Landlords in the United States, for example, have few common interests related specifically to their ownership of farm land. The land tenure system in this setting lacks group interests, and class oppression along tenure lines is limited because other economic opportunities exist, providing social mobility. The reorganization of U.S.

agriculture toward larger farms using more capital and less labor with resulting high family incomes has affected the entire range of tenure classes. Changes in farm size and in the factor proportions (land, labor, and capital) used in farming have been made by owners and part-owners as well as by tenants (5).

The role of present U.S. land tenure institutions contrasts sharply with that in the institutional structure of traditional societies. A traditional society is defined as one where produce markets are not highly developed and where there are almost no markets for land and labor. In this sense, no country is entirely a traditional society, but there are regions and isolated areas within the developing countries where such traditional societies continue to exist.

In traditional societies, there is a stable technology and social order. A person's station in life and his occupation are inherited instead of chosen. The whole structure is one of mutual commitments and obligations. In such a society, the upper classes do not necessarily have despotic power over the lower classes. The relationship may be a beneficial and mutually supporting agreement between lord (or chief) and peasant. Rights and duties become institutionalized, honored, and respected. Tenure rules provide access to a piece of land and often include an obligation to pass on some of the produce or to work for a social superior. Upper classes must seek accommodations with those in lower status because they are so greately outnumbered and because they need help defending themselves against outsiders. The lower classes depend on the upper classes for rights, assistance, contact with the outside world, and maintaining order and resolving conflict. Thus the valuable rights of the upper classes in a traditional society stem from superior status in the social organization rather than from ownership of land per se (5).

This stable order contrasts with the changing technology and more fluid social order in a modernizing (developing) society. Attitudes toward land and labor change. Land itself becomes valuable and exclusive ownership must be secured. The idea gradually emerges that the owner can cultivate the land with tenants or hired workers and establish a social order on his land based on his own choice of terms of labor and tenure agreements. And, of course, since the upper classes are in a better position to take advantage of the new technology, their power is enhanced and mutual dependency relationships are altered.

The upper classes try to gain full control over land and to free themselves of their obligations to the peasants. They recognize the benefits that can be realized only as the power of the state is used to protect private property and to enforce contracts. Wherever the upper rural classes become actively engaged in management, they will seek to shed social obligations, to gain a free hand in controlling land use, and to obtain the services of a "law-and-order" state in protecting their property.

On the other hand, where modernization takes the form of an emerging peasantry, the peasants seek to eliminate the land rights of both the upper classes and the peasant community. Attempts to remove upper-class rights stem from peasant desires for security, from loss of traditional functions of the upper classes, or from shifts in political power to the peasantry. The freedom from community controls finds its rationale in the possibility of individual adoption of technology, the prospect of obtaining credit on the security of their landownership, and the need to free individual innovators from group claims to their gains (5).

Land tenure and ownership arrangements are not confined to economic matters but are inextricably tied to social custom and political interests. Thus, changes in these tenure relations can become major political issues.

MAJOR EXISTING FORMS OF LAND TENURE AND OWNERSHIP. There are many forms of land tenure and operating arrangements, and only key forms can be presented here. Even among these key forms, there is little uniformity. For example, an institution is not defined merely by a name, but by the functions, procedures, rights, duties, and privileges associated with it. Thus, a farm corporation in Iran is in no way comparable to a farm corporation in California. A tenant farmer in the corn-soybean areas of central Illinois has much more in common with an owner-operator in that area than he does with a tenant farmer producing corn in central Luzon in the Philippines. Tenants, sharecroppers, owner-operators, partnerships, corporations, production cooperatives or collectives, etc. in various parts of the world (or even within the same country) are not automatically comparable just because they are called by the same name.

In the following discussion, small and large operating units are distinguished. Throughout much of the world, with major exceptions in most Latin American countries and the collectivized systems in the communist countries, even though land may be held or owned in larger units, farming itself is done by families on small units of land. With the increasing pressures of a growing population, these units are generally getting smaller. Thus, small farm operating units actually represent some what of a continuum from more-or-less subsistence types of farming (with very little produce being sold) to market-oriented farming (with growing proportions of produce being sold). Except for some isolated groups in several areas of the tropics, there is very little strictly subsistence farming. Most farmers (or peasants) do market some produce. Large operating units are, of course, to a much greater degree commercially oriented.

SMALL OPERATING UNITS. A common form of tenure among farmers with small operating units is some form of tenancy. A small operating unit is usually 2 hectares (5 acres) or less, which actually accounts for 70 to 80 percent of all farms in such countries as Indonesia and Bangladesh. But there are many variations in tenancy arrangements. In all instances, however, the operator of the land does not own the land but pays some form of rent for it. The land owner (or landlord) may own no more than the small tract he rents out to a single family. Usually, however, a landlord owns a considerable amount of land that may be rented out (or leased) to a score or more of tenants.

Within this general category, sharecropping (or share tenancy) is the most common, in contrast to a cash rent, which usually, though not always, is a fixed amount of money for the season. In many areas of the world, if water is available for irrigation, climatic conditions permit two or even more crops to be planted and harvested within one year. Thus, rent may not be paid for an agricultural year, but for the specific growing period of one crop within the year.

The share of the crop given in rent varies widely. It may run from one-third to as high as one-half or even three-fourths of the harvest. Much depends on the relative bargaining power of the landlord vs. the tenants. Again, increasing population means increasing competition among landless people for a piece of cultivable land, with corresponding increases in rents. Rents are often determined by the contributions actually made to the production by the landlord and the tenant. If a landlord provides nothing but the land, the rental share would likely be lower than if he provides credit, inputs, power sources, managerial decisions, and marketing services.

Written lease contracts are not common; most agreements are oral. And while some tenants or sharecroppers may operate the same land for years, there is generally a great deal of shifting about of tenants. These conditions are not conducive to long-term investments, and share arrangements may also discourage optimum use of annual inputs.

Besides these tenancy arrangements, there are, of course, many small farms operated by their owners—i.e., owner-operated family farms. Many of these are also 2 hectares or less, but generalizations are difficult. There is a continuum of farm sizes from the very small (fraction of a hectare) to units of 10 to 15 hectares. The larger sizes are considered large operating units in most irrigated areas but are considered small in some less productive areas of dry land farming. Ownership does not always have the same meaning that we generally associate with it. A farmer may claim ownership to a piece of land, and it may indeed have been passed down through generations, yet he may not always possess a legally registered title. This situation can lead to many uncertainties and conflicts. Also, some people settle on what they consider public or unclaimed land, only to be evicted later when someone comes forward with a title or similar document. Having the right political connections may be decisive in having such claims upheld. And, of course, it is ordinarily the more aggressive and economically strong that can avail themselves of such contacts.

Another major form of small farm operating unit is that described earlier for Africa. In this system, use rights are individualized, ownership is not. In many of these areas, slash and burn agriculture (or shifting cultivation) is common, and the major source of power is human rather than animal.

A special problem that plagues many systems of small operating units is multiple plots and scattered fragments of land. That is to say, a 2-hectare farm may not be in one block but scattered in 4 to 6 or more smaller plots, each one separated from the other—sometimes by several miles. In some areas of Africa, the slash and burn system, along with the influences of division through inheritance, the practice of having more than one wife, and deliberate attempts to have land of different types and qualities as insurance against drought or flood, has led to much splintering and fragmentation of land holdings and operating units. In practice it has been nearly impossible to consolidate such fragmented holdings since so many different individual interests and sentiments are involved.

A variety of mixed forms of these small operating units exist, too numerous and complex to give details. People used to U.S. agriculture may consider all these practices highly inefficient. And in terms of labor time involved they are inefficient. But labor is usually overabundant, and thus its efficient use is not the most critical question. The intensity of use of limited land and critically short capital is of much greater importance and significance. And small operating units frequently use land and limited capital more efficiently than overly large ones. A highly labor-intensive agriculture has proven very productive per hectare of land.

LARGE OPERATING UNITS. The exact size of large operating units in terms of hectares is rather difficult to specify. Indeed, size has little meaning since soil quality and the amount and distribution of rainfall or availability of water for irrigation are critical factors in determining effective farm size. Furthermore, the discussion throughout refers to settled agriculture where farmers mainly grow crops. In areas of cattle raising, cattle are frequently grazed over vast areas of range land. Some of it may be held privately, but much of it is public land and ranchers may pay fees for grazing rights. In some more arid regions, nomadic tribes roam over large areas with their animal herds and flocks—a pattern of life especially prevalent in parts of the Near and Middle East and northern Africa.

As with the small operating units, there are also various rental arrangements in large operating units. However, these are usually more commercialized and more sophisticated in a business-contract sense than are those found among small operating units. In some areas of India and Pakistan, where the new high-yielding varieties of wheat have been widely adopted, some more aggressive and well-to-do farmers have purchased and rented additional land to enlarge their units. It may require from 10 to 20 hectares to economically operate a tube well for irrigation purposes. Such farmers are also purchasing more tractors and equipment and thus becoming less dependent on hired labor. While this may make good economic sense for those individuals, it frequently decreases total employment—a serious shortcoming in societies with excess labor and growing populations.

The one region with a concentration of large ownership units is Latin America. Here about 3 to 4 percent of the landowners own 60 to 80 percent of the agricultural land. This system of *latifundia* described earlier is common to most countries in the region. Some of these farms are operated quite intensively and efficiently, but many are not. These large farms are also in various stages of transition. Some remain highly traditional in their methods with low productivity. Some are being divided into several somewhat smaller (though still large) operating units. Others may be highly mechanized and modernized with high productivity. And still others have been broken up into small units or transformed into production cooperatives through land reform programs. Even so, Latin America continues to have mostly large farm operating units—some containing hundreds and even thousands of hectares of cultivable land.

Another form of large operating unit is the plantation. Ordinarily, a plantation is devoted to producing only one or two major crops. It resembles more a factory or industry structure than an agricultural enterprise, and, indeed, plantations are usually owned by a company or corporation. Common plantation crops are: sugar cane, pineapple, bananas, jute, coffee, tea, cocoa, coconut, oil palm, and rubber. Since most of these products require processing, the processing facility is frequently a central part of the plantation. Much of the produce from these plantations is exported. Thus, many of these operations may manage the produce or processed products from the production through the wholesaling stages. Plantations operate largely with a hired labor force and are generally capital-intensive agro-industrial enterprises. Since a large proportion of these crops is normally exported, there has long been interest and influence by foreign companies and governments in the operation of such plantations. Consequently, several research centers devoted to improving plantation crops were established many decades ago while few such centers were established (until relatively recently) for the food crops that are the mainstay of local diets—wheat, corn, rice, food legumes, root crops, and vegetables (7).

Another form of large-scale farm operation is the cooperative farm or collective, and again there is great diversity among such forms. The countries with the most experience in collective farming are the Soviet Union, the People's Republic of China, a number of the countries of Eastern Europe, and Israel. However, in many of the developing countries, there is a growing interest in some form of group or cooperative farming. Sometimes this is advocated on the basis of ideological-political concerns. But in most instances governments are seeking ways and means of reorganizing their agriculture to deal with such pressing problems of development as increased productive employment, a more equal distribution of income, expanded output, including the landless among the beneficiaries of a land reform, and introducing new technologies while avoiding the inequities that frequently accompany such introduction.

There is within this general class of large-scale collectively organized farms a type known as the commune. This type is relatively rare and is frequently associated with religious groups. The kibbutzim of Israel and the Hutterite colonies of North America are two prominent examples. Some of the significant institutional features of true communal organizations are:

1. Communal socialization of children allows individual nuclear families to participate only minimally in this process.
2. Nuclear family units exist, but their activities and interests are subordinated to the collective needs and objectives.
3. All important property (especially land and capital) is communally owned, and personal property is kept to a minimum.
4. The surplus created by agricultural and other productive activities is retained by the collective as capital, with minimal redistribution.
5. Remuneration of labor and services is withheld. Compensation is indirect—i.e., motivational. Necessities and some small luxuries are equally distributed.
6. Consumption is formally restrained and governed by explicit rules (1).

Besides such highly self-disciplined communal forms, there are the state planned and collectivized systems of the communist countries. Land may be owned by the state or by the collective, and individuals usually receive remuneration according to number of days worked or tasks performed, with perhaps a share of the net proceeds at the end of the accounting period or agricultural year. Individual families ordinarily have a private plot of land, own their own house, and have authority and responsibility over their own children. Farm production decisions are made largely by the managers frequently placed on the farm by state authority. But even here, there are many variations among countries and even within countries. Some collectives have more autonomy than others, some have a more democratic organization, etc.

There are also voluntary cooperative farms where people have agreed to join together to manage and operate their lands cooperatively. While not state planned, these usually have considerable support from government agencies. Finally, another form of large-scale operating unit is the state farm. Some state-run farms are found in all countries, but the largest concentration of state farms is in the Soviet Union and Eastern Europe. Such farms are managed by state employees (they may be part of the bureaucracy of the Ministry of Agriculture), and the workers are paid wages just as is hired labor in most large enterprises, public or private. State farms may have a special role in upgrading livestock breeds and providing improved seeds and farming practices for private and (or) collective farms in their area. In some countries these farms represent 10 to 20 percent of all cultivable land and, therefore, are significant factors in the overall production of agricultural commodities.

AN EVALUATION OF MAJOR LAND TENURE AND OWNERSHIP FORMS. What are the relationships between these various forms of land tenure and ownership and some of the basic objectives of development? These are, of course, extremely complicated issues, but a number of generalizations on the various impacts of land tenure arrangements on productivity can be made. The following four points are summarized from reference 4.

INSECURITY OF EXPECTATIONS. Without a clear title to the land, a farmer may be reluctant to invest and to engage in long-term planning since he has no assurance that the land will be his long enough to reap the rewards of such investments. Likewise, without a written lease (or with a very short-term lease) a farmer is unsure how long he will have the land and what the future rent will be, again tending to restrict investments that have a recovery rate of more than one season. Even if there is a written lease for, say, 3 years, investments with a recovery rate of more than 3 years will be discouraged unless there is a compensation provision for the unrecovered portion of such investments.

REWARDS NOT COMMENSURATE WITH EFFORT. If share tenants supply all the inputs but must deliver a share of the produce to the landlord, they have little incentive to use the optimum amount of such inputs since they receive only a share of the added output. This is in contrast to an owner-operator (or a fixed rental payment) situation under which the operator pays the full cost of the inputs but also receives the total benefit of such inputs. Research has shown that production inefficiencies result when variable costs are not shared in roughly the same proportion as the output is shared. In the various forms of cooperative or collective farming arrangements, undifferentiated salaries reduce incentives for labor. If extra effort and skill are not rewarded, they will not likely be forthcoming. Incentives and the complexities of management are two of the major difficulties encountered in group-collective farming organizations. In some systems of tribal organization, although farming may be individualized, a person is nevertheless expected to share produce with his extended family and even beyond this family group. Such a system ordinarily is not conducive to individual effort and initiative. On some very large estates, with subsistence or very low wages, workers will not put forth the extra effort if there is no prospect of their sharing in the extra output.

LACK OF RESOURCE AVAILABILITIES. Land is, of course, the key resource that may be unavailable to people who would have the labor and the incentive to be highly productive. But even people who have access to some land may be hampered by lack of other, complementary resources or services. For example, credit may be restricted because of inadequately developed facilities, lack of loanable funds, nonexistent or faulty land titles, and lack of managerial ability. Limited managerial ability may also be a direct result of tenure arrangements that make acquiring such skills difficult (e.g., a farm worker on a large estate who has never had an opportunity to use his judgment in managerial matters may be denied credit because of his lack of managerial abilities). Land, service, and produce markets are all functionally related to the existing system of land tenure. For example, in a system dominated by large holdings inherited from one generation to the next, there is a poorly developed market for land (both rental and sale). In this same system, because of the greater self-sufficiency of these large estates, service markets are poorly developed, which in turn makes operations for small farmers much more difficult. Likewise, produce markets are geared to the production from the large farms, restricting the commercial enterprise choices of the small farmers. Finally, where agriculture depends on irrigation, the method of distributing water rights and the rationality of such distribution relative to the land resources can be a key factor in determining the level of agricultural output.

THE LARGE ESTATE SYSTEM. It is difficult to explain the reasons for extensive land use by many owners of large estates in such a system. Land ownership under this system seems to provide certain rewards independent of the level of output. The major economic interests of the estate owners may be located elsewhere (e.g., in industrial developments). The land resources are sufficient to provide a comfortable income even if used extensively, and it is evidently simpler to manage a large farm at a more extensive level of production. When such farms do modernize and intensify their land use, there is a great tendency to mechanize and to displace a large part of the labor force.

But of course land tenure arrangements have direct effects not only on production but especially on employment level and the consequent income distribution among the farm population. Large-scale, modernized farm enterprises may be highly productive, but they often remain as islands within a sea of small subsistence farmers. The masses of small farms remain unaffected since the technology is inappropriate for their operations.

A system of widespread ownership of reasonably uniformly sized family farms provides great incentives for investment and the application of labor. Such a system, if properly serviced with research, credit, extension, markets for inputs and outputs, etc., can be highly productive. It is also likely to maximize employment opportunities on the land, and provide for a reasonably egalitarian distribution of income. But few developing countries have such a system. And even if such a system were created through a distributive land reform, it takes many, many years to build the roads, the service centers, the research and extension facilities, and educate the personnel. Another problem, especially where population pressures are great and farms are extremely small, is that small farms have less flexibility in land use and management. They must use land intensively irrespective of soil quality, slope of the land, etc. This can lead to serious problems of deforestation and erosion.

It is because numerous small farms spread over the countryside are so difficult to service that many nations have essentially ignored their small farmers and concentrated development efforts on the large farms. For the same reason many developing countries are experimenting with various forms of group or cooperative farming hoping to introduce more equality into the system and still be better able to service these large units and increase overall productivity. But as noted earlier, cooperative farming poses many management problems, and labor incentives are difficult to maintain under such a system.

To generalize even further, one might conclude that there are two broad classes of institutional structures in the agricultural sectors of the developing countries (with many variations in specifics, to be sure). Many countries today seem faced with one or the other or both of these situations.

The first situation is where existing institutions do not support growth and productivity. For reasons that may be rooted in politics or traditional culture and reflected in the way economic activity is organized and how land is used and distributed, it is difficult to provide the access, the security, and the incentives needed for increased investments in the agricultural sector and for the introduction of new production techniques.

The second situation is where existing institutions support growth and productivity in only part of the agricultural sector, making a relatively small group wealthy and leaving the mass of people behind in abject poverty.

SUMMARY. All is not negative, however. Agricultural output in the developing countries (in the aggregate) grew at about the same rate over the past several decades as in the developed countries. Most of this increase in the developing countries came from bringing new land under cultivation, while in the developed countries practically all the growth came from increased yields. Despite equivalent growth rates of agricultural output, however, population in the developing countries has been increasing at an annual rate of 2 to 3 percent, outstripping recent agricultural increases. Consequently, the developing countries (again there are some exceptions) have become increasingly dependent on imports of grains from a relatively few developed countries, especially the United States. Thus, output performance must be improved, and land tenure arrangements must be altered whenever such alteration offers promise of improving output performance. At the same time employment and income distribution objectives must be given greater weight in the overall development strategies.

These multiple and at times conflicting purposes make the tasks difficult, and no one form of land tenure is best suited to all needs or all circumstances. Development must be a prolonged national effort and multifaceted to work simultaneously on many issues.

Many countries do offer opportunities for increasing output from the existing small farmer sector. International assistance agencies have in recent years begun to direct more of their assistance to small farmers. Tenure security can be offered to more farmers through surveys, land titling, and registration of titles. Although difficult to enforce where many landless people are competing for land, rental arrangements can be made more secure, and the level of rents controlled. In several countries, legislation imposing a ceiling on the amount of land a family can own has been enacted. And in some instances this legislation is also being enforced, making it possible to settle more people on the land and/or to provide more secure rights to tenants currently on the land. There are, however, some instances where only the most drastic reforms can restructure the system and get it onto a more productive and more equitable track. But such reforms involve major power struggles and are not easily achieved. Furthermore, caution must be exercised since frequently in the past too little time and attention was devoted to constructing the new system. It may be relatively simple to tear down an exising land tenure system, but it is exceedingly difficult to construct a viable functioning system to take its place.

## REFERENCES

1. Bennett, John W. The Hutterian Colony: A Traditional Voluntary Agrarian Commune of Large Economic Scale. Proc., Group Farming Conference, June 10–12, 1975. Madison: University of Wisconsin, in press.
2. Carstensen, Vernon. The Land of Plenty. American Issues. The American Association for State and Local History, July 1975.
3. Christodoulou, D. Basic Agrarian Structural Issues in the Adjustment of African Customary Tenures to the Needs of Agricultural Development. Rome: Food and Agricultural Organization of the United Nations, RU: WLR/66/C.
4. Dorner, Peter. Land Tenure, Income Distribution, and Productivity Interactions. Land Economics 40:247–254, 1964.
5. Kanel, D. Land Tenure Reform as a Policy Issue in Modernization of Traditional Societies. In Land Reform in Latin America: Issues and Cases, edited by Peter Dorner. Land Economics Monograph No. 3. Madison: University of Wisconsin Press, 1971.

6. Parsons, K. H. Customary Land Tenure and the Development of African Agriculture. Rome: Food and Agricultural Organization of the United Nations Report No. R.P. 14, 1971. (Reprinted as Land Tenure Center Paper No. 77, Madison: University of Wisconsin.)
7. Wortman, Sterling. The World Food Situation: A New Initiative. New York: The Rockefeller Foundation, 1975.

## BIBLIOGRAPHY

Baraclough, Solon, and Domike, Arthur. Agrarian Structure in Seven Latin American Countries. Land Economics 42:391–424, 1966.

Dorner, Peter. Land Reform and Economic Development. Baltimore: Penguin Modern Economics Texts, 1972.

———. Land Tenure Institutions. In Institutions in Agricultural Development, edited by M. G. Blase. Ames: Iowa State Univ. Press, 1971.

Dorner, Peter, and Kanel, Don. The Economic Case for Land Reform. In Land Reform in Latin America: Issues and Cases, edited by Peter Dorner. Land Economics Monograph No. 3. Madison: University of Wisconsin Press, 1971.

Raup, P. M. Land Reform and Agricultural Development. In Agricultural Development and Economic Growth, edited by H. M. Southworth and B. F. Johnston. Ithaca, N.Y.: Cornell University Press, 1967.

Weitz, Raanan, ed. Rural Development in a Changing World. Cambridge, Mass.: The M.I.T. Press, 1971.

# 6

# Climate and Weather for Food Production

R. H. SHAW

If the ever-increasing number of people in the world are to be fed, food production must increase at least as fast as the population increases. And weather and climate will play an important role in determining how much food the world can produce.

The day-to-day fluctuations in temperature, rainfall, and associated conditions that make up the weather are often the final determiner of crop yields. A farmer or gardener may have excellent soil and follow the best management practices only to have unfavorable weather (drought, hail, excessive rain, frost, etc.) destroy the crop.

Climate is a term used to describe the average weather conditions over several years. Deserts, for example, have dry climates, and Alsaka and northern Canada have cold climates. Climates, therefore, determine generally what crops can be grown in a region. But climates are not constant; they fluctuate around their mean value. The drought conditions of the 1970s in the Sahel region in Africa and in parts of India caused some climatologists (those who study climate) to propose that the world's climate was changing; there is, however, no certainty one way or the other.

Examining climates and where they are found throughout the world is useful to explain why certain crops are grown in certain areas. It also helps to explain many of the problems agriculture faces in each climate area. To compare world climates, however, some kind of classification system is needed. A system allows us to see why Argentina, Rumania, South Africa, and the Corn Belt of the U.S. produce corn while Australia, India, the U.S.S.R., southern Canada, and the Central Plains of the U.S. grow wheat. It will help to show why India and the Sahel frequently have droughts and why cold and dry weather are often problems in the U.S.S.R.

The comparison shows that most of the developed countries are

ROBERT H. SHAW is Professor, Agricultural Climatology, Iowa State University. He has also been teacher, researcher, and consultant on plant-climate-weather interrelationships in several foreign countries.

found in climates that favor agricultural production, while many of the developing countries, with their rapidly expanding population, are found in more severe (wet, dry, hot) climates that are generally less favorable to agriculture.

Before presenting the climate classification system, however, it is necessary to examine the factors that control climate. During this presentation the term latitude, which is simply a method used to divide the distance from the equator (0° latitude) to the poles (90° north or south latitude), will be frequently used. The higher latitudes are closer to the poles and the lower latitudes are closer to the equator, and each degree of latitude represents approximately 70 miles (112.7 kilometers).

CLIMATE CONTROLS. There are nine principal factors that determine the weather and the different climates: the sun, land and water surfaces, altitude, mountain barriers, wind and pressure patterns, ocean currents, storms, human beings, air masses and fronts.

These nine factors seldom act alone, and several usually act together in determining weather and climate. Each of these will be discussed, some only very briefly.

SUN. The sun is the major controller of the world's climate. Some areas of the world receive large amounts of solar energy throughout the year, resulting in the "always warm" climates near the equator. At the other extreme are the polar regions that receive no solar energy in the winter and only low amounts in the summer. These areas never get very warm. In between these extremes are the middle latitudes that have cold winters and warm or hot summers. These areas receive low amounts of solar energy in the winter, but high amounts in the summer.

The two factors that affect the amount of solar energy received are intensity and day length. The sun's intensity varies with position in the sky (Fig. 6.1). When the sun is overhead, it is intense; that is, more solar energy is received per unit of land. When the sun is low in the sky,

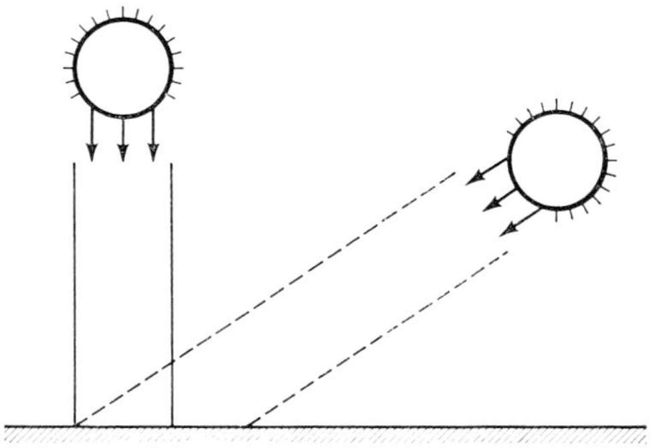

FIG. 6.1. Effect of sun's position on intensity of solar energy received

however, its energy is spread over a larger area, giving less energy per unit of earth surface area. The high sun position corresponds to midday in our summer season when much energy is being received and temperatures are high. The low position would represent the U.S. winter season when the low amount of energy received results in our cold winter temperatures.

Day length also varies with latitude. At the equator (0° latitude), the day is always about 12 hours long. At the poles day length varies from 24 hours in midsummer to 0 hours in midwinter. In the middle latitudes, day length varies from 8 to 9 hours in midwinter to 15 to 16 hours in midsummer.

The total energy received is the result of both intensity and day length. These combine to give the most energy in midsummer near 40° latitude (the southern boundary of Nebraska) and the least in midwinter at the winter pole. In the spring and fall the most energy is received at low latitudes. Remember that in the winter season in the northern hemisphere, the southern hemisphere is having its summer season and vice versa.

Cloud cover decreases the amount of energy a particular area receives. Without cloud cover, all locations on the same latitude of the earth would receive the same amount of solar energy.

LAND AND WATER. Land surfaces tend to warm and cool faster than water surfaces. This causes the climates in the middle of large land areas (continental climates) to have large temperature fluctuations, both daily and annually, compared with islands and areas close to water at the same latitude (oceanic climates). Therefore, crops that grow in continental climates are subjected to greater temperature changes than those grown in oceanic climates. Oceanic climates are often cloudier also.

ALTITUDE. Where mountains are present, temperatures decrease with increasing altitude at the rate of 3.3° F/1000 ft. (2° C/300 m.). The growing season also shortens with increasing elevation. The cooler temperatures can actually benefit agriculture at high altitudes near the equator, but altitude is generally detrimental in the middle and high latitudes, such as in the Rocky Mountains of the United States.

MOUNTAIN BARRIERS. Mountains can act as barriers to the wind flow. For example, in the western United States, the air coming in from the Pacific Ocean loses much of its moisture as it comes over the Rocky Mountains. Therefore, rainfall may be high on the ocean side of the mountains but low on the downwind side causing the dry Great Plains area of the United States and Canada. This dry region is primarily a wheat and grazing area. Further east, where there are no mountains to block the flow from the south, the air flow from the Gulf of Mexico brings moisture north resulting in the increased rainfall of the Corn Belt.

In Europe, the east-west oriented Alps do not have the same effect; air flowing from west to east is not blocked and air masses from the North Atlantic move far inland in Europe creating a large area of oceanic climate. In Australia, mountains again act as barriers reducing the penetration of moist air into eastern Australia and helping make much of the interior very dry. This area is also used largely for grazing, primarily for raising sheep. Other areas of the world also have significant mountain effects.

AIR MASSES. Significant differences exist in air masses over the world. Those that originate in high latitudes are cold; those that originate in low latitudes are warm. Those that originate over oceans may bring significant precipitation to land areas, while those that originate over land tend to be dry.

WIND AND PRESSURE PATTERNS. An idealized pattern of the wind and pressure belts is shown in Figure 6.2. The real pattern is not as uniform as shown, but the figure is useful in showing some important features of world climate. A low pressure area is found around the equator. Low pressure areas are characterized by cloudy, rainy conditions. This region is very wet and much of it is rainy throughout the year. Agriculture conducted in this area has to contend with almost continuous high temperatures and rainy conditions.

The latitudes from 25° to 35° (in both northern and southern hemispheres) are centers of high pressure circulations (called subtropical highs). These areas are characterized by very hot, very dry weather and only irrigated agriculture is possible there. Many of the major deserts in the world are at these latitudes.

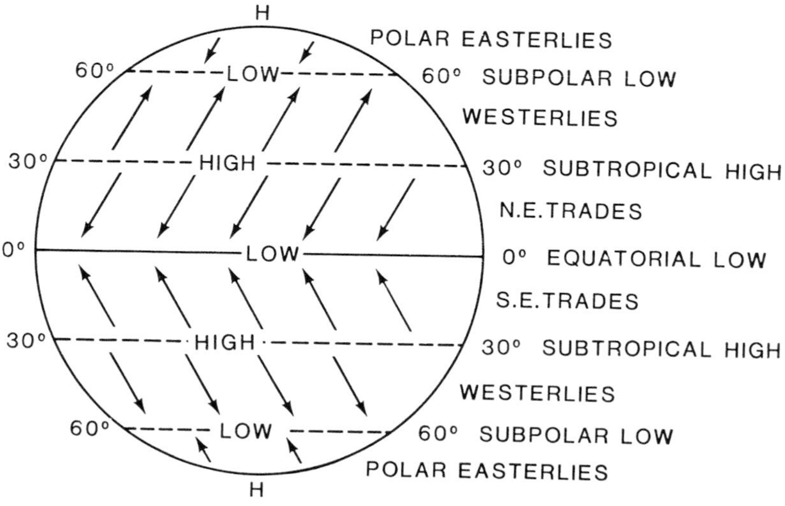


FIG. 6.2. Idealized pattern of wind and pressure belts

Between the equatorial low and the subtropical highs are the trade-wind belts, where surface winds have a general east-to-west direction. This tends to make east coasts wetter at these low latitudes.

Another low pressure area is found about 60° latitude, and is called the subpolar low. Here the warmer air from the south and colder air from the north collide creating a stormy area. This subpolar low moves across the United States, particularly in the winter and results in our periods of cold weather (cold Canadian air). In the mid-latitudes (35°) winds tend to be from west to east, often making the west coasts wetter. Much of the mid-latitude grain producing area of the world has variable weather because of this interchange of the warm and cold air.

OCEAN CURRENTS. Ocean currents have a particularly important effect on coastal areas, but may affect the climate many miles inland if winds are onshore and no mountain barriers are present. Europe is the best example of this. When there is a warm current offshore, the climate of nearby land areas is warmer; if the current is cold, the climate will be colder. Winds that blow over warm water will carry more moisture and give the nearby land areas more rain. On the other hand, cold ocean current reduces rainfall. Cold ocean currents occur on several west coasts at about 25° to 35° latitude, and coastal deserts can exist under these conditions.

STORMS. Storms are an important feature of the climate of some areas because of the heavy rains they create and the damage done to crops and buildings.

Some tropical areas are subject to hurricanes. (These are also called typhoons and cyclones.) These result in very heavy rain and strong winds. In the central United States tornadoes often occur. In warm climates (or warm times of the year) thunderstorms provide much of the rainfall required for agriculture.

HUMAN BEINGS. People's actions are becoming important as a climate control because of the pollution they create. We often think of pollution as being a product primarily of developed nations—smoke, $CO_2$ from burning fuel, etc. But the so-called slash and burn agriculture of developing tropical nations also contributes significantly to atmospheric pollution. Overgrazing in dry areas is causing more dust to get into the atmosphere. Climatologists do not agree as to what the overall effect is, but it may be that people are helping change the climate.

CLASSIFICATION OF CLIMATES. Now that we have examined the factors that control climate, let's look at the climates these controls create. Similar world climates have been grouped together into a few main types to form a climate classification system. The particular system we will use was developed by Professor Glenn Trewartha and is the subject of an entire book. This presentation, however, will necessarily be very brief.

The system identifies six major types. To help identify each climate and where it is located, a colored climate map is shown (see Contents page). All climates in which the evaporation demand (water lost from the ground and plants to the atmosphere) is greater than the precipitation are classified as dry climates. These (labeled B on the map) will be discussed last. All other climates are divided on the basis of temperature, ranging from those that are always warm to those that are always cold. Within each temperature group, subdivisions are made on the basis of the amount and distribution of rainfall during the year. In some, a further subdivision is made using the seasonal distribution of temperature. This may seem complicated at first, but a general picture of the world's climates is soon evident. As you compare the text and the map, you will begin to see the general pattern of world climates.

Tropical Climates (A). These are frost-free climates where plants grow throughout the entire year. There are two types, those that are wet most of the time called tropical wet (Ar on the map), and those that have a very wet season followed by a very dry season called tropical wet-dry (Aw on the map).

Tropical wet climates occur from the equator up to 5° to 10° latitude, except along coastal areas that have moist onshore winds. Here they may extend to near 25° latitude. Although plants grow the entire year, agriculture is hampered by the almost continuous wet conditions. Major areas of this climate are the Amazon Basin, Zaire (formerly Congo Basin), the East Indies, and some of southeast Asia.

To the north and south of the tropical wet climates are areas of tropical wet-dry climates. These climates are dominated by the equatorial low pressure (wet) area during part of the year and by the subtropical high pressure (dry) area the rest of the year. This gives them a tropical wet climate part of the year and an almost desertlike climate the rest of the year. These climates occur from near 0° latitude to about 23½° north latitude (Tropic of Cancer) and 23½° south latitude (Tropic of Capricorn), a band more than 3,000 miles wide. The developing nations of Africa, South America, and the Indian Subcontinent have significant areas of this type climate. Here agriculture must contend with a warm, very wet summer season, followed by a very dry season. Highest temperatures occur in the spring, just before the rain season starts.

Subtropical Climates (C). These climates occur at latitudes just outside the tropics. The frost-free growing season is generally longer than 200 days. The warmest areas with this climate are almost totally frost free. This climate is found from about 25° to almost 40° latitude. Two types are found. The subtropical humid climate (Cf) has no real dry season and is represented by the Cotton Belt climate of southeastern

United States. Frosts, however, do limit crop growth during the cold season. Other major areas of this climate are found in China and southeastern South America. Smaller areas are present in South Africa and eastern Australia. The subtropical, dry-summer climate (Cs), called the Mediterranean climate, is known for vegetable and fruit production and a resort-type climate. It has a very dry, hot summer and only occasional winter frosts. Besides the Mediterranean area, this climate is found in small coastal areas in California, Chile, South Africa, and Australia. The subtropical climates are important food-producing regions of the world.

TEMPERATE CLIMATES (D). These climates have from 100 to nearly 200 days in the frost-free season and are located between 35° and 60° latitude. Two types of temperate climates are found: the oceanic type (Do), which has relatively cool summers and warm winters for the latitude, and the continental type (Dc), which has relatively warm summers and cold winters.

The major area with an oceanic climate is western Europe. Other small areas with this climate are along the west coast of the United States and southern Canada, the west coast of southern Chile, and New Zealand. Summers tend to be cool for long-season grain production, and rainfall is generally adequate in all seasons.

The temperate continental climate is subdivided into two types, those with a warm summer (Dca on the map) and those with a cool summer (Dcb on the map). The warm-summer type is the Corn Belt climate, where long-season grain crops, such as corn and soybeans, are widely produced. This climate extends across the continent from the eastern margin of the Great Plains to the Atlantic Ocean. The cool summer type is found in the northern United States and mostly short-season crops, such as wheat, barley, and rye, are grown. In the warmest areas of this climate, shorter-season varieties of corn and soybeans can be grown. Besides the northern United States, significant areas of this climate are found from eastern Europe into the U.S.S.R. and in eastern U.S.S.R. and China. No temperate continental climates are found in the southern hemisphere.

BOREAL (SUBARCTIC) CLIMATES (E). These climates have a frost-free season of less than 90 days and occur between 50° and 70° north latitude in Canada, Europe, and the U.S.S.R. Grain production is limited by the short growing season, but hay, pasture, forage crops, and some small fruits and vegetables are grown. There are essentially no Boreal land climates in the southern latitudes.

POLAR CLIMATES (F). These climates are present in the polar regions. The areas are too cold to have any significant agricultural production.

HIGHLAND CLIMATES (H). Mountain or highland climates are so variable that they are difficult to classify. If not too cold, some agriculture is possible. In the tropics, special crops (e.g., coffee) and grain are grown, while in the mid-latitudes, these areas are limited to animal production.

DRY CLIMATES (B). Dry climates are those in which the evaporation demand exceeds the average precipitation. They may have periods when moisture is adequate, but drought is a frequent problem for grain crop production, so livestock production is more common. The driest regions have no agricultural production.

The dry climates are subdivided into two groups, a semiarid or steppe type (BS) and an arid or desert type (BW). Certain types of agriculture can be conducted in the steppe climates even though the water supply is limiting, but the desert regions are too dry for any significant agriculture unless irrigation is used. These two dry climates are further divided into hot temperature regions (BSh on the climate map), which occur between 10° and 35° latitude, and cool temperature regions (BSk on the climate map), which occur at latitudes greater than 35°. The cool temperature steppe regions are the major wheat producing areas of the world and occur in the Great Plains area of the United States north into southern Canada and in the southern U.S.S.R. into western China. Extensive areas of the hot temperature type occur in the developing nations. Significant areas occur in northern Mexico, Argentina, north and south Africa, Australia, and southwest Asia.

SIGNIFICANCE OF THE DIFFERENT CLIMATES IN WORLD FOOD PRODUCTION. Previously a brief mention was made of the significance of the different climates on world food production. Now those areas particularly significant to the world food problem will be considered in more detail.

A very important feature for agriculture is the water balance, which indicates whether there might be too much or too little water for food production. The water balance for nine different climate types is shown in Figure 6.3. (Check the climate map for other areas of the same climate type.) For each location, the shaded area represents the time period when evaporation exceeds precipitation (rain and snow). The larger this area, the drier the climate is. Very wet areas are those where precipitation greatly exceeds evaporation.

One factor important in the water balance is not represented in these figures—the amount of water that can be stored in the soil for use by crops during periods of deficient rainfall. A good, deep soil will hold a lot of water. For example, a typical Iowa soil will store 2 inches of plant-available water in each foot of the soil profile, while a sandy or rocky soil may store only a fraction of an inch per foot. This stored water

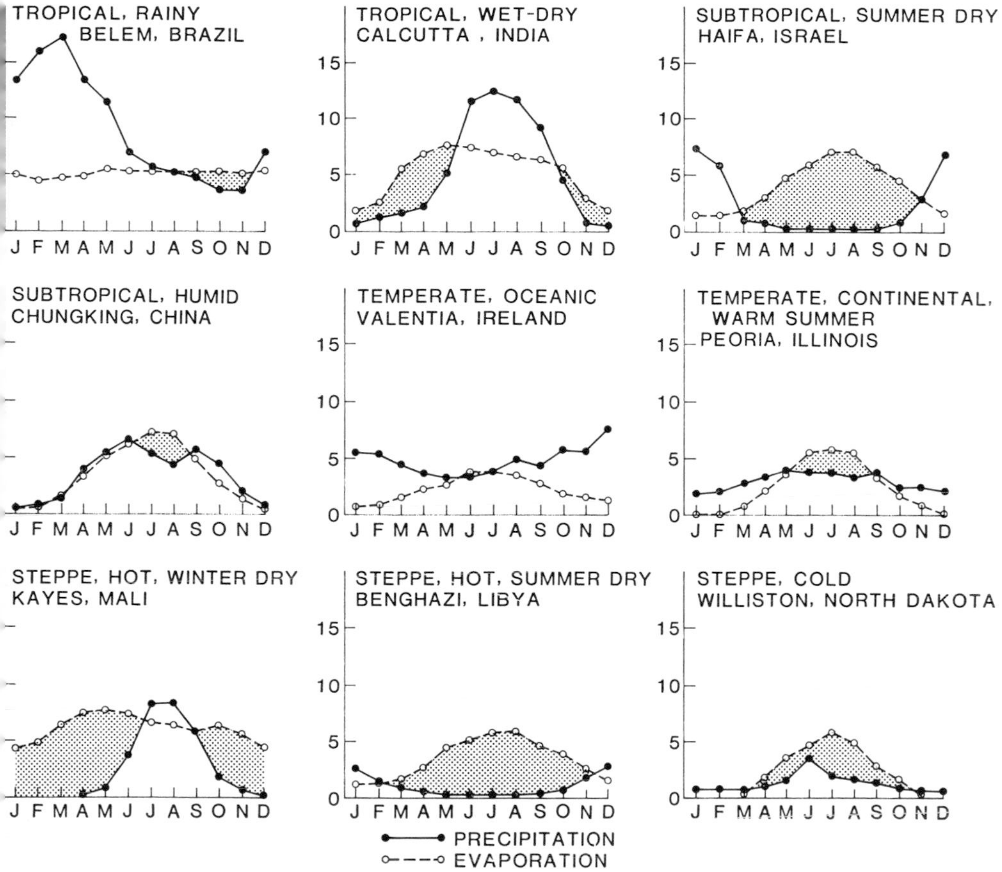


FIG. 6.3. Water balances for nine different climates

can be very important in grain production where a continuous supply of moisture is needed during the crop season.

As the water balances for various climates are examined, it will become obvious that the developed countries have larger areas with better climates for grain production than do the developing countries. The chapter on soils indicates that developed countries also have better soils. The better soils and climates, combined with superior management, result in high yields per acre and account for a large percentage of the world's surplus grain production.

One of the most significant climates for grain production is the temperate continental climate. Areas of this climate with a warm summer are major producers of crops like corn and soybeans. Extensive wheat, barley, and rye are produced in those with a cool summer. The water balance for the temperate continental climate is represented by

Peoria, Illinois. A deficit moisture period occurs in midsummer but a soil moisture reserve helps supply water for this period. As one goes toward the western part of the Corn Belt, however, the moisture reserve becomes more limiting. Moisture is also somewhat limiting in the U.S.S.R. The water balance for the cool summer climates is similar to that of Peoria.

The temperate oceanic climate is important for Europe. The cooler growing season of this climate is generally more favorable for grains like wheat and tubers, like potatoes. These climates rarely suffer from droughts, although they do occur for varying lengths of time, as in the spring-summer of 1976. A typical water balance is shown for Valentia, Ireland.

The subtropical humid climate is also important for agricultural production. This climate has a very long growing season, but most areas still grow only one crop per season. Some effort is being directed to developing a two-crop type of agriculture, e.g., soybeans and wheat on the same land in one season. The water balance for this climate is represented by Chungking, China. Short periods of deficient moisture occur, but they are not usually of major importance. The southeastern United States has more cool-season precipitation than China. Summer temperatures in this climate are not very different from those in the temperate warm summer climates, but winter temperatures are much warmer. Disease organisms and pests overwinter much easier in the tropical and subtropical climates.

The climates just discussed are the "favorable agricultural climates," found largely in developed countries. These countries also have other climates that are not as favorable for agriculture. For example, extensive areas of steppe climate, with its limited moisture supply, occur in the middle latitudes. A typical water balance is shown for Williston, North Dakota. The available moisture will usually support a short-season crop, such as wheat, but is too limited for long-season crops unless irrigation is used. This climate is very important to the world's wheat production, but yields fluctuate considerably from year to year with available moisture. Much livestock is produced in this climate.

The dry-summer, Mediterranean type climate is present in very limited areas of the developed countries and is important for fruit and vegetable production. Irrigated agriculture is extensive in this climate.

Canada and the U.S.S.R. have large areas of subarctic climate. With a 90-day or shorter growing season, cereal grain production is possible only in the warmest regions of this climate. Hay, pasture, and forage crops, however, are produced. Can this climatic area ever become an area of significant agricultural production? Perhaps, but significant agricultural developments will be needed. Climate change could have important effects on this area, but experts disagree on what change is likely. Some evidence indicates the northern climates may be getting cooler, which would further handicap this area. But some climatologists feel that this area is going into a warming period because of carbon dioxide pollution in the atmosphere. A warming would benefit agriculture in these areas.

Most of the developing nations are in the tropical regions where the climate is not generally as favorable for grain production. The amount and distribution of rainfall create problems for agriculture. These climates do have the advantage of being continuously warm. Crops that require continuously warm temperatures throughout the year can be grown in these climates. Multicropping can result in large total production per unit land area, but a different technology from that of the temperate climates must be used.

Tropical rainy climates have periods when they are excessively wet. The water balance for Belem, Brazil, is typical for this climate. Several months have more than 10 inches of rainfall. A "dry" month has 4 to 5 inches. Soil erosion can be a severe problem. The high temperatures and heavy rainfall result in highly leached soils with low organic content. The warm, wet conditions favor the development of many diseases and pests.

The sustained level of production that can be reached in these climates is a debatable point. There is no doubt that the tropical rainy areas of southeast Asia are very important in the world's rice production. Many tropical fruits and vegetables also grow in this climate. But technology specifically adapted for these areas is needed.

The tropical wet-dry climates cover very extensive areas in the developing countries. A typical water balance is like that of Calcutta, India. Some months can be very wet, followed by several very dry months. Agricultural operations must be adapted to this type of seasonal pattern.

Another climate important to the developing countries is the hot steppe climate of the low latitudes. These climates have a short rainy season and a long, very dry season. Any reduction of rainfall below normal is detrimental, and the climate from year to year is extremely variable.

Two areas with significant tropical wet-dry and tropical steppe climates are the Sahelian (south of the Sahara) region of Africa and India. The Sahelian region has recently gone through a very severe drought period. Millions of livestock were lost as famine prevailed across the region. Although this was a serious drought, it was not especially unusual. Droughts are a recurrent problem in these climates. The recent drought in the Sahel had been preceded by several years of relatively good weather. During those years, the population (both human and animal) had increased tremendously, and the combination of the drought and high population resulted in a disaster.

An idea of the variation of rainfall from year to year in this type climate can be seen in Figure 6.4 where a climate index is shown for northwest India. When the solid line is high, the weather is dry; when

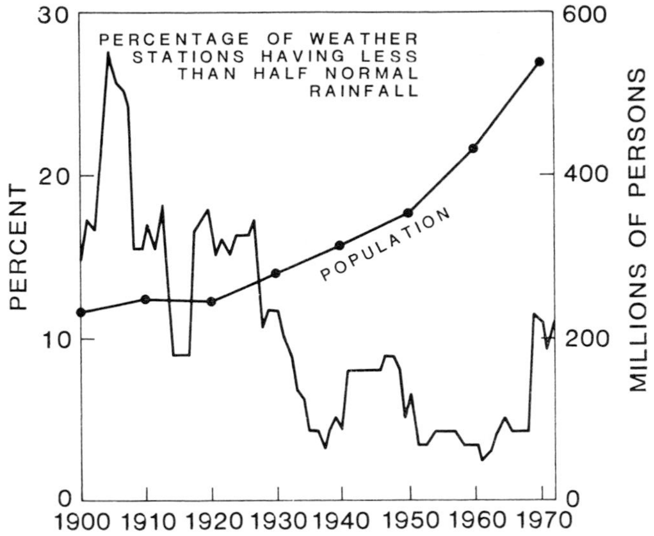


FIG. 6.4. A rainfall index and population trend for northern India, 1900–1972. From Fortune Magazine 1974. Data compiled by Reid Bryson.

it is low, the weather is favorable for agriculture. Notice how rainfall has fluctuated over the years. Weather was relatively good in the 1950s and 1960s when the "Green Revolution" was introduced. In recent years the climate has been drier again. The population factor is also important in India. Early in the century only 200 million people had to be fed; now the number is over 600 million.

India and southeast Asia have what is called a monsoon climate. During the summer season winds blow north from the ocean to the land, and most areas have their wet season. During the winter season winds blow from land to water, and most areas have their dry season. Agriculture depends on the wet monsoon. The rainfall pattern can vary tremendously with the geographical location. An examination of selected stations in India will show how the rainfall pattern varies for tropical climates (Fig. 6.5).

Colombo, Sri Lanka (Ceylon), has spring and fall rainfall peaks with no dry month. It has a tropical, rainy climate. Mangalore has a very dry and a very wet season, with peak rainfall in midsummer. Highest temperatures occur in the spring when the moist air has penetrated far inland. It has a tropical steppe climate. Madras is located on the east coast of India, and gets its rainfall in the fall and early winter season when winds are out of the northeast.

The monsoon circulation is not completely dependable. In some years, the wet monsoon is late in arriving, or it may not even develop. In these cases, droughts may develop, crops fail, and famines occur. Ir-

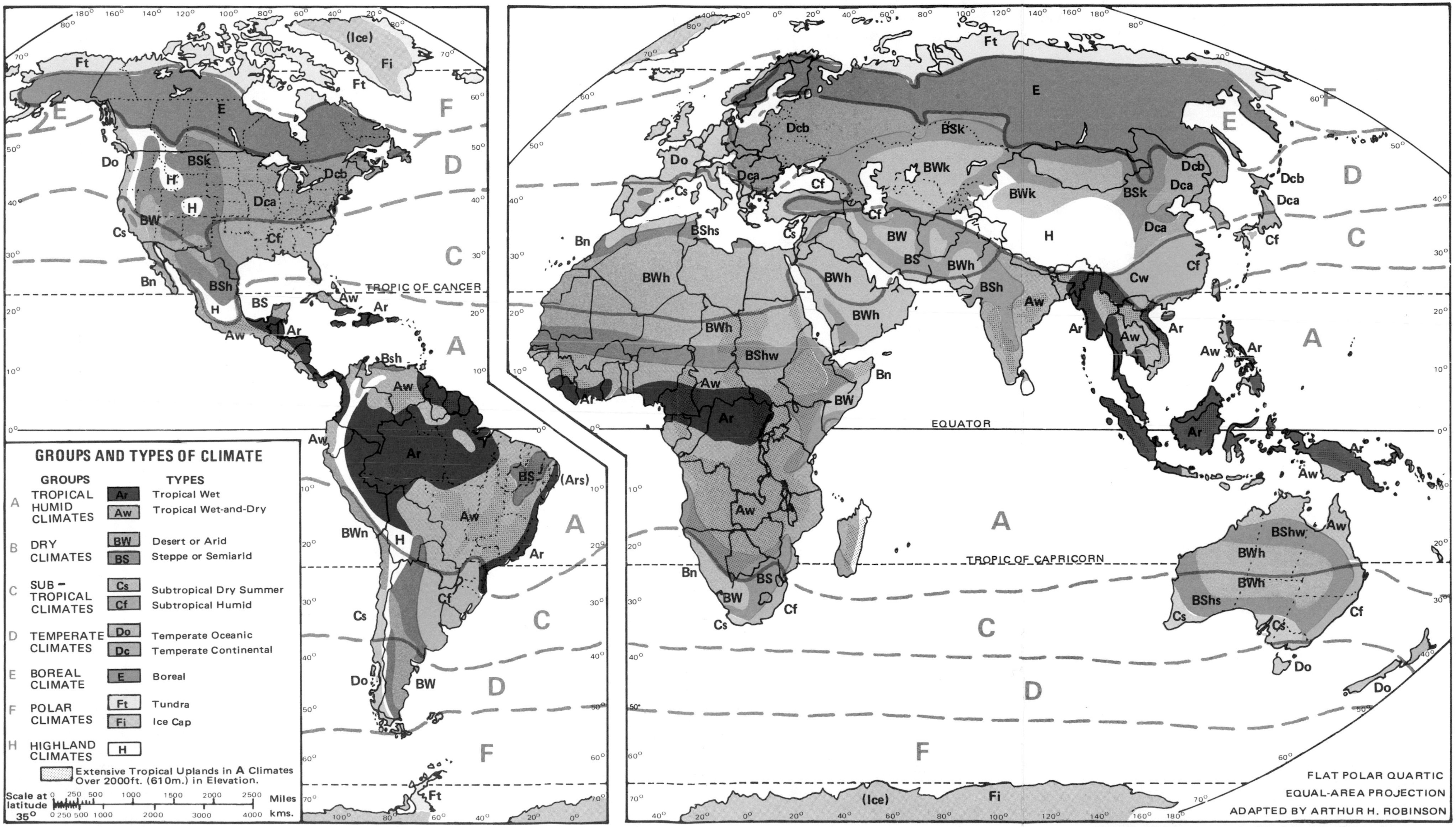


Figure 2. Climates by the classification of Trewartha. From: An Introduction to Climate, by Trewartha, 1968. Copyright McGraw-Hill Book Co., N.Y., 1967. Used with permission of McGraw-Hill Book Company.

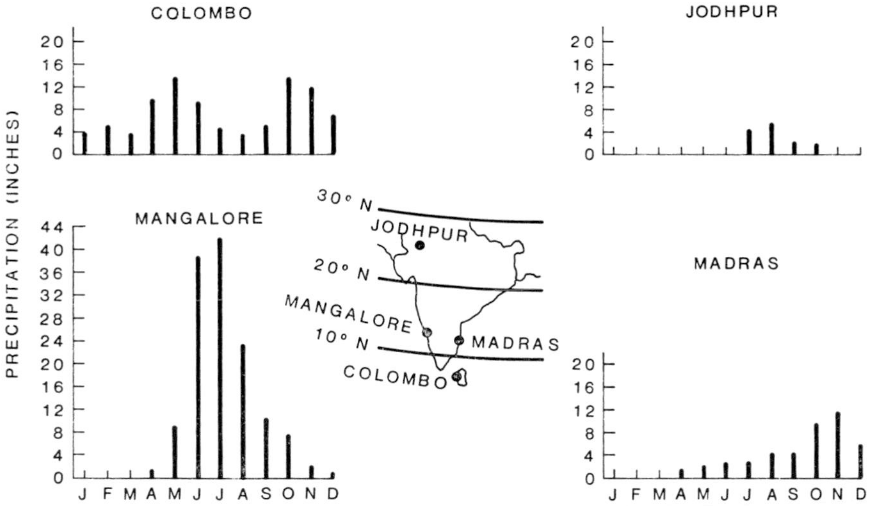


FIG. 6.5. Monthly precipitation at four stations in the Indian monsoon region

regular recurrence of these droughts is a fact of life in these climates. Droughts have occurred in the past and they will occur in the future in both the tropical wet-dry and the tropical steppe climate. This will create severe food problems for the developing nations with these climates.

CLIMATE AND OUR FUTURE FOOD SUPPLY. In the Book of Genesis, Chapter 41, the following can be found: "Behold, there come seven years of great plenty throughout all the land of Egypt: and there shall arise after them seven years of famine; and all the plenty shall be forgotten in the land of Egypt, and famine shall consume the land." Years of plenty and years of famine have occurred for centuries, and no doubt the weather and climate have been a major factor involved. We know that climate has not been constant over the centuries. Has it been changing or only fluctuating? Climatologists are discussing that very question, particularly in regard to the future. But whether climate will change or only fluctuate, events in the future do not seem predictable with our present knowledge. Seven years of feast may not precede seven of famine, but major fluctuations in food production will surely be caused by the weather.

## BIBLIOGRAPHY

Kendrew, W. G. The Climates of the Continents. New York: Oxford University Press, 1942.

Trewartha, G. T. An Introduction to Climate. 4th ed. New York: McGraw-Hill, 1968.

# 7

# Soil Resources—Characteristics, Potentials, and Limitations

WILLIAM D. SHRADER

THE soils of the world and their characteristics affect both present and future food production. Some of the world's soils are being used to their full potential; others are not. This chapter first examines the major soils groups (see Table 7.1) and their locations and then investigates areas where food production might be increased if technical, political, or institutional barriers can be overcome.

## MAJOR SOILS GROUPS

DARK PRAIRIE SOILS. On a global scale, the principal areas of dark-colored soils, known as dark prairie soils or Mollisols are in the midwestern

TABLE 7.1. THE MAJOR SOIL GROUPS AND THEIR CHARACTERISTICS.

| Soil | Characteristics |
|---|---|
| Entisols (including alluvials) | Very young soils that still have essentially the same characteristics as weathered rock or parent materials[a] |
| Vertisols | Black calcareous clays |
| Inceptisols | Reddish soils |
| Aridisols (including alluvials) | Desert soils, brown and reddish brown |
| Mollisols | Dark prairie soils |
| Spodosols | Light-colored sandy soils |
| Alfisols | Moderately weathered[a] light-colored soils |
| Ultisols | Strongly weathered[a] light-colored soils |
| Oxisols | Very strongly weathered[a] soils |
| Histosols | Organic soils, bog soils, peat, and muck |

[a]Weathering refers to the action of elements in altering the color, texture, composition, or form of exposed earth materials. Parent materials are rocks, vocanic ash, etc., from which soil is formed.

WILLIAM D. SHRADER—Professor, Agronomy Department, Iowa State University. Teacher and researcher. Foreign service in Uruguay, Iran, and Thailand. Widely published on soils, soil conservation, and management.

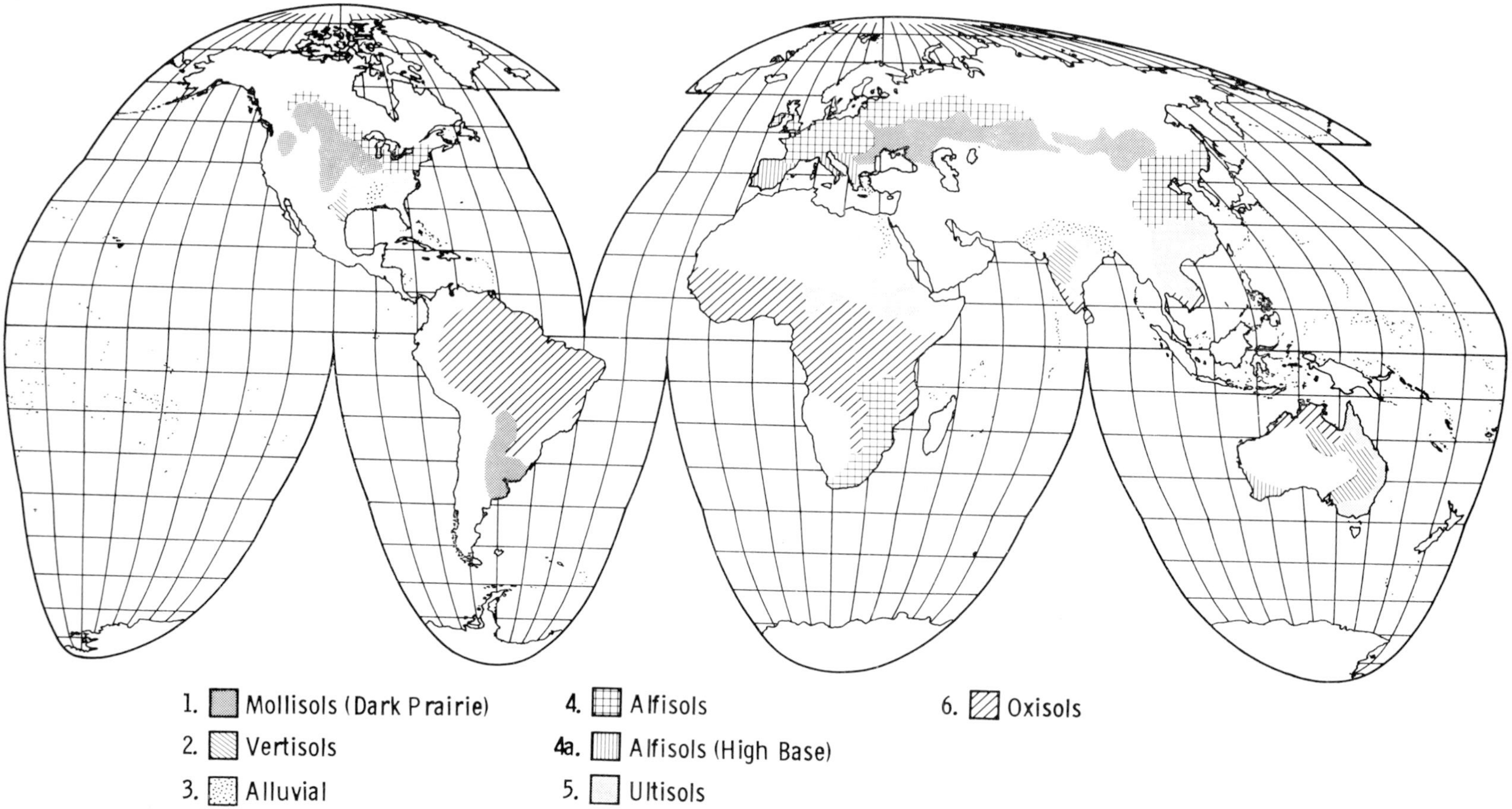


FIG. 7.1. Major soil groups of present and potential crop land

United States and adjacent areas in Canada, the central part of the U.S.S.R., and the Pampas region of eastern Argentina, Uruguay, and southern Brazil (Fig. 7.1). These are also the principal grain-producing areas of the world, with the United States, Canada, and Argentina producing most of the world's exportable surplus of grain.

The soil parent materials (materials from which the soils developed) are geologically young, and most of them are high in nutrients and slightly acid to neutral in reaction. Calcium carbonate (lime) is usually near the surface and often in the surface soil itself.

Until about 1840 prairie soils were largely unused for crop production since these soils occupied the centers of the continents, and transportation to markets and farm equipment were not yet available. Railroads, the steel moldboard plow, drainage tile, and wire fences were necessary before these highly fertile soils could be used.

Prior to 1840, grain was produced mostly on poor, light-colored, acid soils that had developed under forest. Yields were low and always had been low—about 10 bushels of wheat per acre. Any increase in yields was achieved only at great cost and usually only by reducing the acreage of cropland and increasing the amount of pasture or fallow. The land in western Europe was used to its limits and hunger was endemic. By about 1840, however, technology had developed to the point that the prairie soils could be used, and commercial fertilizers became available. Crop yields in western Europe increased dramatically, and with the surplus grains from the prairie soils the Western Civilization as we know it became possible.

The increased crop yields of western Europe, however, were absorbed by increasing populations, and for most of the past 100 years western Europe has had little or no grain to export.

Black Calcareous Clay Soils. Lying on the equator side of the dark-colored prairie soils are about 900,000 square miles of black calcareous clay soils (Vertisols). Extensive areas occur in Australia, India, the Sudan, Chad, Argentina, and Uruguay (2).

Vertisols were developed under prairie vegetation from calcareous (lime containing) parent materials in regions with pronounced wet and dry seasons. During dry periods the clay soils shrink and crack to depths of 3 or more feet. Rains wash the surface soil into the cracks, and with prolonged wetting the cracks swell shut. The entrapped soil also swells, exerting strong pressures that slowly churn and mix the entire soil mass from the surface to the depth of the cracks. Thus, as much as the top 4 feet may be a black calcareous clay. The percentage of organic matter is only moderately high, but the soils are still much more fertile than the red and yellow forested soils with which the Vertisols are usually associated.

In general, Vertisols throughout the world are sparsely settled and underutilized. They are potentially much more productive than the soils traditionally used, but they are very difficult to till with hand tools because of their clay texture. Thus their use has largely awaited the coming of machine power and large-scale commercial agriculture. But even under the best of presently known technology, crop yields are decidedly lower than on the Mollisols. For example, in Texas, where there are about 20 million acres of Vertisols, corn yields on experimental plots average only about 50 bushels per acre as compared with yields of 120 bushels per acre on Mollisols in Iowa (4).

ALLUVIAL SOILS. Alluvial soils were deposited by water. Perhaps the most typical examples are found in the deltas of the Nile, Mississippi, and Ganges rivers. These soils support hundreds of millions of people in India and China. Throughout the humid regions of southeast Asia, rice production is centered on the alluvial lowlands and in the subhumid regions, wheat is grown on these soils. In dry regions, such as in Egypt, crop production is possible only under irrigation usually on alluvial soils. On the Indian subcontinent, alluvial soils are distributed primarily along the Indus and Ganges rivers.

In the United States, the alluvial soils of the Mississippi delta are important for producing cotton, rice, and soybeans. The delta region, which extends southward from southern Illinois, is 650 miles long, averages 70 miles in width and covers an area of 45,000 square miles, or 30,000,000 acres. Most of this region required drainage before it could be farmed, and so large portions of it have been used for crop production only since 1930. Most areas that can be readily used are now cultivated.

DESERT SOILS. Deserts (Aridisols) cover about 15 percent of the earth's surface and, except for very limited grazing, food production is impossible without irrigation.

Even if water were available, most, and frequently as much as 90 percent, of the desert soils are totally unsuited to crop production. They are commonly too steep, too rocky, too salty, or too sandy to be used. The medium textured alluvial soils are usually the most suitable for irrigation and are characteristically the most extensively used. Still, in most deserts there is more land suitable for crop production than there is water for irrigation.

Irrigation in west Texas illustrates how limited water will continue to limit the use of desert regions for food production. On the Texas high plains 5.4 million acres are being irrigated with water pumped from underlying rock strata in amounts far exceeding recharge. Experts estimate that income from irrigation will increase until 1988, peaking at more than one-half billion dollars annually; however, benefits thereafter will decline until 2020 when all the fossil water will have been mined (8).

LIGHT-COLORED FORESTED SOILS OF MIDDLE LATITUDES. The light-colored infertile acid soils of western Europe have been farmed for at least 2,000 years. In ancient and medieval times the ready presence of wood, water, and a measure of protection against invaders made them more attractive than the more fertile prairie soils despite low crop yields.

Similar light-colored acid soils of the Northeast United States were the first soils farmed by Europeans settling America. These light-colored soils are the moderately weathered Alfisols. (Weathering refers to the action of elements in altering the color, texture, composition and form of exposed earth.) Surface soils are characteristically gray, low in clay, acid in reaction, low in organic matter and plant-available nutrients, and have medium to sandy textures. The subsoil is gray or brown and distinctly heavier in texture than the surface.

Throughout the Alfisols, particularly in northern regions, are areas of sandy soils with very light gray surface soils and a zone of accumulated iron and organic matter in the subsoil (Spodosols).

Yields on both European Alfisols and Spodosols were low under subsistence agriculture that depended on hand labor or oxen. But Alfisols responded to fertilizers and remained in cultivation while large areas of the Spodosols, especially in Scotland and Ireland, have gone out of cultivation and the rural population has declined.

In the United States, especially in New England, large areas of the Alfisols and some of the Spodosols were cleared and cultivated prior to the Revolutionary War. Much of this area is stony and steep, but with careful husbandry it could support a family and yield a slight surplus.

Ultisols are strongly weathered soils and are found along the eastern coast from Pennsylvania southward. The surface soils are light colored and the subsoils are bright red and yellow. Strongly acidic to a depth of several feet, these soils are low in nutrients and some of them have toxic quantities of plant-available aluminum in the subsoil. The subsoils often have compacted or weakly cemented zones, known as fragipans, which limit drainage in wet seasons and prevent effective rooting depth causing plants to suffer badly during drought. The Ultisols in the United States are used less for agriculture now than they were 100 years ago but are used extensively for timber production and for pasture.

There are also extensive areas of Ultisols in southeast Asia and in the Amazon basin (6).

Red Tropical Soils. Oxisols are the highly weathered red soils that form in the humid tropics. They are generally high in clay containing kaolinite or oxides of iron and aluminum. The clays do not swell and shrink on wetting and drying as do most clays in temperate regions, and they also have a limited capacity to hold bases or nutrients in a form available for plants. Even though high in clay, these soils usually have an open porous structure and absorb water rapidly. The mineral portion of these soils is much more inert chemically than in most other soils, and thus the organic fraction of the soil is the principal source of plant-available nutrients (19).

Oxisols are acid but because of the relative inertness of the clay the amount of lime required to correct acidity is less than in other soils.

Oxisols occur mainly in Africa south of the Sahara and in the Amazon basin and south in Brazil. They have not been much used for agriculture and many areas are essentially uninhabited. Large areas in the Amazon basin have less than one person per square kilometer.

North of the Mediterranean Sea, the principal soils are brown or red and are shown in Figure 7.1 as high base Alfisols. These soils also make up a subgroup of the Inceptisols.

Many areas have been cultivated for several thousands of years and the rolling to hilly land has eroded extensively. The present surface is usually a brown to reddish brown clay loam that contains varying quantities of stone and is slightly acid to neutral and may be calcareous. Stoniness commonly increases with depth but what soil is present is red and high in clay. These soils developed where winters are rainy and summers are hot and dry. Winter wheat is the common grain crop.

The high base content Alfisols respond to good management and are generally highly productive, but production per person is very low. In the Mediterranean region they have been intensively used since the beginning of recorded history and even under optimum management cannot fully supply the food needs of the present population.

ORGANIC SOILS. Organic soils, peats, and mucks, classified as Histosols, are distributed worldwide and develop wherever climatic conditions permit vegetative growth under water-saturated conditions. These soils occur both on low ground in standing water and on uplands under certain special climatic conditions.

LOW MOORS. Low moors or low ground peats are found throughout the world. Given enough time bogs develop in standing water capable of supporting aquatic vegetation.

HIGH MOOR OR CLIMATIC PEATS. In high latitudes the entire land surfaec may be covered with peats, resulting from the accumulation of Sphagnum mosses. These mosses grow continously upward while the lower portions die and turn into peat. The entire bed thus rises a certain amount annually. Upland peat bogs vary from a few inches to 10 or more feet in depth. Extensive areas occur in Scotland, Ireland, the Baltic region, and in vast areas of the northern U.S.S.R.

The high moors develop where the mosses can grow on rainfall alone and where the ground surface never dries. As the peat layer accumulates, all connection with the water table or with the mineral soil is lost. Nutrients are available only from the recently dead mosses or from rain water. These moors are, therefore, very low in all bases or nutrients and are highly acid.

USE. European peat bogs have been used as fuel throughout history. Peats have also been used as a soil amendment but essentially none of the upland peats has ever been used for more than rough pasturage.

In the United States some areas of lowland peats are drained and used for agriculture. For example, in Palm Beach County, Florida, 350,000 acres of peat soils are used intensively to produce sugar cane and winter vegetables. This peat deposit was about 8 feet deep when drainage and cultivation started 50 years ago, but oxidation of the peat under cultivation has now reduced the deposit to about 4 feet (16).

## POTENTIALS AND LIMITATIONS FOR EXPANSION OF FOOD PRODUCTION

### North America

UNITED STATES. Within the United States about 21 percent of the land area is in cropland (see Table 7.2). It is this cropland that produces most of the food since one acre of Iowa corn land produces 40 times as much meat as one acre of western rangeland.

All lands in the United States have been classified as to suitability for use into 7 classes. Class I is the best, but Classes II and III are both fairly good cropland. For the 48 contiguous states, 76 percent of the soil in Class I land is being cultivated, 66 percent in Class II, and 49 percent in Class III (7, 11).

In total about 230 million acres of privately owned land is suitable for cropland but is not now so used. Some areas are small or isolated, some are not cleared or drained, but if the need for food were great enough, much of the 230 million acres could be used for cropland.

Alaska has only about 30,000 of its total 375 million acres in cultivation. Perhaps as much as 14 million acres might have some limited value for agriculture (1), with the largest potential area on the alluvial soils of Yukon flats in east central Alaska.

Any significant development in agriculture in Alaska, however,

TABLE 7.2. Land use in the United States[a]

| Uses of Land | Millions of acres in each use | Percentage of land in each use |
|---|---|---|
| Cropland | 472 | 20.9 |
| Grassland Pasture and Range Land | 604 | 26.7 |
| Forest Land | 723 | 31.9 |
| Special Uses of Land[b] | 178 | 7.8 |
| Other Land[c] | 282 | 12.7 |
| Total Land | 2,264 | 100.0 |

[a] Based on 1969 census.
[b] Includes urban, highway, parks, wildlife, airports, etc.
[c] Includes land in desert, swamps, glaciers, tundra, etc.

would require developing new crop varieties and new production techniques, and bringing services, such as roads, electricity, schools, and hospitals, to remote areas.

CANADA. Canada is slightly larger than the United States, but only 4.4 percent is improved farmland and probably no more than 10 percent can ever be improved (3). This is because about one-third of the area is underlaid by permafrost, one-half is too cold for forest growth, and two-thirds is too cold for agriculture.

Settlement in the east is confined to a narrow belt adjoining the United States and extending as far west as Lake Huron. North and west of this settled zone is the Canadian Shield, which covers 50 percent of the Canadian land mass and extends some 1200 miles west of Toronto to Winnipeg. This entire area is virtually unsettled and is of little potential value for agriculture.

At Winnipeg, the Interior Plains, with their dark prairie soils open to the west and north, extend several hundred miles north into the interior. These soils are extensions of similar soils in the United States. Rainfall is sparse and the growing season is short, but the area is one of the important wheat producing regions of the world. Manitoba, Saskatchewan, and Alberta contain about 75 percent of all improved land in Canada.

Table 7.3 summarizes soil conditions and agricultural potentials in Canada.

MEXICO. Mexico has relatively small areas of highly productive soils since large areas are various combinations of arid, semiarid, stony, and mountainous conditions. A few large scale irrigation developments have

TABLE 7.3. AREA USE AND AGRICULTURAL POTENTIAL FOR THE PRINCIPAL SOIL ZONES IN CANADA. COMPILED FROM DATA IN (3).

| Soil Zone | Area | Cultivated | Suitable for cultivation | Limitations |
|---|---|---|---|---|
| | | *(millions of acres)* | | |
| Appalachian | 78.0 | 2.3 | 6.5 | Stony and rough |
| Great Lakes and St. Lawrence Lowlands | 29.0 | 26.0 | 24.0 | Competition with industry |
| Prairies | 120.0 | 60.0 | 71.0 | Water, drainage, and soil structure |
| Grey wooded | 200.0 | 10.6 | 18.0 | Drainage, fertility, stony and rough |
| Cordilleran | 273.0 | 0.7 | 3.0 | Stony and steep |
| Shield (south of permafrost line) | 586.0 | ... | 15.0 | Shallow soils or too wet |
| Subarctic | 206.0 | ... | ... | Too cold |
| Arctic | 661.0 | ... | ... | Too cold |
| | 2,245.0 | 99.6 | 135.5 | |
| | | 4.4% | 6.0% | |

improved grain production in some areas, but most farmers still eke out a meager living on small near-subsistence farms. With 60 million inhabitants, a rapidly increasing population, and very limited areas of suitable unused soils, Mexico will not have any appreciable food surplus and probably will need to import increasing quantities of grain.

EUROPE AND ASIA. The naturally poor light-colored soils of western Europe now produce high crop yields only because of advanced technology, large capital investments, and intensive labor use. Any further increases in food production can be achieved only with large investments of manpower and capital since there are no more acres of good agricultural soils that can be readily developed. As long as grain is available at moderate prices on the world market, Europe will likely be a grain importing region.

RUSSIA. Most of the U.S.S.R.'s present agricultural development is within the forest steppe and steppe zones. (See Fig. 7.2.) Limited areas of arid lands are intensively developed under irrigation.

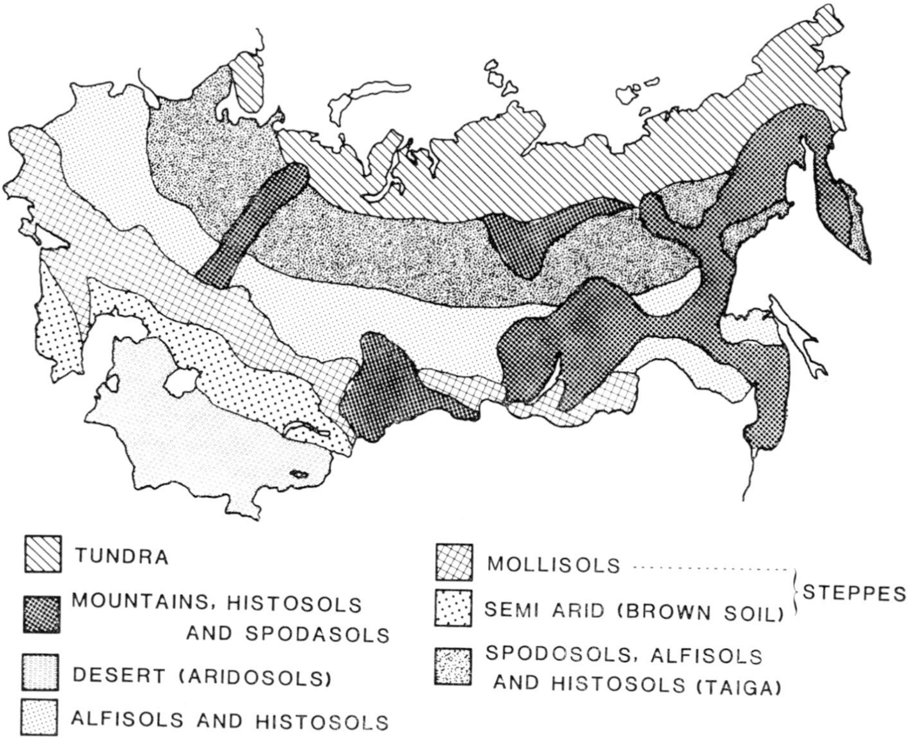


FIG. 7.2. Schematic soil map of the U.S.S.R. Adapted from (12)

U.S.S.R. scientists are reported to be actively researching the agricultural use of cold regions (9), but such use will depend on new technology and major investments in services.

Grain production in recent years has expanded into the semiarid soils—probably the most easily used soils—but risk of drought is high and production costs are also high. Recent purchases of American grain indicate that at present U.S.S.R. officials believe it is cheaper to purchase grain abroad than to try to produce it on their high risk lands.

CHINA. China, with the same land area as the United States, supports a population of about 1 billion. Much of the country is either mountains or deserts not usable for crop production (20). But all lands that can be made arable even with great effort are being used, with food production concentrated on the lowlands on alluvial soils in eastern China.

All lands that can be easily tilled have been cultivated for centuries and have lost most of the original soil characteristics. On sloping lands, several feet of soil have eroded in many areas. The areas of brown earths and gray wooded soils containing extensive loess deposits are the most productive upland soils in China, but these soils have also eroded severely, despite elaborate terrace construction (18).

China is producing enough food for its people only by investing more in agricultural production than any other major nation is presently willing to invest. In terms of production per person, food in China is very high priced. It is unlikely that China will produce any appreciable food surplus.

INDIAN SUBCONTINENT. India, Pakistan, and Bangladesh have an area about half the size of the United States and a population nearly four times as large.

The huge area of alluvial soils along the south front of the Himalayas (Fig. 7.3) is about eight times the size of Iowa and has been fully occupied for thousands of years. As late as 1963, rice yields in India averaged 1047 pounds per acre, the lowest in the world for any major producing area. Recent use of high yield varieties and improved practices show that yield improvement is possible.

Red soils are the most extensive of any soil group in India, occupying about half of the entire area and distributed over much of the peninsula. These soils are dominantly Ultisols and have the same general properties as the red and yellow soils of the southeastern United States. Most land suitable for traditional cultural methods has been used for centuries, and production has also been stable at a low yield level for many years. Any marked improvement in production depends on major changes in technology (14).

The Vertisols or black clay soils occupy an area about three and one-half times the size of Iowa and are extensively developed. These soils are most extensive on the Deccan plateau, where rainfall ranges

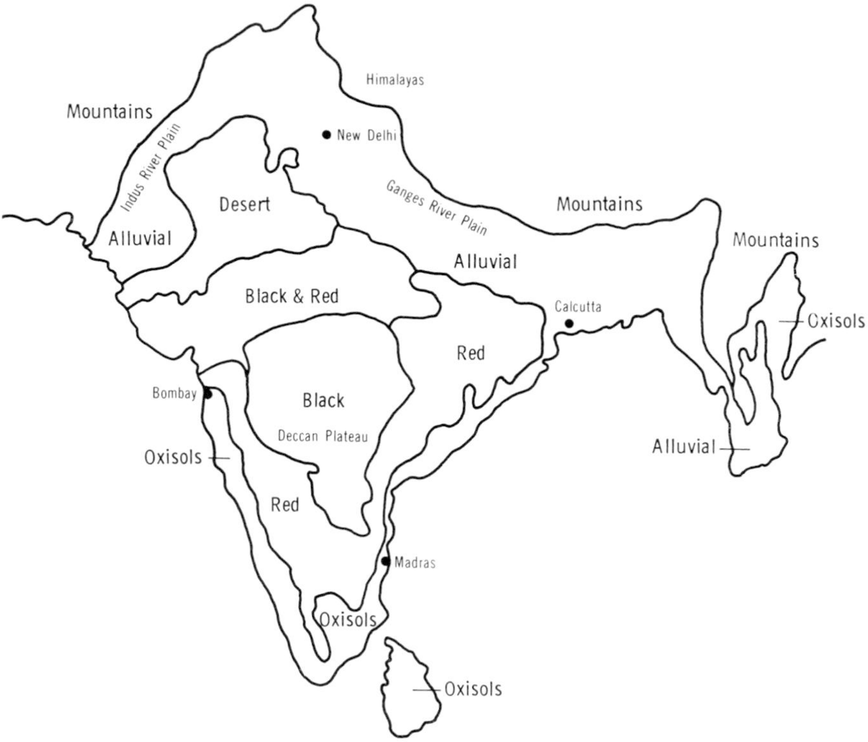


FIG. 7.3. Soil regions of the Indian subcontinent (15)

from about 20 to 60 inches per year and occurs between June and November. The early summer months are very hot, and cracks 4 to 8 inches wide and several feet deep develop. Still these soils can be highly productive especially when deficient nitrogen and phosphorus are supplied. Also, with adequate irrigation during the dry season, a marked increase in production can result.

In summary, there is little land not already in use throughout the Indian subcontinent and increased yields must depend on new technologies. But because of the rapidly increasing population, it is unlikely that this area will be able to sustain any excess food production and massive imports will probably be needed in short crop years to prevent famine.

SOUTH AMERICA. In South America the greatest width of land mass is in the tropics, whereas in North America the greatest width is in temperate regions. South America has a much higher proportion of very highly weathered soils and a more moderate climate in the middle latitudes than does North America. Figure 7.4 shows the distribution of soils in the various areas of South America.

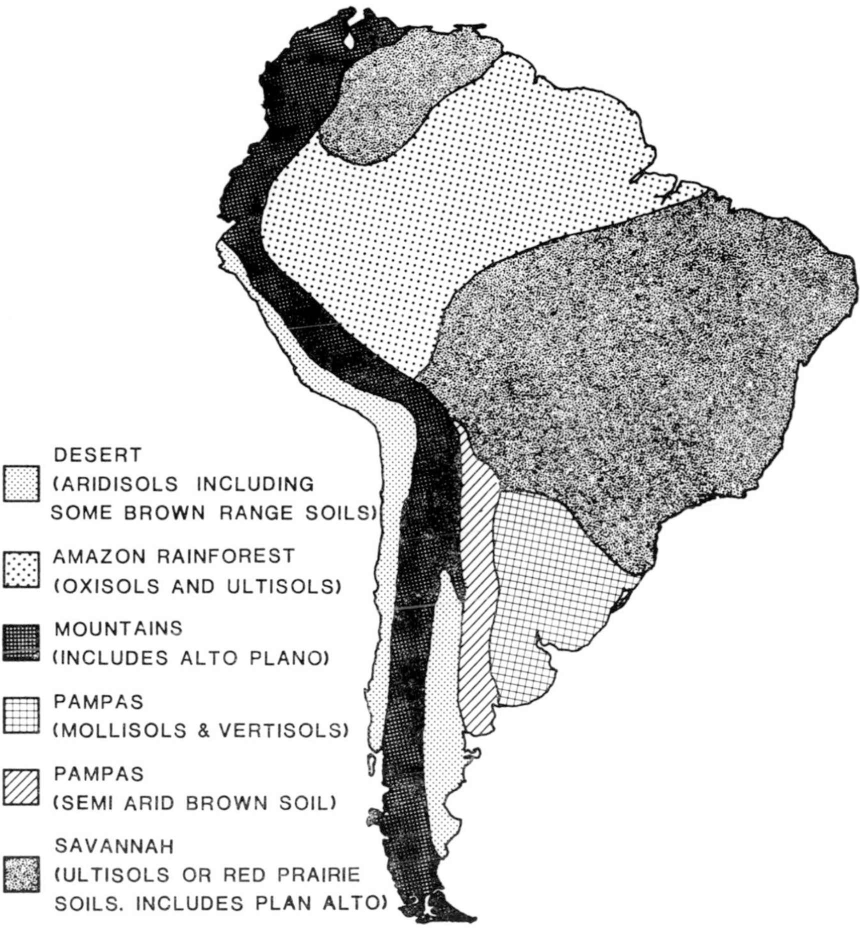


FIG. 7.4. Major land and soil areas of South America

WEST COAST. Only a narrow band of land exists west of the Andes Mountains along the west coast of South America. The northern part of this band is desert, and agriculture is possible only on the 1 to 5 percent of the area that can be irrigated.

ALTO-PLANO. Large areas of almost completely barren, stony, steep, and in places snow-covered mountainous terrain occur along the course of the Andes. But there is also a much larger area of hilly to mountainous plateau, much of it at elevations of 10,000 to 14,000 feet, with stony and shallow soils. This Alto-Plano or high plain is the home of several ancient Indian cultures and has been cultivated for many centuries using hand labor on the steep slopes without benefit of fertilizers or improved seed or tools. The subsistence agriculture is unable to support the growing population and so the impoverished people migrate to the larger cities all along the west coast.

PAMPAS. The prairie regions of eastern South America, known as the Pampas, in contrast to the Alto-Plano are sparsely populated. These are large areas with Mollisols similar to the best soils of the U.S. Corn Belt. Over most of the Pampas rainfall ranges from about 20 to 50 inches per year and relief is generally low.

In northern Argentina, however, there are large areas with highly developed claypans and flat surfaces on which drainage is a serious problem. The summer heat is extreme and there are long and severe droughts at erratic periods. Vertisols and saline soils are also common in this area. To the south, in Patagonia, many of the soils are stony, the rainfall is light and variable, and temperatures are cool. Historically this has been a sheep growing region.

The Pampas has been an important grain-exporting region, and grain production could be increased rapidly and significantly by cultivating more of the land currently held in large ranches and used for grazing. For example, in Uruguay only 8 percent of the total area is cultivated while at least 25 percent is suitable for cultivation. The main restrictions on expansion are political and institutional rather than technical. This is probably the major land area in the world where increased exports could most easily be obtained.

BRAZIL. Brazil occupies half of South America, but only about 2 percent of its land area is presently cultivated.

Southern Brazil has extensive areas of dark prairie soils, extensions of the Mollisols and Vertisols of the Pampas. These dark soils merge into a vast Savannah region characterized by red soils and scattered timber, extending some 1,500 miles north and 2,000 miles east and west. The soils are mainly Ultisols with some areas of red soils similar to those north of the Mediterranean. Most of the area is a plateau (Plan Alto) with an elevation of 2,000 to 3,000 feet, ranging from gently to strongly rolling to hilly. Rainfall ranges from about 40 to 80 inches per year with some extended dry periods. Coffee is produced on the coastal fringes of this area, but the interior is nearly empty and unused.

Isolation, health problems, and political and social customs have all contributed to the lack of development or even settlement of this area. Soils too have been a factor since many are too infertile to support profitable plant growth without extensive treatment. But, because of the relatively level topography, favorable rainfall, and a 10- to 12-month growing season, these soils have a huge potential meriting intensive research.

Technical problems of production can almost certainly be solved, and if suitable institutional arrangements are made, this area can become a major surplus food production region.

AMAZON BASIN. Lying north of the savannah belt is the rain forest that includes much of the Amazon River drainage and extends about 2,500 miles east and west and about 1,500 miles north and south. The inner basin of the Amazon River covers an area about 30 percent the size of the United States.

The soils in the Amazon basin resemble the red and yellow soils or Ultisols of the southeastern United States (12). However, the level of exchangeable aluminum is generally higher in Brazil than in the U.S. soils (5), reaching a level toxic to some food crops. There are also many Oxisols.

The Amazoan basin is thinly settled with large areas containing only two persons per square mile. Most of the farmers practice a slash and burn subsistence agriculture cutting and burning the brush during the dry season. The ashes contain sufficient calcium (Ca), magnesium (Mg), potassium (K), and other bases in the oxide or hydroxide form to raise the pH of the soil, which reduces the aluminum's solubility so that it is no longer toxic to plant roots. The bases in the ashes also furnish needed plant nutrients so corn, beans, squash, cassava, bananas, and other food crops make a fair growth. After 2 or 3 years the nutrients, especially nitrogen, are used up or leached from the soils, the soil's acidity increases, the soluble aluminum increases, yields decline, the field is abandoned to forest for 30 or more years, and a new field is cleared and burned.

The fields can be kept in production permanently if lime and fertilizers are used, but costs are high and prohibitive for most small farmers (6). Government policies can change this, and some subsidies are being provided.

The production potential of this region is enormous, and extensive development of some type will almost certainly come within the next 30 years.

AFRICA. Africa is about one-third larger than North America and three and one-half times as large as the U.S., but about one-third of the area is desert. The Sahara desert has acted as a barrier between the northern and southern parts of the continent throughout history. North of the Sahara the soils are the red high base status soils described in the European section (Fig. 7.5).

South of the true desert, West Africa has a band of brown soils mostly in the Aridisol group that support some vegetation. Where rainfall increases to the south there is a band of savannah. This in turn merges into tropical rain forest. There are many exceptions, but in general African soils are old, highly weathered, sandy, and low in fertility.

A report on the soils of Ghana will illustrate some of the problems and potentials of the soils in West Africa (21): Ghana lies just north of the equator and covers an area about twice the size of Nebraska. The southern one-third is tropical rain forest and the balance is savannah merging in the northeast into the semiarid Sudan.

Rainfall over most of the country is between 40 and 70 inches per

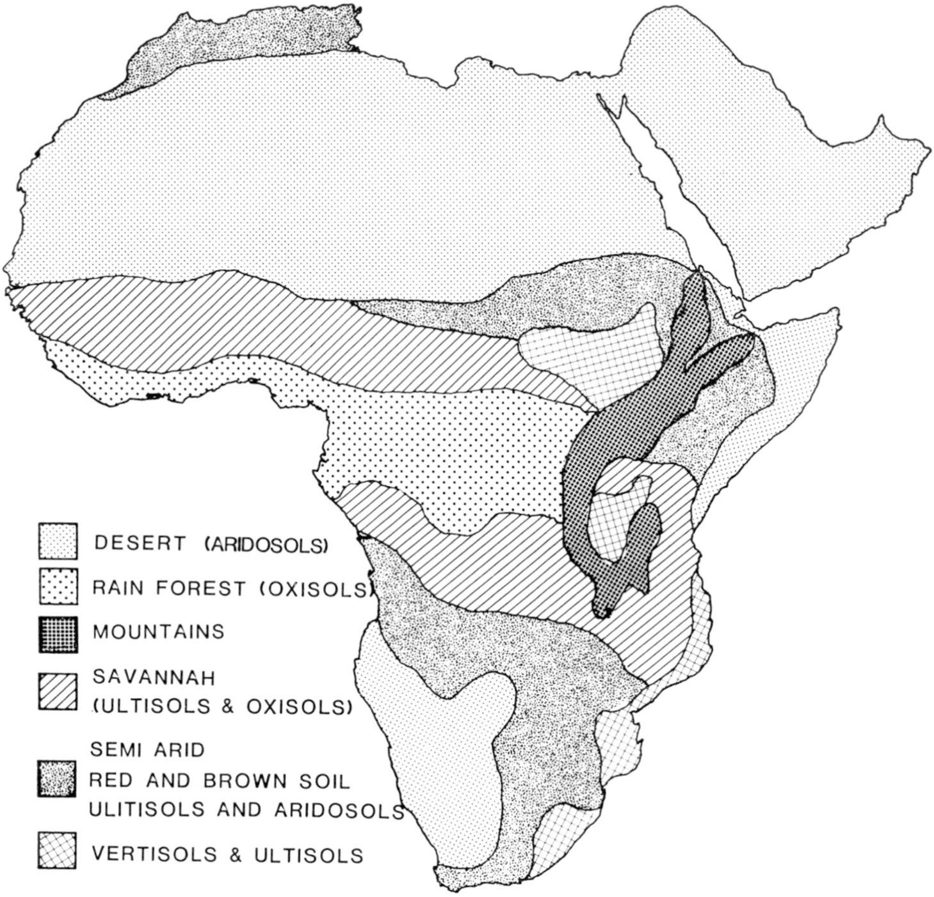


FIG. 7.5. Some major land and soil areas of Africa

year. But the presence or absence of rain forest depends about as much on the duration of the dry season or seasons as on total rainfall.

Most of the soils are Oxisols. The major divisions are between the Oxisols that have at least small quantities of exchangeable bases and those that are almost chemically inert. There are also large areas of iron pan soils, which consist of a shallow infertile silty or sandy surface soil overlying a firmly cemented iron pan horizon that restricts movement of water and greatly restricts root growth. These iron pan soils occupy about 50 percent of the savannah zone and 25 percent of the entire nation. These soils are absent in areas that do not have a dry season (13). To date, only a small proportion of these soils have been used for agriculture since they are not well suited for subsistence farming and even less suited for commercial agriculture.

Throughout much of tropical Africa, population density is about 16 persons per square mile, which is about all that can be supported by a slash and burn system of farming where only 3 to 5 percent of the land is in production at any one time. Keeping the land permanently in crop production would vastly increase the crop production potential but would require greatly increased use of imported lime and fertilizers, machine power, and improved management skills.

The potential for increased food production in Africa in terms of water, sunlight, and space is enormous but technical and institutional barriers are also very great. On the African continent there are more than 400 million people in 50 nations of widely varying sizes speaking hundreds of different languages. Development ranges from the highly industrialized Union of South Africa with modern cities, networks of roads and railroads, and mechanized agriculture to countries like Mauritania, which have almost no roads, no industry, no good harbor, no agriculture, and almost no fresh water.

Thus, for some time to come, it is unlikely that Africa will enter strongly into the world food market except for specialty crops, such as cocoa, and oil seed crops, such as palm oil.

AUSTRALIA. Australia is about 80 percent as large as the United States. While some 60 percent of Australia is either desert or mountains, there is an area about five times the size of Western Germany with at least moderately favorable soil and climatic conditions for plant growth (see Table 7.4).

Most of the arable land is in the eastern part of the continent. The principal grain-producing areas are the areas of Vertisols, the flat areas of Alfisols and Ultisols, and the slightly to moderately weathered red soils of the Inceptisol group. The interior of the continent is desert, and unless irrigated the brown soils of the Aridisol group are used only for grazing sheep and cattle.

Nearly all the best arable soils are in use. And while grain production could be greatly expanded, any pronounced expansion would be on poorer soils and would be at a high cost.

TABLE 7.4. MAJOR SOILS OF AUSTRALIA (17).

| Soil group | Area-in-square miles | Percentage of total |
|---|---|---|
| Aridisols (Desert) | 1,264,170 | 43 |
| Aridisols (Brown soils) | 625,582 | 21 |
| Entisols (Mountains and waste land) | 476,146 | 16 |
| Alfisols and Ultisols (Gray-Brown and Red-Yellow Podzolic) | 247,586 | 8 |
| Oxisols (Laterites) | 122,285 | 4 |
| Vertisols (Black clay soils) | 118,343 | 4 |
| Inceptisols (Terra Rosa and other reddish soils) | 112,748 | 4 |
| | 2,966,860 | |

SUMMARY. Most of the world's undeveloped cropland is found in Africa and the Pampas and tropical areas of South America. Most of the future increase in food production will probably occur in the South American areas if technical, political, and institutional barriers can be overcome. Any development, however, will require large inputs of technology and capital.

## REFERENCES

1. Alaska Rural Development Council. Alaska Agricultural Potential. Cooperative Extension Service, Publication No. 1. University of Alaska, Fairbanks, 1974, p. 40.
2. Buol, S. W.; Hole, F. D.; and McCracken, R. J. Soil Genesis and Classification. Ames: Iowa State University Press, 1973.
3. Canadian Agricultural Institute Review. A Look at Canadian Soils. Ottawa: Agricultural Institute of Canada, March-April 1960.
4. Collier, J. W. Influence of Cropping System-Treatment Combinations and Climatic Factors on Corn Yields in the Black Lands Area of Texas. Agron. Journal 51:587–590.
5. Falesi, I. C.; Vierra, L. C.; Dos Santos, W. H. P.; and Oliveira, J. P. S. Filho. Levantamento de reconhecimento dos solos da regiao bragantina, estado do Para, Pesquisa Agropecuraria Brasileira Vol. 2. 1967.
6. Falesi, I. C. Personal Communication.
7. Frey, H. T., and Otte, R. C. Cropland for Today and Tomorrow. U.S. Department of Agriculture ERS Agri. Econ. Report 291, July 1975.
8. Hauser, Victor. Hydrology, Conservation and Management of Runoff in Playas on the Southern High Plains. U.S. Department of Agriculture Conservation Res. Report No. 8, 1966.
9. International Soil Science Society. Proceedings of the 1960 World Congress.
10. Jordon, R. P. Siberia's Empire Road, the River Ob. National Geographic 149(2):145–183, 1976.
11. Klingebiel, A. A. Land Resources Available to People in the United States. Proc. 16th Annual Meeting. Agri. Res. Inst. Nat. Res. Council, Washington, D.C., 1967.
12. Marbut, C. F. The Soils of the Amazon Basin in Relation to Agricultural Possibilities. Geographical Review Vol. XVI, No. 3, July 1926.
13. Obeng, H. B. Characterization and Classification of Some Ironpan Soils in Ghana. Ph.D. thesis, Iowa State University, Ames, 1970.
14. Randhawa, M. S. Agricultural and Animal Husbandry in India. New Delhi: Indian Council of Agri. Res., 1958.
15. Raychaudhuri, S. P. Development for Classification and Nomenclature of Indian Soils. Journal Indian Soc. Soil Science 10:1–18, 1967.
16. Soil Science Soc. of America. Tour Guide Palm Beach County, Florida, November 1972.
17. Stephens, C. G. The Soil Landscapes of Australia. Melbourne: Commonwealth Scientific and Industrial Res. Organization, 1961.
18. Thorp, James. Geography of the Soils of China. Nanking: Nat. Geol. Survey of China, 1936.
19. Van Wambecke, A. Management Properties of Ferrasols. Rome: Food and Agriculture Organization of the U.N., Soils Bulletin No. 23, 1974.

20. Vilenskii, D. G. (1957) Soil Science. Translated by A. Birron and Z. S. Cole. Jerusalem: Israel Prog. for Sci. Transl., 1960. (Available from the U.S. Department of Commerce, Washington, D.C.)
21. Wills, J. B. Agriculture and Land Use in Ghana. New York: Oxford University Press for Ghana Ministry of Food and Agriculture, 1962.

8

# Animals—Potentials and Limitations for Human Food

N. L. JACOBSON *and* G. N. JACOBSON

THERE is little doubt that sharply reducing the rate of human population growth is essential if world food problems are to be solved and mass starvation avoided. Man will also have to increase the world's food supply—both plant and animal. This chapter evaluates the present and future contributions of animals.

With the current methods of producing animal products in developed nations, animals are fed some feedstuffs, particularly grains, that could be directly consumed by human beings. This is why some people suggest that food shortages could be avoided if everyone would simply consume plant-produced foods directly and eliminate the indirect and less-efficient route of processing these foods through animals. This suggestion has some merit, and the long-time trend in both developed and developing countries will probably be toward reducing animal use of feedstuffs that are directly usable by people. In the more heavily populated areas of the world, human needs will necessitate this change. In other countries people will realize that animal products can be produced using less grain and more forage. The latter adaptation will be hastened by economic and humanitarian considerations.

Animals do not always compete with people for food and therefore can contribute effectively to the human food supply. About 70 percent of the world's land area is too wet, too dry, too mountainous, too cold, or otherwise unsuitable for food crop production. Only about 10 percent is tilled and much of the remaining 20 percent is best suited to growing the high-cellulose plants common to range and pasture areas. Only herbivorous animals, mainly ruminants such as cattle, buffalo, sheep, goats, and deer, can presently convert these plants, that would otherwise be wasted, into useful food. (Even if man should develop a laboratory method of converting these crops, the costs and energy demands would be prohibitive.)

NORMAN L. JACOBSON, Distinguished Professor, Animal Nutrition, Animal Science Department, and Associate Dean, Graduate College, Iowa State University, is a teacher and researcher with experience in several foreign countries.

GERTRUDE N. JACOBSON is Assistant Professor, Iowa State University Library.

We must not ignore animals' many nonfood contributions to the welfare of human beings. Animals are used for draft purposes; they supply products, such as leather and wool and are the source of many pharmaceuticals (e.g., hormones and enzymes) essential to human health. Furthermore, grazing animals return fertilizer (as feces and urine) to the soil; and the excreta from animals raised in confinement can be returned to the soil to improve fertility or used to fertilize fish ponds to improve their productivity. In some countries feces are used for fuel, although the original feedstuffs would have more fuel value than the resulting feces.

Animal agriculture, where suited, can provide farm employment and a source of income throughout the year. Crop farming in the plains areas of North America and in the semiarid regions of the developing world provides employment only a few months of the year. Properly managed, range and pasture animal agriculture also provides an effective means of soil conservation—significantly better than crop farming as it is presently practiced in most of the world.

Animals and animal products certainly have a place in the world today, as they have had throughout history. They will no doubt continue to have a place in the future, but that place will change.

DOMESTIC ANIMAL POPULATIONS. In many developing countries, numbers and classes of livestock are not closely related to their contribution to the human food supply. India, for example, has about a quarter of a billion cattle and water buffalo (almost twice as many as the United States), but they contribute little meat and animal products to its food supply or to that of other countries. The same situation exists among the nomadic tribes of Africa where the farmer's wealth is measured by the size of his herds. In most of the developing world the rate of growth of animals and yield of animal products are very low because of inferior genetic stock, overpopulation in relation to feed supply, marginal weather conditions, diseases, parasites, and a low level of management. While these animals are frequently well adapted to local conditions, the conversion and potential conversion to edible products are very low by developed countries' standards. Still, the number of animals in the world is impressive, their contribution to the world food supply is substantial, and they do constitute a significant food reserve.

The total numbers of animals and recent trends are shown in Table 8.1. These numbers do not represent the total number of animals available for consumption since a large reserve of animals is needed for breeding purposes. A markedly increased rate of slaughter could temporarily increase the supply of meat, but this would decrease livestock numbers and rather soon reduce the supply of meat. The rate of growth and production (milk, eggs, etc.) affects total output from an animal population, as will be shown later.

TABLE 8.1. World livestock numbers.

| | 1961–65 average | 1972 | 1973 | 1974 | 1974/ 1961–65 average |
|---|---|---|---|---|---|
| | | *(million head)* | | | % |
| Cattle and buffaloes | 1,106 | 1,257 | 1,279 | 1,309 | 118 |
| Sheep | 1,006 | 1,043 | 1,020 | 1,032 | 103 |
| Goats | 380 | 392 | 395 | 398 | 105 |
| Camels | 12 | 14 | 14 | 13 | 108 |
| Horses, mules, and asses | 123 | 121 | 120 | 121 | 98 |
| Pigs | 530 | 646 | 655 | 671 | 127 |
| Chickens | 4,272 | 5,596 | 5,722 | 5,901 | 138 |
| Ducks | 92 | 134 | 139 | 141 | 153 |
| Turkeys | 73 | 78 | 76 | 81 | 111 |

Adapted from FAO Production Yearbook, 1974 (4).

The world distribution of cattle (excluding water buffaloes) and pigs and recent changes in numbers are shown in Tables 8.2 and 8.3, respectively. The average percentage increase has been slightly greater in developed countries than in developing countries. Unfortunately, human populations, and therefore food needs, are increasing much more rapidly in the developing countries than in developed countries.

## FOOD PRODUCTION BY ANIMALS

Gross Efficiency of Domestic Species. During the past quarter century, efficiency of animal production has increased substantially, particularly in the developed countries. This has been largely the result of better balanced and more adequate diets, improved management, and

TABLE 8.2. Cattle numbers.

| Area | 1961–65 | 1972 | 1973 | 1974 |
|---|---|---|---|---|
| | | *(million head)* | | |
| World | 992 | 1,131 | 1,151 | 1,179 |
| Africa | 132 | 153 | 147 | 148 |
| North and Central America | | | | |
| Canada and U.S. | 115 | 130 | 134 | 141 |
| Others | 37 | 46 | 48 | 49 |
| South America | 150 | 190 | 159 | 207 |
| Asia | 332 | 347 | 351 | 353 |
| Europe | 117 | 125 | 130 | 134 |
| U.S.S.R. | 83 | 102 | 104 | 106 |
| Oceania | 25 | 37 | 39 | 41 |
| Developed countries | 246 | 275 | 285 | 297 |
| Developing countries | 570 | 656 | 663 | 675 |
| Centrally planned countries[a] | 175 | 200 | 203 | 206 |

Adapted from FAO Production Yearbook, 1974 (4).

[a]Includes China, Democratic People's Republic of Korea, Mongolia, Democratic Republic of Vietnam, Albania, Bulgaria, Czechoslovakia, German Democratic Republic, Hungary, Poland, Romania, and the U.S.S.R.

TABLE 8.3. Pig numbers.

| Area | 1961–65 | 1972 | 1973 | 1974 |
|---|---|---|---|---|
| | | *(million head)* | | |
| World | 530 | 646 | 655 | 671 |
| Africa | 6 | 7 | 7 | 7 |
| North and Central America | | | | |
| Canada and U.S. | 61 | 70 | 66 | 68 |
| Others | 15 | 16 | 21 | 21 |
| South America | 39 | 47 | 49 | 50 |
| Asia | 234 | 281 | 290 | 295 |
| Europe | 114 | 145 | 151 | 155 |
| U.S.S.R. | 58 | 71 | 67 | 70 |
| Oceania | 4 | 5 | 5 | 4 |
| Developed countries | 141 | 175 | 174 | 177 |
| Developing countries | 89 | 109 | 114 | 117 |
| Centrally planned countries[a] | 301 | 362 | 366 | 377 |

Adapted from FAO Production Yearbook, 1974 (4).

[a]Includes China, Democratic People's Republic of Korea, Mongolia, Democratic Republic of Vietnam, Albania, Bulgaria, Czechoslovakia, German Democratic Republic, Hungary, Poland, Romania, and the U.S.S.R.

more effective disease control. The result has been faster growth rates and high levels of production of meat, milk, and eggs per animal unit. Thus, proportionally less feed is needed for maintenance and more can be used for production of desired products. Some further increases, although perhaps less dramatic, can be expected. More efficient reproduction also is likely; e.g., twinning vs. single births in beef cattle; larger litters in pigs; larger lamb crops by using breeds that have a greater incidence of multiple births; and, perhaps most importantly, markedly reduced death losses in the young. Certainly, more attention to disease and parasite control will have beneficial effects.

With the large numbers of domesticated animals (exclusive of poultry, dogs, and cats) almost equal to the human population, a substantial contribution to the human food supply should be expected, and this is the case. As producers of human food from a unit of tillable land, animals are relatively inefficient. More protein and energy can be produced from a given unit of land by growing plants than by raising animals, but plant protein is not as high in quality as animal protein (see Chapter 2).

A high-producing dairy cow will return about one-third of feed protein as milk protein and may convert more than one-third of feed energy to food energy in milk. The milk also contains necessary vitamins, some of which were not present in the original feed. As converters of protein, poultry (broilers, turkeys, eggs) are quite similar in efficiency to the milking cow. Beef animals and sheep are much less efficient and pigs are intermediate when considering feed and food grains. Beef animals and sheep, however, can and do convert high cellulose feeds that have no food value to people into both energy and protein that are useful as human food.

As producers of human food on *nontillable* land (ranges, lightly wooded areas, and rough pasture land), the ruminants especially do not compete with people for food grains and therefore must be considered efficient converters of nonfood vegetation. Land in dry regions, such as the range land in the western United States, is best suited to beef and sheep production. The lush pastures found in parts of northern Europe, Switzerland, and Oceania provide adequate feed even for high-producing dairy animals.

Within reasonable limits, the faster the rate of growth of an animal or the higher the level of output of a product, the greater is the efficiency. This is because the maintenance requirement (feed needed for maintaining body functions) is relatively constant regardless of the level of outputs, such as increasing body weight or milk or egg production. Consequently, a high-producing dairy cow will convert a larger fraction of her feed nutrients into milk than a lower-producing animal. For example, a dairy cow fed only enough for body maintenance will produce no net product. She will either produce no milk or will produce a small amount at the expense of body tissue. On the other hand, if the cow is fed at twice the maintenance requirement, she will use half of the energy for milk production and/or body weight gain. If she weighs 650 kg (1430 lbs) and does not gain or lose weight, she will have enough extra energy to produce about 15 kg (33 lbs) of milk. At feeding levels of three and four times maintenance, the comparable milk producing potential will be 30 and 45 kg, respectively.

The high-producing dairy cow is relatively efficient compared with most meat-producing animals. For example, a holstein cow producing 45 kg (100 lbs) of milk per day will, in about 20 days, produce protein in her milk equivalent in quantity to that in the edible cuts of a 545 kg (1200 lbs) steer. At this level of milk production, the cow is producing an exceedingly large amount of nutrients, about 1½ kg of protein per day plus 2¼ kg lactose (milk sugar), over 1½ kg fat, and ⅓ kg minerals, or a total of nearly 6 kg (over 13 lbs) of milk nutrients daily. But a cow producing at this level would require, under present feeding systems, a relatively high proportion of grain in her diet.

The increasing efficiency in dairy cows has been dramatically shown in the United States. In the past 30 years, the number of dairy cows has been reduced by more than 50 percent while milk production has remained essentially the same. Of course, the present higher-producing cows require more feed per animal so the total feed used for dairy animals has not declined as rapidly as cow numbers. Further modest increases in livestock and poultry efficiency can be anticipated under ideal conditions, but future increases are likely to be less spectacular than those in the past quarter century.

In countries where growth and production rates are very low, the efficiencies and the annual production of edible food per animal unit would be correspondingly low. However, improvements have been made in recent years and further progress can be expected.

TABLE 8.4. Population—human beings, cattle, pigs.

| Area | Population increase, 1963 to 1974 | | |
|---|---|---|---|
| | Human beings | Cattle | Pigs |
| | | *(percent)* | |
| World | 24 | 19 | 27 |
| Africa | 33 | 12 | 17 |
| North and Central America | | | |
| Canada and U.S. | 12 | 23 | 11 |
| Others | 36 | 32 | 40 |
| South America | 35 | 38 | 28 |
| Asia | 27 | 6 | 26 |
| Europe | 8 | 15 | 36 |
| U.S.S.R. | 12 | 28 | 21 |
| Oceania | 24 | 64 | 0 |
| Developed countries | 11 | 21 | 26 |
| Developing countries | 33 | 18 | 31 |
| Centrally planned countries[a] | 18 | 18 | 25 |

Adapted from FAO Production Yearbook, 1974 (4) and Tables 8.2 and 8.3. (1963 data for cattle and pigs are averages of years 1961 to 1965.)

[a]Includes China, Democratic People's Republic of Korea, Mongolia, Democratic Republic of Vietnam, Albania, Bulgaria, Czechoslovakia, German Democratic Republic, Hungary, Poland, Romania, and the U.S.S.R.

Meat Supply. In Table 8.4 the percentage increase in cattle and pig populations over the period 1963 to 1974 is compared with the human population increase during the same period. Because cattle and pigs are the principal contributors to the total world meat supply (nearly ¾ of it), they offer a reasonably good basis for comparison. Table 8.5 presents changes in meat production (based on total carcass weight) from 1963 to 1974. The production of beef-veal and pork has far exceeded

TABLE 8.5. Changes in meat production (based on carcass weight).

| Area | Increase, 1963 to 1974 | | | |
|---|---|---|---|---|
| | Beef and Veal | Mutton and lamb | Pork | Poultry |
| | | *(percent)* | | |
| World | 35 | 6 | 38 | 77 |
| Africa | 46 | 30 | 55 | 63 |
| North and Central America | | | | |
| Canada and U.S. | 31 | —38 | 17 | 47 |
| Others | 36 | 20 | 45 | 129 |
| South America | 21 | — 2 | 31 | 152 |
| Asia | 17 | 26 | 36 | 84 |
| Europe | 38 | 13 | 49 | 112 |
| U.S.S.R. | 84 | 1 | 45 | 87 |
| Oceania | 47 | —10 | 53 | 241 |
| Developed countries | 33 | — 4 | 38 | 73 |
| Developing countries | 23 | 22 | 39 | 105 |
| Centrally planned countries[a] | 60 | 5 | 38 | 75 |

Adapted from FAO Production Yearbook, 1974 (4).

[a]Includes China, Democratic People's Republic of Korea, Mongolia, Democratic Republic of Vietnam, Albania, Bulgaria, Czechoslovakia, German Democratic Republic, Hungary, Poland, Romania, and the U.S.S.R.

TABLE 8.6. MEAT PRODUCTION (BASED ON CARCASS WEIGHT).

| Area | Amount per capita, 1973 | | | |
|---|---|---|---|---|
| | Beef and Veal | Mutton and lamb | Pork | Poultry |
| | *(kilograms)* | | | |
| World | 10.3 | 1.4 | 10.6 | 5.2 |
| Africa | 6.3 | 1.6 | 0.7 | 1.5 |
| North and Central America | | | | |
| Canada and U.S. | 46.0 | 1.0 | 27.5 | 30.5 |
| Others | 10.5 | 0.2 | 5.7 | 2.9 |
| South America | 28.1 | 1.3 | 6.4 | 4.6 |
| Asia | 1.4 | 0.6 | 5.6 | 2.2 |
| Europe | 18.5 | 2.1 | 30.9 | 10.4 |
| U.S.S.R. | 23.7 | 3.7 | 20.3 | 5.2 |
| Oceania | 93.0 | 62.0 | 14.6 | 9.1 |
| Developed countries | 27.4 | 3.3 | 23.7 | 16.3 |
| Developing countries | 5.4 | 0.8 | 1.8 | 1.4 |
| Centrally planned countries[a] | 7.6 | 1.3 | 16.2 | 4.4 |

Adapted from FAO Production Yearbook, 1974 (4).
[a]Includes China, Democratic People's Republic of Korea, Mongolia, Democratic Republic of Vietnam, Albania, Bulgaria, Czechoslovakia, German Democratic Republic, Hungary, Poland, Romania, and the U.S.S.R.

population increases in the developed countries, whereas in developing countries pork has exceeded population increases while beef-veal has been far below population increases. Centrally planned countries have shown a very impressive increase during this period, although the starting point in beef-veal production in relation to human population was quite low.

As shown in Table 8.5, world mutton and lamb production is relatively stable, with very substantial increases in some regions offset by decreases in others. Poultry meat production has increased very greatly in all regions, but the base level (1963) was, in most cases, very low in contrast to beef-veal and pork.

Perhaps a clearer picture of the world's meat supply in a recent year (1973) can be seen in Table 8.6, which summarizes the amount of animal carcass produced per capita in various areas. The gross disparity between the developed and developing countries is obvious. Since there is no major movement of meat between various regions of the world, these data present a rather good picture of the local meat supply. Despite the increases in some developing areas in recent years, the available meat per capita is very low. The four sources of meat tabulated in Table 8.6 represent about 98 percent of the supply tabulated in Table 8.7. Sources other than those shown in Table 8.7, principally nondomestic animals, would contribute no more than a few percentage points to the total.

During the period 1963 to 1974, total world meat production increased by 40 percent while total human population increased 24 percent (4). The greater percentage increase in meat production was due

TABLE 8.7. World meat production for 1973 (based on carcass weights).

| | 1000 metric tons[a] | % |
|---|---|---|
| Cattle | 39,534 | 36.4 |
| Buffaloes | 1,069 | 1.0 |
| Sheep | 5,528 | 5.1 |
| Goats | 1,415 | 1.3 |
| Pigs | 40,642 | 37.4 |
| Horses | 402 | 0.4 |
| Poultry | 20,058 | 18.4 |
| Total | 108,648 | |

Adapted from FAO Production Yearbook, 1974 (4).
[a]A metric ton equals 2200 pounds or 1000 kilograms.

entirely to large increases in the developed and centrally planned countries, however, because changes in meat production and in human population were the same (33 percent) in the developing countries.

World egg production increased 40 percent from 1963 to 1974, with a per capita production of 5.8 kg (13 lbs) in 1974. As pointed out by Borgstrom (2), the temperate regions offer the best protection against poultry diseases; consequently, a large proportion of the eggs are produced (and consumed) in those regions. About three-fifths of the world's eggs are consumed by one-fourth of the world's people (living in North America, Europe, and the U.S.S.R.).

World milk production (Table 8.8) over the period 1963 to 1974 increased modestly (19 percent) but failed to keep pace with human population growth (24 percent). The production per capita is relatively high in the developed countries, very low in the developing countries,

TABLE 8.8. Cow milk production.

| Area | Increase, 1963–1974 | Production per capita, 1973 |
|---|---|---|
| | *(percent)* | *(kilograms[a])* |
| World | 19 | 99 |
| Africa | 29 | 26 |
| North and Central America | | |
| Canada and U.S. | —8 | 258 |
| Others | 48 | 59 |
| South America | 38 | 95 |
| Asia | 23 | 11 |
| Europe | 19 | 334 |
| U.S.S.R. | 44 | 352 |
| Oceania | 1 | 642 |
| Developed countries | 7 | 271 |
| Developing countries | 17 | 26 |
| Centrally planned countries[b] | 41 | 106 |

Adapted from FAO Production Yearbook, 1974 (4).
[a]A kilogram equals 22 pounds.
[b]Includes China, Democratic People's Republic of Korea, Mongolia, Democratic Republic of Vietnam, Albania, Bulgaria, Czechoslovakia, German Democratic Republic, Hungary, Poland, Romania, and the U.S.S.R.

and intermediate in the centrally planned countries. The low level in developing countries is due to a number of factors; e.g., breast feeding of babies, very low consumption of milk by older children and adults due to custom, a high incidence of lactose intolerance (see also Chapter 2), inefficient production methods, and unavailability in much of the tropics. Spectacular increases in production rate per cow have been achieved in many areas of the world, and further increases are not only possible but probable. Nevertheless, the many constraints on consumption and production will likely prevent any spectacular increase in total world milk production in the years ahead.

Furthermore, even though there appears to be a significant increased demand for animal products in many countries, the world supply on a per capita basis will undoubtedly decline in the near future.

PEOPLE VS. ANIMALS: FOOD-FEED COMPETITION CONSIDERATIONS. The difference between what is considered food for humans and feed for animals is quite arbitrary and varies widely among different cultures. Maize (corn) is generally accepted and is used as a staple human food in Latin America, but is neither accepted nor widely used as food in Africa and Asia. Wheat products are generally accepted in most countries as a human food and can also be used as a livestock feed. Most cereal grains can be used as either human food when processed or as animal feed without processing.

The unique stomach of the ruminant animal (e.g., cattle, buffalo, sheep, goats, deer, antelope, etc.) gives it the ability to digest cellulose (a principal component of grasses and other forages) and to convert nonprotein nitrogen to meat and animal products that human beings can digest. The nonruminant herbivores, including horses, rabbits, and many rodents, can also digest cellulose, but less efficiently than the ruminants. The herbivores, ruminant and nonruminant, can use plant materials with little or no direct food value to people, and therefore do not have to consume food that can be used by humans. These animals can then become a food source for humans, establishing a complementary relationship. Grains and proteins, however, are fed to animals primarily to increase the efficiency of animals, including poultry, and to provide the animal products people in developed nations want to eat. This competitive system is likely to continue as long as people have the resources to produce or to purchase such products.

In full recognition that the present system may require modification, steps are already being taken to adjust to the future. By judicious use of forages on the world's marginal and nonarable land plus appropriate supplementation with by-product feeds and nonprotein nitrogen (e.g., urea), the animal industry can make contributions to the food needs of the world's people. (Energy costs of producing nonprotein nitrogen, however, are relatively high.)

If ruminants are to continue to contribute significantly to the world's food supply, they must adapt to increasingly greater amounts of forage and lesser amounts of grains. Even now, forages constitute a major part of the diet. It has been estimated that in the United States forages provide approximately 63 percent of the feed units consumed by dairy cattle, 73 percent of those of beef cattle, and 89 percent of those of sheep and goats (7). On the other hand, the U.S. figures are much lower for nonruminants, being 14 percent for pigs and 3 percent for chickens (exclusive of broilers). In developing countries, food and feed grains constitute a minimal part of the animal diet, especially of ruminants. Cattle, sheep, and goats of the nomadic tribes of Africa, the range and pasture areas of North and South America and Oceania, and the cattle of India usually live entirely on forages.

Some countries, such as North and South America and parts of Africa, have large quantities of unused forages available for ruminant use. For example, an estimated 40 percent of the corn crop in the United States is unused (8). Since this unused portion is largely high-cellulose material, such as stalks, leaves, and cobs, the opportunity of greater use of the products in ruminant feeding is considerable. There also is the possibility of producing much greater quantities of forages on the land not suited to producing foods directly consumable by people. Recent studies have shown that it is possible to use animal wastes (excreta) as feeds for livestock, particularly ruminants. Other research has demonstrated that the food value of some fibrous materials, including wood, can be increased by certain physical and chemical treatments.

Nonruminants, as has been emphasized earlier, are the most direct competitors with people for food. In the years ahead, production methods and the relative proportions of the various types of animals may have to be adjusted to reduce this competition. Even in some heavily populated areas, however, nonruminants are reared in large numbers. For example, an estimated 250 to 260 million pigs are produced in China (6), which is about four times the pig production in the United States. If pigs in China were raised as they are in the United States, there would be very severe competition for human food. But in China many pigs are part of a household enterprise where they are fed wastes, such as "vegetable refuse, ground and fermented rice hulls, corn husks, sweet potato and soybean vines, water hyacinths, and so forth" (6). The amount of grain available for livestock is very limited in China. In addition to meat, the animals provide valuable fertilizer.

## OTHER ANIMAL CONSIDERATIONS

TERRESTRIAL. Attention so far has been directed principally to the domesticated food producing animals of the world. But nondomesticated animals can also contribute to human food supply. This fact was considered in depth at the Third World Conference on Animal Production held in Melbourne, Australia, in 1973 (5). Included were such animals as the kangaroo, gazelle, camel, impala, eland, capybara, and many others. The capybara of South America is particularly interesting because it is the largest living rodent with a mature weight of 40 to 60 kg (100+ lbs), reaches sexual maturity in 1 to 2 years, and produces between 1 and 2 litters of 4 to 6 offspring per year under natural conditions. It eats forage along rivers and in swamps where competition with other animals for food is not great. Nevertheless, there are many problems associated with the development of wild animals as major sources of food (e.g., disease and pest control, management to assure a reasonably dependable food supply, and competition with other species). It is unlikely that wild species will be developed into major sources of a dependable supply of food for people. To be sure, the contribution of wild species may be increased and certainly their potential should not be ignored, but the limitations must also be recognized.

The eating of insects (entomophagy) and insect products by humans has been practiced throughout history, especially in emergency situations. Insects are also considered as delicacies by many. Honey contributed by bees is a widely accepted food. Many forms of insects are consumed today (e.g., insect eggs and larvae, grasshoppers, moths, ants, termites, beetles) in a variety of ways (raw, salted, fried, roasted, etc.). It appears, too, that many insects are quite nutritious, with a high level of protein and fat. It is difficult, however, to conceive of insects as contributing significantly to the total supply of food for the peoples of the world. Foods for emergencies, yes; delicacies, yes; but certainly not ranking alongside major grains, oil seeds, and animal products. Although not major sources, frogs, turtles, lizards, snakes, reptiles, and snails are also a part of the world food supply.

AQUATIC. The oceans and fresh waters of the world supply only a small percentage of world caloric needs, but because of the high protein content of fish and other aquatic animals, they supply almost 20 percent of the animal protein (2). The increased fish catch in recent years (from 22 million metric tons [24.2 million tons] in 1950 to 70 million in 1970) gave hope that the waters of the world might play a major role in providing for the rapidly increasing population. Unfortunately, such optimistic projections may not be realistic. The yearly average catch from 1971 to 1974 was less than in 1970 (4). This has been attributed, at least in part, to overfishing (3). Whether more specific and better managed fish farming in the future can reestablish the upward trend and sustain it over an extended period is a matter of conjecture. It has been shown that phenomenal increases in rate of gain of freshwater fish can be attained by proper cultural procedures. As such methods are expanded, they could greatly increase aquatic food supplies, but much development is still necessary.

As with the world grain supply, not all aquatic catches are used directly by humans. About 40 percent of the total is used for animal feed (2), but not all this could be converted directly to human use. (See also Chapter 3.)

PETS. From the standpoint of competitive use of foods, recognition must be given to the requirements of pets. An estimated 100 million cats and dogs in the United States alone (8), constitute a very substantial demand for food. Although less competitive with humans, the pleasure horse, estimated by Wittwer (8) to be at least 8 million in the U.S., represents a demand that is indeed competitive with meat- and milk-producing animals. In some areas of the world the horse is raised as a source of meat for humans, but the reference here is to those horses used largely for pleasure riding that do not contribute significantly either to draft power or to human food.

NONFOOD CONTRIBUTIONS OF ANIMALS. Although animals are usually viewed in context of their contribution to the human food supply, they have other important functions. In many parts of the world, as was true in the United States until recently, they are a major source of draft power. And this situation is likely to continue long into the future, not only because of agricultural production methods, but also because of the increasing cost of the mechanized alternative with its dependency on fossil fuel. Using animals for draft power reduces the dependency on fossil fuel. However, there is still another way in which domestic animals contribute to a reduction in fossil fuel needs. Harvesting of forages, particularly pasture and range, by animals requires a very low fuel input as compared with the conventional methods of crop production, harvesting, processing, and storage.

Leather and wool are also major contributions to human welfare by the animal population. To be sure, there are substitutes (which require high energy for production), but the demand for leather and wool products still is very substantial.

Another often overlooked contribution of animals is pharmaceuticals, such as hormone and enzyme preparations. For example, over 1 million of the diabetics in the United States alone require insulin that, at present, is available only from the pancreas glands of domestic animals. These glands are recovered from about two-thirds of the cattle and swine slaughtered.

In the past, the excreta of domestic animals represented a valuable source of fertilizer in the United States. It still is a most important fertilizer, as well as a source of fuel, in most countries of the world today. In the future, excreta may once again become an important source of fertilizer in the United States and perhaps a source of fuel as well.

CONSTRAINTS ON USING ANIMALS. Numerous religious, social, and cultural constraints limit the use of all or some types of animals for food. Some groups and individuals for various reasons are largely vegetarians. The people of India use little beef; Jews and Arabs avoid pork; and Americans have an aversion to horse meat, dog meat, insects, and many other items that are valued in certain parts of the world. In some instances, these habits have resulted from a desire to avoid products that might contain parasites or other harmful contaminants. In other instances, the prejudices probably have a less definitive and less sound basis. The customs and habits of people are very significant. Those accustomed to eating rice do not readily become corn eaters and vice versa. But the situation may be more complex. If, for example, the rice eaters are unable to grow corn locally, little would be gained by teaching them to prepare (and like) corn-based foods. They would have access to corn only if it were imported.

Many of the developed countries can still afford to consume a diet rich in animal products because they have an abundance of food for those animals or because they are sufficiently affluent to be able to purchase the animal products or the feeds for locally grown livestock. Most of the developing countries have neither the abundance of animal feed nor the affluence to purchase feeds or animal products. In these countries, most foods usable by people must be consumed by them because the inefficiency of processing them through animals would make the scarcity of food even more critical. About 85 percent of the caloric needs of the earth's human population is provided directly by plant products. Essentially all the remainder is supplied by meat, milk, eggs, fish, and shellfish. But these animal products supply about one-third of the protein consumed by human beings (2). These must be recognized as only rough estimates of nutrients from various sources because exact numbers of animal populations and amounts of animal products are not available. Moreover, nutrients lost and discarded during processing, storage, cooking, and consumption are substantial and can be only crudely estimated.

Animal production in many areas of the world is limited by climatic conditions. Extreme cold increases the cost of housing for animals and limits the grazing season. High temperatures reduce efficiency; this is clearly illustrated by the marked decline of milk production of cows during periods of hot weather. In addition, certain areas of the world have high losses due to disease and parasites. A large section of central Africa (roughly equivalent in area to the United States) is presently unsuited to animal production because of diseases, particularly trypanosomiasis, which is transmitted by the tsetse fly. Food supplies the world over are subject to the vagaries of weather, particularly rainfall. Both plant and animal food supplies have been markedly affected in recent years by severe droughts in many parts of the world.

A uniform, dependable supply of animal products, particularly in developing countries, often is affected by improper grazing management and, as emphasized by Beck (1), the lack of transportation to transfer animals or animal products to market.

LOOK TO THE FUTURE. More than four-fifths of the caloric intake of the earth's human population is provided directly by plant products, principally grains and grain legumes. Nearly all the remainder is supplied by meat, milk, eggs, fish, and shellfish. However, because animal products have a high content of protein, they supply about one-third of the protein used by man. Also, they contribute very significantly to the vitamin and mineral content of the human diet.

Recent trends in animal production suggest that further production increases can be attained in the years ahead. Unfortunately, the increase to date has been less in the developing countries, where the need is greater, than in developed countries.

Although livestock compete with people for some food and processing those foods through animals is a rather inefficient way of providing human food, livestock will likely be reared in large numbers for some time to come. Animals consume many high-fiber crops and crop residues, waste products, and by-products that are not useful to people and convert them into high-quality food. This is particularly evident for the ruminants, which can use both high-cellulose feed and nonprotein nitrogen. Some of the recent spectacular increases in efficiency of livestock production are not likely to be duplicated in the near future, but modest increases can be expected in both developed and developing countries. It must be remembered, however, that even today the per capita supply of certain animal products is declining in some of the developing countries, largely because of rapidly expanding populations. There can be little doubt that our overwhelming concern in feeding hungry people must include population control. Even if all foods usable by human beings were consumed directly without feeding any to animals, the respite provided would be short-lived.

## REFERENCES

1. Beck, Glenn. Africa. In Working Papers: The Role of Animals in the World Food Situation. New York: The Rockefeller Foundation, 1975, pp. 24–27.
2. Borgstrom, Georg. Harvesting the earth. New York: Abelard-Schuman, 1973.
3. Brown, Lester R. The world food prospect. Science 190:1053–1059, 1975.
4. FAO Statistics Division. Production Yearbook. Rome, 1974.
5. Reid, R. L., ed. Proceedings of the III World Conference on Animal Production. Sydney, Australia: Sydney University Press, 1975.
6. Sprague, G. F. Agriculture in China. Science 188:549–555, 1975.

7. Wedin, W. F.; Hodgson, H. J.; and Jacobson, N. L. Utilizing plant and animal resources in producing human food. J. Anim. Sci. 41:667–686, 1975.
8. Wittwer, S. H. Food production: Technology and the resource base. Science 188:579–584, 1975.

## BIBLIOGRAPHY

Bodenheimer, F. S. Insects as Human Food. The Hague, Netherlands: Dr. W. Junk, Publ., 1951.

Borgstrom, Georg. Too Many. Toronto: Collier-MacMillan Canada Ltd. 1969.

Brown, Lester R., and Finsterbusch, Gail W. Man and His Environment. New York: Harper and Row, 1972.

Byerly, T. C. Competition Between Man and Animals. In Working Papers: The Role of Animals in the World Food Situation, pp. 40–45. New York: The Rockefeller Foundation, 1975.

Council for Agricultural Science and Technology. Ruminants as Food Producers. Special publication no. 4. Ames: Iowa State University Department of Agronomy, 1975.

Edmondson, J. E., and Graham, D. M. Animal protein—substitutes and extenders. J. Anim. Sci. 41:698–702, 1975.

Gavan, James D., and Dixon, John A. India: a perspective on the food situation. Science 188:541–555, 1975.

Handler, Philip. Does it matter how many of us there will be? Food Tech. 29:46ff., 1975.

Heady, Earl O.; Faber, Doeke C.; and Sanka, Steven T. A World Food Analysis: Grain Supply and Export Capacity of American Agriculture under various Production and Consumption Alternatives. Ames: Iowa State University Center for Agricultural and Rural Development, 1975.

Jeliffe, Derrick E., and Jeliffe, E. F. Patrice, Human milk, nutrition and the world resource crisis. Science 188:557–561, 1975.

Klopfenstein, Terry J. Unconventional Feeds. In Working Papers: The Role of Animals in the World Food Situation, pp. 56–58. New York: The Rockefeller Foundation, 1975.

Leveille, Gilbert A. Issues in human nutrition and their probable impact on foods of animal origin. J. Anim. Sci. 41:723–731, 1975.

McDowell, R. E. Improvement of Livestock Production. San Francisco: W. H. Freeman and Co., 1972.

McGinnis, James. Potentials of Nonruminants. In Working Papers: The Role of Animals in the World Food Situation, pp. 59–60. New York: The Rockefeller Foundation, 1975.

Nesheim, Malden C. Food Needs in the Future. In Working Papers: The Role of Animals in the World Food Situation, pp. 46–51. New York: The Rockefeller Foundation. 1975.

Oltjen, R. R., and Dinium, D. A. Production practices that alter the composition of foods of animal origin. J. Anim. Sci. 41:703–722, 1975.

Poleman, Thomas T. World food: a perspective. Science 188:510–518, 1975.

Reid, J. Thomas. Comparative Efficiency of Animals. In Working Papers: The Role of Animals in the World Food Situation, pp. 52–55. New York: The Rockefeller Foundation, 1975.

Satterlee, L. D. Improving utilization of animal by-products for human foods—a review. J. Anim. Sci. 41:687–697, 1975.

Spain, James. Alternative Uses of Land. In Working Papers: The Role of Animals in the World Food Situation, pp. 64–65. New York: The Rockefeller Foundation, 1975.

Srivastava, Uma K.; Heady, Earl O.; Rogers, Keith D.; and Mayer, Leo V. Food Aid and International Economic Growth. Ames: Iowa State University Center for Agricultural and Rural Development, 1975.

Steinhart, John S., and Steinhart, Carol E. Energy use in the U.S. food system. Science 184:307–316, 1974.

Steppler, H. A. The Food Resources of Mankind. Montreal: Agri-World Press Limited, 1968.

Turk, Kenneth. Non-Food Uses of Animals. In Working Papers: The Role of Animals in the World Food Situation, pp. 36–39. New York: The Rockefeller Foundation, 1975.

Wortman, Sterling. The World Food Situation: A New Initiative. In Working Papers: The Role of Animals in the World Food Situation. New York: The Rockefeller Foundation, 1975.

JIM HICKS

*Planting groundnuts in Nigeria.*

# 9

# Food Crops—Production, Limitations, and Potentials

D. G. WOOLLEY

FOOD is one common requirement for all humanity. When abundant, it may be wasted, sold, or bartered, but when scarce or absent, it becomes very precious indeed, and its production and distribution become highly emotional issues of international concern (1).

Crops vary from country to country and often within a country, since food producers (farmers) grow crops that produce well in their given climates and for which they receive adequate monetary return. Thus the various diets of the world are basically determined by plant adaptation. Few countries can afford to import their food and ignore the food crops adapted to their climate and soils, even though the only food produced may not be the most desirable.

Surprisingly, the various crops adapted to various areas have usually provided diets with minimum nutritional deficiencies. Conspicious examples are beans and corn (maize) among the American Indians, Chinese cabbage or soybeans with rice in Japan and China, and cassava and beans or coconut in parts of South America and Africa.

A food plant can be any plant that provides nutritive material for growth, work energy, and maintenance of vital body processes. The plant material may be eaten raw or processed and may consist of only parts of or secretions from the stem, leaf, root, flower, or seed and still be classified as a food crop. Some crops serve several functions. For example, corn, cotton, flax, and coconut provide fiber for industrial purposes and oil for human consumption. Crops such as rice, cassava, corn, and potatoes provide industrial starch and food.

Historically the productivity of the world's food crops has been primarily determined by the climate and the soil. But more recently economic factors are having a significant influence. There are fewer subsistence level farms where farmers raise only enough food to live and neither buy nor sell products. Recent inflation and scarcities have made people in the developed nations more aware of cost-price relationships.

DONALD G. WOOLLEY, Professor, Agronomy Department, Iowa State University, has done research on corn grain quality and high-lysine maize in South America and been consultant for the World Bank in Thailand.

TABLE 9.1. Acreage of major food crops, 1974 (3).

| Food Crop or Grouping | World Acreage (1000 Ha) | % of World Acreage |
|---|---|---|
| World Total | 1,472,929 | |
| Cereals—Total | 733,660 | 49.8 |
| Wheat | 224,712 | |
| Rice | 136,791 | |
| Barley | 88,909 | |
| Corn | 116,709 | |
| Rye | 17,482 | |
| Oats | 30,698 | |
| Millet | 68,424 | |
| Sorghum | 42,524 | |
| Roots and Tubers—Total | 56,535 | 3.8 |
| Potatoes | 21,931 | |
| Sweet potatoes | 19,257 | |
| Cassava | 11,878 | |
| Taro | 762 | |
| Yams | | |
| Pulse—Total | 66,287 | 4.5 |
| Dry beans | 27,733 | |
| Dry peas | 9,843 | |
| Chick-peas | 10,473 | |
| Cow peas | 5,071 | |
| Pigeon peas | 2,833 | |
| Lentils | 1,910 | |
| Oil Crops—Total | 130,173 | 8.8 |
| Soybeans | 44,478 | |
| Peanuts | 18,897 | |
| Sunflower | 8,963 | |
| Rapeseed | 9,303 | |
| Sesame | 6,195 | |
| Safflower | 1,039 | |

In recent years people have sought new ways of filling the world's increasing food demands. The reclamation of marginal land such as semideserts and tropical forests, ocean-lake derived foods, and artificial foods have caught the human imagination and given rise to a false sense of food security. But each of these requires great inputs of technology and will be very expensive. The logical and most economical source of future food production is our presently cultivated land. The world's food supply could possibly be doubled if the presently available technology were applied on existing croplands. There are many reasons this has not already been accomplished, but they do not change the ultimate potential of this avenue to sufficiency.

This discussion will begin by examining the world's food crops and then will present some of the current research by scientists that may greatly expand future food production.

WORLD FOOD CROPS. Of the some 80,000 edible plant species in the world, only 50 are actively cultivated, and approximately 90 percent of plant food for people comes from just 12 species. The primary energy source for people is cereal grains, and about half of the world's estimated

1,472 million hectares (3) (one hectare equals 2.47 acres) of cropland is devoted to raising them. Indeed, two grains, wheat and rice, occupy about one-third of the cultivated land (Table 9.1). They also constitute a basic part of the diet (6) for over 90 percent of the world's people. Rice alone is the basic diet component of approximately 60 percent of the earth's inhabitants.

In many regions of the world, animals are not eaten because grains are too scarce to feed to animals or traditions discourage eating meats. People in these areas must depend entirely on plants for the protein necessary for life, which is more difficult than if both plant and animal protein is eaten.

Protein is made up of 22 amino acids, and the human body can synthesize all except 8, which are commonly called the essential amino acids. These essential amino acids must, therefore, be obtained from

TABLE 9.2. NUTRITIONAL CONTENT OF MAJOR PLANT FOODS, FRUITS, VEGETABLES, AND ANIMAL PRODUCTS.

| Product | Calories per 100 g | Protein % | Fat % |
|---|---|---|---|
| Cereal Grains | | | |
| Wheat flour | 350 | 11.7 | 1.5 |
| Rice, milled | 360 | 6.7 | 1.7 |
| Barley, pearled | 346 | 9.0 | 1.4 |
| Corn meal | 360 | 9.3 | 4.0 |
| Rye flour | 341 | 9.0 | 1.8 |
| Oatmeal | 385 | 13.0 | 7.5 |
| Millet | 332 | 6.5 | 1.7 |
| Sorghum | 343 | 10.1 | 3.3 |
| Roots and Tubers | | | |
| Potatoes | 70 | 1.7 | 0.1 |
| Sweet potatoes | 97 | 1.1 | 0.3 |
| Cassava | 109 | 0.9 | 0.2 |
| Pulses | | | |
| Beans, broad | 343 | 23.4 | 2.0 |
| Peas | 346 | 22.5 | 1.8 |
| Chick-peas | 358 | 20.1 | 4.5 |
| Cowpeas | 342 | 23.4 | 1.8 |
| Oil Crops | | | |
| Soybeans | 405 | 37.9 | 18.0 |
| Peanuts, shelled | 546 | 25.6 | 43.3 |
| Other Crops | | | |
| Sugar, refined | 387 | 0 | 0 |
| Banana | 67 | 0.9 | 0.3 |
| Vegetables, fresh | 22 | 1.4 | 0.2 |
| Citrus fruit | 28 | 0.5 | 0.2 |
| Animal Products | | | |
| Beef | 225 | 14.7 | 18.0 |
| Pork | 376 | 9.8 | 37.0 |
| Poultry | 129 | 12.0 | 8.6 |
| Fish | 132 | 18.8 | 5.7 |
| Eggs | 144 | 11.0 | 10.4 |
| Milk, cow's, whole | 65 | 3.5 | 3.5 |
| Butter | 716 | 0.6 | 81.0 |

food. To be well nourished, human beings must consume all 8 in the right quantities. The proportions of essential amino acids found in most animal proteins more nearly match human body requirements than the proportions commonly found in plants. Thus it is considered easier to obtain an adequate diet if some animal protein is included. To get the correct supply of essential amino acids from plants, a variety of plant protein with complementary amino acids should be consumed. (See also Chapter 2.)

In areas that lack meat, pulse crops (edible legume seeds such as peanuts, peas, beans, and soybeans) are important supplements to diets based on grains because they contain large amounts of protein (see Table 9.2). They contain even more protein than animal products even though when eaten alone they do not supply enough of the essential amino acids. Pulses complement the proteins in grains, however, ensuring a near-adequate diet.

Despite the variance in crops grown throughout the world, all food

TABLE 9.3. CHARACTERISTICS OF THE MAJOR FOOD CROPS OF THE WORLD.

| Food Crop | Growth Habit[a] | Growing Season[b] | Moisture | Temperature Type | Photoperiod |
|---|---|---|---|---|---|
| Banana | P | 12 months(m) | High(H) | Warm(W) | Short(S) |
| Barley | A–WA | 90 days(d) | Low(L) | Cool(C) | Long (L) |
| Broad bean | A | 90 d | Moderate(M) | W | L |
| Buckwheat | A | 70 d | L | W | L |
| Cassava | P | 10 m | L | W | Neutral(N) |
| Coconut | P | continuous | H | W | S |
| Corn | A | 5 m | M | W | S |
| Cotton | P(A) | 5–6 m | M | W | N |
| Chick-peas | A | 120 d | M | C | L |
| Cowpea | A | 90 d | M | W | S |
| Dry beans | A | 120 d | M | W | S |
| Dry peas | A | 100 d | M | C | L |
| Lentil | A | 90 d | M | W | L |
| Millet | A | 80 d | L | W | S |
| Peanut | A | 130 d | M | W | S |
| Pineapple | P | 12 m | M | W | S |
| Poppy | A | 90 d | M | W | L |
| Potato | A | 5 m | M | C | L |
| Rape | A | 90 d | L | C | L |
| Rice | A | 130 d | H | W | S |
| Rye | A–WA | 80 d | L | C | L |
| Safflower | A | 100 d | L | W | L |
| Sesame | A | 90 d | M | W | S |
| Sorghum | A | 5 m | L | W | S |
| Soybean | A | 4 m | M | W | S |
| Sugar beet | B | 5 m | M | C | L |
| Sugarcane | P | 12 m | H | W | S |
| Sunflower | A | 5 m | M | W | N |
| Sweet potato | P(A) | 5 m | H | W | S |
| Taro | A | 8 m | H | W | S |
| Wheat | A–WA | 90 d | L | C | L |

[a]WA = Winter annual
P(A) = Perennial grown as annual
[b]For early- to medium-maturing varieties

P = Perennial
A = Annual

production depends on solar energy for the photosynthetic conversion of raw material like water and carbon dioxide into the plant materials, such as grain, tubers, seeds, fruit, stems, and roots, that are primary sources of food. And because of this dependence on sunshine, food production will always remain scattered over the earth to capture the energy where it falls. Each nation has all the essential ingredients of food production it needs, but how well sunshine is supplemented with moisture, warmth, a frost-free growing season, good soils, fertilizers, pest control, and economic incentives, largely determines how well a nation can feed itself. Table 9.3 summarizes certain requirements and characteristics of the world's major food crops.

GRASS PLANTS—THE WORLD'S STAFF OF LIFE. The grass family has fed humanity for centuries. Great civilizations were founded on domesticated grass, in particular cereal grains; for example, India and China on rice, Mesopotamian civilizations on wheat, and the Incas and Aztecs on corn.

The grass family includes the familiar cereals of rice, wheat, sorghum, corn or maize, barley, rye, and oats. Cereal grains produce high yields, are adapted to a wide range of climates, and provide over 50 percent of man's energy. No wonder, then, that three of the world's four major food crops are rice, wheat, and maize. The fourth major crop, sugar cane, is also from the grass family, as are the less-familiar millets. Millets, which include proso, finger, Japanese, foxtail, and pearl, along with sorghum, are the basic food crops in the drier, marginal production areas of Africa and Asia.

The fruit or grain, more commonly called the seed, of the grass plants consists of a pericarp covering a rich layer of minerals and vitamins, called the aleurone (Fig. 9.1). Under this aleurone layer is a rich and relatively large storehouse of starch called the endosperm, which serves as the reserve food supply used by the germinating seed. It also serves as an important source of carbohydrate for people. The embryo or germ of the grass seed is rich in oil and protein.

Besides their role as food, grass plants serve humanity in many other ways. Bamboos provide shelter and furniture, coarse grasses provide thatch for roofs, and turf grasses beautify our yards and protect our land against erosion. Many grasses provide fermented beverages, such as beer from barley, saki from rice, whiskey from corn or rye, and rum from sugar cane.

Because rice and wheat are so important as food crops, their history and production will be considered in some detail.

RICE. Not much is known about the origin of rice, but there is little doubt that it was first cultivated in southeast Asia. It is mentioned in ancient Chinese and Indian writings, and in many Asian languages the word for rice is the same as the word for food or life. There are 24 species of rice (Oryza), but *Oryza sativa* is the only one cultivated widely,

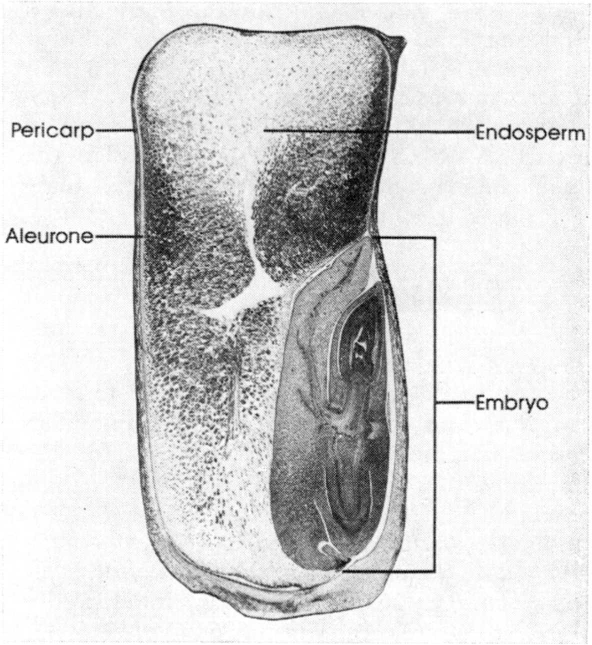


FIG. 9.1. A seed representative of grass plants

and provides virtually all man's rice. Wild rice *(Zizania aquatica)* is a native of and grown only in North America, and is not closely related to true rice. It is harvested from lakes in the north central United States, mostly by Indian tribes whose harvest rights are protected by treaty. Wild relatives of true rice do exist in the tropics and are used in some religious ceremonies, but rarely for food.

Rice is not an aquatic plant although it grows very well under flooded conditions. It can also be grown as other cereal grains, where water for flooding is not available or where the terrain is too irregular for flooding. But upland or dry rice cultivation must have warm temperatures and adequate rainfall to succeed. Even under the best conditions, yields of upland rice are usually about 70 to 75 percent of the lowland or flooded types (Paddy rice).

There are probably several thousand varieties or ecotypes of rice currently grown in the world. These are divided into two groups—the "indica" types, that have long grains and are dry when cooked, meaning they maintain their individual kernel identity, and the "japonica" types, that have short grains and are sticky or mushy when cooked. The japonica types are grown in the northern areas, and while higher in yield than the indica types, they are not grown widely in southeast Asia because of the general preference for a drier rice. The preference of Asiatic and European people for their local varieties and their stubborn refusal to grow or eat other rice has greatly reduced the impact of the new, highly productive rice varieties developed by the International Rice Research Institute in the Philippines. Some of the higher-yielding varieties also have improved protein quality. But adoption has been slow because of the traditional tastes and because most rice farmers lack funds for fertilizer, insecticides, etc., which are necessary to successfully grow the new varieties.

Most rice is grown in paddy fields, and in Asia, for example, the seedbed is prepared for planting with a single furrow plow drawn by a water buffalo. Fertilizer, usually in the form of manure, is then spread and the seedbed is smoothed with a crude type of harrow or a drag made from a tree trunk. These operations are all done with water standing in the field, which destroys the structure of the surface soil and seals the soil so that little water is able to drain through it. The rice is then planted by broadcasting dry or pregerminated seed or by transplanting young seedlings (about six weeks old) from a nursery bed. Transplanting requires more labor but is commonly used because it affords better weed control and increases yields. Weeding, done by hand, is another back-bending activity associated with rice growing. In some regions up to 1000 hours of human labor are required to produce one acre of rice. The water level is kept 6 to 10 inches deep, depending on the height of the plants. The water level never inundates the plants, but it is not allowed to go below 6 inches because weeds are then encouraged.

Harvesting is accomplished with a sickle. The rice is tied in small bundles and left in the field to dry. Threshing is done by beating the plants against a log or having animals walk to and fro over the seed heads. The seed is separated from the chaff by hand winnowing, and then a mortar and pestle are used to remove the hull. The produce is called brown rice, which is the common form of rice for local consumption.

This method of rice culture is common in Asia and Africa and contrasts sharply with the highly mechanized U.S. systems. More than 50 percent of the rice grown in the United States is exported, since the per capita consumption is only about five pounds per year, as compared with southeast Asia where the average consumption exceeds one pound per day. In the United States, the airplane is used to plant, fertilize, and apply herbicides and insecticides to the rice crop, eliminating most of the hand labor. Seedbed preparation and harvesting are completely mechanized.

In processing rice for commerce, the outer (bran) layers of the grain are removed in a process called pearling. The grain is then polished and coated with talc or other substances to seal the grain and improve its storage quality. The final product is appealing to the eye but is much less nutritious than brown rice, since most of the vitamin $B_1$ is lost.

WHEAT. Wheat was one of the first plants cultivated by human beings. Wheat is important today because of its unique facility in bread making.

Wheat has a higher quantity and quality of gluten (a sticky mass of protein) than any other grain. Gluten gives bread dough tensile strength allowing it to stretch (as in rising bread) and retain gas ($CO_2$ produced by the yeast) without breaking and collapsing. The different types of wheat vary in their gluten content and in their bread-making quality.

Before 8000 B.C. wheat was merely one of a number of wild plant types that still abound in the Middle East. Domestication took the form of two separate genetic accidents. First, a wild wheat crossed with a natural goat grass to form a fertile and much plumper hybrid known as emmer. In the language of genetics, the chromosomes of goat grass had combined with a 14-chromosome wild wheat to form a 28-chromosome hybrid. This cross, which is still grown on a limited basis for livestock feed in Asia and the Mediterranean area, spread naturally. Its seeds were enclosed in a husk that could be scattered by the wind. The second genetic accident involved a cross between emmer and another natural goat grass that formed another fertile cross with 42 chromosomes known as bread wheat. This wheat no longer had a husk that carried in the wind, and when the head of the grain was shattered the seeds lay where they fell. Wheat was now completely dependent on people for its propagation.

Another important species, which like emmer has only 28 chromosomes, is durum wheat. It is used to make semolina flour, which is used in making macaroni, spaghetti, and noodles, and thus is often called macaroni wheat.

Wheat migrated to India, to China, and then to Europe before the Christian era and is still an important crop in the temperate areas of these regions, while rice dominates in the warmer, humid areas. The Spaniards brought wheat to the western hemisphere. Today the United States, Canada, and Argentina are among the leading producers of wheat in the world.

There are two general types of wheat, spring wheat (planted in the spring) and winter or fall wheat (planted in the fall). Since it outyields spring wheat, winter wheat is grown wherever the climate will permit. Spring wheat is grown where severe winter weather would destroy winter types, sometimes as far north as the Arctic Circle. Within each of these types are found soft and hard kerneled subtypes. The soft wheats are grown in the humid areas and are more porous and lower in protein than the hard wheats, which are grown in the more arid parts of the world. The soft wheats are lower in gluten and are not used for bread making although they may be blended with hard wheats for this purpose. They are excellent for pastry and other uses where a high tensile strength dough is not required. Hard wheats can be used for bread and pastry flour.

Recently plant breeders in Washington state and in Mexico developed a dwarf form of wheat able to use heavy applications of fertilizers without lodging (falling over). This breakthrough, a cooperative effort of the Rockefeller Foundation and Mexican agronomists, has doubled Mexico's wheat production in less than 20 years. These same dwarf types were quickly adopted in India and other Asiatic countries where yields have also greatly increased. In the western United States, the dwarf wheats, under intense management, have attained yields near 200 bushels per acre. Dr. Norman Borlaug won a Nobel Peace Prize for his role in developing these dwarf wheat types that sparked the "Green Revolution."

In the early 1970s, the first high-yielding wheat hybrid became available, climaxing more than a decade of intensive research. Wheat has minute bisexual flowers designed to self-pollinate. To obtain the wheat hybrid, scientists had to use male sterility because hand pollination of large populations is physically impossible.

Hybrid wheat promises a 25 to 30 percent increase in yield plus a more rapid means of incorporating desirable genetic traits, such as disease resistance or winter hardiness, into commercial size seedlots.

Another recent development is the cross between wheat and rye, which was first accomplished by agronomists in Canada, and is now being worked on at the center in Mexico that developed the dwarf wheats. This cross, Triticale (from the genuses *Triticum* for wheat and *Secale* for rye), incorporates the winter hardiness of rye into wheat. The new grain also has more protein of a better quality than wheat. But since its gluten content is low, it is not a good source of bread flour. Plant breeders are working to improve this, however.

LEGUME PLANTS—THE WORLD'S PROTEIN STOREHOUSE. People began collecting seeds from wild legume plants about the time they were beginning to cultivate the grass species. Not long after the cereals were domesticated, people began to cultivate lentil peas and vetches. As we saw earlier, the legumes are rich protein sources and often ensure an adequate diet for those people, particularly in India, who depend entirely on plant food for their diet. As such, they rank very close to the grasses in their importance as sources of human food.

Fundamentally, however, the legumes may be more important than grasses. Legumes have bacteria *(Rhizobium)* that live in visible swellings, called nodules, on their roots. These bacteria take nitrogen out of the air and make it available to the plants, a process called nitrogen fixation. Thus legumes need less nitrogen from fertilizer than other plants—a definite asset to primitive and developing agricultural systems.

Legume seeds are as important for their oil content as for their protein. For example, peanuts contain 50 percent oil and soybeans about 20 percent. In the industrialized parts of the world, the legumes are often grown for their oil with the protein meal considered as a by-product. This is particularly true of soybeans, which are used as a direct source of food only in the Orient. The protein meal that remains after

TABLE 9.4. MAJOR WORLD FOOD CROPS AND LEADING PRODUCERS, 1974 (3).

| Food Crop | World Production 1000 Metric Tons | Countries (Leading Producers) |
|---|---|---|
| Sugarcane | 665,414 | India, Brazil, Cuba |
| Wheat | 360,231 | U.S.S.R., U.S.A., China[a] |
| Rice | 323,201 | China, India, Indonesia |
| Potatoes | 293,724 | U.S.S.R., Poland, China |
| Maize | 292,990 | U.S.A., China, Brazil |
| Sugar beets | 237,190 | U.S.S.R., France, U.S.A. |
| Barley | 170,858 | U.S.S.R., China, France |
| Sweet potatoes | 134,225 | China, Indonesia, Brazil |
| Cassava | 104,891 | Brazil, Zaire, Nigeria |
| Soybeans | 56,803 | U.S.A., China, Brazil |
| Sorghum | 46,908 | U.S.A., India, Argentina |
| Millet | 46,215 | China, India, U.S.S.R. |
| Bananas | 35,837 | Brazil, India, Ecuador |
| Rye | 32,611 | U.S.S.R., Poland, W. Germany |
| Coconuts | 26,774 | Philippines, Indonesia, India |
| Cottonseed | 25,952 | U.S.S.R., U.S.A., China |
| Yams | 19,137 | Nigeria, Ivory Coast, Ghana |
| Peanuts | 17,590 | India, China, U.S.A. |
| Dry peas (Pisum) | 11,694 | U.S.S.R., China, India |
| Dry beans (Phaseolus) | 11,458 | Brazil, India, China |
| Sunflowers | 11,138 | U.S.S.R., Argentina, Romania |

[a]Includes Mainland China and Taiwan in each reference.

the oil is extracted is used almost exclusively as a protein supplement in animal rations. Soybean flour, however, is used to extend other, more expensive protein foods.

Almost 50 million tons of soybeans are produced each year, mainly in the United States (Table 9.4). Peanuts, chiefly in India, amount to about half as much tonnage. The worldwide production of edible peas and beans equals soybean production. Dried beans come mainly from Latin America, China, and India, while most dried peas come from the U.S.S.R., China, and India. Broad beans are produced mainly in southern Europe, and chick-peas or garbanzos and lentils are important in the Orient and Middle East.

CULTIVATED PEA *(Pisum sativum)*. The cultivated pea *(Pisum sativum)* consists of two main types—the field pea, mostly used as dried peas, and the garden pea, which is eaten fresh either shelled or in the pod. Whole pod peas (sugar peas) are commonly eaten in Asia and are becoming popular in Europe and the United States.

The broad bean, chick-pea, and the cowpea (sometimes called black-eyed peas) are important food beans of Asia and Africa although the cowpea is widely used in the southern United States.

BEANS *(Phaseolus)*. The genus of beans *Phaseolus* provides more edible species than any other genus in the legume family. The Old World members of *Phaseolus* are the mung bean, rice bean, moth bean, the adzuki bean, and the grain or urd bean, which are eaten mainly in

India, China, and Japan. Because their seeds are much smaller than the New World types, they are not grown widely outside of Asia. But most Americans are familiar with the small germinated sprouts of the mung bean (bean sprouts) widely used in Chinese cooking.

Two American types of *Phaseolus,* the scarlet runner bean and the tepary bean, are not grown commercially today but were important in ancient American civilizations. The lima or butter bean *(P. lunatus)* and the common bean *(P. vulgaris)* are, however, grown widely in the western hemisphere. The common bean is known as pinto, kidney, black, great northern, navy, or white, depending on the color of the bean and the locale. The familiar snap and green or wax beans are eaten fresh-in-the-pod. *Phaseolus* beans along with corn and squash were domesticated in Mexico and were the principal foods of the prehistoric civilizations of North and South America.

PEANUT *(Arachis hypogea).* The peanut *(Arachis hypogea),* also called groundnut, pindar, groundpea, and goober, is the most widely grown food legume. The flowers of this unusual plant bloom above ground, but when the seed pod forms, it is pushed into the soil by elongation of the floral stalk (pedicel). The seed matures underground and contains about 50 percent oil and 25 to 30 percent protein. Unlike soybeans the peanut is highly prized for human food the world over. In the United States most peanuts are processed into the American favorite, peanut butter. Peanut oil makes excellent cooking and salad oils and is an important component of margarine as well as numerous industrial products ranging from nylon to cosmetics. The residue left after oil extraction is a valuable livestock feed and in Asia is further processed and used as a human food.

ROOT CROPS—THE WORLD'S STARCHY STAPLES. While the cereal grains are human beings' basic food, some people and civilizations are unable to grow them and have been forced to use other plants, mainly root crops, as the mainstay of their diets. Root crops include the familiar white potatoes, sweet potatoes, and yams, and the less familiar taro and cassava, which are staples of the tropics. Root crops are characterized by a fleshy underground storage organ, often called a root, but sometimes a tuber, a rhizome, a corm, or a bulb. They are high in starch or sugar, low in protein and oil, and more difficult to store and transport than grains and legumes. Thus they tend to be eaten close to where they are produced.

POTATOES *(Solarum tuberosum).* Potatoes *(Solarum tuberosum)* are grown in the temperate parts of Europe, Asia, Russia, and North and South America, often where temperatures are too cool for cereal grains. Grown mainly for human food in the Americas, the potato is grown in Europe and Asia for human and animal consumption and for industrial purposes. The world production of potatoes ranks with the cereal

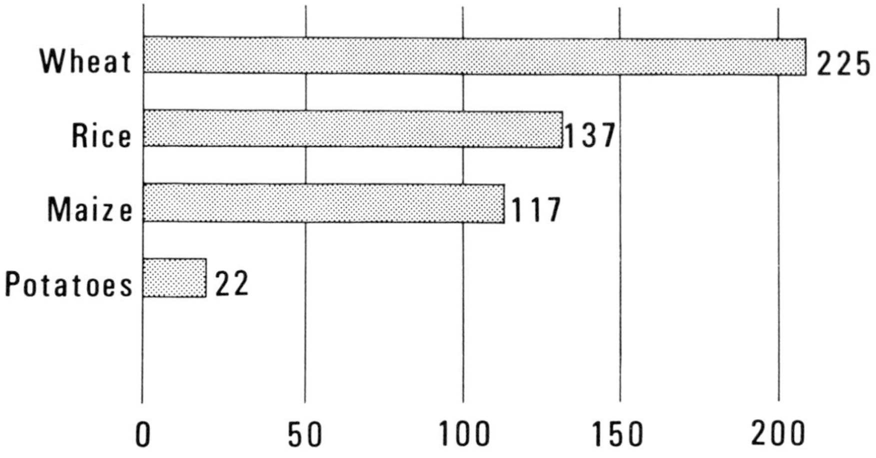


FIG. 9.2. World area planted (million hectares): comparative production area (1974)

grains, as indicated by Table 9.4, even though only one-tenth of the area in wheat is devoted to potatoes (Fig. 9.2). The efficient potato plant produces more than twice the number of calories per hectare obtained from wheat or rice (Fig. 9.3).

CASSAVA *(Manihot esculenta).* Cassava *(Manihot esculenta)* is known in different parts of the tropical world as manioc, mandioca, yuca, sagu, and tapioca, and known to us because of the popular pudding. Cassava is the staple food in many developing nations in the tropics because it can be grown on poor soils with poor management. It is a shrubby

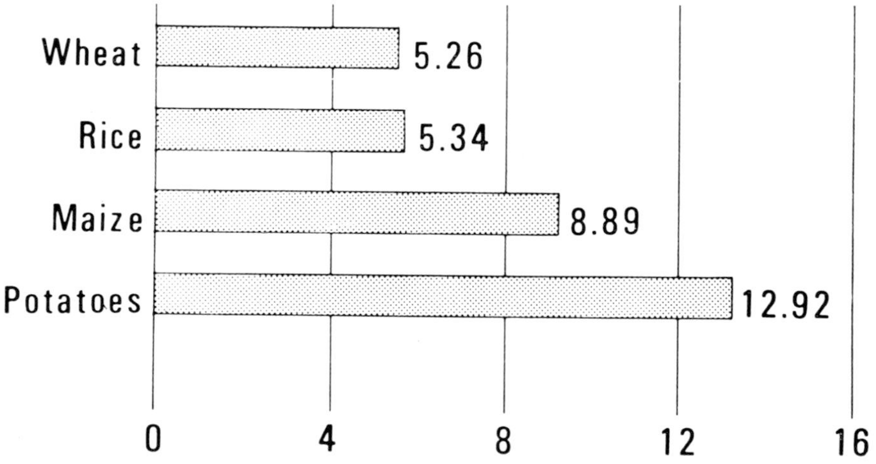


FIG. 9.3. Million calories per hectare: comparative nutritional yield (1974)

perennial that produces swollen roots resembling sweet potatoes that contain 30 percent starch, no oil, and almost no protein (about 1 percent). Young cassava leaves are high in protein (15 to 30 percent) and are used mainly as livestock feed. Recently, however, they have been used for human food in the form of a potherb. Cassava roots may be boiled whole, or dried and shredded into a meal form and mixed with other foods. There are sweet and bitter varieties of cassava depending on how much of the bitter cyanogenetic glucoside (which produces hydrocyanic acid when eaten raw) is present. Sweet cultivars may be eaten directly, but bitter types must be cooked and ground or mashed to rid them of the poison-producing juices.

Tapioca is made from the peeled roots by grating, soaking in water for several days, kneading, straining of the water, drying, and then gentle heating to hydrolize the starch to sugar and form the gel particles while being agitated in a large pan over a slow fire. Indonesia is the main producer of tapioca. Cassava starch is used in the manufacture of adhesives and in sizing paper and textiles.

Perennials. Even though most of our food crops are annuals, meaning the plant dies after producing seed, several perennials are important sources of food in tropical countries, e.g., banana, cassava, coconut, sugarcane, yam, and sweet potato. Perennial crops have many advantages in tropical agriculture. First, since they are planted or established much less frequently than annual crops, the extreme soil erosion common when soils are plowed and prepared for planting in such high rainfall areas is reduced. Second, since perennials are not planted every year, they are not subjected annually to the severe heat during the critical planting and establishment period. Third, of the perennial food crops just mentioned, only sorghum is planted from seed. Indeed, many do not produce seed. Bananas are established by transplanting rhizomes; for cassava and sugarcane stem pieces are used; coconut uses the fruit; and the sweet potato is planted initially with root pieces. This system of vegetative propagation increases the success of plant establishment under adverse conditions such as flooding, heat, cold, poor seedbed preparation, and insect and disease infestations. Finally, storing the plant parts of perennials, such as stems, tuber, roots, and fruit, is relatively simpler and safer than storing grain in such humid climates. In many cases the fruits, roots, and tubers may be stored on a tree, in open structures, or in the ground away from insects, rodents, and diseases while being used or until ready for market.

Rice is the notable exception to this advantage for perennials in the tropics. Rice is an annual that is required daily in the diet of some 2.5 billion people. It is planted from seed and in addition the economic plant part is the seed, which presents some storage problems.

But three factors make storing rice in the tropics more successful than would be possible with most other grain crops. First, it is easily marketed, and excess grain or grain not fit for human consumption can be sold for starch or fermentation processing. Second, it is the number one food preference for most inhabitants of the tropics, so extra care in providing better storage is justified. And, finally, the rice grain when harvested is encased in a very tight and durable hull that protects it from many insects and diseases. Also, only a few weeks' food requirement is hulled and prepared for cooking at one time, greatly reducing the storage losses.

APPLICATIONS OF TECHNOLOGY. Today people are directing changes in all domesticated plants in an effort to increase their productivity and improve the human diet. A plant's heredity is controlled by genes, which are ordinarily very stable and copy themselves exactly from generation to generation. Mutations (spontaneous changes) do occur, however, and they may be passed on to the future generations. Sexual reproduction permits genes to be combined in new and various ways. Mutations and recombinations provide for variations in plant life, which are the important raw materials for the evolution and improvement of a species.

The development of (1) high lysine (an essential amino acid) corn varieties with greatly increased nutritional value, (2) dwarf wheats and rices that can respond to yield-increasing amounts of fertilizers without lodging, and (3) hybrid wheat and high protein cereal grains are three recent major accomplishments of plant breeders.

It is too early to determine the full impact of these "breakthroughs" since there are many underlying sociopolitical factors that affect their adoption and ultimate success in improving the human diet. The major obstacle preventing adoption of these new plant types is the reluctance of most peoples to leave their traditional forms and varieties of food plants. Also, many of the newly developed varieties—such as dwarf wheat and rice—require irrigation, large amounts of fertilizers, and good management for high yields. The cost, therefore, is beyond the means of most subsistence farmers, making government subsidies necessary. Where governments have subsidized new wheat varieties, the results have been truly amazing in favorable seasons. Pakistan became temporarily self-sufficient in wheat production. Mexico went from a major importer to an exporter of wheat, and India has greatly increased its wheat production. The new rice varieties have had less impact because people are more reluctant to eat rice with different textures and taste qualities than their traditional varieties and because cost of production is higher. Plant breeders are constantly working on improving food crops, but they need the assistance of governments, credit institutions, farm extension specialists, and the support of the news media if the fruits of their labors are to be translated into meaningful advances in food production.

Plant breeders face many obstacles in producing a new variety or hybrid. It takes 12 generations to produce a new variety, and where only one crop can be grown per year, this is 12 years. As many as 18 genera-

TABLE 9.5. PRODUCTION OF HYBRID CORN.

| Procedure | Description | Time Required (years) |
|---|---|---|
| Inbreeding | Self-pollination of plants by hand | 3–6 |
| Topcrossing | Crossing inbreds with a synthetic variety | 1 |
| Testing the topcrosses | Yield trials of seed produced in topcross | 1 |
| Single crossing | Crossing inbreds in all combinations | 1 |
| Testing the single crosses | Yield trials of seed produced in single crosses | 1 |
| Adaptability trials | Determining the specific areas of adaptation | 2–3 |
| Double cross | Combining single crosses in all combinations | 1 |
| Testing the double cross | Yield trials of seed produced in double cross | 1 |
| Adaptability trials | Determining the specific areas of adaptation | 2–3 |

tions may be required for double-cross hybrids (see Table 9.5), and pure-line varieties (a self-pollinated variety with none of the undersirable traits of the original parents) take up to 12 generations. Pure-line food plants include beans, peas, wheat (except hybrid wheat), rice, barley, and millets. Once the seed for a new pure-line crop is obtained, it can be grown, harvested, and that seed replanted for the next crop. A farmer need not buy new seed each year. Hybrid seed, however, must be purchased each year because hybrids lose their hybrid vigor after the first year and seed comes only from the crossing of two relatively unrelated parents. Hybrid seed is relatively expensive, and thus not rapidly adopted in poor, developing countries.

Along with high yields, the new varieties plant breeders are developing bring potential genetic dangers for the future. The naturally occuring plant varieties are numerous and varied. No single disease can destroy all varieties. But as local varieties give way to a limited number of high-yielding varieties, this will no longer be true. For example, all the new wheat varieties carry the same kind of rust (a fungus disease) resistance. If a new rust were to suddenly appear, it could devastate the wheat crop. This would be serious in a developed country, such as the United States, but it would be disastrous in a developing country. As the old low-yielding varieties disappear, plant breeders are losing important sources of genes that have protected crops from disease and insects over the decades. In this lies the dilemma of the future. Farmers cannot afford to keep using old low-yielding varieties and plant breeders cannot afford to lose these diverse sources of genes.

BASIC BIOLOGICAL POTENTIALS. Researchers throughout the world are working on understanding and improving basic biological processes. Significant breakthroughs could mean increased food production and improved nutrition.

Some of the areas being studied are:

1. Improving the efficiency of the photosynthetic process.
2. Improving the nitrogen fixation process.
3. Improving protein quality without sacrificing yield—for example, more use of leaf-protein for human food. (See Chapter 11 for a discussion of this.)
4. Improving disease resistance in plants.
5. Growing plant cells in a special nutrient medium (culturing) as a way of expanding sources of genes.
6. Using more undomesticated plants, some of which produce more total dry matter than our current food plants.
7. Producing single cell protein. (See Chapter 11 for a discussion on this.)

Since the first two items listed offer great potential for meeting the world's food needs in the foreseeable future, we will examine them further.

Improving the Efficiency of Plants. If researchers could improve the efficiency of photosynthesis, they could greatly expand the world's food supply. Photosynthesis, sometimes called carbon fixation, is a process by which green plants use light energy to convert carbon dioxide and water into the carbon compounds that are the source of food for all other life. The carbon compounds in plant leaves account for over 90 percent of the dry weight of plants. Therefore, the efficiency of this process is closely correlated with crop yields.

Some plants are naturally more efficient than others. The most efficient plants include sorghum, corn, and sugarcane, and are called $C_4$ species because the first product the plant makes is a compound with 4 carbon atoms. Most other plants are less efficient and are called $C_3$ species because their first product is a 3-carbon compound.

This naturally occurring efficiency is reflected in recent yields of soybeans and corn. Over the past 20 years corn yields have tripled while soybean yields have increased only 20 percent. Soybeans' lower efficiency in converting carbon dioxide to carbon compounds acts as a barrier beyond which yields cannot be increased without altering the basic biological process.

Scientists think that plants such as soybeans are less efficient because they recycle their carbon through respiration faster than other more efficient species. This is called photorespiration. Therefore, large amounts of carbon are wasted that could be used to build leaves, roots, and grain. If researchers could use genetic or chemical methods to decrease the amount of recycled carbon, they could increase the potential yield of many of the world's food crops.

TABLE 9.6. The harvest index of some crop species.

| Crop | Harvest Index (%) | |
|---|---|---|
| | Average | Range of Varieties |
| Maize | | |
| Open pollinated | 24 | |
| Hybrids | 42 | 38–47 |
| Sorghum | 41 | |
| Rice | 51 | 43–57 |
| Oats | 42 | |
| Barley | 48 | 35–52 |
| Wheat | 35 | 23–46 |
| Rye | 28 | 27–29 |
| Soybean | 32 | 29–36 |
| Dry bean | 59 | 53–67 |

Another way of making plants more efficient would be to increase the percentage of the above-ground dry weight of a plant that is useful food material, such as grain. (In root crops, the entire plant weight is used as the base.) This percentage is called the harvest index and ranges from 20 to nearly 70 (Table 9.6). The most efficient plant is dry beans.

Ancient civilizations accidently increased the harvest index by planting larger seeds. Modern people have increased the harvest index by developing hybrids and using better farming methods. Hybrids have increased the percentage of the corn plant that is edible from 24 to 43, and better farming methods and varieties have increased wheat's percentage from 23 to 46.

Improving the Nitrogen Fixation Process. As was discussed earlier, bacteria living on legume roots are able to take nitrogen from the air and make it available to the plant through a process called nitrogen fixation. Legumes are therefore less dependent on nitrogen from fertilizers. If researchers could improve this process in legumes and transfer it to cereal grains, they could greatly increase yields and decrease the need for costly nitrogen fertilizer, which depends on petroleum products for its production. This would be a bonanza of worldwide significance.

Nitrogen fixation has been observed in plants other than legumes, e.g., tropical grasses, sugarcane, and corn. The amount is small, but has led people to look for ways to increase the process in these plants and to try and develop it in other crops, especially cereals.

Scientists have found that they can increase the amount of nitrogen fixed in soybeans over five times by tripling the amount of carbon dioxide available to the plant (4). This increase in $CO_2$ decreases by almost two-thirds the amount of nitrogen needed. The increase is thought to be because (1) the products of photosynthesis are increased, (2) root nodules double in size, and (3) each nodule is more efficient. It is not practical to fertilize the atmosphere with carbon dioxide, but if photosynthesis can be made more efficient, more nitrogen will also be fixed.

This research has not reached the point where it can be applied to field crops, so crops other than legumes must continue to depend on nitrogen fertilizer. But the potential for this kind of basic research is enormous.

CHALLENGE. Food production is a complex energy-demanding process. Many promising factors of great potential are visible on the horizon. Plant breeders are developing more hybrid varieties and dwarf high-yielding, high-protein grains, and scientists are trying to develop nitrogen-fixing cereal grains and to improve photosynthesis in plants. These developments will significantly improve the world's food supplies, but they may not feed more people unless advances are also made on the socioeconomic front. Such things as better food storage and transportation facilities; irrigation projects; availability of fertilizers and pesticides; education on how to use these yield-increasing inputs, and government support for initial implementation are all vital to the success of the world's food production efforts.

Some of the major problems involved in feeding the world do not involve production of food and are beyond the scope of this chapter. For example, the world actually produces enough food to feed its people. The current level of grain and grain legume production is sufficient to feed 6.65 billion people at a level of 2,740 calories per day, which is 20 percent above the current use level. An 8 to 1 ratio of grain to legumes would give a 12.2 percent protein diet of 74 grams of protein per person. This also can be met with current crop production.

People are starving because food is not properly harvested, stored, and distributed, because of poverty, and because 40 percent of the world's grain is fed to animals instead of people. (See the chapters on animals and infrastructure for more discussion.)

The challenge of feeding people can only be met through research, education, economics, and politics. The common language of the world is food. Everyone must eat each day; thus everyone has an interest in meeting this challenge.

## REFERENCES

1. Abelson, Philip H., ed. Food: Politics, Economics, Nutrition and Research. Washington, D.C.: The American Association for the Advancement of Science, 1975.
2. Food and Agriculture Organization of the United Nations. Agricultural Commodities. Rome, 1967.
3. ———. Production Yearbook. Vol. 28-1. Rome, 1974.
4. Hardy, R. W. F., and Havelka, U. D. In Symbiotic Nitrogen Fixation in Plants, ed., P. Nutman. Int. Biol. Program Series, Vol. 7. London: Cambridge Press, 1975.
5. Heiser, Charles B. Seed to Civilization—The Story of Man's Food. San. Francisco: W. H. Freeman Co., 1973.

6. Janick, J., et al. Plant Science—An Introduction to World Crops. San Francisco: W. H. Freeman Co., 1974.

## BIBLIOGRAPHY

Baker, H. G. Plants and Civilization. 2nd ed. Belmont, Calif.: Wadsworth, 1970

Borgstrom, Georg. The Hungry Planet. New York: MacMillan, 1972.

Janick, J. Plant Agriculture: Readings from Scientific American. San Francisco: W. H. Freeman Co., 1970.

Lappe, F. M. Diet for a Small Planet. New York: Ballantine Co., 1971.

Schery, Robert W. Plants for Man. Englewood Cliffs, N.J.: Prentice-Hall, 1972.

# 10

# Crop Production Practices

J. W. PENDLETON

MORE THAN 10 percent of the world's people were malnourished or starving in the mid-1970s. This is difficult for people in the developed countries to comprehend. As Dr. John A. Hannah, Executive Director of the World Food Council, put it, "You have to see it, smell it, and feel it" (1). Hannah went on to say that the solution to world hunger comes in three parts: Food production in food-deficient nations is the first; distributing food to hungry people is the second; and a system of world food reserves is the third.

This chapter will discuss only the first part, specifically the production practices used in producing food. In the discussion we assume that fossil fuels will continue to be available in adequate amounts, but probably at a higher cost, for the next quarter of a century.

Farming as of the mid-1970s varies like no other industry. Some farmers still eke out a bare existence in isolated areas with simple handmade tools, while others are sophisticated businessmen with hundreds of thousands of dollars invested in land, facilities, and equipment. The former may find it difficult to feed his family, while the latter feeds his family and many more.

Scientific achievements have carried human beings to the moon and their equipment far beyond, but we have not found a way to feed the world's hungry people even though the tools are available. Agricultural science has made great progress, but it has been used mainly in the developed countries. Still there is some basis for optimism. In the developed nations, 90 percent of the agricultural scientists who ever lived are alive today; in the developing nations the percentage is even higher. Research information is available. Adaptation and dissemination are needed. The yield potential of most of our crop plants is higher than any one had ever thought, even 25 years ago. The needed inputs for this yield are known, and, more importantly, the scientific principles are also known. An interconnected group of internationally supported re-

J. W. PENDLETON, Professor and Chairman, Agronomy Department, University of Wisconsin, has had foreign assignments in Australia, India, Korea, and Indonesia relating to crop improvement and crop production practices.

search centers is concerned primarily with agricultural food production. More is known about planning and the constraints for development than at any previous time. Many governments are aware of the educational and infrastructure problems and are willing to come to grips with them. And there have been recent national successes in agricultural development.

Even with all this progress, proposals are still being offered that will not solve the problem. A 1975 Rockefeller Foundation report lists three commonly proposed nonsolutions for the world's food problems (8).

First, increasing U.S. food production is not a solution because people of the developing nations do not have money to buy the food and their governments cannot long afford the balance of payments loss needed to purchase it.

Second, production of synthetic foods and single cell proteins is not a solution because people do not have money to buy them, and their production does not offer employment opportunities to the multitudes who need work to earn money to feed themselves.

Third, even though 75 percent of the earth's surface is covered with water, aquatic farming does not appear feasible. Less than 2 percent of the human food supply is derived from aquatic sources.

The food problem can be solved primarily by increasing food production in each developing nation. And increased production will mean individual farmers must adopt new production practices. What requirements must a new practice meet before farmers will adopt it? Here are four; there undoubtedly are many more:

1. The new practice must significantly increase production or significantly reduce labor or cost.
2. The new practice and things that go with it to make a package must be available when needed, must be reasonably priced, and must work. There can be no additional risk involved.
3. The farmer must be shown that the new practice will work. (A field demonstration on his own or a neighbor's farm will be needed.)
4. The farmer must know that there will be a profitable market for the extra produce that comes from using an effective practice.

Farmers and farm suppliers in the United States and most developed countries visualize a new practice as a part of a complex system of farming that will yield greater income given time. The new practice may be anything from an improved variety or use of herbicides, to a $30,000 tractor unit or combine, to a more effective money management system.

Most farmers in developing nations are at or near the subsistence level and do not see new practices in the same way commercial farmers do. They cannot afford to take risks because a smaller yield means hunger for the family, not simply reduced income. Their total money income for the year may be less than $100 and seldom is as much as $300.

They frequently farm less than one acre and seldom as much as three acres, from which they must feed the family and provide income for the family needs. Most use only hand labor. A few have oxen or water buffalo and very crude tools, such as the hoe, machete, cutlass, and ax; usually local varieties of seeds are used, and often the seeds are insect damaged. Very little or no fertilizer and chemicals are used. Farming is still done as it has been for generations and is very strongly guided by local custom.

A new practice for such farmers may be very simple but even then will be accepted cautiously. There are essentially no farm suppliers as we know them, no equipped machine shops, little mechanical knowledge, poor or no storage, costly credit, and poorly developed markets. The farmers and their wives are seldom able to read or write and have no cash reserves. Yet it is these farmers who must provide food for the rapidly expanding populations in the developing nations. Adoption of new or improved practices is essential and urgent.

While this challenge may appear to stagger the imagination, let us review briefly some of the challenges the U.S. pioneers met, or "the way we were" until relatively recently.

THE WAY WE WERE. Much of the world's agriculture today is as backward as U.S. agriculture was in colonial times. America's early settlers were subsistence farmers, producing or doing without. All work was done by hand or with a minimum of animal power. Fields were often cropped until they no longer produced profitable yields then abandoned and new land cleared. The only fertilizers available were animal manure, marl, and oyster shells from along the seashores. Early settlers also used fish—one per hill of corn—as they were taught by the Indian Squanto. Transportation was by foot, canoes, or horses. Neighboring communities were isolated, dictating self-sufficiency. Trade in the backwoods areas was either impossible or minimal. Plantation or estate-type agriculture was developed near the sea for export sales, just as it is in developing countries today.

Until 1775, 98 percent of the U.S. population was involved with agriculture. In 1875, 75 percent of the population still resided on farms. Today the figure is only about 5 percent. Primary education opportunities were extremely limited in early America; the few institutions of higher learning were for the wealthy and emphasized law, theology, and training in the arts.

Witchcraft and strange customs and beliefs influenced U.S. agriculture in those times. Plantings were made according to the sign of the zodiac or phase of the moon. Some believed that during cold winters the wheat plant changed to a weed called cheat. When iron plows were introduced, there were rumors that they would poison the soil.

The American colonist had no place to obtain information about agriculture except from personal experiences and observations of the American Indians' plant culture. Nothing was known in a scientific way about plant growth, fertilizer requirements, pest control, or plant improvement.

DEVELOPMENT PERIOD. Industry, transportation, education, and agriculture advanced during the 1800s. The government recognized the importance of agriculture, establishing the U.S. Department of Agriculture in 1862. That same year President Lincoln signed the Land-Grant College Act to establish institutions for instruction in agriculture and mechanical arts. These colleges had unhappy early histories. Money was limited, few teachers were qualified, and no books were available. There was no agricultural science to teach. This is a familiar story in many developing nations today except that scientific agricultural knowledge is now available.

The Hatch Act of 1887, which provided federal grants to land-grant colleges for research, was the second milestone for agricultural education in the United States. The third milestone was the Smith Lever Act of 1914, which created the extension service that would bring the benefits of agricultural research to all farmers and consumers.

ACCELERATION PERIOD. The big surge in benefits from agricultural science has occurred since the 1940s. Many American crop yields have doubled or tripled during the lifetime of present older farmers. No single production factor or practice has been responsible for this. Instead a number of independent factors on and off the farm caused the increases. The primary characteristic of America's present commercial agriculture is change.

The small farmer in developing countries must essentially go through the same development process as U.S. farmers did. He can do so in less than 200 years or perhaps in less than 40 years. The following sections will discuss several production practices that the traditional farmer must become familiar with. Since the range in climate and soil is so great from region to region and sometimes within a region, general principles rather than how-to-do-it recipes will be discussed.

## CULTURE OF CROPS.

Growing crops is a very complicated process. For greatest success, a farmer must supervise every detail before, during, and after planting. Like an airline pilot, the successful farmer consciously or unconsciously has a checklist, which includes some of the following points:

1. Before planting
   a. Soil, including fertility levels, pH levels, land preparation, and drainage

   b. Plants or crops, including the variety or species to be used, the date of planting, row spacing, population, and planting depth
2. Growing period
   a. Pest control measures, including those for weeds, insects, diseases, and animals
   b. Tillage and supplemental fertility additions
   c. Periodic field observations
3. Harvest, including anticipated date of and method of harvest and provision for drying, cleaning, and processing
4. Storage
   a. Storage for harvested crops
   b. Protection from insects and other pests
   c. Control of humidity
   d. Transportation to market

CROP PRODUCTION SYSTEMS. There are several crop production systems used today in the developing nations. Let us examine three.

SLASH AND BURN. Slash and burn agriculture is a method of shifting cultivation where native plants are cut and burned, seeds planted among the fertile ashes, and the land cropped for 2 to 4 years until the fertility diminishes. The land then is abandoned for long periods before cropping again. This kind of agriculture is practiced in many tropical areas of the world, e.g., in the rain forest areas of western Africa and Brazil. The only energy input needed in this type of agriculture is human labor. The labor, the land itself, and the seeds or vegetative plant parts are the only essentials for establishing the next crop. Tools are crudely handmade, and this is why fire is used to clear the trees and brush. There is air pollution from this burning, and some meteorologists believe that the great amount of smoke added to the atmosphere may influence weather. Even though essentially no fuel energy is required with this system, very little food energy is provided, and so only a small population can subsist by this means.

The slash and burn farmer must be shown a new production practice by someone he trusts, and any new practice introduced must be extremely simple. Perhaps it might be a shaped branch to mark straight rows to receive the seed; the new practice would replace surface broadcasting of the seed. With it, planting depth and soil coverage will be more uniform, which would reduce the amount of seed needed and make weeding and harvesting easier. Seed crops harvested in tropical areas must be carefully stored. One good storage place is in the center of the house or the outside kitchen where smoke and heat from the fire can reach the seeds. The heat and smoke help to control insects, and they also keep the seed dry in these humid areas.

MIXED CROPPING. Mixed cropping, the practice of having several crops randomly distributed in an area, has been characteristic of slash and burn agriculture since antiquity. It is not uncommon to see from six to ten, or even more, crop species in a single mound of soil no more than three feet in diameter. This method attempts to make the most of the environment while providing some insurance against total crop failure. Plants with different growth habits may be better able to exploit the soil nutrients and sunlight because different plant species may compete less intensively with one another than do plants of the same species. Water use may be more effective, the risk of insects and diseases somewhat less, and weeds more effectively shaded. Tall plants can provide support for vining plants, e.g., yams; and early-maturing plants can be harvested before later-maturing ones shade them.

Mixed cropping involving many plants is more commonly practiced near the home than in the principal production fields where no more than two or possibly three different species are mixed. In northern Nigeria, for example, sorghum or millet might be mixed with groundnuts. Research in West Africa has shown that higher yields are possible with certain mixed plantings than with plantings in pure stands. Mixed planting is seldom practiced in the United States since it is easier to cultivate, fertilize, and control weeds and insects in pure stands of crops than in a mixed system. Until quite recently, however, legume plants were commonly seeded with small grains, such as oats or barley, so that a cash crop could be obtained while the legume crop was being established for later use as hay or pasture.

INTENSIVE CROPPING. Agriculture in the temperate zones (see Chapter 9) cannot take advantage of year-round cropping. Double cropping, however, is increasing in the United States, particularly in the southeast and the southwest where the growing season is relatively long. In tropical areas, relay or continuous cropping can be used to produce more food annually from a given land area. The next crop is either transplanted or seeded before the present one matures. For example, tobacco may be transplanted into corn fields in certain areas of Brazil. Irrigation is required during dry seasons but continuous cropping has considerable potential, particularly in areas with abundant labor. It is reported that in parts of China from seven to ten vegetable crops per year are grown on the same plot of land.

Intensive cropping is a very exacting and management-intensive system. No time can be wasted between harvesting one crop and planting the next. Early maturing and day-length neutral varieties are desirable. Multiple cropping may not be possible except where improvements in small machinery have been made.

The International Rice Research Institute in the Philippines has grown as many as five crops in one year on the same piece of land (rice, sweet potatoes, soybeans for grain, sweet corn, soybeans for vegetables). Calculations using the Philippine nutrition standard of 2,600 calories and 55 grams of protein per person per day, indicate that production from one acre continuously cropped could supply enough calories for 29 people and enough protein for 53.

Even without year-round water supply, many areas could grow two or three crops where only one is produced at the present time. To do this, however, the following production practices must receive special attention:

1. Plant short season varieties with high yield characteristics.
2. Plant second crop just before the first matures.
3. Harvest early and on time to prevent serious competition with the following crop.
4. Minimize tillage.
5. Apply pest control measures and fertilizer at the proper time.

Under this intensive system of cropping, plant residues can be used for mulch or fed to livestock, which in turn will increase food supplies. If the animals are confined, the manure can either be used to fertilize crops or to fertilize fish ponds, which will produce additional high protein food. Such systems are already being used in China and in Malaysia and could be used in other tropical areas. But continuous cropping requires abundant labor, good management, and will cost more than single cropping because of the additional fertilizer and agricultural pesticides needed for a successful program.

For several years now scientists have been interested in developing "package programs" of technology for individual crops, and the idea might be extended to the multicropping system. Packaging means including all the elements necessary for a successful crop (seed, fertilizer, and pest control measures) in one "package." Success, however, depends on strict adherence to specific instructions.

The best example of such programs would be those involving the new short-straw high-yielding wheat and rice varieties that have achieved such spectacular success in the Indian subcontinent, Philippines, Mexico, Taiwan, and Indonesia. These package programs have several essentials that must be carefully adhered to:

1. High-yielding varieties with good seed quality must be used.
2. The correct fertilizer must be used and applied at the proper time.
3. Crops must be planted at the time when they can take maximum advantage of available water.
4. Plant pests must be controlled.

A farmer who is successful with the multiple cropping package program must have a passionate zeal for getting things done on time.

CROP AND VARIETY SELECTION FOR PLANTING. The crops selected to be grown on any farm are determined by the needs of the farmer and his family. Even though 350,000 plant species have been identified, fewer than 15 provide for the basic human food needs (see Chapters 2 and 9). Within these few species are found hundreds of varieties.

The variety a farmer chooses is determined primarily by its yield potential and pest resistance and by the local production conditions including cultural practices. For example, a subsistence farmer and his family in Nigeria would usually prefer to eat the rotundata yam, but he will plant cassava because his land is poor and he is more sure of a crop and a higher yield with cassava. He has the choice of planting the local cassava variety, which is quite high in cyanogenetic glucoside, a potential poison, or an improved variety, which is low in the poison, may yield more, and requires less time to mature. The subsistence farmer may choose the local variety, however, because the propagation material is readily available and he knows grasshoppers may destroy the improved variety but will not bother the local variety. This is his form of crop insurance.

A commercial dryland farmer in western Nebraska, Kansas, or Oklahoma might prefer to grow corn, but he knows that sorghum is more drought tolerant and thus in most years his income will be greater from sorghum. This same farmer might prefer to plant a better-yielding white-seeded variety, but because past experience has shown him that severe losses from migrating birds may seriously reduce the yield of the white-seeded variety, he will plant a red-seeded bird resistant (BR) variety.

Similarly, a poor farmer in India may choose to plant the local rice or wheat variety rather than the new higher-yielding varieties (HYVs). He does this because he does not have the money to purchase the seed, fertilizer, and chemicals that must be used as a "package" to obtain the higher yields. Farmers with access to credit and management skills do take advantage of the improved varieties.

One of the major problems plant breeders have is to develop varieties suited to local conditions and needs of farmers. Without higher-yielding crops there is little chance that the overall production needed in the developing nations will be achieved.

SOIL FERTILITY. Soil fertility usually refers to how much nitrogen (N), phosphorus (P), potassium (K), and essential secondary and micronutrients (elements such as copper and zinc, needed in very small amounts) are available to plants. Organic (plant and animal) matter is also important because it is the natural source of N. The level of soil fertility before the land was first farmed was determined by the source of the material from which the soil developed (parent material), the climate, and native vegetation. River valleys and flood plains, such as those of the Nile and the Mississippi, have a high fertility level because frequent flooding brought rich deposits of soil from upstream erosion. Volcanic slopes also have fertile soils. Unfortunately, in many areas erosion removes surface soil and with it much soil fertility. Crops also remove large amounts of nutrients (N, P, and K), especially when all residues are removed.

Low soil fertility is still usually the most limiting factor in crop production in the developing nations. Soil fertility can be improved by adding animal manures, mulches, and leaves; nitrogen can also be added by growing legumes. In the developed nations, the increased use of inorganic (chemical) fertilizers since the late 1800s has helped increase yields substantially.

Legumes have been recognized as soil building crops since ancient times. They were the principal N source in the United States until the 1950s, and since a healthy legume crop can supply an equivalent of 50 to 150 pounds of N they were very effective.

Inorganic fertilizers are relatively costly in developing countries and require good management. Nitrogen, especially, must be applied at the correct time and in a specific manner to maximize effectiveness and reduce potential losses. Often this requires small amounts applied early and a second application made as the plant enters the reproductive stage. Fertilizer is most efficient if applied in the root zone. For example, agronomists at the International Rice Research Institute have recently demonstrated that 60 units of N applied by the hand-placed "mud ball" technique to rice is equivalent to 100 units broadcast on the soil surface. This is a labor-intensive practice and requires more time than transplanting the rice. Time is required to make mud balls, insert the N, and place the mud ball about four inches below the soil surface, midway between four rice hills. Large yield increases can be obtained with small amounts of N with crops that have large growing plants spaced widely apart, simply by poking a hole or making a small furrow alongside the plant and adding fertilizer.

United Nations FAO trials in many developing countries during the 1960s showed fertilizer had a large impact on yield. Increases of over 50 percent were shown. Also, each dollar spent generally increased the value of the harvest by a profitable margin. When improved varieties and pest control were used with the fertilizer, the returns for fertilizer were often beyond a farmer's greatest imagination. Indeed, the great impact of fertilizer is in developing countries. Estimates are that each additional pound of fertilizer increases grain yields by 10 pounds in developing countries but only 5 pounds in developed countries.

The usual method of maintaining fertility in subsistence agriculture is by cropping sequence. The shifting cultivation of the slash and burn agriculture, described earlier, is not very different from ley farming in Britain or Australia where grassland is plowed and planted to grain for a very few years and then returned to grass. When land is fallowed naturally with wild trees, shrubs, or grasses, it is improved in three ways.

First, plant nutrients are brought to the topsoil by the roots; second, legume trees and plants supply N to the soil; and third, soil structure is improved. This favorable condition may last for only two or three years, after which the land must again be fallowed.

When people remove the land's natural vegetative cover, they reduce the ability of soil to resist erosion, particularly on sloping land and forest areas in hot climates. Crops that form a continuous cover (such as grasses, pastures, legumes, and sugarcane) are generally more effective in reducing erosion than widely spaced plants like cassava, yam, tobacco, or maize. Crops that are intermediate in their ability to reduce erosion are small grains, millets, and taro.

Farmers also protect the soil from erosion by planting row crops around the slope (contouring), constructing terraces and channels across the slope to catch or slow the water, or by covering the soil's surface with a mulch. Elaborate bench terraces and erosion-control devices built by hand are found in many parts of the world, and some are very old.

WATER MANAGEMENT. Many agricultural regions in the wet-dry tropics and in the subtropics have seasons of excessive rainfall followed by essentially dry seasons (see Chapter 6). Since these regions are essentially frost free and could produce crops much of the year, water management is especially important. Irrigation during the dry season would mean additional food. Irrigation water can be obtained by gravity flow from dam impoundments, by diverting water from rivers or streams, and from dug or drilled wells.

Crops, other than rice, are usually irrigated by gravity flow and furrow irrigation. This method requires exacting land leveling and grading; drainage is also important. Sprinkler irrigation is more commonly used in temperate climates where the water is pumped from drilled wells. Pumping and water distribution costs are high, but crop production is also high.

Among new methods of irrigation under study are subsurface and trickle systems. Trickle systems use water efficiently by providing water only to the root zone of widely spaced plants. The space between rows, or between plants, is not irrigated. While installation costs are high, this method has great promise for trees and other widely spaced plants in arid regions.

Paddy rice requires irrigation and since rice culture in developing countries is labor intensive increasing irrigation offers a major opportunity for increasing crop production and employment in these countries. Because of the costs involved, however, government participation in construction, leveling, educating farmers, and establishing credit facilities is essential.

Besides providing water for irrigation, reservoirs and wells can often supply badly needed clean water for direct human use.

PESTS. Estimates vary, but must authorities agree that 25 to 35 percent of agricultural produce is lost to insects, birds, rodents, and molds before it reaches the consumer. In some tropical countries, where food is already scarce, grain losses may approach or even exceed 50 percent. The high temperatures and humidity of these countries particularly favor the multiplication of the molds, and also create a favorable habitat for insects, birds, rodents, and other pests (see Chapter 11). Selecting or developing resistant crop species or varieties is the most economically important and environmentally sound crop protection practice available. But the practice of growing only a single variety on each piece of land (monoculture), even a resistant variety, can lead to serious losses if new races of pests arise through genetic mutation. Thus, monoculture usually depends heavily on pesticides.

Crops in tropical countries are particularly susceptible to animal damage. For example, squirrels and monkeys seriously damage certain fruits and food crops, and birds take a heavy toll in grains, particularly rice. The ever-present rat attacks many crops from the low-growing seed legumes, to intermediate-height crops like rice, to tree crops, such as oil and coconut palms. The mongoose was introduced on certain Caribbean islands to control rats in sugarcane, but trapping or poison baits are most often used as control measures. Much biological research has been devoted to trying to control animal pests using diseases, but the only notable success has been in Australia, where the virus disease myxomatosis was used against rabbits.

We will examine three other categories of pests: weeds, insects, and diseases.

WEEDS. Weeds compete with crops for food, water, and light; they also harbor other pests. Removing weeds has often increased yields up to 25 percent in temperate zones and 100 percent or more in tropical areas.

Subsistence farmers control weeds by fire, flooding, mulching, hoeing, or hand weeding since labor is usually cheap and abundant. As labor costs increase, mechanical or chemical methods have usually been used.

Another effective weed control measure used is shade. Some annual crops grow rapidly, shading the weeds, and thus limiting their growth. Annuals that grow slowly form less shade and require other weed control methods. Perennial crops often present serious weed-control problems, particularly when invaded by perennial weeds.

Row planting allows easier access for weed control, particularly for cultivation with animals or tractors. Cultivation, if not necessary for weed control, however, does not seem to be necessary to improve yields. Thus, commercial farmers are using less mechanical cultivation and more chemicals to control weeds.

Increased use of herbicides (weed killers) has resulted in greatly improved application equipment. Numerous kinds of both hand and power operated spray equipment are presently available. Some tractor-drawn applicators can cover 40 to 60 feet at one time, and are capable of covering immense areas in a single day. Conversely, more and more small backpack sprayers are being used by small farmers in developing countries. When the cost is shared by several farmers, they are relatively inexpensive.

Because chemical pesticides may be dangerous to the environment and are relatively expensive, biological weed control by weed-eating insects is avidly being sought. Two spectacular successes have occurred. One species of cactus in Australia was destroyed effectively by a moth, and St. John's Wort has been partially controlled in arid U.S. regions by a beetle.

INSECTS. In primitive agriculture, farmers must often resort to hand picking the larger insects off crops; they also grow crops with a natural resistance to insects. Cassava, for example, is highly resistant to most insects.

Before chemical insecticides, the principal control practices available to farmers were cultural, including planting date, clean cultivation, flooding, burning, sanitation, crop rotation, and trap crops. Good seed-bed preparation and fertilizers speed up emergence and plant growth, which tends to reduce insect damage.

The earliest insecticides were mineral oils, soaps, and resins. Sometime later arsenicals (calcium, lead, and copper) were developed. Lime sulfur was used both as an insecticide and a fungicide. Certain insect poisons were obtained from plants. For example, rotenone comes from a species of *Derris* and has been used as an insecticide and fish poison for hundreds of years. Pyrethrum is made from the dried flowers of certain species of chrysanthemums. Other insect poisons come from tobacco and sapodilla.

Curtailment of the supply of such plant-derived insecticides during World War II actually hastened the development of modern chlorinated hydrocarbons (DDT, aldrin, dieldrin, etc.), organophosphorus compounds (parathion, malathion, etc.), and carbamate compounds (carbaryl) as insecticides.

An exciting new development is the systemic insecticide, which the plant absorbs, making it toxic to feeding insects but not to humans. Developments have also been made in application methods. For example, rice entomologists have recently shown that only one-fourth of the amount of insecticide is needed when it is applied in the root zone instead of to the soil surface. Researchers are also investigating new biological methods of insect control, including insect predators, sterile insects, or sex attractants.

The most practical and cheapest method of insect control, however, is through breeding resistant varieties. Examples of this are varieties of wheat that resist the Hessian fly, corn varieties that resist corn borers, and cotton varieties with hairs on the leaves that resist the feeding of jassids (leafhoppers). Small farmers in developing nations need such varieties because chemicals are costly and require careful use.

DISEASES. Throughout agricultural history plant diseases have destroyed people's crops. In the 1800s, the potato blight devastated Ireland's potato crop. Today, Dutch Elm disease is ravishing one of the world's most beautiful shade trees.

Cultural methods can be used to control disease. Crop rotation makes it more difficult for disease to persist. All plant materials left after harvest can be removed, buried, or burned. Diseased plants can be destroyed, and plants other than the crop plants that harbor the disease can also be destroyed; e.g., the barberry was destroyed because it harbored cereal rust. Practices that promote healthy plants and rapid growth also help reduce disease attacks.

The Bordeaux mixture (a fungicide) was discovered in the mid-nineteenth century and was the forerunner of many chemicals. Previously, formaldehyde, sulfur, Paris green, lead arsenate, tobacco juice, and soapsuds, were used to control plant diseases. Today many improved chemicals are available, including systemic ones.

As with insect control, the most important and lowest cost method of disease control is breeding resistant varieties. All crop breeding programs include this as an important objective. Native varieties in developing countries frequently have some disease tolerance.

TOOLS. One of the most difficult questions facing farmers in developing countries is when, where, and how crude hand tools can be replaced with more efficient hand tools; efficient hand tools by draft animals; and draft animals by small tractors. The needs will vary with farmers, farming areas, and the crops grown. Tools, draft animals, and machines supplement a farmer's muscle power. With them, he can farm a larger area or a small one faster. He may also use the new machinery or animal power for transportation. He can then transport his purchases and his produce more easily. People do not walk far to market especially with heavy loads on their backs or heads. The process of adopting more efficient tools begins with improved hand tools and ends with motorized tools. A woman in India who cuts grass all day for cattle feed could harvest more if the sickle blade were larger and sharper. The farmer who uses a small, narrow-bladed hand tool to control weeds could change to a hoe or a weeder with a wider blade. Sickles and scythes could replace small knives and palm knives, hastening the harvest of rice and other cereal grains. Foot-operated threshing machines could replace the much slower hand beating or animal treading. All such tools must be cheap, simple, and easy to manufacture and repair by the farmer or village blacksmith.

Any mechanization must be accompanied by all other improved cultural practices; otherwise, the increased costs are not covered by the increased production. As long as incomes remain low and labor overabundant, mechanization may not be practical. Much remains to be learned about production practice transition for tropical subsistence agriculture.

SUMMARY. Development of improved, useful production practices and equipment elsewhere does not assure that they will be used by farmers in the developing nations. Biophysical (soil fertility, water, pests) and socioeconomic (knowledge, credit, transportation, traditions) constraints must be overcome first. The latter constraints may be overcome slowly, so changes in production practices that could increase food production may also be made slowly.

It is slow and difficult even to present a new idea to people who can neither read nor write. It is also difficult to bring about changes that require modifications in customs and habits. Very poor, uneducated people often prize their tribal religions, local holidays, and customs more than the possibility of a little more income.

Appropriate education will speed understanding and adoption of useful practices. Although many developing nations have an agricultural extension service, its effectiveness is often low. Extension workers often have little training and little or no farming experience. To be effective in working with farmers, their skills must be improved.

Developing agriculture can be improved and production increased but only through significant changes. These changes will take time and will need the commitment of many governments. But these changes must take place or all humanity will suffer.

## REFERENCES


1. Hannah, John A. Address given at The World Food Conference, Iowa State University, Ames, July 1, 1976.
2. Krantz, B. A., and Hills, F. G. Role of extension, research with a mission. Spec. Publ. 14. Madison, Wis.: Amer. Soc. of Agronomy, 1969.
3. National Academy of Sciences. Agricultural production efficiency. Com. Report. Washington, D.C.: National Academy of Sciences, 1975.
4. ———. Plant studies in the Peoples' Republic of China. A trip report of the American plant studies delegation. Washington, D.C.: National Academy of Sciences, 1975.
5. National Science Foundation. Potential increases in food supply through research. Agriculture Reports. Washington, D.C.: National Science Foundation, 1975.
6. Stakman, E. C.; Bradfield, R.; and Mangelsdorf, P. C. Campaigns against hunger. Cambridge, Mass.: Harvard University Press, 1967.
7. Streeter, C. P. Reaching the developing world's small farmers. Working paper. New York: The Rockefeller Foundation, 1975.
8. Wortman, S. The world food situation: A new initiative. New York: The Rockefeller Foundation, 1975.
9. ———. Strategies for agricultural education in developing countries. Agri. Education Conf. II. New York: The Rockefeller Foundation, 1975.
10. Willet, J. W. The world food situation and prospects to 1985. U.S. Department of Agriculture, ERS, Foreign Agr. Econ. Rpt. No. 98.

# 11

# Food Losses—Situation and Opportunities for Improvement

HARRY E. SNYDER

THE COMMON PROCEDURE for determining the amount of food available is to divide the amount of food produced by the number of people who consume it. But there is a third factor that must be considered. During production, harvesting, processing, and marketing of food, from 10 to 20 percent is lost or discarded in developed countries and as much as 50 percent may be lost in the developing countries.

Most people think of food losses as occurring only in the field because of flood, drought, disease, or pests. But losses also occur because food is not adequately stored, processed, or preserved, and it is with these losses that this chapter will deal.

After harvest, food must be stored until processed or eaten. Some foods store well without prior treatment, but others must be preserved for effective storage. The skill with which food is stored and preserved will determine how much is lost to spoilage. This chapter will first consider the methods used to store and preserve food in the households and small villages of developing countries.

Next, the possibility of economic gain through food processing will be explored. When grains are milled or food oil is recovered and refined, the new food products are more valuable than the raw materials. The skill with which food is processed will determine how much food is wasted, how much food quality is lost, and whether valuable byproducts can be recovered. Both village scale and large-scale processing will be considered.

For developing countries, a significant economic opportunity may be lost when raw agricultural products, such as coffee, tea, cacao, and groundnuts are exported. If these raw materials were processed into consumer products for export, a developing country would gain more profit, generate needed foreign exchange, and create needed jobs.

HARRY E. SNYDER is Professor, Food Technology and Biochemistry, Iowa State University, whose primary research has been on use of soybeans for food products. He has served on the staff of Food Resources Laboratory, Korea Institute of Science and Technology, Seoul, Korea.

The final section of this chapter will examine how needed nutrients, and even new foods, can be developed by specially blending foods and by processing raw materials not normally considered as foods.

STORAGE, PRESERVATION, AND PROCESSING OF FOOD IN VILLAGES AND HOUSEHOLDS. In the rural areas of developing countries, there are well-established and time-honored practices for storage, preservation, and processing of foods. People often depend on a single grain crop, such as rice, wheat, maize, or teff, as a basic food, and since the grain may be harvested only once each year, storage to provide food for the rest of the year is essential (see also Chapter 9).

STORAGE. Grains and grain legumes are important foods because they can be stored for long periods without extensive treatment. The primary requirements are to keep moisture content at, or below, 14 percent, to keep the temperature low (preferably below 70° F), and to protect the grain from adverse weather, molds, insects, and predators.

Moisture of harvested grain can range from 10 to 30 percent depending on grain type, whether the harvest is early or late, and the weather conditions immediately preceding harvest. Therefore, if moisture is too high, the grain must be dried. In the developed countries, this may be done mechanically, but in rural farms and villages of developing countries, grain is usually spread on the ground in the sun to dry for several days.

Keeping moisture and temperature low prevents rapid fungal and insect growth. Fungi are always present during normal agricultural production and harvesting. If moisture is high enough, fungi start to grow, and as growth continues, heat can be generated to make conditions suitable for insect growth. Once insect infestation is noticed, the only effective control practice is to fumigate the grain. In rural households this is seldom done. Frequent inspection and turning of stored grain are useful to avoid hot spots and moisture accumulations that lead to rapid fungal and insect growth. Obviously, people living in temperate climates find it easier to control temperature and moisture than those living in the hot humid tropics.

Protection from the weather and predators is best accomplished by selecting proper storage containers. Usually each individual household stores its own grain using wooden bins, boxes, sacks, earthenware jars, wicker baskets, or underground pits. Sometimes, however, grain is stored collectively in a village (Fig. 11.1).

Many of the containers used in rural areas can resist rodents for only a short time; eventually mice and rats gnaw their way into the grain. But even here losses can be minimized if spilled grain is constantly cleaned up to avoid attracting rodents.

When grain harvests are good, rural areas do not have enough im-

FIG. 11.1. An example of grain storage structures used by a village in northern Africa. Such storage gives minimal protection from weather and predators.

mediate storage space to hold excess grain. Grain is usually just piled on the ground in these situations. And indeed, grain will not deteriorate badly in a week or two, particularly if the pile has a smooth continuous slope with no depressions to hold the moisture. Most rain will run off and will not penetrate further than a couple of inches into the pile.

PRESERVATION. Many foods have a higher moisture content than grain, making them susceptible to bacterial spoilage in addition to the problems just described for grain. Bacteria can not only render foods unpalatable within a short time, but actually make them dangerous to eat. Meat, eggs, fruits, and vegetables are all more susceptible to bacterial spoilage than grain, but milk, with its extremely high moisture content, is particularly susceptible to this kind of spoilage. All these foods require extensive treatment before they can be stored safely, and since the ability to store these foods may be synonymous with the ability to avoid hunger, people throughout history have searched for food preservation methods. Some of the more important methods are pickling, fermenting, drying, salting, canning, and refrigerating.

PICKLING. The process of adding edible acids to food to lower the pH and inhibit bacterial growth is known as pickling. Vinegar, which contains acetic acid, is the most common pickling agent. Vegetables and even meats can be pickled, but because of their acid flavor, they are used not as main dishes but as condiments or side dishes.

FERMENTATION. Fermentation is an ancient way of controlling the growth of microorganisms. As the microorganisms grow, they produce a chemical product such as an organic acid (e.g., vinegar) or alcohol. This product then stabilizes the food and prevents further growth of microorganisms. Hence fermentation is a way of converting what might be food spoilage into food preservation. Some fermented foods familiar in western cultures are sauerkraut, cider, beer, wine, and yogurt. Less familiar are gari, kimchi, and soy sauce.

Gari is an African food produced from cassava (from which we get tapioca). The cassava root is chopped, washed extensively, and allowed to ferment for several days. The resulting product is then dried, ground, or grated and made into paste or bread. Gari is not only more stable than fresh cassava, but has a reduced concentration of cyanogenetic glucoside, which when eaten can produce hydrogen cyanide (a poison). Because of the hydrogen cyanide, eating fresh cassava is deleterious to humans.

Kimchi is a Korean food, very similar to sauerkraut but less acidic and more highly spiced. Kimchi seems to be fermented more for flavor than for preservation, however, since it is only stable for a few days during warm summer weather.

Soy sauce is another oriental product that is fermented for months instead of days and is used as a condiment rather than a basic foodstuff. The fermentation of soy sauce starts with soybeans and is caused mainly by molds although yeasts and bacteria are probably active.

Alcoholic fermentation is used by all cultures as a way of preserving barley (beer), grapes (wine), rice (rice wine), honey (mead), and several other foods. The alcohol is produced by a yeast fermentation of sugars in fruit or of glucose from starch in grains. Alcoholic drinks, if not clarified by filtering, can have considerable nutrient content. And many native beers and wines, in contrast to western varieties, are not clarified before use. Therefore, if not diluted with contaminated water, they can supply needed nutrients.

DRYING AND SALTING. Drying and salting are combined frequently to preserve meats and fish, and drying alone may be used to preserve fruit. Both processes remove the water necessary to support bacterial growth and thus prevent food spoilage. Drying removes water physically, and salting binds water chemically. Sugar can also bind water chemically and so is used to preserve fruit or fruit juices as jams or jellies.

HEAT. A Frenchman named Nicholas Appert discovered in the early 1800s that food could be preserved by extensive heating in a closed container. This process of heat sterilization or canning (named for the metal canisters used as packages) results in food that is remarkably stable even after years of storage at ordinary temperatures. The heat effectively kills all microorganisms in the food, and the package prevents any recontamination. In this way, surplus fruits and vegetables as well as meats and fish can be preserved with essentially no storage losses.

Canning did not come into widespread use until the late 1800s and even today little canning is done in the villages and households of the developing countries. Attempts to introduce this process into rural areas of these countries has met with little success for two main reasons. First, the cost of either glass or metal containers may be equal to, or greater than, the food's cost, and poor people in developing countries cannot afford the extra cost. Second, considerable knowledge and equipment are required to ensure that food is sufficiently heated to prevent harmful or even fatal food poisoning. Despite these drawbacks, there is considerable potential for using heat sterilization to preserve food in developing countries, particularly if inexpensive packaging that could withstand heating under pressure could be developed.

Refrigeration. Even more recent than heat sterilization is refrigeration. Of course, people have used low temperatures to preserve food throughout history, particularly during winters in temperate climates. Natural ice can also be cut into blocks and used as a cooling agent during hot summers, but mechanical refrigeration has made the process much more reliable and introduced the possibility of frozen foods. Cooling and freezing food slow the growth of bacteria or insects and also retard the normal ripening processes in fruits and vegetables. These processes also maintain a fresh state of food that is frequently more desirable than the cooked state of canned food.

Refrigeration is important in preserving pasteurized foods since food is heated only briefly to kill most, but not all, microorganisms. Pasteurization, named for the famous French scientist Louis Pasteur, is used extensively to preserve fresh milk. Any mishandling of refrigerated foods, particularly pasteurized foods, may lead to microbial growth, food spoilage, and possible poisoning.

While effective, refrigeration, like canning, is expensive and usually requires electricity. Consequently, it is not a solution for those poor people who most need help preserving food. While people in developed countries may have home refrigerators and freezers, the usefulness of refrigeration in developing countries will probably be limited to retail and wholesale food outlets. For example, some warehouses in Korea are mechanically cooled to maintain 75° F (24° C) to prevent deterioration of stored rice.

PROCESSING. Agricultural products frequently need to be processed to change their form or purity before they can be used as foods. This kind of processing can increase the value of agricultural products and provide jobs for people. Because it increases food's utility, processing is equivalent to avoiding food losses since in both cases, more food becomes available.

Home Preparation. Much food processing is done in households for meal preparation (Fig. 11.2). Foods must be ground, peeled, washed, pitted, diced, skinned, or mixed, and then cooked. Cooking is universal

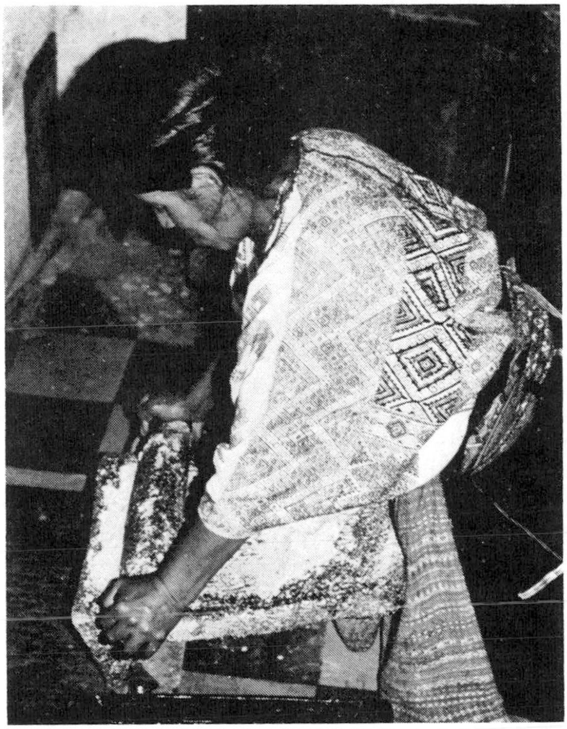

FIG. 11.2. Food processing in the home: grinding corn for making tortillas.

throughout human cultures and has much to do with the palatability, nutritive value, and safety of food.

Cooking depends on fuels for heat, and a serious problem in many villages and households is obtaining enough cooking fuel. Wood is often scarce, and cutting wood from hillsides may result in rapid erosion. In some cultures dried dung is used for fuel.

Heating causes very complex chemical and physical changes in foods. Flavors are changed because chemical compounds are destroyed, lost, or changed into new compounds. Enzymes are inactivated, stopping other chemical changes. Proteins are denatured, making them more easily digested and making their amino acids available to people as nutrients. The starch in grains and beans is gelatinized, making these foods much softer. Cooking also kills microorganisms and destroys some of the toxic substances produced by microorganisms, greatly decreasing the chance of food-borne illness. By carefully controlling the amount of heat used to cook vegetables and by saving the water in which they are cooked, loss of B and C vitamins can be avoided.

The women, who in most cultures select and prepare food, have an important job since their skills affect the health of those who eat the food and may determine if it is eaten or wasted. They deserve substantial recognition for their skills, but unfortunately recognition is not often given. Perhaps if people better understood the importance of food to health more emphasis and care would be given to food preparation and more recognition to those who prepare it.

Two important food processes are frequently done outside the home on a village scale. They are milling grain and pressing oil seeds.

MILLING. Milling prepares grain for eating by a dry grinding to remove outer hulls and make fine flours or by polishing the bran from the outside of the grain. Both of the grains most used as food in the world—wheat and rice—must be milled before they are edible. Rice is usually milled in small village mills, whereas wheat is either ground in households with crude tools or milled on a large scale with machinery.

After threshing, rice has an outer hull and is called rough rice or paddy. Milling removes the hull to produce brown rice, or rice with the bran layer intact. The miller then removes the bran layer by an abrasion process called pearling or polishing. If the polished rice grains are unbroken, they are called head rice. The proportion of head rice in the final yield depends on the miller's skill and his ability to adjust the milling machinery. And since people prefer head rice, some food may be lost because of poor milling skills.

The rice hulls are often burned as fuel for the mill but can be used as soil conditioners, packing materials, and roughage in livestock feed. The bran removed from brown rice is high in vitamins, minerals, and protein, but these nutrients are not readily available because of the indigestibility of rice bran. Rice bran also contains oil, which is attacked by inherent enzymes and can quickly become rancid. New milling methods can remove this oil, make it a valuable by-product, and upgrade rice bran as a feed ingredient. Unfortunately, the new milling method is not practical on a small scale for village millers and will become available only to large millers who can afford the capital investment.

Wheat is milled to produce a flour rather than whole polished grain. Industrially this is accomplished by crushing the wheat berry between steel rollers and then sifting the crushed material into several size categories. The larger particles are then crushed and sifted further resulting in a finely divided wheat flour. To produce white flour, the bran is separated as completely as possible. White flour with low ash and bran is generally considered to be the most desirable.

Since the bran contains more protein, minerals, and vitamins than the endosperm used for white flour, some people object to removing the bran. It is, however, less digestible than flour so that its vitamins, minerals, and protein are not readily available to humans although it does contain dietary fiber that may be helpful in avoiding digestive tract problems.

Before roller milling was introduced in the latter part of the nineteenth century, wheat was ground by passing the grain between flat revolving stones. The ground wheat was then passed through a reel covered with a series of bolting cloths. The best quality flour was recovered from the first reel section with the finest cloth, middlings was the coarser flour with more bran recovered from the middle portion, and tailings or lowest quality came from the final reel section. In rural villages some of these mills are still in use.

In addition to use for leavened bread, wheat flour is formed into the various pasta products used throughout the world. Some examples are macaroni, spaghetti, noodles, and flat pan breads like the Indian chapattis.

OIL EXTRACTION. Fats and oils are important components of the food supply since they are concentrated sources of calories, and have flavors, textures, and nutrients that make eating enjoyable. Sources of edible fats and oils include cattle, hogs, fish, oil seeds (soybean, peanut, cottonseed), palm fruit, olives, and coconut. Oil is usually removed from seeds by a hydraulic or screw press, and acquiring such a press is a first step for villages that want to improve their processing of oil seeds.

The processing of seeds for oil begins by grinding or flaking to reduce particle size. (Seeds may or may not be hulled first.) Seeds are next cooked to help release the oil and then pressed.

Pressing greatly increases the temperature thereby decreasing the protein quality of the oil seed cake that remains. Also, the oil remaining in the press cake may quickly become rancid. Therefore, the press cake may be unsuitable for anything but fertilizer or fuel. By improving oil processing, oil press cakes can be used for animal feed and may even be suitable as ingredients in human foods thereby eliminating a significant food loss. Likewise, better recovery of oil will decrease the food loss.

Animal fat is processed (or rendered) on a small scale by cooking the fat-containing material in water. As the fat melts and is released from the tissues, it rises to the top of the container and can be recovered by skimming. (Rendering was common on U.S. farms until about 1940.) Commercial processes are similar but include pressure and stirring to increase the rate of heating. The fat is recovered by centrifuging rather than by skimming. The recovered fat may be used as food and as a starting material for soap manufacture.

PROCESSING DAIRY PRODUCTS. Milk is often processed in rural villages and households to produce butter and cheese. In butter production, the butter fat is first concentrated by centrifuging milk or by letting the cream rise. Low-fat skim milk is a by-product of this process that has high food value. If commercial processing equipment is available, this by-product can be converted into nonfat dry milk. Often in developed countries the skim milk is fed to animals. This is another example where a food loss can be avoided if adequate technology and equipment are available.

Cheese retains the fat and much of the protein from milk in a unique and stable product that is eaten in many countries. The by-product of cheese manufacture is whey containing protein and lactose (milk sugar). Lactose is good food but many people in developing nations become ill after eating it because they lack the proper digestive enzymes. To prevent complete loss in villages or households, whey is often fed to animals. On an industrial scale, whey may be recovered as a valuable food ingredient, and even the lactose can be removed.

The food preservation and processing done throughout the world in villages and households is of great value in reducing food losses and in recovering valuable foods. As knowledge, skills, and money become available, improvements will be made that can greatly increase food availability even with the same levels of agricultural production.

STORAGE, PRESERVATION, AND PROCESSING OF FOOD ON AN INDUSTRIAL SCALE. In developing countries, raw agricultural materials often are valuable exports. For example, coffee, tea, cocoa, groundnuts (peanuts), tropical fruits, and spices are sources of foreign exchange to the developing countries. One way to enhance a country's development is to process the agricultural commodities in the producing country and export the finished product. This greatly increases the product's value and also provides jobs. Following is a discussion of large-scale storage and its problems and some examples of large-scale, industrial treatments of foods that would be valuable assets for developing countries.

STORAGE. Large-scale grain storage and transportation facilities are needed for countries that import large amounts of grain and for countries that raise grain as a cash crop. Some storage facilities may be on the farm, as in the United States, but usually grain is stored in bulk in storage bins or elevators serving a community. Elevators take their name from the continuous chain of small buckets that move the grain. Warehouses in developing countries usually store grain in sacks. Labor often determines how grain is stored. If cheap labor is available, sacked grain can be moved in and out of storage on the backs of men, but if labor is expensive and capital is available, it may be cheaper to store grain in elevators and use machinery to move it.

As discussed before, grain must be dried to 14 percent moisture for safe storage. But large volumes complicate moisture problems because the grain comes from many different sources. Adequate sampling and accurate analyses are very important to ensure that grain is dry enough to store safely. Large storage facilities must be able to constantly monitor temperature and have a way to aerate and turn the grain to avoid heating. Grain can be fumigated to kill heavy insect infestations, but the only way to control mold is to keep moisture and temperature low.

Even with large, well-constructed storage facilities, predators can still be a problem. Rodents, in particular, will usually gain access to grain stores. The best control methods are trapping, using rodenticides, and keeping spills cleaned up.

Another problem in grain handling and storage is the dust produced by friction between grains. If the dust accumulates over time, it may create an extremely dangerous explosive hazard. The smallest spark coming from shovels or nailed boots striking metal, a careless cigarette smoker, or a welder can ignite an explosion large enough to destroy a storage facility. Removing dust through cyclone separators or filters and avoiding any source of sparks will minimize explosive dangers.

Large-scale storage of grains in developing countries can prevent losses caused by mold, insects, and predators if good management practices are used. And for countries that are spending scarce foreign exchange to import grains, it is important to minimize losses with modern and efficient storage facilities. Unfortunately, modern facilities are expensive; therefore, rich countries can afford to avoid food losses while poor countries cannot.

PRESERVATION AND PROCESSING. Presently, many agricultural products are raised in developing countries and then shipped to developed countries for further processing. Much of the profit in these products is in the processing, and keeping the processing in the developing countries could improve their economies and provide jobs. Following are suggestions for these processing opportunities.

Coffee is produced mainly in Central America, Brazil, Colombia, and certain African countries (Ivory Coast, Angola, Uganda, and Ethiopia). After handpicking the coffee berries, machines partially remove the pulp surrounding the beans, and the remaining pulp and mucilaginous layers are removed by washing or by microbial fermentation (Fig. 11.3). The beans are then dried from about 55 percent moisture to about 12 percent moisture by the sun or by heated air. At this stage, the beans still have an outer hull that must be removed, and then they are inspected and sorted for size and color. Processing to this point is done in the country of origin. The green coffee beans are then exported to the country where the coffee will be further processed and consumed.

In the importing country, coffee beans are roasted using dry heat to develop the desired coffee color and flavor. After roasting, most beans are ground, blended, and vacuum packed for sale. A few roasted beans are sold for grinding in households, and an increasing proportion of coffee is being brewed under industrial conditions, dried, and sold as instant or soluble coffee.

If coffee-producing countries could do the roasting, grinding, and packaging of coffee, they, rather than the developed countries, would re-

FIG. 11.3. Washing coffee beans to remove mucilage prior to drying.

alize the profit. Of even greater value would be the preparation and shipment of soluble coffee since the saving in shipping costs should be considerable. To become involved in these kinds of processing, developing countries would have to import processing equipment and packaging materials. The countries would also be limited to blending only coffees produced in their own country. Even so, there is an opportunity for coffee-producing countries to be involved in limited processing.

Most tea, like coffee, is grown in developing countries and exported to developed countries, although much tea is grown and consumed in

India and in China. Unlike coffee, however, except for final packaging and the production of instant or soluble tea, most tea is already being processed by the exporters.

Tea processing starts by slight drying or withering of the tea leaf. Next, rolling breaks the leaf and allows enzymatic action to take place. Then the leaves are heated (fired) to further dry them and stop the enzyme action. For black tea, the enzymatic action is intense over a 2 to 5 hour period. For green tea, the leaves are steamed before rolling to prevent enzyme action and then are fired. Oolong (a partially fermented green tea) has some enzymatic action but less than that for black tea.

The major way for developing countries to expand their tea processing would be to produce soluble tea if the demand for it continues to grow.

Chocolate and cocoa are produced from cacao beans grown in the tropical countries of Africa and South and Central America. The cacao bean, like the coffee bean, grows in a pod surrounded by pulpy and mucilaginous layers. First the pod is removed and the beans allowed to ferment briefly (3 to 5 days) to remove remaining pulp and mucilage. The beans are then dried, usually in the sun, to about 7 percent moisture. At this stage, the beans are stable and are shipped to consuming countries for further processing.

The manufacture of chocolate and cocoa begins by roasting the cacao bean to develop color and flavor. After hulling, the roasted beans, called nibs, are ground and heated until a liquid stream, called chocolate liquor, is produced. This liquor has a high fat content and can be processed in two ways. First, the fat (or cocoa butter) can be removed with hydraulic presses yielding a press cake that can be further processed by grinding and sifting into cocoa. Second, the chocolate liquor can be mixed with other ingredients, such as milk, sugar, and more cocoa butter, to form various types of chocolate.

The raw materials for such products as sugar, spices, and gums are also grown in developing countries and undergo a preliminary processing in these countries. Again, the final processing or refining is done in developed countries. The value added in the final processing may equal the value of the raw materials plus the preliminary processing. And so further processing into consumer products represents an excellent opportunity for developing countries to earn foreign exchange and to provide jobs, both of which may be needed as badly as food.

Other opportunities for developing countries exist in processing of tropical fruits. Bananas and pineapples are currently marketed in developed countries either as fresh fruit or as processed products, but as more is learned about how fruit ripens and how to care for fruit after harvesting, markets for fresh or processed mango, papaya, breadfruit, guava, plaintain, and others could be developed.

Some finished consumer food products are already being produced in developing countries. Two examples are mushrooms and oysters in

Taiwan and Korea. Still, as indicated, more opportunities exist.

Some people question producing food in food-deficient countries and shipping that food to countries that have sufficient food. This might be a valid concern if the only consideration were food. But economic development in poor countries also must include earning foreign exchange and providing jobs even when it sometimes involves producing and shipping food out of those countries.

NUTRITIONAL GAINS AND NEW FOODS. As just discussed, food losses can be minimized by preservation and the economic value of food increased by processing. A third matter to examine is how nutritional value is changed by processing. Generally, preservation or processing of food decreases its vitamin and mineral content. A common example is removing the bran from grain to make flour. But even such simple home preparation procedures as peeling remove nutrients. Most processing is done to remove parts people consider inedible or do not like. And usually the outer covering of fruits, vegetables, grains, and animals are less digestible than the inner parts.

Processing may preserve nutrients that would otherwise be lost. For example, the canning of peas destroys half of the thiamine (vitamin $B_1$) content. Presently no practical way is known to avoid this loss, but if the peas were not canned, thiamine would also be lost to consumers because only a small amount of peas could be grown and marketed fresh during a short period each year. Where laws allow it, food can be fortified with vitamins and minerals to make up for some preservation losses.

Fortification is a complex technology, but there are other simpler ways in which food processing can be used to increase nutrient availability. Consideration will now be given to blending of high-nutrition low-cost foods to increase amino acid availability and to production and processing of new food sources.

HIGH-NUTRITION LOW-COST FOODS. Recent advances in nutrition have increased our ability to design foods with good protein nutrition built into them. Proteins supply the eight essential amino acids needed for good nutrition. Human beings must have specific amounts of each of these eight essential amino acids to be well nourished. Some protein sources, particularly plant sources, do not have enough of one or more essential amino acids to ensure satisfactory protein nutrition. Therefore, diets based on a limited range of plant protein sources may be deficient in essential amino acids. (See also Chapter 2.)

By carefully choosing plant proteins or by blending several proteins in special foods, however, one can ensure that sufficient amounts of the essential amino acids are being ingested. These blended foods can be produced using a minimum of expensive animal proteins and thus have been called high-nutrition low-cost foods. Some examples of such foods are corn-soy milk (CSM) and wheat-soy-blend (WSB). These foods are not generally commercial products but are dry mixtures used by the United States mainly as gruels for infant and child feeding in food relief programs.

There have been many attempts to produce commercial products that could be described as high-nutrition low-cost foods, but none has enjoyed much success. Incaparina is a blend of plant proteins, vitamins, and minerals originally conceived by the Institute for Nutrition of Central America and Panama (INCAP) and later marketed by companies in Guatemala, El Salvador, Honduras, and Colombia. Incaparina has had more success than many similar products but still is not widely used. No easy explanation exists for why these products have not been accepted, but people tend to avoid new foods and are generally unwilling to accept a food that is used only by poor people. Also, these products have been relatively expensive because they are commercially produced.

New Foods. When food is in short supply, it is necessary to search out new supplies. Considerable effort has gone into this search, and three examples—single cell protein (SCP), leaf protein, and fish protein concentrate (FPC)—will be discussed briefly. As with high-nutrition low-cost foods, none of these new foods is yet a commercial success, but we do know a lot about the technology of producing them.

Eating microorganisms, usually yeasts or bacteria, is not new, but has never been widely practiced. Microbial cells, just like the cells of higher plants and animals, contain protein, fat carbohydrate, vitamins, and minerals and can be used to supply the nutrients humans need. These cells may contain as much as 50 percent protein on a dry weight basis, which accounts for the name single cell protein (SCP).

SCP production can be controlled much more closely than general agricultural production. The microbial cells can double in weight in one hour under ideal conditions in fermentation tanks. These ideal conditions include a carbon source, a nitrogen source, and large quantities of air or oxygen. The carbon source is often a waste, such as sulfite waste liquor from the paper industry, lactose in whey from the cheese industry, molasses from sugar refining, and most recently long-chain hydrocarbons from petroleum. When hydrocarbons are used to grow SCP, the result is sometimes referred to as protein from petroleum. The nitrogen source can be inorganic, and ammonium salts are frequently used.

SCP has the disadvantages of (1) being relatively high cost compared with agriculturally produced foods or feeds, (2) occasionally causing toxicity because of its high content of nucleic acids or residual hydrocarbons, and (3) having no well-defined food use for humans. Most advocates of SCP are promoting its use for animal feed, particularly for chickens and hogs. Some large-scale processing plants capable of producing 100,000 tons of SCP per year are being planned or built in Italy, Russia, and Japan.

Leaf protein refers to the protein recovered from any green leafy plant and processed for use as a food ingredient. This protein can be produced through conventional agriculture or by gathering plants already growing in tropical forests or in waterways. Even though we generally do not consider green leaves a rich source of protein, two tons of dried protein per hectare (2.47 acres) can be produced in a temperate climate like England and three tons per hectare in India is possible. For comparison, maize yields about 0.5 ton of dried protein per hectare in North America and rice yields about 0.3 ton of dried protein per hectare in Asia. The protein must be removed from leaves before it can be efficiently used by humans, and this can be done in a special processing plant designed to crush the leaves, extract the protein, and then dry it. The cellulose left over could then be used for cattle roughage.

Leaf protein has a green color that must be removed at extra cost before the taste is acceptable for incorporating into foods. Also, there is presently no ready market for the high cost leaf protein; whether it can be produced economically on a continuing basis is not known.

Fish protein concentrate (FPC) is produced from fish not normally used for food. Whole fish are ground and then the fat and malodorous compounds are removed. This mixture is then heated, dried, and milled to produce a bland nutritious product of low bacterial count.

At one time FPC or some similar nutritious source of inexpensive protein was thought to be what developing countries needed most. But people in developing countries are reluctant to use a new food, especially one that is not used regularly by another country or culture. Therefore FPC is not widely used.

Another possible addition to our food supply that is not actually a new food, but still is not widely used, is soy protein. After oil is removed from soybeans, a high protein meal remains. Even though it is not as nutritious as animal protein, soy protein quality is better than that of other grains and could contribute substantially to human nutrition. Soy protein has been used as human food for centuries in China, Japan, and Korea. And while almost 95 percent of soy protein currently goes to animal feed, it will make an increasing contribution to the food supply of all countries as we learn more about making it palatable. Considerable progress has been made with textured soy protein (TSP) in recent years in the United States, but it is still relatively expensive.

SUMMARY. The principles for avoiding losses of food through storage, preservation, and processing are well known. They may have to be adapted to new foods and different cultures, but killing bacteria that spoil food with heat or preventing their growth by drying, salting, or chilling will work just as well in Zaire, Laos, or Bangladesh as in France, Japan, or the United States.

For people in rural villages of developing countries, probably the most effective way to decrease food losses is by educating the people. Once they know what they can do to avoid food losses and what is being done by others, people will quickly take advantage of those savings for themselves. People must be able to read, to write, and to calculate needs or savings as well as have the opportunities and motivation to make improvements in the food system.

On an industrial scale, developing countries could gain valuable foreign exchange and provide needed jobs by developing plants to further process some of the raw agricultural products they supply to the developed world.

## BIBLIOGRAPHY

Christensen, C. M., ed. Storage of Cereal Grains and Their Products. 2nd ed. St. Paul, Minn.: American Association of Cereal Chemists, 1974.

Houston, D. F., ed. Rice Chemistry and Technology. St. Paul, Minn.: American Association of Cereal Chemists, 1972.

A Hungry World: The Challenge to Agriculture. Report of Food Task Force, Div. of Agricultural Sciences, University of California, Berkeley, 1974.

Orr, Elizabeth. The Use of Protein-Rich Foods for the Relief of Malnutrition in Developing Countries: An Analysis of Experience. London: Tropical Products Institute, 1972.

Pomeranz, Y., ed. Wheat Chemistry and Technology. 2nd ed. St. Paul, Minn.: American Association of Cereal Chemists, 1971.

Potter, N. N. Food Science. 2nd ed. Westport, Conn.: AVI Publishing Co., 1973.

# 12

# Constraints to Change—Social, Political, and Economic

LOYD K. FISCHER

THE TECHNICAL ASSISTANCE PROGRAMS of the U.S. have tried for many years to carry to the farmers of the developing countries the production technology of the industrial world. Yet after three decades and despite some quite spectacular increases in the yields of a few crops in a few areas, traditional production methods and widespread malnutrition persist in most of the developing world. One viewpoint, which may be inferred from this chapter's title, is that archaic social and political institutions in the developing nations prevent, or at least severely inhibit, the adoption of improved agricultural technology and thus are responsible for the persistence of malnutrition. The implication is that such institutions should be modified to be compatible with the agricultural technology of the developed nations.

However, another viewpoint is that the fundamental problems of the developing countries are not indigenous. On the contrary, some hold that their poverty is a consequence of international political and economic institutions that permit the world's wealthy countries to exploit the poor. Furthermore, some would argue that current U.S. agricultural technology is inappropriate in most developing countries and may even be short-lived in the developed world.

While these issues are being debated, people continue to die of malnutrition and hunger. Yet irrefutable evidence establishes that the world's natural resources, if used with appropriate technology, are more than adequate to provide sufficient food for all people now living. It follows then that the existence and persistence of world food problems are a consequence of defective social, political, and economic institutions. Therefore, the problem will be solved, if at all, not primarily by new technology but by improved human institutions. On the other hand,

LOYD K. FISCHER, Professor, Agricultural Economics Department, University of Nebraska, works largely on land tenure systems and economic and legal problems of water use. He has had assignments in Colombia and Bolivia. He has also been visiting professor at the University of Missouri.

the best of human institutions will fail to solve the problem without appropriate technology.

THE PROBLEM: POVERTY. For too long the world food problem has been addressed as the inability of the developing nations to produce sufficient foodstuffs to provide every person with some minimum number of calories per day. The effect of the deficiency in food production has been described in terms of some number of millions of people who die each year from malnutrition or starvation or who are on the verge of starvation. Solutions prescribed include reduced consumption of livestock products by the affluent and distribution of the grain products saved to the hungry. Also often advocated is increased support for technical assistance programs with the objective of "improving" farming practices in the developing countries. Most advocates of more technical aid seem to have in mind the type of assistance that has historically been directed toward inducing farmers to adopt "modern" production techniques, which depend heavily on machines, chemical pesticides, and commercial fertilizers.

MORE THAN MALNUTRITION. Unfortunately, the description of the problem and the proposed solutions just presented are much too simplistic. Attempting to measure the magnitude of the food problem in terms of people starving to death is to look at only one gruesome symptom of a condition that is far more complex and pervasive. Not all malnourished people are starving in the sense that the term is usually defined. Varying degrees of malnutrition, reflecting deficiencies of amino acids, vitamins, and minerals, adversely affect a major portion of the world's population, including many who have sufficient calories in their diets (see Chapter 2). Subtle and pernicious effects of qualitatively inadequate diets include reduced resistance to infectious diseases, weak bones, lack of physical and mental vigor, and permanently impaired mental capacity; all reduce the productivity of those so afflicted. In this sense, the malnourishment of the poor perpetuates and accentuates their poverty.

Furthermore, the hungry people of the world lack much more than adequate food. They are also ill clothed and badly housed. They usually lack even the most rudimentary facilities for waste disposal; their water is polluted and their surroundings are crowded, cluttered, and contaminated. Particularly in tropical and subtropical regions, where most of them live, the poor are plagued by rodents, insects, and various internal and external parasites. Medical and dental care and educational opportunities are deficient, if available at all. In short, not only are they malnourished, but they also lack many of the other necessities of life and virtually all the amenities.

Hungry people are inadequately nourished because they are so poor that they are unable either to produce or to purchase what they need. Therefore, the basic problem addressed in this chapter is poverty, of which malnutrition is just one consequence. Social and political institutions are obstacles to improved nutrition to the extent that they help perpetuate poverty. If effective development assistance were simply a matter of encouraging economic growth within given social and political structures, the vicious circles of poverty that bind millions into seemingly perpetual squalor would long since have been broken. But poverty is not necessarily eradicated, or even reduced, by economic growth. Nor does increased capacity to produce food assure a reduction in the number of hungry people. Robert McNamara, president of the World Bank, has stated on several occasions that even with very satisfactory rates of growth in the GNP in several developing nations, the welfare of the poorest 40 percent of their populations has not improved.

The development process involves far more than improving production techniques. Not only are changes in social, political, and economic institutions required for economic development, but they are probably the largest and most difficult part of economic development. At a conference on American foreign policy, Robert Heilbroner, an economist, presented four realities of the development process:

> One of these is the certainty that the revolutionary aspect of development will not be limited to the realm of ideas, but will vent its fury on institutions, social classes, and innocent men and women. Another is the great likelihood that the ideas needed to guide the revolution will not only be affirmative and reasonable, but also destructive and fanatic. A third is the realization that revolutionary efforts cannot be made, and certainly cannot be sustained, by voluntary effort alone, but require an iron hand, in the spheres both of economic direction and political control. And the fourth and most difficult of these realities to face is the probability that the political force most likely to succeed in carrying through the gigantic historical transformation of development is some form of extreme national collectivism or Communism (6).

Kenneth Boulding, another economist, has written that "economic development . . . involves teaching people to look at the world in different ways, to have different values, and to develop different images and skills . . ." (4). Nor are economists the only ones who view widespread malnutrition as more than a technological problem. Norman Borlaug, a noted plant breeder, cautioned that the Green Revolution would not solve the hunger problem but would only buy perhaps three decades of time. He states that

> there remains the unsolved social-economic problem of finding effective ways to distribute the needed additional food to the vast underprivileged masses who have little or no purchasing power. This is the great unsolved problem with which the economists, sociologists, and political leaders must now come to grips (3).

RELATIVE POVERTY. Poverty is defined in both relative and absolute terms. In relative terms, differences in levels of living between the inhabitants of the world's poorest and richest countries are immense and are increasing. On the one side are two dozen or so industrialized states whose 750 million affluent inhabitants consume most of the annually available world's resources and enjoy history's highest level of living, at least in terms of the consumption of goods and services. On the other side are more than 100 underdeveloped states with 2 billion people whose average incomes per capita are only a tiny fraction of the average incomes in the developed nations.

Not surprisingly, those who view poverty from positions of wealth perceive the problem quite differently than do the poor. Also defining the problem in terms of the disparity in wealth between the affluent and the poor leads to different conclusions than does viewing the problem in terms of human beings trapped in a state of misery and degradation. Furthermore the concept of a poor country is quite different from the concept of poor people. Paradoxically, some of the world's poorest people live in countries that possess great wealth, and some of the world's richest people live in countries that are heavily populated and poorly endowed with natural resources.

The leaders of the poor nations have emphasized the disparity between rich and poor states, although they usually appear less outraged by even greater disparities among their own citizens. They resent having to solicit aid from wealthy countries, since in their view it is the low prices paid by the wealthy nations for the products exported by the developing countries that make aid necessary. The view that poor countries are poor because the western industrialized states monopolize the resources of the world is propounded by virtually all leaders of the developing nations. This diagnosis of the problem leads to the conclusion that poverty would be solved if poor countries were adequately rewarded for what they produce.

But wealthy countries, like wealthy people, have the economic power to retain the riches they have and to acquire more. Neither wealthy countries nor wealthy people in poor countries seem inclined to make major sacrifices to reduce the gap between the rich and the poor. On the contrary, rich people contend that the existence and persistence of poverty and malnutrition is explained, not by an inequitable sharing of resources, but by the ignorance, superstitions, apathy, and indolence of the poor. The message from the wealthy to the poor is "Believe and behave as we do and you will be rewarded as we have been."

The leaders of the industrial states advise the citizens of the poor countries to emulate the wealthy countries, socially, politically, and technologically. In addition, the industrial countries, and especially the United States, have provided military, technical, and economic assistance, as well as food aid, to many developing nations with the stated objective of helping them escape the poverty trap. These efforts have not been notably successful, nor do the people receiving the aid appear particularly grateful for the assistance. Their view is that the aid returns to them only a tiny fraction of what is rightfully theirs and does so in ways that demean and humiliate them.

Conflicts between the rich and poor countries have up to now remained in the realm of international politics. The leaders of the poor nations recite a familiar litany of sins that they believe are being committed against them by the wealthy, western, industrialized nations: imperialism, unjust exploitation of resources, and neocolonialism. Within the United States and elsewhere the leaders of the developing nations are demanding a "New International Economic Order." Although this term has no precise definition, in essence it calls for a more equal sharing of the world's resources and of the products resulting from using those resources.

ABSOLUTE POVERTY. The absolute poverty problem goes beyond the glaring contrast between the life styles of the rich and the poor to actual physical deprivation. Approximately 25 percent of the world's inhabitants exist in conditions of poverty, misery, and despair. An estimated one billion people are suffering in some degree from malnutrition; perhaps half a million die each year of malnutrition and its consequences. Yet despite their high mortality and diminished life expectancy, the populations of most developing nations are literally exploding with more than 200,000 new mouths to feed every day. Simultaneously the cultivated land available for growing food is diminishing. Productive farm land is being engulfed by urban sprawl or destroyed by soil erosion or advancing sand dunes.

DIFFERENCES IN POVERTY AMONG DEVELOPING NATIONS. Poverty is a problem that afflicts all underdeveloped countries and is not absent from the developed nations. However, the various developing nations do differ markedly in their capacity to cope with the problem. At the bottom of the economic scale are perhaps 200 million people who live in countries that appear to be in a state of perpetual catastrophe. These countries include Bangladesh, Haiti, and a number of African countries, such as Ethiopia, Mali, and Chad. Their populations far exceed the numbers commensurate with their apparent resources. They have demonstrated no capacity to construct or operate social, economic, or political systems that will muster their people and natural resources to do battle against grinding poverty. Furthermore, they have few easily exploitable raw materials to sell abroad and are unable to grow enough food to adequately feed themselves. They seem destined to remain on a permanent dole or to be abandoned as hopeless. In either case they will in all likelihood remain into the forseeable future in a state of abject poverty with their populations being limited by the means of subsistence their production can supply.

In less desperate straits are another billion people living in the developing nations that have some raw materials, a reasonable land base for their current populations, some modern economic institutions and systems, and some trained technicians and administrators. These countries, unlike the poorest of the developing countries, appear to have the physical potential eventually to achieve self-sustaining economic growth; but not without (1) drastic changes in their social and political systems, (2) significant reductions in their rates of population growth, (3) financial help from the developed countries, and (4) basic change in the international economic system. This group includes Peru, Bolivia, Ecuador, most of Central America, Egypt, Jordan, India, Thailand, Pakistan, and Liberia.

A third group of developing nations, with perhaps 700 million inhabitants and with somewhat greater potential, includes the revenue-rich members of OPEC (Organization of Oil Exporting Countries) as well as countries whose development may be facilitated by other raw materials essential to the industrialized nations; for example, Zaire and Zambia (copper), Morocco (phosphates), Malaysia (tin, rubber, and timber), and Jamaica (bauxite). This group also includes nations like Taiwan, Singapore, South Korea, Mexico, Brazil, Colombia, Greece, and Turkey, which are developed enough to attract foreign investment and to borrow on commercial terms. Countries that are borderline between this group and the developed nations include South Africa, Portugal, Spain, and Argentina. These countries need time, appropriate technology, population control, and political will rather than massive foreign aid to escape the poverty trap. Clearly the countries that have been designated as developing nations are by no means homogeneous. Yet except for the globe's most difficult cases, such as Bangladesh, most of the poverty and malnutrition in these countries is explained not by a paucity of productive land and other natural resources, but instead by defective human institutions.

## ATTEMPTS AT COPING WITH POVERTY

THE GREEN REVOLUTION. Most of the developing nations do have land and other natural resources, which if properly managed could yield at least enough goods to provide for the basic needs of their current populations. Many have, in fact, substantially increased their output of goods and services (GNP) during the last couple of decades. In the late 1960s and early 1970s spectacular increases were achieved in the output of agricultural products by farmers in some areas of a number of developing countries. The development and adoption of new varieties of wheat and rice coupled with machines, fertilizer, irrigation, and pesticides were dubbed the Green Revolution. Many people hailed the developments as the beginning of a new era of abundance for all humanity. Behavioral scientists were persuaded that the new varieties offered such large potential rewards that the peasants' resistance to change, deemed by many the major obstacle to eliminating widespread malnutrition, would be overcome.

Others like Borlaug, who were better informed or more perceptive concerning the social and economic environment of the developing nations, were much less optimistic. No great insight was required to predict how the benefits from the Green Revolution would be distributed. First, those farmers with substantial land holdings, with access to capital, and with a voice in community affairs were able to acquire the fertilizer, pesticides, and irrigation water without which the new varieties yielded little if any more than the old. Only rarely were these inputs available to the small, peasant farmers. Furthermore, the impact on those who did not adopt the new technology was by no means neutral. Since the Green Revolution did little to improve the purchasing power of the malnourished, the increased output depressed the market price for agricultural products, thus reducing the income of the already poverty-stricken peasant farmer and landless laborer bypassed by the new technology.

The Green Revolution had equally adverse consequences on the international scene. Since the additional output of wheat and rice was being produced mostly for internal consumption, not for export, the importation of fertilizers, pesticides, irrigation pumps, fuel, etc., threw a heavy burden on the balance of payments of the developing nations. This effect was intensified by the energy crisis of 1973, when the price of crude oil quadrupled and rapid inflation occurred in the prices of other purchased inputs, particularly fertilizers that depend on petroleum for their production. Consequently, those countries where the transition had been most rapid found themselves unable to finance the necessary imports. Not surprisingly, the output of agricultural products in India, Mexico, and many other developing nations has increased little beyond 1973 levels while their populations continue their relentless growth.

THE CONCEPT OF CARRYING CAPACITY AND LIFE-STYLES. When addressing issues concerning human population pressures, ecologists, economists, demographers, environmentalists, and others often refer to "carrying capacity." The term is borrowed from livestock producers or game management specialists who attempt to determine the maximum number or density of creatures that can live perpetually in a given habitat without destroying it. When applied to humans, as is often done, the term "carrying capacity" may be seriously misleading. In the first place cattle may be satisfied with the minimum biological necessities of life; people are not. At least they are not if they have ever experienced or observed a more abundant life. Second, people have not been limiting their consumption of products to a level that can be maintained indefinitely. On the contrary, much of the world's current agricultural production depends upon rapid exploitation of exhaustible resources, which now appear all too finite.

Nor is depletion of irreplaceable natural resources solely the result of excess consumption by the affluent. On the contrary, with heavy population pressure or in fragile ecosystems, the most technologically backward people despoil their environment even while living in abject poverty. Not only the declining world reserves of petroleum and minerals but also the advancing sand dunes in the Sahel of Africa and the denuded landscape in the high plains of Bolivia give grim testimony to the proposition that people are not just living on the earth's surface; they are using it up.

The concept of "carrying capacity" can be legitimately applied to humans only when a population is producing and consuming in a manner that can be sustained indefinitely, at an acceptable level of living, from the inexhaustible resources to which it has perpetual access. Those who view Japan, or the densely populated areas of Western Europe, as evidence of the earth's immense "carrying capacity" are being seriously mislead. The appropriate analogy for these countries is not that of a pasture but that of a feedlot. Their populations and economic systems, like those of the United States, are being sustained not by their own renewable resources but by consumption of the world's exhaustible (nonrenewable) mineral and energy resources.

With a very different life-style, approximately 20 percent of the world's population lives in China. They occupy only about 5 percent of the habitable part of the earth's surface, a portion that is likely no better than average in terms of natural resource endowment. Yet, despite a population density perhaps four times that of the world as a whole, the 900 million Chinese people are apparently well enough nourished, housed, and clothed to maintain physical and mental vigor. Furthermore, that massive population is being sustained with a minimal use of exhaustible resources for the production of food and fiber, although synthetic nitrogen fertilizer is being produced and used in increasing amounts (5).

Given the life-style, level of living, and techniques of agricultural production of China, the "carrying capacity" of this planet might be approximately 16 billion people, or four times the present population. This potential would appear to give humanity a large cushion. However, at current growth rates, world population will quadruple to 16 billion by the year 2050, or within the life expectancy of children already born. If population were to rise to that level, the increase in output necessary to provide adequately for the biological necessities of life must occur primarily where land resources are abundant relative to the number of people being sustained. Furthermore, to avoid intolerable distribution costs the people must live near the source of products. In other words, world population can increase to 16 billion people only if a major portion of that increase occurs in North America.

If 16 billion people is accepted as the "carrying capacity" of the earth on the Chinese system, how many people can be sustained indefinitely with a level of living that is less onerous and austere? Of particular interest to most people is the viability of their own life-styles and levels of living. The various accessories of modern life, such as central heating and air conditioning, airplanes, automobiles, tractors, automatic washing machines, television sets, etc., are currently all made and operated from resources being rapidly exhausted. Only to the extent that such contrivances can be produced and operated from resources not being exhausted will they be available for an indefinite period.

But perhaps human welfare is not well measured in terms of mechanical contrivances. Alternatively, the good life could be defined in terms of (1) surroundings that are uncrowded, serene, and pleasing to the senses, (2) food, clothing, and shelter adequate in quantity and quality for health, (3) time for contemplation, study, and communication with other people, (4) the opportunity to work at tasks, the products of which are beneficial, physically and spiritually, to the producer and to others, (5) security of person and property, and (6) a wide latitude for individual decision making. The population of the earth already appears to be too numerous to permit all mankind to enjoy for all time either of the life-styles just described. Clearly neither is compatible with 16 billion people.

The foregoing, which argues that current levels of population neither explain nor excuse poverty and malnutrition, should not be construed as a rationalization for ignoring the rate of population increase. On the contrary, continued rapid population growth foredooms every effort to relieve human misery. In fact, at some point not far removed, the rate of population growth in the world will be reduced to zero and may well become negative. Either birth rates will fall or death rates will rise until the two equate. The human species, as is true of every other organism, cannot continue to proliferate indefinitely in a finite world.

Presumably human beings, unlike the lower animals, can predetermine the maximum population compatible with their environment and avoid exceeding that limit. Most people would likely agree that the maximum number of people that could be physically sustained is beyond the optimum population, although opinions may differ widely as to what is the optimum. Also, the social and political institutions appropriate for the life-style and production technology of the industrial state are very different from those appropriate for China. The important issue that seems to have been largely ignored in past technical assistance programs is that the U.S. social and political system is not only unattainable but is also inappropriate for most if not all of the developing nations of the world. In fact, the free enterprise system and emphasis on individual rights may well be a casualty in the western world before the year 2000 unless life-styles are made more compatible with the environment.

Foreign Aid. An assessment of U.S. economic and technical assistance programs does not present an encouraging picture. True enough, U.S. aid to Japan, Britain, and Western Europe, after the devastation of World War II, contributed substantially to the spectacular recovery of those countries. On the other hand, among the developing nations, those that have received U.S. aid seem to have made less progress on the average than those that have not. One need only view the recent history of the two most populous countries in the world, India and China, to question the efficacy of U.S. aid. Clearly U.S. assistance to Indians has not resulted in their being freed from malnourishment or even the threat of famine (see Chapter 17). Conversely, during the same period China has apparently been able to eliminate malnutrition as a significant problem. China's progress has been achieved despite (1) an even larger population than that of India, (2) somewhat inferior land resources, and (3) economic strictures imposed by the United States. Could it be that U.S. aid to India has impeded rather than facilitated progress toward the goal of adequate food for all Indians? Conversely, has the mutual hostility between China and the developed countries contributed to China's success by persuading the Chinese to look to their own resources to solve their food problem?

It goes without saying that only the most poverty-stricken would find the lot of the Chinese peasant an enviable one. On the other hand, his condition is by no means as pitiable as that of the hopeless, starving peasant of Bangladesh. Furthermore, if the U.S. population were four times its present level, or roughly equal to that of China, it might be unable to match the Chinese accomplishment in providing for the biological necessities of its people, particularly after the oil wells run dry. Also, with a population density equivalent to China's, U.S. citizens would likely be no less regimented since freedom of individual action is a luxury that is among the first casualties of resource scarcity and overcrowding.

UNDERLYING CAUSES OF POVERTY. As illustrated by the Chinese example, technical knowledge and natural resources are available in the world to produce the biological necessities of life for perhaps four times the number of people currently living. Furthermore, this goal could be achieved with only a minimal input of exhaustible resources. But with much of the developed world's agriculture currently based on irreplaceable energy and material resources, many people suffer from malnutrition. Why are people severely deprived in an abundant world? Surely no one can believe that hungry people would rather starve than work. The explanation must be that the social, political, and economic systems of the world and of individual nations do not permit human and natural resources to be combined in ways that will yield the required goods and distribute them to those in need.

A number of issues are disputed concerning the role of the developed nations, and particularly of the United States, in the existence and persistence of malnutrition and general poverty in the developing nations. Some of the charges leveled against the developed nations by the developing nations are as follows:

1. Aid programs and investments from the industrial nations have undermined their dignity and cultures;

2. Foreign aid has further enriched the already wealthy, helped the middle class, and intensified the impoverishment of the poverty-stricken;
3. The international economic system has been rigged to keep the developing nations dependent;
4. The industrial West has systematically plundered the developing countries, exploiting their natural resources and their people; and
5. Efforts by the industrial states to induce the developing nations to limit population growth are intended to (a) keep the poor countries weak and (b) save their natural resources for the wealthy.

Two questions concerning these charges need to be examined. How valid are they? And to what degree do they explain the existence and persistence of poverty in the developing nations? Certainly ancient social systems are disrupted if and when "modern" technology is adopted. Overwhelming evidence establishes that in most of the developing nations the social and political systems function to promote and protect the interests of a wealthy minority at the expense of the masses. Barnet and Müller describe the typical underdeveloped country this way:

> What a curious contradiction of rags and riches. One out of every ten thousand persons lives in a palace with high walls and gardens and a Cadillac in the driveway. A few blocks away hundreds are sleeping in the streets, which they share with beggars, chewing-gum hawkers, prostitutes, and shoeshine boys. Around the corner tens of thousands are jammed into huts without electricity or plumbing. Outside the city most of the population scratches out a bare subsistence on small plots, many owned by the few who live behind the high walls. Even where the soil is rich and the climate agreeable most people go to sleep hungry. The stock market is booming, but babies die and children with distended bellies and spindly legs are everywhere. There are luxurious restaurants and stinking open sewers. The capital boasts late-model computers and receives jumbo jets every day, but more than half of the people cannot read. Government offices are major employers of those who can, but the creaky bureaucracy is a joke except to the long line of supplicants who come seeking medical help or a job. (For supplicants with money for a bribe the lines shorten miraculously.) (1)

Galeano, a Latin American, Marxist writer-journalist, also decries disparity in wealth not only among nations but also within the developing nations. According to the United Nations, six million Latin Americans at the top of the economic and social pyramid possess as much wealth as the 140 million at the bottom. Commenting bitterly on the behavior of the wealthy, Galeano writes:

> Adding insult to injury, they squander in sterile ostentation and luxury, and in unproductive investments, the capital that Latin America could devote to the replacement, extension, and generation

> of job-creating means of production. Harnessed as they have always been to the constellation of imperialist power, our ruling classes have no interest whatsoever in determining whether patriotism might not prove more profitable than treason, and whether begging is really the only formula for international politics (5).

Barnet and Müller describe further the social and economic malaise that suffocates enterprise in the developing nations.

> Nationalist slogans are prominent, but the basic industries are in the hands of foreigners. The houses behind the walls are filled with imported cameras, TVs, tape recorders, and fine furniture from the United States or Europe, but the major family investment is likely to be a Swiss bank account. There appear to be three groups in the country distinguishable by what they consume. A tiny group lives on a scale that would make a Rockefeller squirm. A second group, still relatively small in number, live much like the affluent middle class in the United States—the same cars, the same Scotch, the same household appliances. The vast majority eat picturesque native foods like black beans, rice, and lentil soup—in small quantities. The first two groups are strong believers in individual development for themselves and their family, but they see no solution for the growing plight of the third group. So they fear them, and their walls grow higher. For the third group, disease, filth, and sudden death are constant companions, but there is an air of resignation about them. Life has always been full of pain and uncertainty and it always will be. The only development they see is the same journey from cradle to an early grave that their fathers and their grandfathers took (1).

The conclusions of these writers are closely parallel. Barnet and Müller are describing what they perceive to be the impact on the world economy of the operations of the multinational corporations. Galeano, in much more emotional terms, protests what he sees as the exploitation of the many poor by the few wealthy inherent in the capitalist system.

These writers believe that whether the blame is placed on corrupt and greedy ruling classes in the developing nations, or on the machinations of the managers of immensely powerful, multinational corporations, the result is obvious. Power over the wealth produced in the developing countries has been largely in the hands of foreigners and consequently has not been used to expand local economies. The result has been a process of wealth depletion in the developing nations and wealth generation in the developed nations. Galeano expresses the view widely held in the developing nations that ". . . our wealth has always generated our poverty by nourishing the prosperity of others . . ." and ". . . the history of Latin America's underdevelopment is . . . an integral part of the history of world capitalism's development" (5).

The conclusion that must be drawn is that the social and political systems of the developing nations must change and change drastically if the poor of the world are to be relieved of their misery. However, changes must also occur in the international economic area. These changes, which are already occurring, will cause social, political, and economic disruptions of no small magnitude in the developed world as well. What would be the consequences in the industrial world if the leaders of the developing nations were knowledgeable, incorruptible, and dedicated to the goal of promoting the interests of their own people?

Historically, the international economic system has not functioned according to the classic model of a competitive market. Trade between the developed countries and the developing countries is conducted mainly by huge multinational corporations. Each of these giant, vertically integrated companies controls assets and revenues that exceed those of most of the world's countries. Typically they have extracted or produced raw materials in the developing countries and transported the commodities to their plants for processing and/or fabrication, then sold the brand-name products throughout the world. Evidence exists that these corporations do manipulate markets and governments to their advantage, and often to the advantage of those able to buy their products.

RECENT CHANGES IN INTERNATIONAL ECONOMICS. Although most of the multinational corporations are U.S. based, the allegiance of their management is to their companies and not to any nation. Yet few would deny that the principal victims of their machinations have been the developing nations. Historically the prices of their products, whether agricultural or mineral, have been established almost unilaterally by the multinational companies. Only very recently has OPEC gained control of prices of a commodity being produced in their countries. The drastic increases in the price of crude oil in 1973 were rationalized by OPEC partly by the fact that the producing countries had been unable to achieve gains before that time. OPEC is now attempting to establish the principle of indexing. They propose that future oil prices be maintained in approximately the current relationship with the prices of the industrial products being purchased by the petroleum-exporting countries. Not surprisingly, the oil-importing states, led by the United States, oppose this action.

The success of OPEC has not only delighted but also enlightened the developing nations. Their leaders are now conscious that the world's industrial nations have become as dependent upon the developing nations as the developing nations are upon them. The increasing awareness within the poor countries of the vulnerabilities of the rich means that their leaders are likely to make greater use of their bargaining power (2). Although the multinational companies are trying to strengthen their international alliances, the competition for raw materials and profits among the United States, Japan, and Western Europe is apparent to every sophisticated leader in the developing countries.

The poor countries with scarce raw materials and cheap labor now have a choice of customers. Perhaps they are finally heeding the advice that they behave as we do. Their attempts to ensure that a major share of the fruits of their labor and natural resources are returned to them to build their economies and feed their people is a new development in international affairs. The "New International Economic Order" may arrive sooner than expected. Furthermore, its establishment will be in response not to rhetoric but to reality. And when it does arrive, the social and political adjustments required of the developed nations may well be as far-reaching and painful as those required in the developing nations.

SUMMARY. The world's resources, if properly used, are capable of yielding more than enough goods to provide adequate food and other biological necessities of life for all people now living. A major problem is that the natural resources are distributed unevenly among the nations of the world. A further complication is that the poor people in the developing nations have few opportunities for gainful employment even in those countries well endowed with land and other natural resources. Also, the rapid population growth in the developing countries leads (1) to an overabundance of labor, (2) avid competition for the available jobs, and (3) low wages for those who are employed.

Virtually everyone agrees that changes must occur in social and political systems if widespread poverty and malnutrition are to be eliminated or even substantially reduced. However, opinions are by no means uniform as to which institutions must change, and the nature, urgency, and magnitude of the changes required. Within the developing nations, stultifyig social systems, mishandling of public affairs, concentrations of wealth and political power, and rapid rates of population growth all combine to trap perhaps 40 percent of their people in conditions of grinding poverty.

However, not all the problems lie within the developing countries. Just as the economic systems within the developing nations are geared to favor the wealthy, so too the world economic order operates to exploit their raw materials and labor to provide cheap and abundant goods for the developed nations. However, for those developing countries that possess abundant mineral and energy resources, the prospects for change in international markets appear bright. The success of OPEC in quadrupling the price of crude oil can be attributed to neither the shrewdness of their leaders nor the altruism of their principal customers. It reflects instead the insatiable appetite for energy in the developed world.

As the developed nations compete more avidly for raw materials and cheap labor, the developing nations find themselves, for the first time, with a choice of customers. They have the opportunity to derive greatly increased revenues from what they export, and the wealth generated will be controlled by their governments and citizens. If significant portions of the increased revenue are not used to improve the productivity and welfare of the poverty-stricken, the blame can no longer be placed on the wealthy nations or on the multinational corporations. For the first time, the destiny of some of the developing nations will be largely in the hands of their own citizens.

The frightening prospect is that the revenue obtained from the exportation of minerals and fossil fuels will be used not for investment but instead to produce or purchase goods for consumption by ever-growing populations. If this is the course followed, then in the years to come, as their natural resources become depleted, more and more of the developing countries will join not the developed world but the permanent paupers.

The inescapable prospect is that in the forseeable future, only those developing nations that possess sufficient wealth or productive capacity to provide for their people's needs will be able to free themselves from the bonds of poverty. Nor is such an outcome certain even in the wealthiest of them. The paradox is that higher prices for the products of the developing countries with something to sell takes income away from the poorest developing countries—as well as from wealthy countries. Even the oil- or mineral-rich developing countries are likely to find that inflated prices of their imports will offset higher revenues from their sales.

The problems associated with making all people productive are far from solution. Furthermore, we are even further from a world in which those who possess neither wealth nor the capacity to produce will fare well. Clearly eliminating widespread malnutrition from the developing countries requires that (1) their populations be limited to a density that their resources can support, (2) their people be prepared and given opportunities to be gainfully employed, and (3) their people's productive efforts be rewarded at levels that permit them to live with dignity and invest for the future.

## REFERENCES

1. Barnet, Richard J., and Müller, Ronald E. Global Reach, pp. 133–134.
2. Bergsten, Fred C. A New OPEC in Bauxite. Challenge 18 (3): 112–120.
3. Borlaug, Norman E. The Green Revolution, Peace, and Humanity. Presentation given on the Occasion of the Award of the Nobel Peace Prize for 1970, Oslo, Norway, December 11, 1970.
4. Boulding, Kenneth E. The Knowledge Boom. Challenge 14 (6): 57.
5. Galeano, Eduardo. Open Veins of Latin America, pp. 12–13.
6. Heilbroner, Robert. Counterrevolutionary America. Commentary, April 1967.
7. Sprague, G. F. Agriculture in China. In Food: Politics, Economics, Nutrition and Research, ed., Philip H. Abelson. Washington, D.C.: American Association for the Advancement of Science, 1975, pp. 57–64.
8. Whyte, William Foote. Organizing for Agricultural Development.

## BIBLIOGRAPHY

Abelson, Philip H. Food: Politics, Economics, Nutrition and Research. Washington, D.C.: American Association for the Advancement of Science, 1975.

Adelman, Irma, and Morris, Cynthia Taft. Economic Growth and Social Equity in Developing Countries. Stanford, Calif.: Stanford University Press, 1973.

Barnet, Richard J., and Müller, Ronald E. Global Reach. New York: Simon and Schuster, 1974.

Black, C. E. The Dynamics of Modernization. New York: Harper and Row, 1966.

Caprihan, S. P. Fight Against Hunger in Developing Countries. Bhopal, India: J. K. Jain Brothers, 1975.

Galeano, Eduardo. Open Veins of Latin America. New York: Monthly Review Press, 1973.

Paddock, William, and Paddock, Paul. Time of Famines: America and the World Food Crisis. Boston, Mass.: Little, Brown & Co. 1975.

Whyte, William Foote. Organizing for Agricultural Development. New Brunswick, N.J.: Transaction Books, 1975.

E. R. DUNCAN

*Feeder roads are needed for agricultural development.*

# 13

# Institutions and Facilities—Development Considerations

MELVIN G. BLASE

THE JOB of feeding a nation is only half done when farm products are harvested. There still remains the task of getting the produce to the ultimate consumer. Even that is not as simple as it sounds because it must get to the consumer at the time and in the place desired and be processed and packaged properly, too. Someone must provide the capital and management to furnish the services needed for this important task.

Businesses, cooperatives, individuals, churches, and other organizations provide the direction and inputs required to get the farm products to the consumer as needed. But the job is even bigger than that, for the farms and the rural areas must have supplies and services that will not only allow them to farm efficiently but also result in their sharing in the good life on a level equal to that enjoyed by city residents. All the marketing, farm supply, and rural services both public and private are required, and in the right combinations, to assure sufficient food production and a prosperous rural community.

For an efficiently functioning economy in any nation, a foundation of social and physical institutions and facilities must be available and well organized. These institutions and facilities include *transportation* (roads, railroads, air and water carriers, etc.), *communication networks* (telephone, radio, etc.), *credit* (banks, both private and government, available money, credit supervision, etc.), *education and research* (all levels of education and at least adaptive research), *markets and marketing* (locations where products are bought and sold, and a system for efficiently moving products from the producer or manufacturer to the consumer), and *irrigation and drainage*. *Planning units* of government may also be included. These things and others like them are taken for granted in the developed nations because they have been established over the past century or more and are available for use. These make up

MELVIN G. BLASE is Professor, Agricultural Economics, University of Missouri-Columbia, and Acting Executive Director, MIAC (Midamerica International Agricultural Consortium of the University of Nebraska–Lincoln, Kansas State University, Iowa State University, and University of Missouri–Columbia). He has had foreign research assignments in Africa, Asia, and Latin America.

what is commonly called, for want of a better term, *infrastructure.*

Infrastructure investments are largely made by governments from tax funds because individuals and small segments of society can seldom afford the cost. Such investments are usually paid for from taxes. Private individuals and groups formed into cooperatives and private businesses may make significant contributions to the infrastructure of a country.

Infrastructure is necessary for economic growth of an agricultural economy, but will not by itself guarantee development. As Yudelman has pointed out, increased agricultural productivity comes only when farmers themselves increase investments and expenditures (6). Infrastructure supplies the farmer with services and facilities he needs. Thus the need for investments in infrastructure is seen as only one of a series of factors necessary to expedite development (3).

Even so, infrastructure investments are extremely important to agricultural development. For example, Mosher, in his widely used book on agricultural development, has identified five factors necessary for any agricultural development to take place: (1) markets for farm products, (2) constantly changing technology, (3) local availability of supplies and equipment, (4) transportation, and (5) production incentives for farmers (5). Four of these five essentials are items of infrastructure, the fifth being the exception.

In addition, Mosher contends that there are five accelerators necessary for rapid agricultural development: (1) education for development, (2) production credit, (3) group action by farmers, (4) improving and expanding agricultural land, and (5) national planning for agricultural development. All five have implications for infrastructure investments.

Two unique characteristics make infrastructure investments more important to agriculture than to other industries: First, farms are widely dispersed geographically to take advantage of the various soils and climate conditions that support plant life. Second, the numerous farmers are not organized into any centralized organization. Each of the millions of farms represents an individual decision-making unit that depends on the public sector for adequate transportation, communication, and other physical and institutional infrastructure.

In traditional economies where infrastructure does not exist, farmers have no support in trying to develop beyond subsistence agriculture. This, plus the farmers' dependence on the vagaries of weather, has reinforced their tendency toward fatalism, merely accepting whatever happens as what was meant to be.

This presentation will begin by considering the various physical and institutional investments of infrastructure and then examine how countries can best determine their investment priorities to expedite agricultural development.

## PHYSICAL AND INSTITUTIONAL INVESTMENTS

TRANSPORTATION—WALKING IS A POOR ALTERNATIVE. In many developing countries, walking is the only means of transportation available for farm families. A high percentage of Ethiopia's farm families, for example, are at least a 4-hour walk away from the nearest road. In such a situation, it is at best difficult to transport heavy, bulky farm inputs, such as fertilizer and seed, and outputs, such as grain. Consequently, subsistence agriculture tends to continue.

Transportation, of course, can be provided by facilities other than roads. In addition to paved highways, a transportation system can include paths, dirt roads, canals, highways, rivers, and railroads. But these different kinds of local and long distance transportation facilities must add up to a well-integrated system of transport serving the widely dispersed farms by bringing supplies and equipment close to each farm and taking products from the farms to urban consumers (5).

New transportation facilities have often had a marked impact on communities. For example, in one area of the Philippines, one year after roads were built sales of corn and tobacco nearly doubled and those of chickens increased by two-thirds. Not only did the roads provide a way of physically moving the increased production, but they resulted in lower costs for transportation. Thus more of the profit went to the farmers. The village price of maize (corn) increased by almost 25 percent. Roads made the community more accessible, so government officials responsible for education, social welfare, and medicine visited more frequently. Even more important were the much more frequent visits by the credit agency representative and the extension service representative.

Improved transportation can also result from improvements in other infrastructure elements. For example, in an Indonesian community, the research and extension institutions developed a new package of practices that increased maize production 600 percent. In turn, farmers in the area were motivated to improve a road to the major highway so that the 35 tons of fertilizer required and the 200 tons of maize produced each year could be hauled by truck.

These are just two illustrations of how transportation facilities that enable low-cost movement of both inputs and outputs aid in the transformation from subsistence to commercialized agriculture.

COMMUNICATIONS—SILENCE CAN BE DEADLY TO DEVELOPMENT. Communication is especially important in agriculture because farms are widely dispersed. Two primary types of communications are needed for transforming traditional agriculture: (1) information on production techniques, and (2) information about prices.

In subsistence agriculture, production practices tend to remain the same from generation to generation. Thus, introducing new technology requires effective communication. In the United States and some other relatively developed countries, both mass media and the "trickle-down" process are used to introduce new practices. In the "trickle-down" process, new technology is introduced to community leaders whose subsequent experiences can then be emulated by others in the community. In many developing countries, however, neither the "trickle-down" process nor the mass media is effective. Frequently, leaders have such large farms that small farmers feel it is futile to attempt to duplicate the experiences of large farmers. Mass media use, particularly the written word, is limited because most people in many rural areas cannot read.

Communications concerning prices are equally inadequate. In many developing countries, the price of the same agricultural product in one area may often be double that in another area nearby. Whenever price information does not move swiftly, therefore, opportunists can make windfall profits.

Both of these communication problems are particularly prevalent in countries with multiple languages. In Peru, for example, technical and market information must be translated from Spanish into Quechua and then communicated by radio to be useful to most farmers living in the mountains. This translation process is one more complication in establishing an effective communication network.

DAMS—PUTTING WATER TO WORK. Dams are used to impound water for generating electric power and for irrigation. These highly visible structures exemplified development activities early in the post-World War II period. Dams were desirable since they represented means for dramatically increasing production on irrigated acreages and they made electricity available in villages and on some farms. Unfortunately, the dams were also very expensive. Consequently, much less emphasis has been placed upon them recently, even though it is still relatively easy to get financing for such visible developments (see Chapter 15).

The costs of providing electricity in rural areas tend to be quite high. A World Bank study recently indicated that these costs are sensitive to the level and growth of demand, the level of use, the distances between demand centers, and the difficulty of the terrain. At the same time, revenues are usually low in the early years of rural electrification programs, even when the response has been good. Nevertheless, with rising petroleum prices, alternative energy sources may become so expensive that hydroelectric power will again become a high-priority need for infrastructure investment.

In many parts of the world, especially in tropical areas with pronounced wet and dry seasons, irrigation provided by dams can play a major role in increasing agricultural production. For example, in Taiwan, investments in irrigation and flood control have materially helped development in agriculture. During the 1920s the total investment in irrigation facilities rose sharply, accounting for nearly 15 percent of Taiwan's total capital investment. By the 1956–60 period, investment had doubled; but, because the nonfarm sector of the economy was so much more important by that time, the investment represented only

7.5 percent of the country's total investment. Nevertheless, investments in irrigation facilities enabled Taiwan to make some of the most rapid strides in increasing agricultural output of all the developing countries.

Investments in dams alone are not sufficient to supply needed irrigation water, however. Without a distribution system, irrigation water will not reach farmers. For example, in Turkey, only dam construction has been emphasized. Consequently, water is still behind the recently completed dams waiting for a distribution system that may not yet even be on the drawing boards.

Good distribution systems require that (1) farmers along the distribution canals know when water will be available, (2) sufficient water be available at proper intervals to maintain crop growth, and (3) excessive water that will only evaporate be avoided. A frequent problem in water distribution is that farmers near the source take most of the water while those at the end of the canal are unsure of water supplies.

Drainage—Putting Water in its Place. Investments in drainage facilities have been important in both arid areas that are irrigated and in humid areas where flooding frequently occurs. The advantages in flood areas are obvious, but drainage is also vital to irrigation projects, as described by Milikan and Hapgood.

> Many irrigation projects fail because of lack of drainage. Excess water, instead of draining off the irrigated fields, simply seeps underground and raises the water table. The water table may also be raised by canal leakage. When the underground water has risen sufficiently, water is sucked up by capillary action and evaporates at the surface, a residue of salt accumulates in the fields, and the productivity of the land gradually diminishes. Drainage of excess water to control salinity is as important in the long run as providing the water in the first place. This principle was neglected in the Indus plain in West Pakistan, the world's largest irrigation scheme, and as a result large areas have been lost to production (4).

Clearly these highly visible investments are beyond the capacity of most individual farmers and require some type of public investment through government or groups for particular development purposes. These kinds of development projects still need other less obvious support, particularly from institutions.

INSTITUTIONAL INFRASTRUCTURE—THE LESS OBVIOUS. As mentioned earlier, only recently has the importance of institutional infrastructure in development been recognized. Indeed, its role in expediting agricultural development may be more important than physical infrastructure.

The following institutions will be discussed in some detail: markets for agricultural inputs and products, credit institutions, research institutions, agricultural education institutions, planning institutions, local government institutions, and legal systems.

MARKETS—THE LIFEBLOOD OF AN EXCHANGE ECONOMY. In a subsistence economy, markets are relatively unimportant because inputs are not bought and farm output is not sold. As development proceeds, however, the availability of inputs, such as improved seeds and fertilizer, as well as of markets for farm produce, becomes increasingly important. Development of marketing institutions is often difficult, however, because in many countries those who only buy and sell what others produce ". . . are despised as social parasites" (5). Often these "middlemen" are members of another race or country—"the Chinese in southeast Asia, the Indians in east Africa, and the Lebanese in west Africa" and "it has been too easy to underrate both the importance and the real costs of marketing" (5).

Closely related to the recognition of the importance of marketing is the need for farmers to have confidence in the marketing system. If farmers have an unfavorable experience with a marketing system, they tend to develop a long-standing suspicion of it. Especially in the early stages of development this severely retards development. For example, in one Latin American country, farmers attempted to form a cooperative to purchase a truck to haul their potatoes (their entire farm output that was sold) to the central market in the country's major city. When the truck arrived at the market, however, it was denied entry to the central marketplace. Forced to park some distance from the market, the farmers had to sell their potatoes for less than if they had been selling in the central market. These farmers were reluctant to be so venturesome with their marketing activities in subsequent years.

Confidence in the marketing system must be built upon a perceived equity and fairness, which is absent from many markets in developing countries.

There are several essential functions that must be performed in conjunction with marketing. The first is *transportation*. Again, because farms are widely dispersed, the need to assemble and transport large quantities to make their handling efficient is an essential part of the marketing process. Closely related to this process is *storage*. Obviously, products available at harvesttime are needed by consumers all year round. Storage with a minimum of waste is difficult in developing countries. For perishable crops, storage is impossible without *processing*. Most grains also require some processing before consumption. Rice must be milled and wheat ground into flour. Thus, processing, storage, and transportation widen the market for farm products. In turn, this increases the likelihood that the profitability of production will be enhanced.

Before processing, storage, and transportation can take place, there must be provisions for *financing*. Someone must finance the marketing function if farmers are to be paid when they deliver their products to the local buyer. The final essential function is *managing* the whole marketing operation. Those who assemble products must have contacts to whom they can be shipped. Likewise, buyers must have sources of supply available to them. Getting the right commodities to the right places at the right times with a minimum of waste is the intricate task of market organization.

CREDIT—THE MOBILIZER OF PURCHASED INPUTS. In May 1975, the World Bank estimated that there were outstanding institutional loans for agriculture in developing countries of approximately $15 billion. The actual total is unknown because much of it originates in informal sources, but the Bank estimated that the total amount outstanding is at least five times the estimated outstanding institutional credit. Thus, agricultural credit is big business, even in developing countries where a considerable amount of subsistence agriculture still exists.

The Bank reports that the availability of institutional credit in the developing world varies widely. In certain African countries, only about 1 percent of all farmers were believed to use institutional credit, while in Taiwan nearly all farmers have access to it. Overall, about 5 percent of the farmers in Africa use institutional credit as compared with about 15 percent in Latin America and Asia (excluding China). As expected, larger farmers have been the main beneficiaries of institutional credit. Frequently, 70 to 80 percent of the small farmers in a developing country have virtually no access to credit. Even when institutional credit is accessible, it may be available only for short-term loans, often one cropping season.

An indication of the growing importance of agricultural credit is found in the agricultural lending program of the World Bank. In the first 15 years of the Bank's existence, about 20 percent of the total lending for agriculture went for agricultural credit purposes, whereas in a recent 5 year period the amount grew to 56 percent. Further, the total amount of agricultural lending during this period grew approximately fivefold. Consequently, the amount of World Bank funds going to agricultural credit multiplied many times during the period. Other international lenders also expanded their agricultural credit lending during this period.

Expanding use of agricultural credit reflects the growing needs for purchased inputs to increase agricultural production. Yield-increasing technology can be mobilized only if liquid resources are available to buy the necessary inputs to apply the technology. In most instances credit is needed.

RESEARCH—THE CREATION OF TECHNOLOGY IS NOT ACCIDENTAL. The creation of new technology via research is also one of the essential ingredients necessary to transform traditional agriculture to a commercial state. This process is neither accidental nor inexpensive. Nevertheless, recent experience indicates that some of the highest payoffs can be found in this area. In addition to considering the recent impacts of new technology, it is important to understand how research institutions can be created and developed.

The recent expansion of farm output in a number of countries, e.g., Mexico, Taiwan, Pakistan, and India, has been based on increases in yields associated with the use of new high yielding varieties (HYVs) and fertilizer. The work of Nobel prize winner Norman Borlaug and associates resulted in the development of these HYVs of wheat; they are short-stemmed, stiff-strawed, and fertilizer-responsive, and have made possible greatly increased yields. This research breakthrough was one of the most, if not the most, productive investment made in increasing agricultural production anywhere in the world in the post-World War II period.

Another spectacular breakthrough was the development of high yielding rice varieties at the International Rice Research Institute (IRRI) in the Philippines. Combining the expertise of scientists from several nations and several disciplines and working closely with professional resources available at the University of the Philippines, IRRI concentrated resources available on rice production technology. Within six years of its establishment in 1962, the institution had developed a series of new rice varieties with yield potential roughly double those varieties previously available to farmers in southeast Asia.

Building of research institutions capable of making these types of breakthroughs is not simple. Besides staffing these institutions with highly competent scientists and providing them with adequate resources to address problems, the more subtle requirement of establishing research as a permanent part of the agricultural economy must be recognized as essential. Strategies for developing such institutions have been developed elsewhere (1), but this time-consuming, expensive process is clearly an essential element in breaking the stranglehold of traditional agriculture.

International research by itself, however, is not sufficient. Equally as important is the research carried out in the developing nations themselves. The new varieties and cultural practices need to be adapted to local conditions. Particularly important is protective research designed to find ways of making new varieties less susceptible to local diseases.

EDUCATIONAL INSTITUTIONS—LITERACY UNLOCKS A LOT. Relatively few of the decisions required in technical agriculture can be made by illiterate farmers. The sophisticated, technologically complex agriculture of pesticide dosages, fertilizer analysis, and nutrition in livestock rations is not compatible with illiteracy.

But a basic education in reading, writing, and arithmetic is not enough. Advanced agricultural technology even though not complicated requires that farmers be able to integrate technical material in making decisions. For example, the application of proper amounts of fertilizer and herbicides is related to plant populations, price expectations, and climatic conditions. The ability to place all the relevant variables in perspective and evaluate them properly requires a relatively sophisticated decision-making capability. Hence, the development of functional literacy is only a very modest beginning in terms of meeting the educational requirements of technical agriculture.

Developing agricultural educational institutions, like those just mentioned for research, is a time-consuming, complicated business. Developing and establishing schools, from grammar schools through graduate agricultural programs, requires a major effort by developing countries, since developing only a single educational level within the total system is not enough. Instead, the educational programs must build upon one another, culminating in the most advanced, scholarly work associated with developing new agricultural technology.

PLANNING—AVOIDING GROWTH "LIKE TOPSY." Agricultural planning is the process of deciding what government agricultural policies and actions will be effected during a given time period. Such planning must be done not only at the national level but also at the regional and local levels. Government must decide what is needed to transform traditional agriculture and what future preparations are needed to effect this transformation process. An implicit part of this planning process is determining what resources in what amount, especially money and manpower, will be required to meet the needs of a developing agriculture. Since resources are never adequate to do all things, relative priorities must be established for policies and programs. These priorities will keep changing, and so planning must be continuous.

Recent changes in Pakistan provide an example of what is involved in planning. Encouraged by drought conditions and dwindling supplies of food aid, the Council of Ministers decided in the late 1960s to set up a program to make Pakistan self-sufficient in food grains.

Its Planning Commission and appropriate ministries then began to organize the program. Examination of the requirements for carrying out such a program revealed the need for fertilizers, new seeds, irrigation water, and other inputs. These needs raised questions about how to supply electricity for irrigation pumping, transportation for fertilizers and crops, credit facilities, and storage. The programming units began implementing the projects and examining possible incentives to decide which to use to persuade farmers to increase their food grain production.

Much has been learned about planning for agricultural development, and Mosher has identified 14 specific lessons:

1. The "essentials" deserve the highest priority.
2. The accelerators can help where the essentials are present.
3. Only part of agricultural development can be planned.
4. Planning should be by agricultural regions.
5. Production and market possibilities must be considered jointly.
6. Planning should be directed more at increasing the profitability of

farming than at increasing production of specific farm commodities.
7. Many investments require time to be productive.
8. The quality of each activity is more important than its quantity.
9. Certain activities should be coordinated locally.
10. Important relationships related to agricultural development cannot be expressed in numbers.
11. Planning should take account of the desires and complaints voiced by farmers.
12. Plans for agriculture and industry should be jointly considered.
13. Planning should include critical assessments of what is already being done.
14. Planning should be continuous (5).

LOCAL GOVERNMENT—PUBLIC SERVICES AT THE GRASS ROOTS. Probably more lip service and less action have been devoted to the need for decentralizing government in developing countries than to any other single policy question. The countries in which decentralization has actually taken place are rare indeed. There are many reasons for this.

In developing countries many forces cause central cities to be a leach on the countryside rather than a service center for it. Many owners of farmland actually reside in the central cities since this is where the best medical facilities, schools, and amenities are located. And since he does not live on his farm, a landowner has few incentives to pay taxes to improve local institutions, such as schools and medical facilities, in the area of his farm. There is also a natural tendency to invest the capital accumulated in the agricultural sector in the urban center. Once this pattern of leaching by the central city becomes established, the task of decentralizing government functions becomes almost impossible. Local governments in rural areas are relatively powerless; they lack the resources and political power of key decision makers among the landowning group. Even agricultural professionals are attracted to the central cities rather than rural villages since most of the highest-paying government jobs are located there. Under these conditions the central city cannot function as a service center for the needs of the agricultural community.

One of the few countries to actually undertake a government decentralization program has been Tanzania. Tanzania established government positions in outlying regions comparable to those in the central city. Capable personnel were assigned to these posts. Further, the personnel working in government ministries assigned to regions were made responsible to regional governments rather than to their ministry headquarters in the capital city. This decentralization was designed to make the government more nearly serve the needs of farm people. The reorganization has taken place too recently to be evaluated, but it represents a valuable exception to the rule of highly centralized governments in the noncommunist developing countries.

LEGAL SYSTEMS—MESHING WITH THE REST OF THE WORLD. Modifying legal systems in developing countries to meet both the needs of the society and the commercialized developed world with which it must interact is a complicated process indeed. Despite these complexities, the basic requirements of an effective legal system for a developing country have been identified: (1) fairness, (2) predictability, (3) rapid adjudication, (4) similarity to systems of developed countries, and (5) similarity to local traditions (2).

There are difficulties in establishing a system that is compatible both with local traditions and with the complexities of the developed world. For example, the concept of a contract is basic to commercial activities. In many tribal societies, however, the concept of a contract is a foreign one. But if that tribally based society is to interact with the commercial world, it must be able to incorporate the concept of a contract into its legal system.

Developing a fair, predictable, responsive legal system in which farmers have confidence is indispensable to the development of commercial agriculture, and requires time and persistence.

INTERACTIONS AMONG INSTITUTIONS—A COMPLEX NETWORK. All the elements we have discussed so far are dependent on each other to form an effective agricultural infrastructure. The strength of this infrastructure, however, is only as great as the strength of its weakest link. For example, if a country possesses a well-developed transportation network but has an inadequate marketing system, the prices farmers receive are unlikely to be high enough to encourage increased output. Similarly, if a research program has developed a highly productive technology but there exists neither an education program to carry this to farmers nor a credit program to enable them to purchase the required inputs, the new technology will be of little avail.

In the final analysis, even though infrastructure is necessary for development, increased agricultural production must come from the individual farm. The individual farmer makes the crucial decisions about increasing production. Infrastructure simply provides the individual farmer with the necessary services and facilities he cannot provide economically for himself. In the language of the theater, infrastructure does not play the lead role, but no one else can play the lead role if the infrastructure is not adequate.

As an example of this, Millikan and Hapgood describe the role infrastructure has played in Taiwan's agricultural development (4). In 1948, the Joint Commission on Rural Reconstruction (JCRR) was created by the governments of Taiwan and the United States. An organization separate from both governments, JCRR views itself as a catalyst in rural development and agricultural growth, helping those who help themselves. This organization deals on a national scale with all factors affecting agricultural productivity.

Since the formation of JCRR, agriculture has progressed rapidly with production doubling between 1952 and 1964. JCRR has brought farmers increasingly into the development process and relies heavily on farmers' associations. The agricultural four-year plans drafted by the organization are revised in consultation with farmers' associations and local governments. Many activities started by JCRR are turned over to farmers to manage. Typically, there is a period of study followed by an action program managed by JCRR or the central government and then farmers take over full or partial management. Farmers assume the main burden of extension work. Farmers' associations hire extension agents, bearing two-thirds of the cost; the rest is paid by the government and the JCRR. The many farmer cooperatives employ some 13,000 persons, many trained by the JCRR.

The JCRR has been so successful because of several reasons. Taiwan is small when compared with other developing nations, and its central government has had both the will and the means to reach the people. For example, land reform succeeded in Taiwan while it has failed in most Asian nations. The special relationship between Taiwan and the United States assured large amounts of aid and also allowed the formation of the joint Chinese-American venture JCRR which would have been politically unacceptable to many nations.

> When JCRR began, the farmers of Taiwan already were relatively highly skilled, used to working throughout the year, and open to innovation. Perhaps most important, Taiwan had an abundant supply of trained manpower—so abundant, in fact, that Taiwan is sending technicians to other nations. . . .
>
> The lesson from Taiwan and the JCRR is that agriculture is capable of rapid growth, but only if all the necessary factors are present. This underlines the importance, to governments of underdeveloped and aid-giving nations alike, of investing in the physical and human infrastructure that made Taiwan's success possible (4).

In most developing countries, needs are so vast and resources so limited that someone must decide the priorities in which investments are made for development to proceed.

THE PROBLEM OF CHOICE CRITERIA—WHAT IS IMPORTANT. The crucial first step in the decision-making process is determining what criteria should be used in deciding what one element of the infrastructure should be developed before others. The development of such criteria requires that a set of objectives be established for the agricultural sector. Frequently, these objectives are grouped into the following categories: (1) increased agricultural production, (2) increased employment opportunities, (3) improvements in the distribution of income, and (4) improvements in the participation of farmers in group decision making. Unfortunately, frequently these conflict with one another, e.g., increasing agricultural production may result in a less equitable distribution of income. But even when objectives do not directly compete with each other, the relative emphasis to be given each objective must be established. For example, a government might decide that increasing employment opportunities in the agricultural sector is twice as important as increasing agricultural output. Thus, when evaluating road construction as compared with the development of a research installation, the government would undoubtedly emphasize labor-intensive road construction projects. Hence, once the alternative objectives have been identified and weights placed upon them, the criteria for evaluating alternative infrastructure investments can be determined, and priorities established.

This is not, however, a "once and for all" process. Countries usually find it necessary to reevaluate their investment decisions at least annually. Some of the reasons for this are discussed later.

THE CONCEPT OF LAYERED INSTITUTIONAL CONSTRAINTS—THERE ARE NO PANACEAS. Frequently, efforts to improve an agricultural economy's infrastructure center on one or, at best, a few elements. Unfortunately, although designed to remedy a constraint within the agricultural sector, this approach does little more than provide an opportunity for another poorly developed infrastructure element to become the effective constraint. This layering of institutional infrastructure constraints often misleads and frustrates individuals who feel the elimination of one institutional barrier represents a panacea for transforming traditional agriculture.

ORDERING INVESTMENTS—THE MESSY BUSINESS OF COST EFFECTIVENESS ANALYSIS. Having identified criteria and recognizing that constraints vary over time, analyses can proceed to determine the priority of infrastructure investment. This analysis requires that the cost of each investment be matched against its effectiveness, measured in terms of the objectives of the agriculture sector. Consequently, such things as the cost per job created or cost per million dollars of increased agricultural income can be calculated for each investment, assuming that all other expenditures are adequately rewarded. Finally, since both the costs and benefits will accrue over time they must be discounted to present value. That is, income generated five years from the date of the investment must be recognized as having a smaller present value than if the same amount were forthcoming next year. The process of ordering investments is a complex and specialized undertaking.

FINANCING INFRASTRUCTURE INVESTMENTS—SOMEONE MUST PAY. In many developing countries, funds for investing in infrastructure are unavailable. Consequently, funds must be borrowed, frequently from multilateral lending agencies such as the World Bank and regional development banks and from bilateral lending programs of individual countries. Regardless of the loan source, the borrowing government will also have to raise funds.

Just as an individual farmer borrows, fully anticipating the need to repay the loan, so countries must also enter loan agreements for infrastructure investments. In most instances these investments require not only that tax revenue be generated to repay them, but also that the long-run profitability of the investment will help generate tax revenues that will sustain the infrastructure over time. Needless to say, careful investment decisions are a "must."

**Building in Flexibility Over Time—Avoiding the Unreal World of Fixed Needs.** Unlike many physical relationships in production agriculture, infrastructure needs change over time. To assume that a fixed infrastructure will suffice for all stages of development is to put the agricultural sector in a straitjacket that will make further development impossible. Hence, pragmatism is needed in viewing the needs of an infrastructure over time. As the improvements in infrastructure generate improvements in the agricultural economy, these in turn will make new demands on the sector's infrastructure. Just as development implies change, so too must the infrastructure possess the needed flexibility for the development of an agricultural economy to be sustained.

## REFERENCES

1. Blase, Melvin G., ed. Institutions in Agricultural Development.
2. Church W. Lawrence. Legal Systems. In Institutions in Agricultural Development. Melvin G. Blase, ed.
3. Johnston, Bruce F., and Kilby, Peter. Agriculture and Structural Transformation. New York: Oxford University Press, 1975.
4. Millikan, Max F., and Hapgood, David. No Easy Harvest.
5. Mosher, A. T. Getting Agriculture Moving.
6. Yudelman, Montague, Agricultural Development and Economic Integration in Latin America. London: George Allen and Unwin Ltd, 1970.

## BIBLIOGRAPHY

Blase, Melvin G., ed. Institutions in Agricultural Development. Ames: Iowa State University Press, 1971.

Millikan, M. F., and Hapgood, David. No Easy Harvest. Boston: Little, Brown, and Company, 1967.

Mosher, A. T. Getting Agriculture Moving. New York: Praeger, 1966.

# 14

# Food Policies of Governments

ROY D. LAIRD *and* BETTY A. LAIRD

THE PROBLEM. To avoid disaster, people (and thus their governments) will have to cope successfully with exploding populations and lagging food output.

Unless profound policy changes are adopted by the governments of most developing nations (and some major developed nations as well), over the next few decades starvation could reach crisis proportion. Failure to avert such a tragedy will rest primarily on the shoulders of political leaders, thus a subtitle for this chapter might be *"The Dismal Political Economy of World Hunger."*

Stated bluntly, a review of national policies as of the mid-1970s leads to the inescapable conclusion that if the nations of the world, and thus their leaders, had given food production highest priority, there would be no reason for alarm, with present levels of world population. Mass hunger is concentrated in the developing nations, but the potential for greater food output there is also large. Current estimates are that from 400 to 800 million people suffer from serious malnutrition in such nations (26). Some assert that nearly half of humanity is malnourished to some degree. Indeed, the average intake of calories has been estimated at 3,150 per day in the developed nations, compared with only 2,200 in the developing nations (25).

From the base period 1961–65 until 1974 food output in the developing nations with market economies increased by some 2 percent (5), but so did their populations. Therefore, as Table 14.1 illustrates, output of food per capita has stagnated, and increased demand has had to be met by increased food imports from the developed nations. Developing countries have become net food importers (Table 14.2). Indeed, only New Zealand, Australia, and North America remain net exporters of grain.

ROY D. LAIRD, Professor, Political Science, and Graduate Director, University of Kansas, writer and international lecturer on Slavic and Soviet studies, especially agricultural policies in the U.S.S.R. and developing nations.

BETTY A. LAIRD is Independent Research Analyst and former Research Associate on Slavic and Soviet studies, University of Kansas.

TABLE 14.1. PER-CAPITA CHANGES IN WORLD FOOD PRODUCTION (5) (1961–65 = 100%).

| | 1961–65 | 1970 | 1972 | 1973 | 1974 |
|---|---|---|---|---|---|
| | | | *(percent)* | | |
| Developing nations | 100 | 103 | 99 | 100 | 99 |
| Developed nations | 100 | 107 | 111 | 113 | 113 |

Some encouraging developments have taken place, but far too little has been done. Perhaps the most encouraging change has been the so-called Green Revolution that produced the new high-yielding varieties (the HYVs) of wheat and rice, which have been a prime factor in recent production increases by the developing nations. Certainly, both the scientists who labored and the politicians who backed their efforts deserve great credit. Nevertheless, Norman Borlaug, often referred to as the "father of the Green Revolution," has warned that improved technology is not enough to avert future tragedy.

> By the Green Revolution we have only delayed the world food crisis for another 30 years. If the world population continues to increase at the same rate we will destroy the species (22).

Grain (including rice), consumed either directly as bread and cereals or indirectly as livestock products, is the world's major source of food; and if world hunger is to be alleviated, it will be through increased grain production. But calculations by Borlaug indicate that increasing population will require an additional "28–30 million metric tons of grain every year" (2).

An examination of some factors and policies that account for the present world food situation is necessary to make sound judgments.

TABLE 14.2. AVERAGE ANNUAL GRAIN EXPORTS (+) AND IMPORTS (—) (7).

| | 1934–38 | 1973 | Projected Possible[a] 1985 |
|---|---|---|---|
| | | *(millions of metric tons)* | |
| North America | + 5 | +88 | +128 |
| Australia and New Zealand | + 3 | + 7 | + 17 |
| Total | + 8 | +95 | +145 |
| U.S.S.R. and Eastern Europe | + 5 | —27 | — 55 |
| Africa | + 1 | — 4 | — 9 |
| Asia | + 2 | —39 | — 53 |
| Latin America | + 9 | — 4 | — 8 |
| Total (developing and Japan) | +12 | —47 | — 70[b] |
| Western Europe | —24 | —21 | — 20 |

[a]Tentative projects based on USDA, AID, and Laird studies.

[b]Including an additional 10 million for Japan, although one source includes 1985 projections for Japan at levels more than twice that amount.

GOVERNMENTS AND THE IMPACT OF THE INDUSTRIAL REVOLUTION. More than any other thing the Industrial Revolution (which started in England in the 1760s) has been responsible for the present state of affairs in world food. The medicines and techniques it produced resulted in an enormous population growth. It was primarily responsible for urbanization in the developed nations, since a small percentage of people using labor-saving machinery is able to feed the rest. For example, in the United States only some 4 to 5 percent of the population produces the nation's food; the average American farm worker feeds a total of 52.4 persons—42.0 at home and another 10.4 abroad (22).

Even the large numbers of farmers in developing countries have been profoundly influenced by the Industrial Revolution. Most of these nations in their development have emphasized industrialization at the expense of small farm agriculture. Thus in a very real sense much of the backwardness of the Asian, African, and Latin American farmers can be related to their being the neglected, sometimes deprived, orphans of industrial aspirations.

Only the most isolated food producer in the most remote regions of the world can escape from being profoundly affected by policies dictated in some distant national capital. Some nations have practiced policies of "benign neglect." Many have required agriculture to subsidize industrial expansion, by keeping prices paid the farmer-producer deliberately low to satisfy demands of the urban masses. Other, more positive, policies have included subsidies, price supports, and tariff protections, which sometimes are beneficial to rural producers.

Modern farmers, wherever they are found, increasingly find that decisions made in Washington, D.C., Moscow, and other national capitals can be as influential over their welfare as the weather. No longer is the success of the U.S. farmer largely a matter of just being a good farmer. Now he must be also a first-rate manager, coping with government controls and directives in the most favorable manner possible.

POLICYMAKERS. Few U.S. farmers, even those faced with unreasonable standards, would argue that all regulations and controls should be eliminated. They, too, wish to market products that meet high quality and health standards. Nevertheless, most farmers argue that excess controls are a major problem today. Increasingly, farmers must face local, state, and federal laws, often fashioned by urban politicians and their allies who (through misconceptions and misunderstandings) too often impose regulations that discourage production. Many such decision makers are agriculturally illiterate, ignorant of the special demands of food production and of what it takes to nurture living plants and animals successfully. Many decisions are based on the idea that the Industrial Revolution has changed food production in the same fundamental way that it has altered urban manufacturing. Schultz has described this misconception as "industrial fundamentalism" (19).

But a farm cannot be run like a factory. A farmer cannot entrust the agricultural process to machines, adding only necessary ingredients and using no decision making powers. Brewster and Wunderlick have emphasized that there has really been no agricultural industrial revolution:

> With minor exceptions of certain specialized poultry and livestock operations, a shift to machine farming leaves relatively undisturbed the sequential pattern of operations that has prevailed in farming since the domestication of plants and animals. . . . thus in farming the Industrial Revolution is merely a spectacular change in the gadgets with which operations are performed, whereas in industry it is a fundamental revolution in the sequence of production operations (3).

Blindness on the part of Washington, D.C., London, and Paris lawmakers and bureaucrats to the special needs of farmers dealing with living plants and animals has extracted its toll in the developed nations. However, nowhere has the price been higher than it has been in the U.S.S.R.

THE DEVELOPED NATIONS. In the short run, the surplus food production of the developed nations (particularly the United States) can buy time in the face of rising world demand for food. However, if recent policies are not changed, America's contribution to alleviating hunger will probably not increase. Let's examine these policies, and how they are affecting world food supplies.

MARKET ECONOMIES. Food productivity has reached the highest levels in the developed nations where a combination of relatively favorable physical environment and governmental policies have encouraged production. But even though the yields of food per unit of land in nations such as Japan and those of western Europe are among the highest in the world, there is just not enough arable land to feed the populations. This has greatly influenced their agricultural policies.

Unlike the western European nations, Japan is not a member of a major economic consortium. Only some 15 percent of the land can be cultivated. Because of the size of its population and its demand for a better diet, Japan has turned to fishing the sea and importing food (6).

Until recently, with one exception, Japan's food policy has been benign neglect at home, while maximizing imports, especially from the United States. Domestic agriculture was neglected with the conviction that ever-expanding industrial exports would pay for needed food imports. The one major bright spot was the change in land tenure arising out of World War II. Immediately after that war, nearly half the farmers did not own the land they farmed. Today, however, as a result of the reform, some 95 percent of the farmers own their land (6).

But Japan must still import much of its food. This reality is a source of serious concern, and efforts to reduce its dependence as much as possible have resulted in recent policy changes favorable to farmers, and so in a most unusual situation, rural incomes have now come to surpass those of urban dwellers. Moreover, although modern Japan is not satisfied with a predominantly rice diet, high artificial domestic price supports have stimulated the farmers to produce enough rice to meet current consumption needs (6).

Most recently, the Japanese leadership stimulated by U.S. embargoes on grain exports is broadening their source of supply. Specifically, new programs of agricultural investment have been initiated in both Asia and in Latin America. Such programs are designed not only to diversify Japan's source of food, but also to allow a more direct control over the sources. Whatever the changes, however, Japan seems destined to become even more dependent on the outside world for food.

The nine nations in the European Economic Community (EEC) make up much of western Europe. Internal and external trade in foodstuffs as well as production is determined by CAP (the EEC's Common Agricultural Policy). The CAP arrangements are most complex reflecting at once attempts to balance the membership's consumer desire (primarily for inexpensive food) against farmer demand for high prices and/or subsidies, along with an overall goal of reducing food imports to the lowest levels possible. Agreements must be unanimous among the nine, and negotiations are constantly going on. A major long-run goal of the community is to be able to produce enough grain to supply consumption demands (17). However, given the prices that surely must be paid if such an achievement were to be realized, there is a question whether the goal is economically feasible. Key policies have included high subsidies for member farmers, substantial levies on some exports and a 1974 ban on beef imports.

Serious complaints can be heard from time to time. Certainly the community's farmers chafe under what must be the most complex set of agricultural controls anywhere. Nevertheless, on balance, EEC policies have been in their favor. Farmers' welfare has improved, and they have responded by producing agricultural growth in the post-World War II era that has surpassed industrial growth (8).

Until the early 1970s the United States, which currently produces nearly one-fourth of all the world's major field crops (Table 14.3), was primarily concerned with overproduction. Various programs were devised (including the Soil Bank Program of the ASC) to induce U.S. farmers to hold down output. The possibility of accumulating unmanageable surpluses was the major concern. Efforts were also made to expand sales to the developed nations who could afford to pay for their

TABLE 14.3. WORLD PRODUCTION AVERAGES IN 1973–74 (23).

| | Wheat | Corn | Rice | Soybeans | Total |
|---|---|---|---|---|---|
| | | | *(millions of metric tons)* | | |
| U.S.S.R. | 96.8 | 12.7 | 1.9 | 0.4 | 111.8 |
| China | 27.9 | 24.9 | 103.0 | 6.7 | 162.5 |
| U.S. | 47.6 | 130.1 | 4.7 | 37.8 | 220.2 |
| Total | 172.3 | 167.7 | 109.6 | 44.9 | 494.5 |
| World Total | 356.4 | 295.1 | 310.1 | 54.5 | 1,016.1 |

purchases. In addition, the United States participated in unprecedented food-aid programs. Between 1954 and 1973, under the Public Law 480 (the Food for Peace Program), the United States supplied $25 billion in donations and concessional sales. The United States supplied 46 percent of all world food program aid since it began in 1962, providing some 143 million tons of wheat, rice, and other grains (14).

Since the early 1970s, a whole new situation has come to prevail, and many U.S. farmers feel caught in an increasingly precarious position. With world and U.S. grain reserves reduced to precarious lows and demand for U.S. grain mounting, the government removed virtually all its programs designed to hold down production, called for U.S. grain farmers to go all out, and encouraged them to expand further their foreign markets.

Believing that they faced a new prosperity unfettered by marketing controls, U.S. farmers did go all out producing record crops. The resulting expanded foreign grain sales were a prime factor in bringing the U.S. balance of payments into the black for the first time in years. Wheat prices increased to over $5 a bushel, and in 1973, for the first time, net disposable personal income per person on U.S. farms actually surpassed that of the balance of the population.

Unfortunately, not only for the farmer's welfare but probably also for the nation's, 1973 seems destined to have been an isolated phenomenon. Since 1973, inflation has hit the farmer worse than the balance of the population. Fertilizer, fuel, and equipment costs have soared while grain prices have fallen back significantly. Many grain farmers believe the primary cause of the reversal was the embargoes on grain exports, which they fear will be reinstated if urban cries for lower food prices are again raised.

As of early 1976, government agricultural policies are contradictory. Even though the administration and Congress seem to realize that increasing world demand requires expanded production, no serious moves have been made to reduce the mounting cost-price squeeze that the farmer is facing. The mass communication media may have played a major role in holding down prices paid to farmers. Consumers' groups, television commentators, and newspapers systematically report the weekly and monthly price of the average food basket. Periodically, scare stories are published including one about the possibility of a-dollar-a-loaf bread. Seldom is the voice of the farmer-producer heard saying that his cost of production has been rising while his return has been decreasing.

Caught in a cost-price squeeze, dairy farmers have been drastically declining in number. As of 1975, grain farmers received only 4.7¢ as their share of return for a 16 oz. loaf of bread costing 35¢: this, in a situation where if the price of wheat were to have risen 70¢ a bushel, it would have increased the price of that loaf only one penny. Yet as of January, 1976 wheat on the farm brought only $3.20 a bushel, "a price that in most cases is below the cost of production" (9). The world needs more U.S. grain, yet U.S. farmers increasingly find themselves faced with costs and prices that discourage expanded production (1).

As noted earlier, U.S. farmers are the most labor-efficient food producers in the world, each one feeding more than 50 individuals. Estimates are that given the proper incentives, U.S. farmers' output could increase some 50 percent (24).

All indications are that Japan, Western Europe, and the other well-to-do nations (including the oil-rich Arab states) will want increasing amounts of U.S. food and will pay hard currencies that could help keep our balance of payments in the black. Additional amounts of food will be needed for the hungry developing nations. As of 1976, however, farmers are holding back. For example, 1975–76 Kansas press reports reveal that farmers' purchases of mineral fertilizer are down some 10 percent over previous years. The grain producers believe that the depressed wheat prices will not make it economical to attempt to optimize their yields.

The U.S. farmer is subject to increasing controls. For example, if adopted, a proposed change would allow the Corps of Engineers to control irrigation, regardless of its source. However, the 1975 embargoes on foreign sales were one of the most frustrating obstacles for farmers. They saw this action as an attempt to depress food prices and considered it unfair since the U.S. consumer pays far less for his food and still eats better than virtually any other country in the world, as Table 14.4 shows.

COLLECTIVIZED AND CENTRALLY PLANNED ECONOMIES: THE SOVIET MODEL. In a world greatly in need of more food, the Soviet agricultural model

TABLE 14.4. AVERAGE PERCENT OF PRIVATE INCOME SPENT FOR FOODS: 1972 (1).

| Country | % |
|---|---|
| Sweden | 20.6 |
| France | 22.0 |
| Yugoslavia | 39.5 |
| Honduras | 47.9 |
| Ghana (1970) | 62.8 |
| United States | 14.5 |

(which has been copied to varying degrees by most of the new communist states) is one of the most depressing aspects of the food problem. True, in the past two decades Soviet food output has increased substantially, but compared with the achievements of other developed nations or when measured against the potential of the land, the U.S.S.R. achievement is not good.

Grain yields per unit of land are far below those of North America, and recent yield increases have been less than those of Canada, which shares a comparable climate to much of the producing area of the U.S.S.R. For example, when yields in Saskatchewan, Canada, where much of the Canadian wheat is grown, are compared with yields in Kazakhstan, U.S.S.R., which has a comparable climate and produces some one-fifth of Soviet grain, Canadians far outproduce the Soviets. Although yields have increased in both areas, in 1958–62 Saskatchewan spring wheat yields were 32 percent greater than those in Kazakhstan, while by 1970–74 the gap had increased in favor of the Canadians to some 63 percent (12).

There is also strong evidence to indicate that because of "systems costs" (i.e., losses rooted in faulty policies), Soviet grain yields lag some 15 percent below the potential of their land (13).

Central direction and control is the key to Soviet agricultural policy. The bulk of the Soviet agricultural system is based on huge bureaucratized state *(sovkhozy)* and collective *(kolkhozy)* farms. Although the *kolkhoz* peasants theoretically are co-owners of the buildings, the implements, and the output (the land itself is nationalized), in practice, they merely do what their farm leaders tell them to do. For most purposes they are in a similar position to that of workers on an assembly line in a factory. Therefore, these peasants have little incentive to increase production.

Current Soviet leadership wants very much to increase output and currently subsidizes the farms at an estimated 20 billion rubles a year ($24 billion). Unfortunately, added investments alone will not promote a solution.

From the beginning, the collectivized system was not designed to maximize production. However, much greater output may be needed and desired, maximum central controls, which are rooted in a combination of ideological, political, and economic factors, often work against increasing productivity.

Ideologically one cannot build a communist society without sharing its benefits with the farmers. Thus, the peasants had to be collectivized. Further, Lenin was convinced that the agricultural problem could be solved by adapting the entire industrial model to farming, including machines and organization. An urban intellectual, Lenin never perceived the special needs of living plants and animals nor the farmer's need to deal with life processes, which are quite unlike urban industrial processes. Still, Lenin's successors have fully accepted the view that the whole of outdoors can be transformed into some sort of rural factory.

Economically, the Soviets have rejected the market system, insisting instead on centrally controlled prices and adherence to centrally directed plans. Soviet farmers plant and husband not what their best judgment might dictate but what the plans impose upon them, whatever the cost in terms of lost potential.

The collective or state farm is the primary rural political unit, led by a party member chairman aided by an active party unit of some 30–40 individuals where first priority is assigned to controls. The price paid for such control includes both low yield and low labor productivity. Thus, the average area of land cultivated by a Soviet farmer is nearly eight times less than that of an American farmer (11). If the U.S.S.R. farms were to match Canadian yields, which their land has the potential for doing, they would more than amply feed their populations.

Since the recent improvements in relations between the United States and China, visitors to the agricultural sector have added to and confirmed the limited information already unearthed by students of the Chinese collectivized system.

Drawing on the Soviet model—but taking vital intermediate steps calculated to prevent the massive livestock and crop losses suffered in the Stalin period—the Chinese communists combined a myriad of intensively cultivated, tiny peasant farms (averaging one hectare or 2.47 acres) into huge collectives (and some state farms). This consolidation of land, labor, and animal power was to increase efficiency and bring Chinese agriculture under central control, allowing maximum extraction of the agricultural surplus. Collectivization was completed in 1956, reducing the resource losses of small and fragmented landholdings and initiating massive irrigation and flood control projects, which increased acreage as well as the land's productivity. By requisitioning the enormous labor force and with little or no investment of scarce capital, the Chinese leadership was able to increase agricultural production at a rate approximately equal to that of the population growth (21).

But as the first five-year plan drew to a close in 1957, Peking imposed the Great Leap Forward because of diminishing agricultural returns that threatened to affect the rate of industrialization. The already large collectives were combined into monstrous communes, households were socialized, all private land plots were abolished, and an industrialization plan that depended on a minimum of resources, was applied to the countryside. The result was social upheaval and huge shortfalls, first in agriculture and then spreading to industry, that nearly collapsed the economy (21). Fortunately, Chinese agriculture rallied during the 1960s under a government policy of relaxation and modernization that restored private plots and other incentives and increased investments. Imports of chemical fertilizer were increased, seeds improved, and selective mechanization introduced. By the early 1970s, however, the Green Revolution of the 1960s had spent its initial impetus and China's growth rates appear to have tapered off (21).

An appalling number of problems obstructs the further development of Chinese agriculture, not the least of which are the sheer size and numbers involved. (Some 75 percent of the population is engaged in agriculture (15).) Difficulties other than those that can be labeled political, however, are beyond the scope of this chapter. The Great Leap Forward, for example, certainly carried political implications, greatly advancing the role of party leaders in agriculture, and further centralizing controls. Also clearly under attack was the autonomy of the family unit.

Whether collectivization as an organizational method has increased or reduced the potential of Chinese agriculture remains an open question, which will remain unanswered until its performance can be compared with other world systems and analyzed. (Some scholars believe that comparison is impossible and that the question will never be resolved.) Certainly the performance of Chinese collectivized agriculture has not been spectacular, particularly when compared with production on the peasants' individually owned plots.

As in the U.S.S.R., the peasants in China are permitted tiny (averaging 0.03 hectares or 0.07 acres) kitchen gardens on which they grow mostly vegetables and raise pigs and chickens. These holdings make up only about 5 percent of the country's cultivated land, but they produce some 20 percent of the total output (21). They also provide 25 to 30 percent of the peasants' total net income. As such, these little bits of private enterprise remain an important and embarrassing ideological, as well as economic, anomaly within the collectivized system. Periodically there have been grumblings against this form of residual capitalism, and peasants have been discouraged from spending too much time in cultivating their holdings. But the peasants' right to farm their plots was reaffirmed in the 1975 Constitution, and Peking, like Moscow, seems reluctant again to test the consequences of outlawing the household plots.

Another government policy seems to be proving costly for Chinese agriculture; that is the anti-elitist attitudes of the Cultural Revolution that have led to the neglect of research and university education for technicians. As a result, the potential of technological development in agriculture could well be limited (21).

These periodic political upheavals generally have proved expensive for Chinese agriculture, and other such movements will probably take place in the future. The price they could extract cannot be predicted.

Finally, policies of political interference in farm activities by party officials present at the commune and brigade levels (4) must pose additional difficulties for both the directors and the workers. This certainly has been true in the collectivized U.S.S.R.

Despite multiple cropping, intensive labor application, expanding irrigation and flood control, construction of fertilizer plants, increased mechanization, and injunctions from Mao (a combination of which have produced outstanding results in specific areas), Chinese agriculture

TABLE 14.5. YIELDS OF WHEAT AND RICE IN TONS PER HECTARE (23) (1971–73 AVERAGES).

| | Wheat | Rice |
|---|---|---|
| World | 1.6 | 2.2 |
| Developed | 2.6 | 3.8 |
| Developing | 1.1 | 1.8 |
| United States | 2.2 | 5.0 |
| Japan | 2.6 | 5.5 |
| South Korea | 2.1 | 4.9 |
| Western Europe | 3.7+ | NA |

is generally plagued with natural and economic difficulties. These are further complicated by government policies strongly motivated by political considerations. Thus, it is a constant battle to provide adequate food for China's own growing population. It is unlikely that Peking can have collectivization, strong central controls over agriculture, and efficient production too.*

THE DEVELOPING NATIONS. It is impossible to deal adequately with the complexity of the food problems of the developing nations of Asia, Africa, and Latin America in this limited space. Therefore, we will only touch on some of the most serious problems of many of the nations.

> The world food problem is really a problem of political will or rather the lack of it in all but a handful of the developing countries (16).

Most developing nations are as underdeveloped agriculturally as they are industrially. The yields of wheat and rice—the world's two major grains—in the developing nations lag far behind those achieved by the developed nations (Table 14.5). Also, some (although not all) of the developing countries have substantial areas of additional land that could be brought under cultivation if the farmers were given the proper encouragement.

If needed policies were adopted, and they must be if disaster is to be averted, the developing nations could feed themselves adequately at present population levels. But in most such nations, indications are that needed policies are not being adopted and populations are increasing. Unfortunately, agricultural policies in most developing nations discourage agricultural production. The policies are such that their farmers, who are living at poverty levels, cannot afford to expand production. The prices they are offered for their produce often will not cover costs. Table 14.6 presents a list of the major policies practiced in the developing world that discourage production.

* The authors wish to thank Professor Anthony M. Tang for his helpful suggestions in the preparation of this section of the chapter.

TABLE 14.6. POLICIES THAT DISCOURAGE AGRICULTURAL PRODUCTION IN THE DEVELOPING NATIONS (10, 18).

| Policies | Number of Nations Involved |
|---|---|
| Governments artificially holding down prices farmers are paid for their produce | 38 |
| Governments artificially holding down prices consumers pay for food | 35 |
| Governments demanding farmers to deliver certain produce to the state | 26 |
| Export taxes on food | 22 |
| Export controls on food | 22 |
| Restrictions on farmers' credit and land holdings | 19 |
| Subsidization of food imports | 17 |
| Restrictions on movement of food within the nation | 11 |
| Adverse exchange rate controls | 6 |

Why do nations that need more food impose such policies? Some argue that the various food-aid programs have encouraged political leaders to neglect agriculture and direct scarce investment resources elsewhere. Certainly many leaders are convinced that industrial growth is a major road to salvation and have assigned their priorities accordingly. Infatuation with industrial development combined with the easy availability of food aid probably has had its impact.

But the causes of lagging food output in the developing nations are complex. Perhaps the most important force working against the increased productivity of food is urban consumer pressure demanding that governments hold down food costs. This state of affairs involves a triple irony. First, in most such nations the rural poor are a majority but they are outvoted in the making of economic policy. Second, although rural people usually are poorer than city dwellers, the policies of cheap food mean the rural poor are subsidizing the urban consumers. Third, and most crucial, even though higher food costs would very likely result from ending policies that discourage agricultural production, increased food productivity should in the long run raise the standard of living for all, e.g., the export of surplus food could help pay for imports needed by the entire population.

Unfortunately, whatever human justice and economic sense might suggest, political reality in the developing nations has dictated something else. Most peasants are not organized and thus have relatively little voice in their national capitals. Urban workers, however, are often highly organized, vocal, and capable of determining who stays in political office. Few things cause stronger reaction among urban dwellers (even in the United States) than increases in food prices. Citations from a 1970 FAO study support this view.

> In almost all developing countries there has been considerable reluctance to raise producer prices for basic food products because of the effect on consumers' food prices. . . . It is clear, however,

> from recent experience that reluctance to raise food prices (encouraged in some cases by the ready availability of food aid) has contributed to food shortages in many countries by providing producers with insufficient incentive to increase production. The resulting shortages have brought increases in food prices that are perhaps greater than those that would have been necessary to bring forth a sufficient increase in domestic production (10, 18).

What are specific adverse effects of such policies in several nations? In Argentina, policies have resulted in production cutbacks to the point where that nation is no longer a major food exporting country. India continues to spend hard currency on developing her military power (including a nuclear capability) and on inadequate food imports. India could feed her current population from her own lands, but she too practices policies that discourage increased farmer production. Farmers are not paid enough for their grain to allow them to purchase adequate amounts of fertilizer, while black markets in food abound in the cities. Pakistani farmers are faced with problems similar to those of their Indian neighbors.

Recently, the Peruvian government set prices for potatoes (a major food in that nation) so low that many farmers were unable to cope with rising inflation and ceased raising potatoes. In Kenya, a government official admitted that the combination of low prices set by the government for food and inflated fertilizer costs resulted in many farmers losing money. Finally, although Thailand has considerable potential for expanded rice production, farmers have not used their production potential because the government holds down the prices they receive for their product to about one-fifth the world price (10, 18). These are only a few of the seemingly endless number of examples. The result is much agriculture in the developing countries remains at near subsistence levels.

THE DISCOURAGING FUTURE OUTLOOK. Given the political realities that shape agricultural policies in most developing nations, their future is hardly cheerful. Few leaders in such nations have the vision, conviction, or will to change policies to help farmers increase production when such actions must involve increased food costs for urban consumers. Nevertheless, one must hope that mankind is capable of using intelligence to do what must be done to avert calamity.

Most observers of the world agricultural scene would agree that beyond assuring farmers adequate prices for their produce, the most important need is agrarian reform. In some nations, land reform or redistribution is a necessary first step of the needed rural development. Real agrarian reform, however, involves much more than just land redistribution, as the following points make clear:

1. A genuine agrarian reform should effect substantial improvement in the abilities, capacities, and performances of those who cultivate the land to bring them more into line with human potentiality.
2. Any worthwhile agrarian reform should result in a substantial increase in the amount of agricultural and livestock products secured from a given amount of land and the efforts of those who work it.
3. A real agrarian reform should result in the replacement of wasteful, inefficient, demeaning and stultifying ways of producing agricultural and livestock products by methods of agriculture that are efficient, dignifying or enobling to those engaged in agriculture and stock raising (20).

Needed economic inputs are a vital part of the food equation. However, as recent Soviet experience underscores, greater investment in agriculture is not enough in itself. Agricultural specialists from thirteen nations met in Urbino, Italy, in the summer of 1975 to discuss the problems of agricultural modernization. There it was agreed that the miracle of production increases in the developed nations of the West since World War II was primarily a matter of research coupled with farmer education. The agrarian reform, so drastically needed in the developing world, must include farmer education. For example, AID reports reveal that in India, even among the peasants who have had the HYV seeds responsible for the "Green Revolution," only some 12 percent have followed fully the recommendations for their cultivation (27).

Japan, now a developed nation, has shown the way. There, tiny farms averaging less than 2 hectares (5 acres) are among the most productive in the world. In some nations, Brazil, for example, larger farms probably are part of the answer. However, "four-fifths of the farms in poor nations are less than twelve acres," and it is from these farms and their farmers that most of the world's needed food output increases must come (16).

As simple as it may sound, any significant increase in the world's supply of food must result from governmental policies designed to induce farmers into performing the extraordinarily difficult and demanding work that results in bountiful harvests. Tiny as the farms are in Egypt and Taiwan, according to Edgar Owens, agricultural policy reform has been the key to the exceptional achievements of agriculture in those two nations.

> Egypt and Taiwan have combined . . . [an] unusual use of farm machinery (selected to supplement the human effort but not replace it), land reform protection of their tenant farmers, cooperatives that work, high taxes to finance the cost of rural public investment, integrity in public administration, and the accounting of farmers' funds and other activities which make up what the experts call rural development (16).

In summary, then, the major problems in developing nations involve largely nontechnical matters, such as prices and the will of national leaders to tackle head-on the political forces that stand in the way of achieving the land's potential.

Before concluding this review, however, we must return to the role of the United States, its policies, and the future. Even if the developing nations are able to significantly improve their food output per capita over the next few decades, the demands for U.S. grain exports will continue to rise. Already, the United States supplies some three-fourths of the world's food exports. Thus it is the major present and future source of food both for the nations that can well afford to pay market prices and those poorer nations who must have assistance or face mass starvation.

Ironically, as we have seen, although enormously better off than peasant farmers, the average U.S. farmer faces the same cost-price squeeze, inflation fueled by energy shortages, and urban consumers' demand for low-priced foods. Farmers will not and cannot produce grain without a profit to feed, clothe, and house their families. Thus, without adequate food prices they will not and cannot increase production to meet projected future world requirements. The United States needs an agricultural policy that will increase output for at least four purposes:

1. to improve farmers' welfare so that they can afford to produce more to meet domestic and world needs
2. to assure more than adequate supplies of food at relatively low costs for the domestic consumer (but probably at higher than current levels)
3. to assure maximum availability of food for export sales, which surely will become an even more vital factor in the U.S. balance of payments. (Increasingly, we need food dollars to pay for the oil and other items we must import.)
4. to assure that there will be ample stocks to aid developing nations when they are faced with periodic famine caused by unavoidable natural disaster

Many planners believe that a major key to any such change involves the creation of major reserves. Such reserves are needed, but unless some new, unforeseen guarantees can be devised against the probable abuse of reserves held by the government, they should be held by the farmers. For reasons discussed earlier (particularly the forces responsible for embargoes on grain exports), there is every reason to anticipate that large government grain reserves could not be insulated from domestic political pressures. Should powerful consumers' groups conclude that food prices were rising too rapidly, their pressures on politicians to release the grain on the domestic market (to drive down prices) would be irresistible. Of course, in the short run, food prices would be forced down, but as past U.S. experience would show, such actions could only cause the nation's farmers to reduce output. The end result, a year or so later, would be new, more serious food shortages, Eventually, food prices would move rapidly to ever higher levels. The United States would not have the reserves to help poor nations faced by drought and famine and the domestic consumer would eventually pay more for food at home.

Politicians must persuade the nation's consumers that just as the price of energy has increased, so must the price of food if needed additional production needs are to be met. Indeed, in relative terms, if done properly, policies so designed should result in U.S. food prices remaining among the lowest, if not the lowest, in the world. Moreover, on balance, added earnings from food exports (thereby reducing the balance of payments) could more than counterbalance any rise in food costs so that the overall standard of living would improve.

America's capacity for food production is probably a far greater asset than the oil reserves of the OPEC nations. However, the U.S. public and its political leaders have much to learn if the full U.S. food production potential is to be best realized for both national and world interests. Neither the developing nations nor the United States will meet future world demand for food unless governments are willing to make significant changes in their agricultural policies.

## REFERENCES

1. America's Agricultural Illiteracy. Agricultural World. December 1975, p. 19.
2. Borlaug, Norman. Kansas City Times. December 13, 1975, p. 10B.
3. Brewster, John M., and Wunderlich, Gene. Farm Size Capital and Tenure Requirements. In Adjustments in Agriculture—a National Basebook, ed. Carlton Christian. Ames: Iowa State University Press, 1961.
4. Champeau, Harold C. Five Communes in the People's Republic of China, Part I. Foreign Agriculture Vol. XIII, No. 29. July 21, 1975, p. 3.
5. FAO. Monthly Bulletin of Agricultural Economics and Statistics. Vol. 24, No. 4, April 1975, p. 3.
6. Gallager, Charles F. Japan and the World Food Problem. American Universities Field Staff Reports. East Asia Series Vol. XXII, No. 1.
7. Hathaway, Dale E. Food Prices and Inflation. Brookings Papers on Economic Activity 1:1974.
8. Johnson, D. Gail. Unpublished paper presented at the International Conference on Agricultural Modernization, Urbino, Italy, July 1975.
9. Kansas City Times. January 29, 1976, p. 2C.
10. Kiewit, Fred. Nations Policies Discourage Production. Kansas City Star. March 14, 1975, p. 1.
11. Laird, Roy D. Soviet Farmer Productivity 1950–70 as measured by a U.S. Barometer. In Economic Development in the Soviet Union and East Europe, Vol. 2, ed. Zbigniew M. Fallenbuchl. New York: Special Studies, 1976, pp. 241–60.
12. ———. The Widening Soviet Grain Gap and Prospects for 1990. Revised unpublished paper prepared for the American Association for the Advancement of Slavic Studies, October 1976.

13. Laird, Roy D., and Laird, Betty A. Soviet Communism and Agrarian Revolution, Appendix B.
14. Lofton, John D., Jr. U.S. Saves Millions from Starvation. Kansas City Times, November 25, 1975, p. 11E.
15. Morse, Joseph L., ed. Funk and Wagnalls Standard Reference Encyclopedia, Vol. 6, New York: Standard Reference Library, Inc., 1970, p. 2062.
16. Nash, Helen. Today's Small Farmer—Can He Succeed? War on Hunger. AID, February 1975, pp. 5–7, 19.
17. Phillips, Donald M., Jr. West Germany Study Sees European Community Grain Sufficiency Soon. Foreign Agriculture, April 15, 1974.
18. Saleh, Abdullah A. Disincentives to Agricultural Production in Developing Countries: A Policy Survey. Foreign Agriculture, March 1975.
19. Schultz, Theodore W. Transforming Agriculture. New Haven: Yale University Press, 1964.
20. Smith, T. Lynn. Agrarian Reform in Latin America. New York: Alfred Knopf, 1965, p. 46.
21. Tang, Anthony M. Organization and Performance in Chinese Agriculture. Unpublished paper presented at the Allied Social Science Association, Dallas, Texas, December 1975.
22. United Nations World Population Conference. Department of State Bulletin, Sept. 30, 1974. Publication 8783 International Organization and Conference series 116, October 1974.
23. U.S. Department of Agriculture. Agricultural Statistics, 1975. Washington, D.C.: U.S. GPO, 1975.
24. ———. American Agriculture: Its Capacity to Produce. ERS–544, February 1974.
25. ———. The World Food Situation, Prospects for 1985. ERS, Foreign Agricultural Report No. 98, March 1975, p. 48.
26. War on Hunger. AID, April 1975.
27. Willett, Joseph W. Unpublished speech at the Canadian Agricultural Economic Society, August 6, 1974.

## BIBLIOGRAPHY

Brown, Lester R., with Eckholm, Erik P. By Bread Alone. New York: Praeger, 1974.

Disincentives to Agricultural Production in Developing Countries. Report to the Congress by the Controller General of the United States, November 26, 1975. ID–76–2.

Foreign Agriculture. A weekly issued by the U.S. Department of Agriculture.

Laird, Roy D., and Laird, Betty A. Soviet Communism and Agrarian Revolution. Middlesex, England: Penguin Books, 1970.

Smith, T. Lynn, ed. Agrarian Reform in Latin America. New York: Alfred A. Knopf, Borzoi Book, 1965.

Schultz, Theodore W. Transforming Traditional Agriculture. New Haven: Yale University Press, 1964.

The State of Food and Agriculture. An annual publication of the Food and Agricultural Organization of the United Nations.

# 15

# Credit and Credit Systems for Food Production

MERVIN G. SMITH

PEOPLE who hunt for or produce just enough food and other essentials to live, seldom borrow money. They do not buy or sell anything, but merely have a subsistence level of living.

People start producing more than is needed for their own consumption when they see how they can barter the extra for other commodities or services. As a marketing system develops they begin to sell their products and buy other products and services. In this simple way, people begin to move from subsistence to commercial farming.

Gradually farmers perceive how they might expand production and further increase income. But they begin to encounter the problem of enough money to pay for such items as seed, fertilizer, and small tools needed to expand production. The solution to this problem is to borrow extra money for short periods or until their crops are harvested and sold, at which time the money would be returned to the lender.

Very soon a farmer may need to borrow for more fertilizer, insecticides, essential livestock facilities, and feed, and eventually, he may want credit for farm equipment and improved livestock. Credit could allow him to purchase land and to make improvements on land and buildings. There will be times when he may need to borrow to meet emergencies and consumption needs such as food, clothing, and health care.

Without available credit, personal and national development is stymied—and with perhaps 90 percent of the world's 600 million farms still barely above the subsistence level the demand for credit has just begun.

The greatest concern in meeting credit needs is that policies be established that ensure that efficient credit systems are developed that meet the needs of the numerous small farmers in developing countries. Proper credit can help increase food production and improve the quality of life for many rural poor people. Existing credit systems will need to

MERVIN G. SMITH is Professor, Agricultural Economics, and Assistant Dean, International Affairs, Ohio State University. He has worked in Latin America, South America, and Africa.

be improved as well as new systems developed. Governments will play an important role in ensuring that not only efficient credit systems are developed but also complementary services that support agriculture, such as education, research, transportation, and marketing facilities, are developed.

Before discussing the development of credit in developing countries. the various uses for, and sources of, credit must be considered.

NEEDS AND USES FOR CREDIT. The most common uses and needs for credit in agriculture are for current operations, emergencies, and capital investments.

Credit to finance current operations is usually short or intermediate term, that is, usually for one season or one year. A farmer uses such credit for the following purposes:

1. Buy seed, fertilizer, insecticides, and other materials for crops
2. Hire extra help (labor), especially for planting, harvesting, and marketing
3. Store farm products
4. Purchase livestock, feed, and veterinary service
5. Buy tools and farm machinery

Much of this credit is made necessary because of the seasonal characteristics of farming: A farmer needs money to put in his crop and take care of it, but he will not receive money back until the crop is harvested and sold. Occasionally, a farmer may need to borrow for a short time to provide his family with food, clothing, and shelter.

The farmer also faces unpredictable cash demands because of emergencies, such as drought, floods, disease, poor markets, death, and health problems. When he cannot obtain enough money to meet these emergencies, he may become bankrupt. At the very least he may be forced to sell products at low prices and borrow on extremely harsh terms. To protect himself, the farmer needs to remain in a liquid position by having cash reserves, resources that can be converted to cash, and existing credit on satisfactory terms. Low income farmers in developing countries tend to keep their limited assets in a liquid state. Whatever they possess is usually converted to jewelry, gold, or money and kept hidden ready for any emergency. Some have their assets almost entirely in livestock.

Credit used for capital investment is usually needed for many years. Such long-term investments include the purchase of land, the purchase, construction, and remodeling of buildings, and the development of drainage or irrigation, wells, fencing, and other improvements. Generally the amount of credit needed increases as farms become larger and more specialized. In the United States, the estimated capital investment

TABLE 15.1. U.S. FARMERS' ASSETS, DEBTS, AND NET VALUE, IN BILLIONS OF DOLLARS.

| Item | 1940 | 1950 | 1960 | 1970 | 1975 |
|---|---|---|---|---|---|
| | | | *(billions of dollars)* | | |
| Assets: | | | | | |
| Real estate | 33.6 | 75.3 | 130.2 | 206.9 | 374.1 |
| Physical assets other than real estate | 15.1 | 41.3 | 55.2 | 76.3 | 126.8 |
| Financial | 4.2 | 15.9 | 18.1 | 22.8 | 30.0 |
| Total assets | 52.9 | 132.5 | 203.5 | 306.0 | 530.9 |
| Debts: | | | | | |
| Real estate | 6.6 | 5.6 | 12.1 | 29.2 | 47.4 |
| Nonreal estate | 3.0 | 5.1 | 11.6 | 27.0 | 46.7 |
| CCC[a] | 0.4 | 1.7 | 1.1 | 2.7 | 0.8 |
| Total debts | 10.0 | 12.4 | 24.8 | 58.9 | 94.9 |
| Equity | 42.9 | 120.1 | 178.7 | 247.1 | 436.0 |

[a]Commodity Credit Corporation, U.S. Department of Agriculture.
Source: U.S. Department of Agriculture, Fact Book of U.S. Agriculture (Washington, D.C.: Misc. Pub. 1063, 1976).

per farm varies from $60,000 to well over $1,000,000 and the annual operating expenses vary from $10,000 to several hundred thousand dollars per farm. Without huge amounts of capital and credit, such commercial farms could not exist. Thus, there is a close relationship between credit and development. This relationship is so close that the change in the amount of agricultural credit used in a country is one indicator of development and economic growth of a country.

Table 15.1 shows the parallel growth of credit and farming in the United States. The value of farmers' assets increased from 52.9 billion dollars to 530.9 billion dollars or multiplied ten times in the 35 years from 1940 to 1975. During the same time farmers' debts or *credit* increased from 10 billion dollars to 94.9 billion dollars.

Marketing and purchasing credit is needed to establish organizations to market agricultural products and to provide needed farm supplies (feed, seed, fertilizer, etc.) and farm equipment. Local merchants, especially in developing countries, usually are not able to provide these services, or if they do, very high interest rates are charged. Likewise, individual small farmers are often not able to obtain credit themselves, so they may join together and form credit associations or cooperatives to provide these services. In different countries and cultures, credit is needed for different things and present sources of credit vary widely.

SOURCES OF CREDIT. The main source of credit in the world is the savings of individuals and businesses. A lender's function is to transfer these funds to farmers and others who need to borrow them. Transfers are made within a local community, from one part of a country to another part, or even from one country to another. Thus, lenders are critical links in any credit system. Lenders may be individuals, institutions, and governments and may be classified into two groups, *informal* and *formal* lenders. Every country has both groups.

INFORMAL LENDERS. Informal lenders are the farmers' friends, neighbors, relatives, landlords, village storekeepers and merchants, itinerant traders, and moneylenders. Except for the moneylender, credit is not these peoples' primary business and interest. Some farm supply dealers, merchants, and manufacturers, however, have organized nationwide to provide credit in addition to their main business. In this way, they provide a more systemized form of credit. These informal lenders either have their own funds or obtain the funds from their business connections, such as the supplies and manufacturers of products that they sell. Their sales are increased by providing credit.

The informal lenders provide the largest proportion of rural credit in most of the developing countries, especially in Asia and Africa (1). The proportion of informal credit decreases as agriculture and food production develop but will continue to be a significant part of total credit. For example, the informal lenders in the United States still provide about 40 percent of the real estate credit to farmers and about 35 percent of the other credit.

FORMAL LENDERS. Formal lenders are institutions or systems, both private and government-owned, that provide credit through formalized procedures. They mobilize funds from individuals farther away, from local businesses and governments, from other parts of the country, and even from other countries.

The major formal agricultural credit institutions in the various countries of the world fall into three types:

1. Government and private commercial banks, which provide credit to all forms of business including agriculture
2. Agencies, such as government cooperatives, which may involve shared ownership between private and public authorities
3. Institutions and organizations such as cooperatives, which may be multiple purpose, providing supplies, marketing, extension education, and technical advice, as well as credit

The developed countries tend to have a cross section of nearly all types of credit institutions. Developing countries, however, may not have many credit institutions and generally it is the small farmers who require special services who are not adequately served. For example, commercial banks, the most common credit sources in developing countries, tend to concentrate their services in the urban areas. Each country needs all three types to serve all the different needs of agriculture.

DEVELOPMENT OF CREDIT SYSTEMS. Developing countries are presently struggling to expand existing credit systems and develop new ones. Whatever systems are developed must help meet each country's specific goals and objectives for development. Some of the development objectives that credit programs are being established to meet include:

1. Increase credit for expanding agricultural production and for meeting critical food consumption needs.
2. Strengthen and improve infrastructure (basic framework of institutions and services serving a country), including banks, merchants, processors, cooperatives, and associations that serve the rural areas.
3. Increase the use of new farm technology, improved seeds, fertilizer, livestock, and machinery.
4. Develop and increase production of a specific crop or kind of livestock.
5. Increase production of commodities to meet specific needs, e.g., cereal needs and products for export.
6. Improve and develop a specific area or group, e.g., a new area or a special group such as small farmers.
7. Facilitate resettlement and employment.
8. Mobilize rural savings for use as credit.

Each country must carefully study its own situation to determine which agricultural credit system will meet its needs best. Which particular system is developed is not important as long as it helps meet the country's development goals, is dependable, and meets the following specific criterita:

1. Provides enough credit to meet the various increasing needs of large numbers of farmers
2. Provides the funds when needed, such as at planting time and for storage
3. Offers convenience to farmers in obtaining and repaying loans, such as being close by and requiring little paperwork
4. Is closely related and coordinated with other services needed by farmers, such as supplies, and equipment, marketing services, education, and planning that contribute to improved farm incomes
5. Provides credit at low cost by keeping administrative and overhead expenses at the minimal level

No one type of credit institution meets all these criteria. Countries will usually need all three types of institutions described earlier (shared ownership, multipurpose, and those that supply credit to all businesses) as part of any credit system they develop.

Next for consideration are some of the credit organizations that developing countries might include in any credit system, how they operate, and how they might be used to provide funds to small farmers.

BANKS. Banks, both private and government, are the major formal source of credit in countries that are just beginning the development process. Unfortunately, banks generally do not serve the small farmers (1) because they are usually located in urban centers, and (2) because they provide few services with their loans. Small farmers need assistance in farm planning, technical assistance, and supervision as they increase their use of credit to prevent incorrect credit use and subsequent default on loans.

All these services are expensive, require trained people, and increase the costs of administering loans. Unless government subsidizes these services, most banks cannot afford to provide them. When banks are partly or totally owned by the government, part of the cost of providing such services can be considered a free public service.

The costs of administering credit to small farmers by banks might be reduced in developing countries if decisions could be made at the local level instead of sending them through many other state, regional, and national offices for action. The local banker or agent, if well trained and well acquainted with the people, could then make decisions on loans and payments. This would be more like the local moneylender who has personal understanding of the people and their needs and would decrease costly paperwork and time. This has been done in the United States with the Production Credit Associations and attempts to do this are being made in Taiwan, Korea, and Colombia.

SUPERVISED CREDIT AGENCIES. Institutions set up explicitly to provide assistance in farm planning, technical assistance, and supervision with loans are called supervised credit agencies. Costs still limit the amount of credit these agencies can provide since the cost of supervising this kind of farm credit is estimated to average about 20 percent of the loan and it varies from 2 to over 100 percent (2). Such agencies must be subsidized by, and often are owned by, the government.

These agencies are also limited by the shortage of qualified personnel to administer the credit. In some countries such as Brazil, Dominican Republic, and Philippines, attempts are made to have the agricultural extension service provide the supervisory and technical service for the credit agency. But this too has had limited success because of the shortage of well-trained and understanding personnel and because of difficulties involved in coordinating agencies.

Despite the expense and difficulties, supervised credit is an important system for developing countries to establish as they begin agricultural development. Farmers should gradually improve their managerial and technical skills and thus be able to use other credit sources, but illiteracy remains a serious constraint in most developing countries.

In the United States, supervised credit has been and continues to be successfully provided by the Farmers Home Administration (FHA). FHA has offered credit to young beginning farmers and to others with limited resources who have been unable to obtain credit from commercial lenders. This agency is providing about 5 percent of the farm real estate credit and 2 percent of the nonreal estate credit for farmers.

GOVERNMENT DEVELOPMENT AGENCIES AND MARKETING AGENCIES. Governments occasionally set up development agencies that provide multiple programs, including agricultural credit, that together are expected to bring about the development. One such organization in Chile was established to divide large estates, combine small farms, and organize agricultural production. Other agencies have been established in other countries to administer development in a particular region or for a certain group in a country. The development agency may use existing credit institutions or set up its own system.

Governments also sometimes establish marketing agencies or boards to market farm products, e.g., the cocoa marketing board in Nigeria. They may control and administer the product for export or for domestic use and have responsibility for distributing the production equitably and controlling the price both for producers and consumers. The agencies may also provide such services as transportation, storage, and credit for farmers. Credit may take the form of providing production supplies, such as seed and fertilizer, that the farmer is required to use. Repayments are assured by compulsory delivery of the farm products to the organization. These agencies have had limited success in situations where shortages exist and where the government gives high priority to increasing exports. The tight government control can lead to economic distortions, political manipulation, disruptions, and other unfavorable changes. Inept leadership may also be a problem.

COOPERATIVES, ASSOCIATIONS, AND CREDIT UNIONS. Cooperatives, associations, and credit unions are formal organizations owned by and operated for the benefit of those using their services. Cooperative credit institutions have had more failures than successes in developing countries. An example of serious failure was in the Philippines (3). Examples of cooperative credit successes are in Taiwan, Japan, Korea, and with the Coffee Cooperative in Kenya. Credit Savings Unions (type of cooperatives) in Latin America have had considerable success.

One reason for the failures is that agricultural credit services of cooperatives are often regarded as a form of "relief" or subsidy to farmers and then they become public welfare agencies instead of cooperatives. Credit is not really credit when it becomes an income substitute and when repayment is not required on schedule.

Where credit co-ops have been successful they have adhered to strict financial discipline and good management and have tied credit closely to farm supplies, marketing, extension services, and planning and supervision. Management of such multipurpose cooperatives is critical and success is more likely if credit services are a separate program that is then coordinated with the other services.

Cooperatives have a greater chance of success if they grow out of a felt need of a local group or association, rather than being directed by the government. Village Cooperatives formed by force in India have not performed well. The Production Credit Associations in the United States are successful and have about 20 percent of the agricultural production credit in the country. Cooperatives, however, are often underfinanced and are unable to mobilize needed funds.

The government's role in promoting cooperatives, associations, and credit unions is often difficult to determine. Cooperative credit programs have been most successful where the government had little interference and control but was generally supportive. However, they have also been successful in a few countries where the government has compelled farmers to be members of the association, has subsidized them, and given them monopoly control over supplies and services.

GROUP CREDIT. In some developing countries, a group or association is formed primarily to obtain a loan. Apparently such groups for credit are operating well in Malawi, Mexico (Ejido), and Panama. This kind of group credit has several advantages. Since one large loan is granted instead of many small loans, this means that more farmers can obtain credit at a lower cost. The group or association takes some responsibility in obtaining the loan, distributing it among individuals, managing it, and repaying it, and so less supervision is required. Formation of such groups can stimulate local leadership, provide more effective administration, reduce defaults on loans, initiate the use of new technology and marketing, and help community development.

Group credit is most successful with groups of farmers that have similar farm sizes, tenure status, and other similar characteristics. Combining large and small farmers has not been as successful unless there were other strong social factors to unify them.

Credit groups tend to work better if they include a savings program that can be used to repay loans and to preserve and increase capital. Some credit groups force beginning savings by requiring a small percentage of each loan to be held back as savings.

Some government support and encouragement is usually needed to initiate these credit groups. Minimally government should give legal recognition, training, and assistance in organizing and developing leadership for management.

Group credit, as with other forms of credit, is not likely to be successful unless other related services are provided, such as marketing, farm supplies, extension, and technical services. These services may become group owned and operated enterprises, but if not, they should be provided by outside agencies and government and very closely coordinated with the credit. Group credit, therefore, may be the basis for forming small cooperatives that would have good chances of being successful.

Mobilizing Funds in Rural Areas. In the early stages of development the savings of individuals and businesses in the rural areas are the main sources of borrowed funds. These funds will have to be mobilized and transferred to farmers and others who must borrow them.

As indicated, much of the savings of rural people in the developing countries exists as gold, jewelry, and money that individuals keep hidden. These hidden assets earn no interest and are seldom used as funds from which others can borrow. Studies in countries such as Taiwan, Korea, and Japan indicate that rural people will invest their hidden savings and save more if given the opportunity and if they can see the advantages of using the savings to increase their incomes, obtain more education, improve health, improve housing, satisfy other needs and desires, and have confidence in those in charge (4).

The banks and other regular financial institutions generally do not provide rural poor people with these opportunities. Therefore, small savings associations and credit unions may be successful in rural areas if leadership is organized and people can be educated about savings and credit. Both adults and young people can be involved in these savings groups and associations. With such associations not only are needed funds mobilized, but also responsible community leaders are developed, all of which will help stimulate agricultural development.

Savings programs should also be encouraged as part of any multipurpose agricultural association or cooperative formed. Such organizations would benefit from having increased funds for purchasing agricultural production supplies, marketing agricultral products, and providing other services.

As development proceeds, other institutions would be needed that can mobilize funds from individuals farther away and from businesses and governments in other parts of the country and even from other countries.

Eventually, funds are mobilized from many different and sophisticated sources; for example, deposits in commercial banks, savings banks, savings societies, credit unions, insurance funds, pension funds, securities, bonds, mortgages, notes, and stocks. Governments can obtain funds to use for credit through taxation, by borrowing from the public (public securities), or through loans from a foreign government or international agency.

Government Influence. Government policies have a profound effect on the success or failure of credit systems in developing countries. How interest rates are set, for example, determines if private funds, which are the major source of all loanable funds, can be mobilized. A more profitable agriculture will attract more funds and be able to pay more for credit. Thus, anything government does to make agriculture more profitable will increase the funds mobilized. But interest rates on savings and credit must be high enough to attract investors and there must be little risk of losing the investments. Subsidies to farmers, tax exemptions, and providing insurance on life, loans, and crops are examples of government actions that could promote the mobilizing of funds for agriculture.

The government can provide funds or loan them at low interest rates, and it can absorb losses by obtaining more money through taxation or by further borrowing. Additional funds can also be obtained from foreign governments and international banks. Too much indebtedness, however, can weaken the government. In the long run, therefore, most of the available funds to be used for agricultural credit in a country must be mobilized within that country.

Government policies on interest, supplying supplementary services, and subsidies are so critical to success of credit systems that they will be discussed in more detail.

INTEREST RATE POLICY. Interest rates charged for credit to farmers vary from 4 to 50 percent or more in developing countries. The higher rates usually occur during emergencies and are provided by the informal lenders, while the lower rates of 4 to 10 percent are for government-subsidized loans. Surprisingly, these subsidized interest rates may be one of the important reasons small farmers are still receiving limited amounts of credit and that credit systems are not functioning well in developing countries. Interest rates of 15 to 20 percent are probably needed to pay administrative costs and to attract funds from private savings and investors that are so necessary to any successful credit system.

Subsidized low interest rates in developing countries have disadvantages; (1) they make it easy for farmers to buy equipment instead of using the abundant and often less costly local labor; (2) they may increase consumption expenditures (housing, food, etc.) thus reducing expenditures for increased and more efficient production; and (3) they continue to channel credit to large farmers who are more favorable credit risks and already have access to other credit.

Thus, unrealistic interest rate policies convert credit into a welfare program and may actually hinder rural development and increased food production. Politically, however, it has been dangerous to oppose low interest rates. People and their governments must be clearly shown why cheap credit policies generally have not been successful in increasing credit use by small farmers in the developing countries.

A more successful policy usually includes interest rates high enough to attract more savings in the rural areas and to pay for the institutional costs of mobilizing the funds, delivering the credit to the farmer, and supervising the loans.

ESSENTIAL COMPLEMENTARY SERVICES. In the long run, governments may increase agricultural production more efficiently by emphasizing services that complement credit services instead of providing low interest rates.

Agricultural credit programs are not successful unless the following services are also provided or available:

1. General education
2. Extension education and technical assistance
3. Agricultural research
4. Land, water, and irrigation development
5. Public roads, transportation, health, and other services
6. Production supplies and equipment and institutions that provide them
7. A good market and marketing institutions and organizations

The first five of these programs and services are usually provided mostly by the government. Items 6 and 7 are usually initiated and provided initial assistance by the government but should eventually become self-supporting. Some of these programs are developed separately, but others may be organized in various combinations along with credit. (See also Chapter 13.)

Very little development can take place if farmers are illiterate since commercial farming requires basic mathematics and communication skills. Basic education is desperately needed by the farming and rural population of developing countries. Beyond basic education, agricultural extension education services, provided largely by the governments of developing countries, are also necessary to increase production. To train new generations of farmers more agricultural education is needed in the elementary schools. Agricultural higher education at secondary and the college level is also essential to train agricultural educators, credit agency personnel, researchers, agricultural farm supply managers, and marketing business people. As indicated earlier, a major limiting factor in developing credit systems and other programs in agricultural development is the dearth of trained people who are essential for successful development.

Agricultural research stations and programs are needed to help solve farmers' problems and to develop improved crop varieties, animals, and new agricultural technology. This must be linked closely with a strong agricultural extension service.

In the United States agricultural extension, higher agricultural education, and agriculture research are conducted and coordinated by agricultural colleges or universities. In many developing countries, however, these three agricultural functions are weak and not well coordinated and therefore are ineffective. It is extremely important, therefore, for improvement in the use of credit that education, extension, and research be improved and coordinated in the developing countries.

GOVERNMENT SUBSIDIES. Governments often provide other forms of subsidies besides credit that may influence the farmers' success in the use of credit. These government subsidies can be grouped as follows:

1. Production costs: Fertilizer, seeds, chemicals, tubewells, irrigation facilities and water, land development and improvement, tools and equipment, breeding animals, veterinary services, crop insurance, etc.
2. Marketing of agricultural products: Price supports, storage, processing, transportation, marketing facilities, handling of products, etc.

Such subsidies may be needed and should be provided in a way that will promote increased food production and rural development. Some may be provided along with credit. Subsidies may be provided through farmers' associations or cooperatives for the purchase of farm production supplies or for marketing agricultural products and they often are included in comprehensive government agricultural development and agrarian reform programs.

Subsidies of production supplies can complement credit services by encouraging farmers to start new activities, adopt new technology, and stimulate production expansion programs. But problems arise if these subsidies continue for a long time and the government is pressured to expand and continue them after they have accomplished their goals. Subsidies become very costly to governments, and the programs may become corrupt with benefits going to farmers who do not need them. After an extended time, farm production costs and returns become dependent on the subsidy; if it is withdrawn, the production system may collapse. As an example, in the United States tobacco subsidies eventually resulted in large increases in the price of tobacco land. Price supports and marketing subsidies can be important in initiating special projects and programs, but if they are continued for a long time serious problems may develop.

Development programs must be economically sound in the long run and must stand on their own once they are established. Extension, education, and research, however, should be part of the programs for increasing agricultural production and rural development and funded on a continuing basis. Unfortunately, these activities are often neglected and weak in developing countries.

FOREIGN ASSISTANCE. Many of the foreign assistance development programs have an agricultural credit component, and the developed countries are providing substantial amounts of loans to foreign governments. The World Bank and USAID, in particular, are providing loans to developing countries for agriculture credit development.

Most governments seem to be emphasizing government borrowing to obtain large amounts of loanable funds. Not enough emphasis has been given to developing the complementary and allied programs necessary if more credit is to be used successfully. More attention should also be given to mobilizing funds from within the country. Manpower development must receive high priority if credit agencies are to have competent trained people and efficient credit systems are to be developed.

Considerable emphasis is being given in providing foreign assistance for training personnel to work in agricultural credit institutions in developing countries but much more is necessary. The developing countries must give more attention to training people in agricultural credit within the country. Training is also important for all the other agencies and programs in agricultural development. Education and educational institutions must be expanded and developed to increase the trained manpower needed for development.

Some foreign assistance has been provided in the organization, administration, and operation of agricultural credit institutions. More attention probably is needed to assist in mobilizing funds within the developing countries and in improving government policies for developing agricultural credit.

Past programs of foreign assistance and other credit development programs are being evaluated and studied. New information is becoming available that should be helpful in planning new assistance programs. In developing agricultural credit programs, the total array of complementary programs must be examined and the planning should consider all the factors and programs that contribute to the success of credit and credit systems.

SUMMARY. An increasing amount of credit is essential for rural development and increased food production in developing countries. The greatest concern in most countries is to provide credit for the large number of small farmers who are not presently well served by credit systems. A variety of credit institutions tailored to meet each country's specific development goals will be needed. Funds will have to be mobilized in rural areas, old credit systems will need to be improved, and new systems developed. Government will play an important role in ensuring that efficient and economically sound credit systems are developed and that complementary services, such as extension, education, research, transportation, and marketing facilities, are also developed.

## REFERENCES

1. International Bank for Reconstruction and Development, Report No. 436.
2. Long, Millard F. "Conditions for Success of Public Credit Programs for Small Farmers," AID, Spring Review of Small Farmer Credit, Vol. XIX, No. SR 119, June, 1973.
3. Sacay, Orlando J. "An Analysis of the Crop Loan Program of the Agricul-

tural Credit Financing Administration" (Philippines). Ph.D. diss., Cornell University, New York, 1961.
4. Ong, Marcia L.; Adams, Dale W., and Singh, I. J. "Voluntary Rural Savings Capacities in Taiwan, 1960–70," American Journal of Agricultural Economics, Vol. 58, No. 3, August 1976.

## BIBLIOGRAPHY

Agency for International Development. Spring Review of Small Farmers' Credit, Vol. I–XX. Washington, D. C.: PPC/PDA AID, June, 1973. Recommended for general reading: Vol. XIX, Analytical Papers, and Vol. XX, Summary Papers.

———. Agricultural Credit and Rural Savings. AID Bibliography Series, Agriculture No. 7, and later additions. Washington, D.C.: AID, 1972. A list of significant writings on agricultural credit with brief summaries.

Hopkins, J. A.; Barry, P. J.; and Baker, C. B. Financial Management in Agriculture. Danville, Ill.: Interstate Printers and Publishers, Inc., 1973.

Johl, S. S., and Kapur, T. R. Fundamentals of Farm Business Management. Ludhiana, Punjab, India: Lyall Book Depot, Chaura Bazar, 1973.

Lele, Uma. The Design of Rural Development—Lessons from Africa. In Agricultural Credit, Inc. Baltimore and London: The Johns Hopkins University Press for the World Bank, 1975.

Nelson, Aaron G.; Lee, Warren F.; and Murray, William G. Agricultural Finance. 6th ed. Ames: Iowa State University Press, 1973.

Upton, Martin. Farm Management in Africa: The Principles of Production and Planning. London: Oxford University Press, 1973.

World Bank. Rural Development. Sector Policy Papers, February, 1975.

E. R. DUNCAN

*Extension worker shows how to weed maize and side dress fertilizer, but few farmers adopt the practices.*

# 16

# Education and Training for Adoption and Diffusion of New Ideas

JOE M. BOHLEN

FOOD PRODUCTION in the developing countries has been barely meeting or falling behind the rising demand for food caused by rapidly increasing populations. To adequately meet the rising demand for food through increased food production, new ideas and practices will have to be introduced, since perhaps 90 percent of the world's farms are still at or near subsistence level. They raise just enough to feed themselves and their families, using the same farming practices their ancestors used.

If these multitudes of farmers are to develop their food production capabilities beyond subsistence level, they will need to accept and use (adopt) new ideas and practices. These new practices may not be, and probably should not be, those of energy- and capital-intensive agriculture. Nevertheless, the ideas will be new to the subsistence farmer (see Chapter 10). If leaders from both the developed countries and the developing countries are to find effective ways of educating these farmers and getting them to adopt new ideas, they will need to understand the elements and processes of adoption. (The term *adoption* refers to the process that any given individual goes through in accepting a new idea. *Diffusion* is the term applied to the spread of an idea within a social system, such as a village, neighborhood, community, or state. The term also applies to spread of an idea from one culture to another.)

Much of the research on adoption and diffusion of new ideas has been done in the United States, but many of the principles apply to all cultures. These general principles will be discussed first. The differences between adoption and diffusion in developed and developing countries will follow, along with discussion of education and change agents.

GENERAL PRINCIPLES. Only man changes and manipulates his environment to suit his will. Except for minor adjustments in their habi-

JOE M. BOHLEN, Professor, Rural Sociology, Iowa State University, is widely recognized for innovative work on dissemination of ideas. He has had foreign assignments in Latin America, Africa, Asia, and Near East.

tats, such as burrowing holes in the earth, building nests or building dams in streams, other species adapt to the local conditions, migrate to more favorable environs, or become extinct.

Modern man with this tremendous capacity for controlling and changing his environment is still an enigma. On one hand he changes and adapts in his physical environment with ease and rapidity, and on the other hand he ignores or resists the social, social-psychological, and economic changes that are inextricably a part of those physical changes. This is as true of people from the developed countries as it is of those from the developing countries, because human beings wherever they are found have certain traits in common.

Man has three special sets of traits that distinguish him from other life forms and affect his adoption or rejection of new ideas:

1. Man is a symbol creator. He creates a language, oral and written, which allows him to share the experiences of other men who lived in other places at other times. He doesn't have to "reinvent the wheel" each generation.
2. Man is an organizing being. He puts his subjective universe into a pattern of meaningful relationships and then makes choices about the actions he wishes to take in regard to the alternatives that he perceives available.
3. Man is telic being. He can look into the future and weigh alternatives and set goals.

Because of the uniqueness of his intelligence, man is inclined to place all the phenomena he perceives into patterns of meaningful interrelationships. Man is an organizing being. He organizes the world around him into cause-effect relationships that appear rational to him. In many instances he does this without considering all the data known or available. Hence, he sometimes assigns relationships between and among phenomena that cannot be verified by research.

Man is able to go through the process of perceiving interrelationships because he has the ability to think in terms of abstractions. He can create symbols in his mind, to which he can respond without being in immediate sensory contact with the phenomena the symbols represent. Man can respond to a stimulus not only on the basis of his own past experiences but also on those of other men who met similar stimuli in other places and at other times.

Because of his ability to deal with abstractions and to communicate via symbols, man is able to plan for the future. "Future" has no meaning to an animal that must have immediate sensory contact with phenomena to respond to them. "Future" is an intellectual concept that has meaning for creatures who use symbols to conceptualize the relationships that can or could exist between that phenomenon with which they have immediate sensory contact and the universe in which they place this phenomenon.

Thus, man never responds to a stimulus per se, but to his interpretation of it based on his past experiences, his future expectancies or goals (ends) and the means available, and his perceived relationships of this stimulus to both. He deals with the realities of the situation as he perceives them, taking into consideration the possible outcomes resulting from choice of alternative responses he might make to the stimulus. Since he thinks in symbols, he can project himself into the future and choose the alternative that in his judgment will help him to maximize his satisfactions.

Since man is this kind of being, his personality, i.e., the bundle of beliefs, feelings, values, and attitudes that are unique to him, is a result of the hereditary package with which he was born and the unique experiences he has had since then.

When man reacts to a stimulus, two residues remain: (1) physical changes (change in muscle tonus, fatigue, organic changes, etc.) and (2) the memory of the experience. Man remembers both the details of his actions and interactions and his judgment about the experience. For each experience, man tends to assign a normative factor, i.e., it was good or bad, satisfactory or unsatisfactory, pleasant or unpleasant, or rewarding or unrewarding. Out of this intellectualizing about experiences, man develops a set of values, beliefs about what *should be* the relationships between the phenomena in his perceived universe and how he *should* relate to the rest of this universe. This value system is the basis of a set of tendencies to act in given directions toward various categories of stimuli and is a major influence in determining man's behavior.

As a man receives stimuli and contemplates alternative responses, he organizes both ends and means into hierarchies of favorableness to himself as an individual. In this process, a lower level or less favorable *end* may be selected because the *means* of attaining the higher level or more favorable *end* was too unsatisfactory. When a given *end* exists with alternative *means* of attaining it, an individual invariably (unless he is mentally ill) chooses the means that he considers most consistent with his value system; i.e., the most satisfactory one. In many instances, man segments his total attitude pattern. He may act rationally and consistently within a given area of values although these actions may be in conflict with another area of values that he also holds.

It follows from these premises that whenever man receives a stimulus he tries to recall if he has ever received a similar stimulus before. If he has, he attempts to reconstruct his previous actions and judgments about the outcomes of his actions; this is done both in terms of the ends or goals and the means or methods he chose. He then relates his past to the future by asking himself if he still desires the same ends, goals, or outcomes. If he decides that these desires have changed, he asks himself what different ends and means are possible and which is most desirable. Only then does he choose a final alternative (end and means).

Man's personality is molded by the series of events in his experience world. When he receives a similar stimulus repeatedly and each time responds in a similar manner, one that gives him satisfaction, he gradually changes the procedure of response. At first much thought may go into the interpretation before he makes a response, but as each additional interpretation is made and the results are satisfying, man puts less and less thought into interpreting the stimulus. He reaches a point where, after only cursory scrutiny of the stimulus, he responds in a pattern that in the past brought satisfaction. When this has taken place, an individual has formed a *habit*—a convention by which he copes with relatively similar and familiar stimuli with a minimum of intellectual effort. This allows an individual to do many routine things very quickly, and to use available time for interpreting new or unique stimuli. It usually takes a major change in the stimuli toward which man has routinized a behavior response before he will discard this response and think through another. When an individual has developed a habitual pattern of response to a recurrent pattern of stimuli, he frequently neglects to notice that at each recurrence the pattern of stimuli and (or) the circumstances surrounding it have changed very slightly so that after a period of time he is responding to a stimulus pattern so altered that his habituated response is completely nonrational.

The above attributes are widely accepted as being universal, the starting place for understanding the behavior of humans wherever they live and whatever their experiences that make them appear different from culture to culture.

ADOPTION PROCESS. The adoption of new ideas and practices is in many ways a part of this universal behavior because it is an intricate series of mental activities involving the basic human skills not limited by cultural boundaries.

The amount of research on adoption and diffusion of new technology has increased so greatly in the past 20 years that it is impossible to present all the findings. Therefore, only those data that have wide application will be presented. Where significant differences exist, they are indicated.

One way of viewing adoption is from the viewpoint of one trying to get someone else to change his behavior. Using this approach, adoption involves the following key factors:

1. The change agent
2. The adoption unit
3. The type of adoption behavior desired
4. The characteristics of the innovation

A *change agent* is anyone who is trying to get others to change what they are now doing by adopting new ideas, new practices, or new products. An *adoption unit* may be one person, e.g., a farmer, or it may be two or more people, e.g., a family, a partnership of some kind, a corporation, a cooperative, a local change agent, or any combination of these. In food production and storage, the main adoption unit is the individual farmer or farm family.

To be effective in bringing about change, a change agent needs to understand his adoption units, particularly the amount of knowledge about the practice the potential adopter possesses. The change agent needs to remember that changes take place not in his own mind but in the mind of the adopter and that change will be made within the context of the adopter's knowledge, values, and attitudes. Research has shown that there is a wide variation among adopters in their knowledge of new products and also their basic value-attitude patterns, such as risk aversion, attitudes toward science, traditionalism, and feelings of security in decision making.

The kind of *adoption behavior* the change agent wishes to bring about is also an important factor to consider. Change agents are usually concerned with direct action, i.e., getting the adoption unit to actually use the practice, but *symbolic adoption* is also important. This is the mental state where an individual has decided to use an idea but because of lack of money, landlord resistance, or other factors he cannot take up the practice immediately. Creating this attitude of favorableness at every opportunity may make future adoption easier.

One of the most important factors affecting the rate at which new practices and products are adopted is the potential user's perception of the practice, for example, its complexity. Researchers have categorized the levels of complexity of practices and products on a continuum from the most simple to the most complex. Complexity is determined not so much by the product itself as by the number of variables that the ultimate user has to manipulate simultaneously in his mind in the process of deciding whether to accept the product.

The simplest of these categories is what is called *a simple change in materials and/or equipment.* Examples of such changes are increasing application rate of broadcast fertilizer of a given analysis from 100 to 200 pounds per acre or changing from a four-row to a six-row corn planter. In both the old and the new, the basic principles are the same; thus there are a minimum of variables to consider.

The second category of complexity is referred to as *an improved practice.* Changing from broadcasting to side-dressing of fertilizer or from a standard draw-bar tractor to one with a three-point hitch are examples in this category. The adopter has accepted the basic idea of fertilizer use or a tractor for power but new principles and methods of use are involved.

The next category of complexity is called *innovations,* that is, changes that involve not only a change in materials but also a change in basic beliefs and a change in the basic principles involved. A good example of an innovation is hybrid seed corn. Using hybrid seed corn involved changing from a seed selected by its appearance to one selected by scientists on the basis of the reproductive potential of its genes. Using it involved radical changes in seed sources and selection procedures, and meant dependence upon a nonlocal source of seed supply. There was resistance to the hybrid in many areas because certain farmers had attained status, satisfaction, and extra incomes from being good judges of seed corn. "They knew which ears to put in the box in the front of the wagon." When these farmers adopted hybrid seed corn, they had to give up this prestige and go to an outside source of seed. Corn was the first hybrid to be used extensively by farmers. Approximately 5 years passed from the time that the average farmer in the Corn Belt first heard about hybrid seed until he tried it. Since most of them tried one bushel the first year, it was 6 years from awareness to adoption. It was more than 13 years from the time hybrid seed corn was introduced before most farmers had adopted it. Once farmers accepted the idea of hybrids, new varieties were adopted much more rapidly because now changing from one hybrid variety to another was a simple change in materials!

Many farmers in the developing countries have not accepted hybrid varieties because of strong traditional beliefs about seed selection from the field. In many areas hybrid varieties are inadequate or unavailable, and in most instances, using the best hybrid varieties demands changes in related cultural practices to ensure successful use. The additional costs involved may also be a barrier to adoption.

Innovations take longer to get adopted because people have to change their conventional and traditional ways of trying to solve a problem to adopt them. Besides complexity, four other attributes affect the rate of adoption:

The first is *divisibility*. If a useful product can be available in small units so that most farmers can try it out with a risk of only minimal loss if they have a failure, it will be adopted much more rapidly than those products that involve higher risks because they do not provide ease of trial.

The second attribute is *visibility* of the results. When results are highly visible, products get adopted more rapidly. Preemergent weed killers were adopted more slowly because of low visibility of results. The same is true of preventative medicines such as vaccines, vitamins, and antibiotic feed additives. If they work perfectly all that one can see is *no* weeds and healthy animals. Many see this as "the way nature intended things to be!"

To be prepared to provide the necessary information and explanations, a change agent has to constantly consider how potential adopters will look at a new practice or product.

A third factor is the perception that the potential adopter has of the practice's *compatibility* with his ongoing operations or beliefs. For example, the potential adopter considers the following: Will the new practice demand additional time at periods when time is at a premium? Will the new practice or product help the individual to maximize his goals? Is it contrary to his beliefs about what is proper? Many farmers were reluctant to use antibiotic feed additives when they were first introduced because of concern over using "medicine" in feeds. In some primitive cultures, farmers refuse to use fertilizer and agricultural chemicals because they are unnatural or against their god's will.

Finally, *accessibility* enters into the speed of adoption. If the adopter can always easily obtain the product, he will adopt more rapidly than if he must delay ongoing operations or suffer any inconvenience.

New products and practices vary in their *relative advantage*. There are three aspects of relative advantage: usefulness, economic costs relative to benefits, and pay-off time.

Usefulness is defined by the potential adopter in terms of his basic values. If he is concerned with labor saving, he places high priority on that aspect of usefulness. If he is convenience oriented, he places high value on that.

The economic costs or benefits are measured in several ways by potential adopters. Some will hesitate to adopt a new product if it has a high unit cost. Others look beyond the initial cost to the ratio between initial cost and the additional profits that will result from usage. Still others operate on the theory that if a new product is low in cost it cannot be very effective. The change agent needs to keep these different approaches in mind when dealing with his clientele. In general, the higher the cost, the less likely the farmer is to adopt. Likewise, the lower the costs-to-benefits ratio, the slower the adoption.

These kinds of rational economic approaches are used only by the top grade farmers in the developing countries. Most of the farmers think in terms of traditional rather than rational models.

As indicated earlier, adoption is the process that an individual goes through in accepting a new idea or practice. Researchers have identified at least five stages or steps that an individual goes through in adopting a new idea or practice. Individuals are also aware that they go through these stages in adopting ideas that are new to them.

The stages and a description of each are discussed in the following paragraphs and summarized in Table 16.1.

## ADOPTION STAGES

AWARENESS. The *awareness* stage begins for an individual when he first finds out about the existence of some new practice or product. At this stage, he lacks details concerning the way it works, how to use it, and its

TABLE. 16.1. Stages in the adoption process and sources of information used.[a]

| Awareness | Information | Evaluation | Trial | Adoption |
|---|---|---|---|---|
| Knows about it; lacks detail | Develops interest; gathers general information and facts | Mental trial, application to personal situation: Can I do it? | Small-scale experimental use; how to do it | Large-scale continued use; satisfaction |
| 1. Mass Media: Radio, TV, newspapers, magazines | 1. Commercial[b] | 1. Commercial[b] | 1. Commercial[b] | 1. Neighbors, friends |
| 2. Neighbors, friends | 2. Neighbors, friends | 2. Neighbors, friends | 2. Neighbors, friends | 2. Commercial[b] |
| 3. Commercial[b] | 3. Govt. agencies | 3. Govt. agencies | 3. Govt. agencies | 3. Govt. agencies |
| 4. Govt. agencies: Extension, voc. ag., etc. | 4. Mass media | 4. Mass media | 4. Mass media | 4. Mass media |

[a]The ranking of information sources in their order of importance applies primarily to U.S. samples. This table is included as an illustration of the fact that potential adopters use different sources of information at various stages in the adoption process. If the change agent is to be effective he must become familiar with the credible information sources as perceived by his clientele.

[b]The commercial category includes dealers; technicians employed by commercial companies; publications, such as magazines and pamphlets that are sent free to selected mailing lists by commercial companies; and meetings, demonstrations, and/or seminars conducted by commercial companies.

costs and benefits. He knows little more than its name and that it is available. Many people become aware of new ideas without much actual conscious effort on their part. They are "bombarded" by the idea via radio, television, farm magazines, and conversations with others.

INFORMATION. At the *information* stage, the individual is actively seeking additional facts about the practice or product. He wants to know what it is, how it works and what its potentialities are. He is interested in the cost factors and the time it will take for him to get his investment back if he decides to adopt it.

EVALUATION. At the *evaluation* stage, the individual puts the new practice or product through a mental trial. He applies to his own situation all the information he has gathered. He asks himself: "Can I do it?" "Do I have the type of farm, the capital, the labor resources, and the management skills to use this?" "If I do use it, will I be better off than with what I am now using?" After answering these questions, many potential adopters consider the importance of this practice to themselves or their families and weigh the capital outlay against what else they might do with the same amount of money and the satisfactions they would get from each alternative.

The flow of the discussion and Table 16.1 may leave the impression that individuals go through each stage in sequence and are completely through one stage before going on to the next. This is true for most of the stages but not for the information and evaluation stages. Man tends to evaluate after gathering each new bit of information. Thus, the typical person may mentally shuttle from information gathering to evaluation many times before concluding that he has all the information needed to answer satisfactorily all his questions.

TRIAL. An individual finishes the evaluation stage by making the decision either to reject or accept the practice or product. The majority of those who decide to accept any idea usually go through a *trial* stage where they try out the practice in an experimental way to determine the answers to such questions as: "How do I do it?" "How much do I use?" "How do I operate it?" "How can I make it work best for me?"

The majority of the potential users try out the practice on a small scale if it can be obtained in small units (is divisable). More than 75 percent of the farmers adopting hybrid seed corn planted only one bushel during the first year they used this type of seed. The adoption of 2-4-D and other chemicals shows similar patterns of behavior. The farmers purchased small amounts and applied them in areas where they could check results before using them on a broad basis. When the practice cannot be used on a small scale, farmers move much more cautiously. For example, before they purchased and used tractors, combines, cornpickers, and haybalers, many farmers went through the trial stage by visiting fairs where the equipment was exhibited, or by visiting dealers where they saw demonstrations, or by having the dealer bring the equipment to their farms where they could try it. Many also visited neighbors or relatives who had this type of equipment and were able to operate it or ride with the owner while it was being used. About 20 to 25 percent of the farmers do not need to go through the trial stage to adopt. These people are different in the way they make decisions and will be discussed later.

Most people, however, must go through this stage. No matter how long they have known about the practice and how much information they may have gathered, they still must actually have sensory contact with it and use it themselves before they can really decide to adopt it for their own continued use.

ADOPTION. The final stage in the process is the *adoption* stage. This is characterized by large scale and continued use of the idea, and most of all, by satisfaction on the part of the user. This doesn't mean that an adopter will use a practice or product forever, but he will tend to use it until something newer comes along to make him dissatisfied with what he now has. It does mean that he thinks he has a good thing and will make it a part of his ongoing program.

To reach the adoption stage on any practice or product, the user must have satisfactorily answered the following questions: "What is it?" "Is it good for me?" "How can I use it and make it work?" As previously indicated, individuals may go through these stages at different rates. Also, any given individual will go through the process at different rates for different practices and products.

INFORMATION SOURCES AND ADOPTION IN DEVELOPING COUNTRIES. Up to this point the basic principles apply to the variety of cultures where man grows plants and animals for food. The real differences in adoption and use of new technology arise not from the differences in men themselves but in the differences in the sociocultural worlds that men and their ancestors have created and in which they live out their lives.

If one looks at the world of farmers on a continuum whose polar points range from the highly educated commercial farmer operating a heavily capitalized, extensive holding in an urban-industrial society to the cultivator on a small acreage in an agricultural village, in a developing country, there are several major differences that may be pointed out, as well as some generalizations that apply to all.

The majority of the people use different sources of information at the different stages in the adoption process. This is quite reasonable to expect since different kinds of information are being sought at each stage. Generally, studies indicate that (1) many people use more than one information source at each stage in the process, and (2) those people who adopt later tend to use less expert sources and depend more on face-to-face conversations for their information.

The use of the term "majority" in this discussion is deliberate. Farmers do not form a uniform category. In any social system (i.e., village, neighborhood, or community), there is a wide range in the behavior of individuals toward new ideas. The speed at which they adopt new ideas is a good indicator of the differences in these economic, social, and personal characteristics.

Therefore, in many of these studies, the farmers in the samples have been categorized on the basis of the speed with which they adopt a new idea after it has been introduced. A typical classification used is Innovators, Early Adopters, Early Majority, Majority, and Laggards.

The Innovators and Early Adopters that make up only about 15 percent of the midwestern populations studied usually hear about new ideas from agricultural experts and specialized technical publications, but all the rest, except the late end of the Majority category and the Laggards, usually hear about new ideas and get some general information from mass media (about 60 percent). The Innovators tend to use the more expert sources at all stages in the adoption process while the Majority and Laggards tend to use peer sources.

Education level also affects the choice of information source. Those with lower levels of education tend to depend more upon neighbors, friends, and relatives, and those with higher levels of education use more expert sources, such as agricultural technicians, printed mass media, and government bulletins.

In developing countries, the development and aggressive marketing of the inexpensive battery powered transistor radios combined with government programming in local dialects may be having an impact that still has not been researched enough to evaluate. Studies made in developed countries, however, indicate that mass media devices, such as farm magazines, radios, and televisions provide a very inexpensive way of making the majority of farmers aware of new ideas.

DIFFERENCES BETWEEN DEVELOPED AND DEVELOPING COUNTRIES. One of the major differences between the functioning of the agricultural change agent in the developed countries and in the developing countries is the role definitions and social distances between the technically competent sources of information and the potential users of the new technology.

In most developed countries, especially North America and northwest Europe, the man with the doctor's or master's degree has no status problems in going to the fields or stables and actually demonstrating to the farmers the new idea and its proper use. He does not lose any status or "face" with farmers because he does so. Agriculture as a science has gained wide acceptance and every community knows one or more farmer's son or daughter who is a university-trained specialist in agriculture. The overwhelming majority of the agricultural scientists in the United States are sons and daughters of farm families. There is no stigma attached to getting one's hands dirty.

This is not true in many of the developing countries where food production is lowest and where modern technology is needed most (not necessarily the same modern technology as in the advanced urban industrial societies). Agricultural scientists with excellent training from the best agricultural universities of Europe and North America exist, but most lack farm experience comparable to that of the farmers they would work with. This lack of experience plus their advanced degrees are actually barriers in their communications with the potential users. These highly skilled scientists are in many instances blocked from working directly with the local small farmers because it is considered as a mark of distinction by themselves, their peers, and the farmers to be a person who does not perform manual skills. To do so is to lower one's status and may even cause the validity of the degrees held to be suspect!

Communications research has indicated that communication takes place between individuals only within the arena of their commonly shared experiences. One of the ways this gap between the scientists and the small farmers of the developing countries may be bridged is by training at lower level institutions, sons and daughters of small farmers who have had enough formal education to accept the scientific bases of the technology and could bring about change. These people could then demonstrate the proper uses of new technologies.

Using people as change agents who identify with the adoption units is of ultimate importance because research has shown that whether any given change agent is used as an information source is determined mainly by the potential user's belief in the source's credibility. To the potential user, credibility is composed of trustworthiness and valid knowledge. A source is considered trustworthy when the potential user believes that the source is putting out information that is beneficial and in his best interest. A knowledgeable source is one considered to have understanding and skills.

Farmers always use the source they consider trustworthy. In U.S. research the top 20 percent of the farmers always use expert knowledgeable sources of information because they consider them trustworthy. The majority of farmers consider neighbors, friends, and relatives the most trustworthy and so go to them for information rather than to more knowledgeable sources of which they may be fully aware, but whom they do not trust.

Another major difference between the developed countries and the developing countries is the role that men and women play in the actual production of the crops and the care of the livestock. In advanced agricultural areas, men play the dominant roles and have the need for information. In developing countries, women take an active role in production and decision making and also need information.

A third difference between farmers in developed countries and those in the developing countries is the perception of and availability of markets. An estimated 40 percent of the world population live in barter economies where money as such is nearly nonexistent. In many of these societies the perception of distribution of surplus production is that growing too much means sharing with less fortunate relatives or being bilked by tradesmen. The incentive to produce beyond immediate needs is quite different from that in an economy where farming is perceived as a business rather than as a way of life.

A final difference between the developed countries and the developing countries is the existence in the developed countries of the capabilities to create and operate complex organizations that provide for production, preservation, and distribution of food. These organizations exist in the public sector as well as in the private. Despite the disclaimers and cynicism, most of the organizations that make up the infrastructures (institutions and services) of the developed countries are operated with a relatively high level of efficiency, honesty, and trust.

Because developed countries have such things as farm credit systems, farmer-owned and -managed cooperatives, government loans and crop insurance, Social Security programs, and government price support programs, the production costs and the risks involved in adoption of new techniques, new breeds of livestock, and new varieties of seed involve much different problems of risk than in the developing countries. If a commercial farmer tries a new seed and it does not yield well, he suffers some financial loss. If a farmer living in a barter economy of a country with no infrastructures to back him tries a new variety and it fails, at best he loses "face" and at worst his family goes even hungrier!

THE ROLE OF EDUCATION. Education has a major role to play in bringing about change and adoption of appropriate new technology in the developing countries. This is best illustrated by the universal awareness that a major gap exists between the valid usable technology and what is now being used. In the developed countries this gap has been closing at a rapid pace, e.g., Midwestern corn growers are getting average yields that are within 90 percent of those at the Agricultural Experiment Station Farms. In the developing countries this is far from the case.

Education, in or out of the classroom, is the process by which ideas, understanding, and skills get transferred from one man's mind to that of another. Education is nothing more than communication. There is a sender, a message, a medium, and a receiver.

From the viewpoint of the change agent (the sender) it must be understood that a receiver is not taught. He learns. No man receives any idea unless he is voluntarily ready to do so. Potential adopters prefer some senders, messages, and media and reject others.

The advanced societies have attempted to transfer their education systems; lock, stock, and barrel, from kindergarten to graduate school to the developing countries. But is this system really adequate for solving their problems?

The major emphasis in the educational goal structure of advanced societies has been mobility. One is encouraged to better himself by developing occupational skills that will place him higher in status than his parents and provide him the opportunity to leave the less desirable surroundings of the farm or village to go to new and greater opportunities. If this is the major emphasis in a world of 8 billion people, it could be that the major end product of the educational systems will be increased dissatisfaction and frustration. Western educational systems have always been based on the assumptions of unlimited social and geographic frontiers. What happens when the education systems instill mobility goals and there is no place to go?

If the important contribution of education is to be fully used in the developing countries, the educational systems must have several important traits that will distinguish them from the systems of developed countries.

Since a large proportion of the agricultural scientists are trained in the universities of the developed countries, there should be special attention paid to the training of those who plan to work in developing countries. In the developed countries, the agricultural scientists are only a part of a network of support systems that take their laboratory findings and carry them to the ultimate users.

The agricultural scientists in developing countries must be trained to understand the basic communication theories in the fields of sociology, social psychology, and communications (media use).

In the developing countries, there is a need for a dualistic approach in education, i.e., there is a need for governmental support for programs that upgrade the competencies of the on-the-job agricultural agents and there is need to train young people, both boys and girls, who grew up on farms and have developed skills in reading and writing to act as demonstration agents. These people will have credibility among the farmers and can extend the limited resources of time that agricultural scientists have available.

These training programs should be designed to take into account the unique aspects of farming in that country. For example, in many countries women do much of the work with livestock and make decisions regarding the relevant practices. Male-oriented programs are dysfunctional under such circumstances.

In many developing countries, the women do the marketing and deal with the tradesmen in buying supplies. Change agents need to understand the various roles played by the different sexes in various countries if they are to be effective.

Probably there will be no significant changes in food production capabilities of the developing countries until there is a commitment to channel more resources into training both local change agents and small farmers in the use of appropriate technologies.

All too frequently, well-meaning individuals from the developed countries have recommended using technologies that have been useful in their countries, which have a scarcity of labor and a relative abundance of land and capital. But most of the countries where people are going hungry have shortages of capital, scarcity of land, and at least seasonal underemployment in agriculture. These countries need technology innovations that can be best used in their own situations.

The world population went from under 1 billion in 1850 to more than 4.2 billion in 1976. It could easily become more than 7 billion by the year 2000 A.D. given the current growth rates. There is general agreement that this rate of growth may well outrun the capacity of the earth to provide food for all even under ideal conditions. Closing the hunger gap includes population growth regulations, but it must also include approaching more optimum production levels in developing countries. This is the most serious crisis ever faced by mankind.

## BIBLIOGRAPHY

Beal, G. M., and Bohlen, J. M. The diffusion process. Iowa Agr. Ext. Serv. Spec. Rpt. 18, 1957.

Beal, G. M.; Rogers, E. M.; and Bohlen, J. M. Validity of the concept of stages in the adoption process. Rural Sociology 22 (2): 166–168, 1957.

Beal, G. M., and Rogers, E. M. The adoption of two farm practices in a central Iowa community. Iowa Agr. Exp. Stat. Spec. Rpt. 26, 1960.

Beal, George M.; Coward, Walter, Jr.; Bohlen, Joe M.; and Klonglan, Gerald E. Factors related to adoption progress. Rural Sociology Rpt. 64, Iowa State University, Ames, 1967.

Berlo, David K. The Process of Communication. New York: Holt, Rinehart and Winston, 1960.

Bohlen, J. M. The adoption and diffusion of ideas in agriculture. In Our Changing Rural Society, edited by J. H. Copp. Ames: Iowa State University Press, 1964.

Bohlen, Joe M., and Beal, George M. Sociological and social psychological factors. In Capital and Credit Needs in a Changing Agriculture, edited by E. L. Baum, et al. Ames: Iowa State University Press, 1961.

———. Market information and radio use. Iowa Agr. Exp. Stat. Bull., 1966.

Bohlen, Joe M. Needed research on adoption models. Sociologia Ruralis, Vol. VII, No. 2, 1967.

Bohlen, J. M., and Breathnach, T. Study on adoption of farm practices in Ireland. Dublin, Ireland: An Foras Taluntais, 1968.

———. Irish farmer's uses of information sources. Irish Journal of Agricultural Economics and Rural Sociology, Vol. 3, 1970–71.

Copp, J. H. Toward generalization in farm practice research. Rural Sociology 23 (2): 103–111, 1968.

Fliegel, F. C., and Kivlin, J. E. Differences among improved farm practices as related to rates of adoption. Pennsylvania Agr. Exp. Stat. Bull. 691, 1962.

Frawley, J.; Bohlen, Joe M.; and Breathnach, Thomas. Personal and social factors related to farming performance in Ireland. Irish Journal of Agricultural Economics and Rural Sociology 5:157–181, 1974–75.

Griliches, A. Hybrid corn: An explanation in the economics of technological change. Econometrica 25:501–522, 1957.

Klonglan, Gerald E., and Coward, E. Walter, Jr. The concept of symbolic adoption: A suggested interpretation. Rural Sociology (1):77–83, 1970.

Klonglan, Gerald E.; Coward, E. Walter, Jr.; Beal, George M.; and Bohlen, Joe M. Conceptualizing and measuring the extent of diffusion of innovations. Sociologia Ruralis (Journal of European Society of Rural Sociology), Vol. XI, No. 1, ISU AES Journal No. 6061, 1971.

LaCasa-Gomar, Jaime. The sender-linker-receiver communication model. Unpublished Ph.D. Thesis, Iowa State University, Ames, 1970, copyrighted.

Lionberger, H. F. Adoption of new ideas and practices. Ames: Iowa State University Press, 1960.

Ryan, B., and Gross, N. Acceptance and diffusion of hybrid corn seed in two Iowa communities. Iowa Agr. Exp. Stat. Res. Bull. 372, 1950.

Warren, D. M. Disease, medicine, and religion among the Techniman-Bono of Ghana: A study in cultural change. Unpublished Ph.D. Thesis, Indiana University, 1974.

Wilkening, E. A. Acceptance of improved farm practices in three coastal plains countries. North Carolina Agr. Exp. Stat. Tech. Bull. 98, 1952.

JIM HICKS

*A farm in Africa "ready for planting."*

# 17

# Assistance to Developing Nations

DOUGLAS ENSMINGER

HISTORICAL PERSPECTIVE. If we will only do so, we can learn much from history that will guide us in the future. Understanding the policies and processes of giving and receiving technical assistance and economic aid over the past 28 years will help the developed countries as the "givers of aid" and the developing countries as the "recipients of aid" evaluate experience and formulate appropriate future policies and strategies.

A critical look at past experience should not, however, concentrate on fault finding and condemnation. Twenty-eight years ago, the United States was without experience in helping newly created independent, later to be called developing, nations in formulating policy and planning and carrying out nation-building programs The new nations had just emerged from colonialism and lacked leadership experience and the institutional structures and experienced manpower essential to plan and carry out developing programs. Finally, the people, most of whom were rural and poor, in the developing countries had, out of their bitter experience with colonial rule, developed a strong mistrust for governments —all governments. Most of the people were illiterate; and they used their land to meet family survival needs by following handed-down, proven traditional practices.

The governments of the newly independent countries followed very closely the policies of the colonial powers and emphasized earning foreign exchange through exporting their mineral resources. Within agriculture, crops with high export potential (basically coffee, tea, cocoa, cashew nuts, and for some countries cereals, especially rice) were stressed —again to earn foreign exchange. Thus, small-farm agriculture, which was in essence family subsistence and mostly food grain agriculture, was given only minor attention by the new, independent developing nations.

Douglas Ensminger is Professor, Rural Sociology, University of Missouri-Columbia and President, Mid-Missouri Associated Colleges and Universities. He has had foreign assignments with the Agency for International Development and the Food and Agriculture Organization in Latin America and spent twenty years with the Ford Foundation in India.

Two other circumstances, both largely political, also help explain the lack of attention to small-farm agriculture by the developing countries. First, as the new countries emerged as self-governing political entities, the political institutions and political power base rested on a minority of economically elite, educated people. This elite population supported the new political leaders, and the political leaders upheld the elite's control over the wealth-producing resources and institutions.

Second, as the developing countries needed food, U.S. food surpluses were readily available at concessional prices, which made possible low and consumer-oriented food prices. More will be said about this effect later.

Assistance to the developing countries by the developed countries originated in Point IV of President Truman's 1948 inaugural address. What President Truman had in mind was a very fundamental, simple, and highly humanistic approach for sharing United States "know how," i.e., experience in problem solving—analyzing problems, understanding the factors that contributed to these problems, and developing alternative strategies for solving problems. Most important, the United States was not to impose its institutional structures nor buy policy changes by tying strings to aid.

But the Point IV Program was not to be kept simple and self-help oriented for long. Pressures were brought by those involved with the European Recovery Program to add economic aid to the original concept. The basic philosophy changed to one of emphasizing economic growth measured by GNP (gross national product). And this in turn influenced the developing countries, as recipients of U.S. aid, to change their policies and emphasis from improving the living conditions of their masses of poverty-ridden rural poor to investing in big development programs. The new aid policies were to rely on economic growth to generate employment opportunities, and there was to be a trickling down of the benefits of economic growth to the poor.

With few exceptions, the U.S. aid policies that emphasized GNP found favor among the elite in the developing countries since these policies strengthened the elite's economic hold and allowed them to further exploit the poor. The rich got richer; the poor increased in numbers; and the poor's deprivation became greater as the gap widened between the haves and have-nots in the developing countries.

An early and major input into U.S. foreign assistance to the developing countries was the "food for peace" program carried out through Public Law 480 (PL–480) legislation. There have been many pluses and minuses with this law, and these must be examined and needed policy changes made.

Initially, U.S. food grains were relied upon by the United States as well as the recipient countries, to meet urgent humanitarian needs. In the early fifties, India appealed to the United States for food grains to stave off a possible famine caused by a monsoon failure. Country after country looked to the United States for emergency food grains, and the United States responded.

U.S. food grain surpluses mounted and the developing countries' needs for food imports grew. The developing countries built into their plans and development policies a dependence on procuring U.S. food surpluses. And the United States counted on the PL–480 agreements to provide needed markets for its grain surpluses. In essence, what initially was conceived as a short-term emergency arrangement between the United States and the developing countries became institutionalized, affecting the developing countries' national policies as well as their agricultural price policies.

Developing countries used scarce financial resources for industrial development and developed agricultural food grain pricing policies that supported cheap food for the consumer. And because these pricing policies held his profits down, the farmer had little incentive to invest in new agricultural inputs and increase production.

Largely because of the speed with which Europe recovered after World War II with massive inputs of economic aid, neither the United States nor the developing countries were prepared for the slow, difficult task the developing countries faced as they emerged from colonialism. In the struggle for freedom, political leaders blamed the mass poverty on their status as colonies. They promised that once the people were freed from the problems that created it poverty would vanish and all would achieve a higher level of living. When this did not happen, leaders tried to create the illusion of development by investing in visible signs of development, such as dams and big industries.

Twenty-five years ago, neither the United States nor the political leaders of the developing countries understood that the masses of illiterate poor people constituted the countries' most important potential development resources. Experience has documented that material development and rise in people's level of living follow the education of people and the development of people's institutions.

This information should not have surprised the United States since its agricultural history is one of developing rural and farm people's competence to analyze problems and to examine alternative solutions. American agriculture has advanced because the farm family has had the needed resources and managerial competence to apply the technology. Supporting and sometimes leading this advance has been a national institutional infrastructure (credit, transportation, etc.) capable of responding to all the farmers' needs. Today U.S. agriculture is the complete opposite of agriculture in the developing countries. U.S. agriculture is big business, commercial, scientific, management efficient, profit motivated, and market oriented. Agriculture in the developing countries is small farm, subsistence, traditional, and an integral part of the rural culture.

Not realizing these vast differences, the United States persisted in pushing the transfer of its advanced, complex agricultural technology on the developing countries. This emphasis influenced the developing countries to support agricultural development on their larger farms. The result has been a widening of the agricultural gap with the larger farmers becoming more prosperous and the small farmers remaining poor, subsistent, and traditionally oriented.

Continuing these development policies, which emphasize GNP and rely on the trickling down of development benefits to the poor in the developing countries, will assuredly encourage widespread social and political unrest. This is because the poor, whose numbers are increasing and whose plight grows more hopeless, have nothing to lose by joining revolutionary movements that demand a more equal sharing of the two basic agricultural production resources, land and water.

All is not negative, however. The world's poor have had in Mr. Robert McNamara, President of the World Bank, an effective advocate. In his address to the World Bank Directors in Nairobi, Kenya, in 1973, he presented convincing documentation that the GNP development approach had failed to benefit the poor. Indeed the poor had increased in numbers, and their plight had worsened. He called for a change in the Bank's lending policies to support programs that would directly benefit the world's bypassed people, estimated to be more than 400 million. His two priorities for aiding the world's poor directly were then, and still are, integrated rural development and small-farm agriculture. Integrated rural development involves all the social, cultural, institutional, and economic aspects of a defined rural area in the development project and has as its objective improving the quality of life of all people. The rural areas usually have a growth center or market town. The priorities of integrated rural development include (1) developing the economy by developing agriculture and off-farm employment and (2) providing needed supportive institutions and services.

The U.S. Congress followed the Bank's priorities and in 1974 wrote into the USAID legislation two conditions that required aid to contribute to improving the living conditions of the rural poor and to focus on improving production on small farms.

A review of the past 28 years of giving and receiving technical assistance and economic aid would be incomplete if it did not recognize the significant contribution the land-grant universities and many private foundations and institutions have made in institution building and manpower development. The land-grant universities have concentrated most of their assistance on developing agriculture-related institutions directed toward developing advanced agricultural technology and manpower development.

Compared with governments and international institutions, the monetary contribution of foundations to developing countries has been minor. But foundations have been able to operate free of government rules and regulations and are essentially not political. The foundations have demonstrated they can be of great assistance in highly sensitive areas and in providing funds to initiate innovative programs that frequently must be tested before government funds can be assigned. In a few cases these programs have been rejected by the host countries.

WORLD CONFERENCES ON POPULATION AND FOOD. The changes in development priorities and the new development strategies were strengthened and solidified by the two 1974 U.N. Conferences: The World Population Conference held in Bucharest, Romania, in August; and The World Food Conference held in Rome, Italy, in November. These conferences emphasized that:

1. The world population would double early in the twenty-first century, reaching between 7 and 8 billion people.
2. The food surpluses, largely held by the United States, Canada, and Australia, were depleted because of poor weather and large grain sales to Russia. The 1970 world market reserve of about 217 million metric tons or food for 69 days had dropped by 1974 to 90 million metric tons or 26 days, where it remained until at least mid 1976.
3. The political leaders from the developing countries who attended the Rome World Food Conference should heed three clear messages:
   a. Each country should include in its future agricultural plans the additional food required to meet its growing population.
   b. Countries could no longer depend on the United States to bail them out when they had food import needs.
   c. Increasing production per hectare on their small farms is the principal way the developing countries can meet their growing food needs.

The U.N. Conferences pointed out two additional avenues to the developing countries for increasing their agricultural production: increasing acres in production and acres under irrigation. But these additional acres exist only in Africa and Latin America, and bringing them under the plough will cost billions of dollars and will take decades to achieve. Likewise, bringing additional acres under controlled irrigation, which is essential to multiple cropping, will cost billions and take decades.

FUTURE DEVELOPMENT STRATEGIES. Thus, in the latter half of the decade of the seventies both the donors and receivers of aid are nearing a consensus that future emphasis should focus on involving all the people in the development process and improving the quality of life (level of living) for all people.

Program strategies to do just that are now emerging with the increasing support of the developing countries, the World Bank, USAID, the Food and Agriculture Organization, and the U.N. The emphasis is on assisting the developing countries plan and implement national integrated rural development programs that give first priority to the development of small farm agriculture.

There is a wealth of well-documented experience representing the past 28 years and encompassing almost every conceivable development strategy, and most of it supports the newly emerging strategy of rural development and small farm agriculture. Dramatic evidence is found in the differing experiences of India and China after independence.

India emerged committed to democracy; China to communism. India started with a commitment to rural development that had three objectives—to involve all the people, to improve the level of living of all the people, and to make the country self-sufficient in food.

China, with early assistance from Russia, emphasized industrialization, following the Russian model of big industries.

Over the past 28 years India's political commitment to involve all the people in development and to have all benefit from development changed to an emphasis on industrialization and approaching agriculture through introducing advanced technology.

On the other hand, China's political emphasis changed from development of large industries to integrated rural deveopment using communes to involve all the people and to assure that all would benefit from development. Under the communes, land and water are equitably available to all the people.

Today, 28 years later, the following conclusions seem pretty well supported by the facts: By its change, China has achieved for its 900 million peasants food, employment, health, education for all, and a new sense of security never before known to them.

By its change, however, India, with more than 650 million people, currently has a food deficit of between 9 and 12 million tons. About 40 percent of its rural people and 50 percent of its urban people live in poverty, lacking the income to provide a minimum nutritional diet.

Japan, Taiwan, and South Korea, like China, all provide solid guidelines for policies in support of the small farm agriculture. The part of the developing world that, like India, changed from its commitment to small farm agriculture finds itself with similar, if not as drastic, problems.

In the initial years of emergence from colonization, many of the new nations emphasized rural community development. Pakistan, Nepal, the Philippines, Indonesia, and the Latin American countries all supported community development programs. And while few countries have completely abandoned community development, during the decade of the sixties most did change the emphasis away from *integrated* rural development, retaining only rural development *projects*. This change in emphasis is explained largely by four factors, mentioned earlier in the historical review.

First, the developed, aid-giving countries pressed the developing countries to use the offered economic aid on projects that promised rapid economic gains and early return on the investments.

Second, the political leaders, who had promised their poor people relief from poverty after independence, began to lose interest in community development after 10 years. Impatient with the slowness and complexities involved in such development, political leaders began to search for a faster, less complex development strategy.

Third, the economically elite in developing countries exercised political muscle, and they saw community development as a threat to their power structure. The lessons of the first 10 years very clearly indicated that major, if not revolutionary, institutional reforms were needed if community development was to succeed. Far-reaching land reform was needed to make land and water more equally available and to ensure just rental arrangements. Existing institutions would have to be made responsive to all the people instead of just to the elite.

Fourth and finally, the easy availability of U.S. food grain surpluses eliminated incentives for small farmers to change and improve their traditional subsistence agriculture. This opportunity to expand agricultural production and strengthen the economic base, essential to improving the social and economic well-being of all the people, was lost.

LESSONS FROM EXPERIENCE. The past 28 years in and out of political commitment and support for community development provide a new understanding that can now be used in implementing the policies of integrated rural development.

Important lessons can be drawn from this period for both the givers and the receivers of technical and economic aid. These will be examined first from the viewpoint of the developing countries and then from that of the developed countries and institutions.

FOR THE DEVELOPING COUNTRIES.

1. To involve all the people in nation-building programs and assure that all will share in the benefits of development will require great depth of political commitment and strong political muscle.
2. Effectively implemented legislation will be mandatory to make the two basic resources, land and water, more equitably available to small land holders and tenants.
3. Social and economic institutions must be transformed, not just changed, to encompass and serve the needs of all the people.
4. Government development policies will have to strongly support development and application of technology that is labor intensive, makes labor more productive, is within the resources and managerial capability of most people, and benefits most of the people. Even though technology must be labor intensive, there must be less drudgery.
5. The early and continuous emphasis must be on educating and de-

veloping all the people as human beings and developing people's competence for leadership in all phases of development.

6. Developing countries' policies should clearly specify that all outside economic aid should contribute to policies and strategies for improving the quality of life for all people.
7. For integrated rural development to improve the level of living of all the people, three conditions must be met:
   a. Agriculture must provide the needed initial economic base for integrated rural development.
   b. There must be an equal distribution of finances, institutions, and manpower resources to all regions within the countries.
   c. Besides agriculture, integrated rural development must provide alternative employment opportunities first by creating institutional services and small industries related to agricultural production and food processing, and second, by creating small industries to produce consumer goods—but only after agriculture generates needed new purchasing power to assure markets.
8. Past experience dictates that initially, integrated rural development strategies should use limited financial resources for such key approaches as:
   a. Developing farm-tested research that is labor intensive, makes labor more productive, and can be easily adopted locally, i.e., developing multicropping and making animal and human power more productive.
   b. Developing the physical infrastructure (roads) and institutions essential to serve small-farm agriculture.
   c. Inventorying all constraints (biological, social, economic, and political) that inhibit moving small farm agriculture from traditionalism toward an acceptance of agricultural science and technology. Programs to remove these constraints should be developed on a priority basis.
9. Education should be for all the people and directed toward helping people more effectively earn a living and make their lives more meaningful. Political and educational leaders will sooner or later have to accept that traditional education has not served the needs of developing nations. Larger investments in primary and secondary education, which is achievement- and promotion-oriented and at best serves only a small minority of the population, help develop an elite class and leave the great masses of people deeply entrenched in traditionalism and a cultural poverty web.

   Each developing country will have to examine alternatives to traditional education and agree upon acceptable educational strategies. The search for an alternative to Tanzania's political commitment to a revolution in primary and secondary education is worthy of careful study.
10. Because pressures will be great to rapidly expand service, educa-

tion and administration must be persuasive to prevent adding too many services before the economy can support them. Many rural development programs have failed during the past 28 years because they failed to do this.

11. Improving quality of life calls for rural women being full partners with men in all phases of integrated rural development. Women are to have strategic roles in agricultural production, family planning, and family nutrition. They must be key change agents in transforming the traditional rural cultures.
12. Nutrition must be a priority. Nutrition cannot wait until after production is adequate to meet market needs. Good nutrition is as essential for human output as gasoline is for engine power. Good nutrition for pregnant women and nursing mothers contributes to both the survival and health of newborn babies, which in turn has a positive effect on limiting family size.

    The rate and quality of development directly relates to the alertness and capacity of people to understand and solve their problems. Brain, not muscle, power is required, and it starts with good nutrition.
13. Food grain losses must be reduced if nutritional needs are to be met. Food losses range from 17 to 26 percent, with the higher figure probably being more realistic. More effort is needed to control the losses that occur at all stages in the food cycle; specific programs are needed to control rodents, diseases, and insects, and to prevent loss during harvesting and storage.
14. Each country must formulate and implement comprehensive national policies supporting integrated rural development and small farm agriculture. The traditional set of agricultural policies that emphasizes prices, inputs, and resource allocations will not suffice. Tanzania's national policies are a good example of the kind of comprehensive policies needed; in summary they are:
    a. To emphasize food crop production to the same extent that cash crops were emphasized in the past.
    b. To encourage change and development measures as necessary to make the country self-sufficient in food.
    c. To treat agricultural development as an integral part of integrated rural development.
    d. To encourage, promote, and facilitate the development of agricultural production through villagization.
    e. To encourage village development.
    f. To enable all people to participate in development programs and benefit from them.
    g. To support a one-channel marketing system for food crops through a cooperative structure.
    h. To foster the development of the agricultural cooperatives into "multiservice" cooperatives distributing agricultural inputs, con-

sumer goods, and credit, as well as assembling and marketing agricultural products.

i. To delegate significant responsibility for planning an agricultural development of district and regional character and for implementing those plans (within guidelines) at regional and district levels.

j. To foster geographic specialization in production to maximize production increases.

k. To use price incentives to encourage increased food crop production.

l. To develop local field plot demonstrations and credit programs for ujamaa villages (basically communes) and for cooperative efforts by individual farmers.

m. To base an individual's credit worthiness on his intent to carry out improved practices and subsequently on the extent to which he has carried out or is carrying out improved practices plus his record of repayment.

n. To develop primary societies (in the cooperative structure) into socially and economically viable entities.

o. To increase food crop production and storage facilities to meet the nation's needs during the most severe failure or other unavoidable food production crises.

p. To encourage improved storage at the primary society level and farm level to avoid the additional expense of moving food crops into regional storage at harvest time and back to production areas for later consumption.

q. To improve feeder roads in agricultural producing areas.

r. To develop the road transport facilities and equipment to the point that the National Haulage Company will be capable of handling the long distance truck transport needs of the nation. To encourage a Regional Union truck fleet sufficient to handle the bulk of within-region transport needs.

s. To increase production by using improved seeds, fertilizer, and plant protection technology, rather than by increased land input.

t. To provide adequate supplies of fertilizer for food crop production, primarily through internal production but by allocating foreign exchange for import if necessary.

u. To subsidize agricultural production inputs as a method of encouraging early farmer adoption.

v. To review agricultural production subsidies each year with the expectation that subsidy levels will be reduced. The import subsidy level will be influenced by changes in the commercial prices of inputs and the price the farmer receives at the market.

FOR THE DEVELOPING COUNTRIES. For the aid givers, whether developed countries or institutions, there are equally important lessons to be drawn from the past. Some of the more important guiding principles for improving the quality of life for all people in a developing country are:

1. A successful relationship depends on making absolutely clear what a developing country's political commitments are and the depth and strength of commitment to programs and strategies that will improve the quality of life for all their people.
2. Aid-giving should, without exception, be in response to an expressed need for assistance. Offering aid on conditions of changing policies should be a "no-no."
3. An important requisite for accepting a request to assist should be a mutual understanding that the assistance will contribute in a specific way to improving the quality of life for all the people.
4. Aid in helping improve institutional competence must recognize the need that technology be labor intensive, make labor more productive, be appropriate, and be within the resources and managerial competence of small farmers.
5. Since integrated rural development depends on developing people and people's institutions to transform rural culture, the aid givers should take a long-term view about both their commitments and expectations.
6. If integrated rural development is to improve the quality of life for all the people, the aid givers will need competence in a wide variety of areas, including agriculture, health, nutrition, education, industry, communication, rural development, policies, credit, and marketing. They will need to be astute students of culture and possess great skills as change agents.
7. For the aid sought and agreed upon to be effectively programmed, there should be a written agreement clearly stating the problem for which aid is sought and the country's commitments to solving the problem. The specific aid and how it will be used should be clearly stated. A written agreement avoids misunderstanding and provides needed continuity throughout personnel changes.
8. Both the aid givers and the receivers must press for evidence that the aid sought can meet the following criteria:
   a. Is it appropriate technology for the country to build into its culture?
   b. Can the country provide competent leadership to strengthen or develop the program?
   c. Can the country afford to integrate the new program into its financial structure?
   d. Does the aid giver have the built-in institutional competence to deliver the requested aid?

PROBABLE CONSTRAINTS. Past experience indicates that the following four constraints are the most likely to inhibit success in implementing inte-

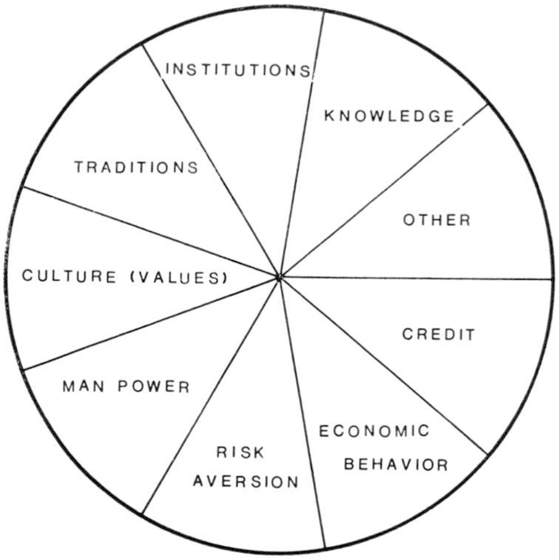


FIG. 17.1. Socioeconomic constraints to agricultural production

grated rural development and small farm agricultural programs:

1. Weak and shallow political commitment to using resources to bring about needed institutional changes
2. Lack of administrative proficiency to plan and implement national programs
3. Shortage of manpower capability (administrative, technical, educational, and operating) to plan, organize, administer, and service programs

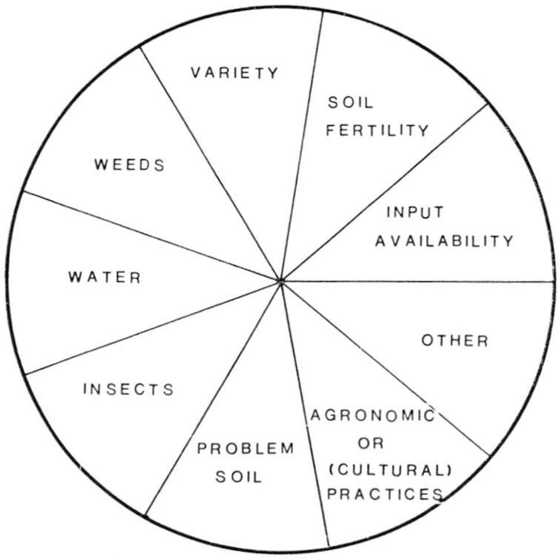


FIG. 17.2. Biophysical constraints to agricultural production

4. Lack of comprehensive national policies supporting national commitment to integrated rural development and small farm agricultural programs

Besides these four constraints, there are other specific constraints—both socioeconomic and biophysical—that inhibit agricultural production (see Figs. 17.1 and 17.2). These will vary by countries, but it is necessary to understand how they relate to programs formulated to remove or minimize their influence.

Even though those providing assistance to the developing countries cannot be expected to influence political commitments, aid givers would be well advised to ascertain the country's political commitment to integrated rural development and small farm agriculture as a condition for their commitment to help.

The lack of strong political commitments by the aid-receiving countries can be frustrating for those who want and try to help. Still the leadership for change and development must come from within the country needing and asking for aid.

Even though specific needs will vary for each country, success in aiding the developing countries will be greatly enhanced if assistance includes strengthening administration and increasing manpower competence and needed policies are assured.

SPECIAL ROLE FOR LAND-GRANT AND OTHER U.S. UNIVERSITIES. Title XII of the December 20, 1975, International Disaster Assistance Act establishes the special role of land-grant and other universities in aiding the developing countries. The Act states:

> The Congress declares that, in order to prevent famine and establish freedom from hunger, the United States should strengthen the capacities of the United States land-grant and other eligible universities in program-related agricultural institutional development and research, consistent with sections 103 and 103A, should improve their participation in the United States Government's international efforts to apply more effective agricultural sciences to the goal of increasing world food production, and in general should provide increased and longer term support to the application of science to solving food and nutrition problems of the developing countries.

Past experience tells us the most important contribution U.S. land-grant universities can make is in helping the developing countries find solutions to farmers' problems and in contributing to the development of institutional infrastructures and services oriented to the family farm. With few exceptions, the agricultural technology now so widely applied throughout the United States is too advancd, too complex, and beyond the resources and managerial competence of the millions of small farmers who must now be looked to for increased agricultural production.

The U.S. land-grant universities, largely through the Colleges of Agriculture, are uniquely equipped to assist developing countries to develop all the institutions and services, such as research institutions, credit, and farm-to-market roads (integrated institutional infrastructure), needed to serve the needs of the small farmer (see Chapter 13). People from numerous U.S. Colleges of Agriculture and Home Economics have worked abroad and have made major contributions in developing research and training institutions. College after college has on its staff as many as 50 faculty members with solid experience of working in the developing countries. The Colleges of Agriculture know from U.S. experience how important a total integrated institutional infrastructure oriented to the needs of the family farm is. They can, therefore, assist the developing countries to produce their own culturally oriented institutional infrastructure to serve the needs of the small farmer with less cost and greater acceptance by the developing countries than can the U.S. Government or some other agency that might send uncoordinated teams of consultants to attack the problem piecemeal.

Other things, of course, need doing. Fertilizer plants must be built. Available productive land must be brought under cultivation. Irrigation schemes that are economically feasible must be undertaken. These and other big schemes can be done through loans with built-in technical and manpower assistance.

What the United States knows about agricultural development and the essential role of institutions to service agriculture can help bring the small farmer to center stage. Over the next 10 years the small farmer can, if effectively assisted, increase agricultural production to help meet the nutritional needs of all the world's people.

NEW REASONS FOR AID. Most arguments for the U.S. aid to developing countries have been based on humanitarian grounds. Sharing and helping people in need were deeply ingrained in American culture; they still are.

While humanitarian and ethical considerations remain important, we are now confronted with very important economic and international reasons for U.S. farmers to support aid policies and programs.

The American farmer knows from experience that the decisions he makes are influenced by what happens beyond his fence boundaries. And American agriculture is increasingly interlinked with the world's raw resources, the world market system, and the strength of the economies of the countries deficient in food.

There is much about the past and present that is taken for granted: our status as a highly industrialized nation, our agriculture as the most productive in the world, our high level of living. U.S. agriculture has contributed to the development of U.S. industries; and U.S. industries, in turn, have contributed to the development of agriculture. Both have contributed to the American level of living. What is not generally understood is the way the world's mineral resources have contributed to the present development of American industry, agriculture, and family levels of living. Today, America, with 6 percent of the world's population, is annually consuming between 38 and 42 percent of the world's resources.

Throughout our industrial growth and agricultural development, we looked upon the world's mineral resources as ours for prices we determined. But the oil-producing countries drastically altered this situation; in two years oil prices increased 400 percent. Many of the developing countries, which are the primary producers of the world's mineral resources, are following the lead of the oil-producing countries, seeking to make their pricing policies producer-oriented. The mineral-producing countries are evolving policies to conserve their rapidly depleting resources and to channel more of them into industrial development within their own boundaries. The policies now being evolved, both with respect to pricing and to deciding how resources will be shared among the countries that produce them and the United States, will have a direct bearing on American agriculture. Inevitably, the availability and cost of energy for power and the critical agricultural inputs, especially fertilizer, herbicides, and insecticides, will affect U.S. production and prices. Thus, American agriculture is increasingly interlinked with the world markets.

In the future, American agriculture will find that the manner in which the United States shares food with the mineral-producing countries will influence the policies of these countries in sharing their mineral resources with the United States. As the mineral-producing countries earn more from selling their resources, their economies will be strengthened resulting in their buying more U.S. agricultural products on the world market. Thus, in the long run, U.S. agriculture will be strengthened by the United States paying more for needed imported mineral resources.

OTHER COUNTRIES AND AID. As has been true with the United States, there is great variation in the way other countries have approached assisting the developing countries over the past two decades. While increasing numbers are making their contribution to and through the United Nations, many continue direct bilateral assistance arrangements.

When viewed in terms of percentage of the country's Gross National Product, each contributes to development assistance; the range is from a high 0.8 percent for Sweden to a low of 0.12 percent for Italy. Only four countries (Finland, Switzerland, Italy, and Austria) contribute a lower percentage of their GNP than the U.S., whose share was 0.24 percent in 1975 (Fig. 17.3).

OTHER ASSISTANCE NEEDED. For the developing countries to (1) provide the conditions for the small farmers to increase their production, (2) build the needed physical infrastructures (mainly roads) and the in-

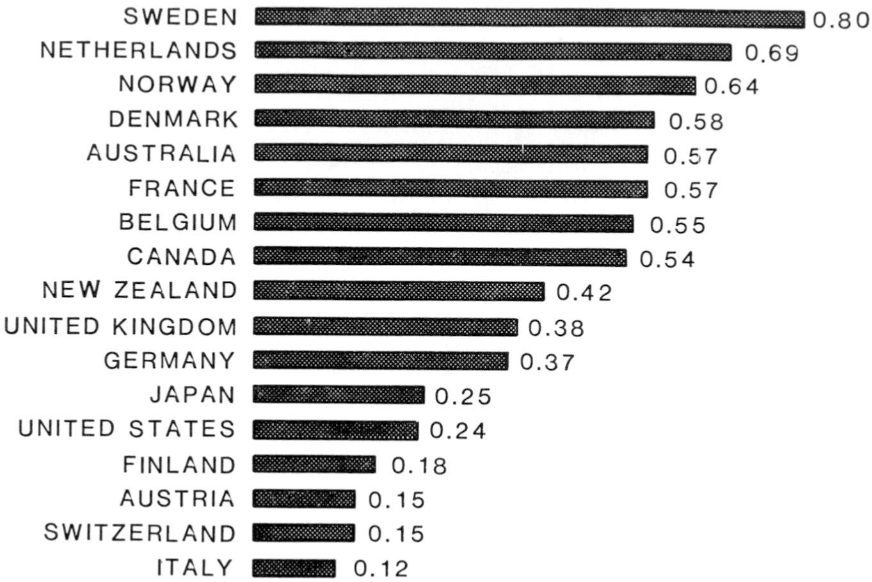


FIG. 17.3. Estimated official development assistance from industrialized countries as a percentage of their gross national product in 1975 (based on World Bank Data)

stitutions to serve small farmers, and (3) generate needed foreign exchange to purchase food grains when needed, they will need aid beyond technical assistance with integrated rural development and small farm agriculture. They will need loans and grants to augment the needed physical and institutional infrastructures, including roads, irrigation, and credit. They must also receive a more equitable price for their exportable minerals, and existing U.S. trade restrictions must be eased so they can sell their industrial and selective agricultural products to generate needed foreign exchange.

Even though significant economic inputs from both developed countries and international lending agencies will be mandatory, a word of caution is appropriate: Past experiences indicate that outside monetary inputs must be made available only in direct relation to the developing country's political, administrative, institutional, and manpower competence to effectively apply the loans or grants to its basic development objectives of improving the quality of life for all people.

The political pressures will be great for massive economic inputs. But too much injected money, especially for low priority projects, has probably done more harm over the past 28 years to the developing countries than it has contributed to sound and balanced development. Political pressures are always present for visible development (big industries, dams, etc.). Still the political payoffs in the future will be seen in the growing capacity of the people to do things for themselves and not wait for government to solve all their problems.

Much is being accomplished through U.S. and international forums to define the new world order. The debate is about the need for a more equal sharing of world resources between developed and developing countries. But even though these issues are important, a more urgent issue facing the developing countries is that of land reform and transforming economic and social institutions. The poor and deprived people in the developing countries, about 40 to 60 percent of the population, will remain poor if the developing countries receive a large share of the world's resources but fail to transform institutions and legislate and implement land reforms.

If solid progress is to be gained in the next two decades in making the aid-giving-and-receiving process rewarding to the developing countries and satisfying to aid givers, realistic projections must be made about the kind of a level of living developing countries seek for their people. Regardless of how this sought-for level of living is defined, it must meet the following requirements:

First, the level of living sought will have to be culturally acceptable to and economically achievable by most of the people.

Second, preliminary objectives should include:

1. Opportunities for all to be employed and earn enough to meet minimum family needs.
2. A nutritional diet and freedom from fear of hunger.
3. Shelter that meets the family's needs.
4. Continued education for the family.
5. Health services for the family.
6. Economic and social security for a sense of well-being.

The choice of how to improve the quality of life (level of living) for the people can only be made by the political leaders from within the developing countries. The decisions and commitments on this will, more than any other world issue or decision, determine whether we can look forward to a generation of satisfied people or to a future of uprisings, revolutions, and worldwide political instability.

POPULATION—THE OTHER SIDE OF THE COIN. Any discussion about assisting the developing countries must also recognize the important role of population. World agricultural production is plateauing and unless presently unforeseen breakthroughs in new agricultural technology are made, it seems unlikely that agricultural production can meet the minimum nutritional requirements beyond the 1980s of a population growing at a rate of 2.4 percent per annum in the developing countries. The time has come for educational programs and institutional services to be equally supportive of programs to increase agricultural production and family planning. Agricultural people and public health and family planning educators cannot continue to execute their programs separately. Integrated rural development must include educational programs on the importance of family limitation if all children born are to have adequate diets. And family planning programs must stress the importance of enough food and a nutritional diet.

Without food enough to meet minimum nutritional needs, the quality of life will be substandard. A balancing of population with resources is desperately needed.

## REFERENCES

1. Ensminger, Douglas, ed. Food Enough or Starvation for Millions? Chapters 16, 19, 22, 24, 26–28, 33.
2. Illich, Ivan. Celebration of Awareness. Chapters 8, 9.
3. Parmar, Samuel L. Self-Reliance and Development in an Interdependent World.
4. McNamara, Robert. Addresses to the World Bank Board, 1973, 1974, 1975.
5. Nyerere, Julius K. Education for Self-Reliance.
6. Schumacher, E. F. Small is Beautiful.

## BIBLIOGRAPHY

Bennis, Warren G.; Benne, Kenneth D.; and Chin, Robert, eds. The Planning of Change. New York: Holt, Rinehart and Winston, 1962.

Blase, Melvin G., ed. Institutions in Agricultural Development. Ames: Iowa State Univ. Press, 1971.

Dandekar, V. M., and Rath, Nilakantha. Poverty in India. Economic and Political Weekly, Bombay, Vol. VI, Nos. 1 and 2, January 2 and 9, 1971.

Ensminger, Douglas, ed. Food Enough or Starvation for Millions? New Delhi, India: Tata McGraw-Hill, 1976.

Illich, Ivan. Celebration of Awareness. Chapters 8 and 9. New York: Doubleday & Co., 1970.

Leagans, J. Paul, and Loomis, Charles P., eds. Behavioral Change in Agriculture. Ithaca, N.Y.: Cornell University Press, 1971.

Lele, Uma. The Design of Rural Development: Lessons From Africa. Baltimore: The Johns Hopkins University Press, 1975.

McNamara, Robert. Addresses to the World Bank Board, 1973, 1974, and 1975.

Nyerere, Julius K. Education for Self-Reliance. Printed by the Government Printer, Dar es Salaam, Tanzania, March 1967.

Parmar, Samuel L. Self-Reliance and Development in an Interdependent World. In Beyond Dependency, ed. Guy F. Erb and Valeriana Kallab. Washington, D.C.: Overseas Development Council, 1975.

Pearson, Lester B., chairman. Partners in Development—Report of the Commission on International Development. New York: Praeger Publishers, Inc., 1969.

Schumacher, E. F. Small is Beautiful. New York: Harper and Row, 1975.

Sen, Lolit K.; Wanmali, Sudhir; Bose, Saradinku; Misra, Girish K.; and Ramash, K. S. Planning Rural Growth Centres for Integrated Area Development, ed. V. R. K. Paramahamsa. Hyderabad–30, India, 1971.

U.S. Foreign Aid Legislation. Public Law–480 and Title XII Famine Prevention and Freedom From Hunger. Washington, D. C., 1974 and 1975.

Webster, R. Lyle, ed. Integrated Communication—Bringing People and Rural Development Together. Honolulu, Hawaii: East-West Communication Institute, East-West Center, 1974.

World Bank Rural Development—Sector Policy Paper. Washington, D.C., February 1975.

# INDEX